A GUIDE TO HISTORIC PLACES IN LOS ANGELES COUNTY

Prepared under the auspices of the
History Team of the City of Los Angeles
American Revolution Bicentennial Committee

Editor-in-Chief
Judson A. Grenier

Associate Editors
Doyce B. Nunis, Jr.
Jean Bruce Poole

Researchers
Abraham Hoffman
John O. Pohlmann

Contributors
William A. Mason
Abraham Hoffman
Richard Lillard

Introduction
John Walton Caughey

Cartography
Lawrence G. Jones

KENDALL/HUNT PUBLISHING COMPANY
2460 Kerper Boulevard, Dubuque, Iowa 52001

Special Acknowledgments

Research for this guide book was made possible by a grant from the MANUFACTURERS LIFE INSURANCE COMPANY of Toronto, Canada. Without this initial contribution this guide book would never have been realized.

The Manufacturers Life Insurance Company

Printed in the United States of America

407501   01

Contents

LOS ANGELES: A SHORT HISTORY

TWELVE ZONE MAPS AND SITE DESCRIPTIONS

Acknowledgments

The editors wish to express their appreciation to the following for special assistance in bringing this guidebook to publication. First, to Thomas Sitton, Curatorial Assistant, Los Angeles County Museum of Natural History, for his constructive and critical reading of the site entries, and to the Los Angeles Cultural Heritage Board for making their existing files available for our use in preparing certain entries. It is with genuine gratitude that we express our appreciation to the Associated Historical Societies of Los Angeles County for their helpful assistance, encouragement, and support. Much of the basic information for the guide was secured through the cooperation of the County's many historical societies. Several members of these societies participated in the original site selection and evaluation process. Many individuals also cooperated by providing pertinent photographs for site illustrations. In particular, we wish to thank Elva Meline and Kay Wright for helping to coordinate much of this exchange of information.

In addition to the three editors, the following members of the History Team of the Los Angeles City Bicentennial Committee made valuable contributions: John W. Caughey, Marcia Erickson, Dudley Gordon, Marie Harrington, Donald and Nadine Hata, Harry Kelsey, Helen Lawton, Miriam Matthews, Leonard Pitt and Betty Welcome. Two other History Team members, William A. Mason, Curator, Los Angeles County Museum of Natural History, and Victor L. Plukas, Historian, Security Pacific National Bank, gave yeoman service in providing numerous site illustrations and historic photographs. Security Pacific Bank's photographic collection is renowned in southern California and we are grateful for its use. The bank also provided maps which were adapted by cartographer Larry Jones for use as our twelve unit maps. The freeway map which serves as the end paper for the Guide was donated by the Automobile Club of Southern California.

A special acknowledgment goes to Abraham Hoffman and John O. Pohlmann, who researched most site entries and verified relevant data. Their work was made possible by a generous grant from the Manufacturers Life Insurance Company of Toronto, Canada. Without that support, this guide book would not have been possible. This grant also made possible the typing of the final manuscript copy, a task executed with attentive care by Roberta A. Johnson, and verification of contemporary logistical data by Roxanne Frye. The County Museum of Natural History generously permitted us to use some two dozen negatives of historic sites taken in recent months by Thomas Sitton; they were printed by Judson Grenier, who photographed an equal number of sites especially for this Guide. Generous donations also were received from the Los Angeles City American Revolution Bicentennial Committee, the Atlantic Richfield Foundation and El Pueblo de Los Angeles State Historic Park which made it possible for the guidebook to be published. A word of appreciation is due to Bruce Baily of Kendall/Hunt for his editorial guidance and enthusiasm.

Lastly the editors wish to express their thanks to the Los Angeles City Bicentennial Committee, the Los Angeles County American Revolution Bicentennal Commission, the Los Angeles City Council, and the Los Angeles County Board of Supervisors for their endorsement of the project. Our only regret is that the book could not be published during the bicentennial year. Unfortunately, the demands for historical accuracy and high editorial standards required more effort and time than first envisioned when the project was originally planned. We hope, however, that the end result, four years in preparation, this Guidebook, will continue to light and point the way to this historical past of the greater Los Angeles community in the years to come. For that was what the 1976 Bicentennial was all about—an examination of our historic past coupled with an expectation of things yet to come. We anticipate that spirit also will motivate commemoration of the bicentennial of the founding of the city in 1981. By looking at the past, we can build for the future.

Note to User

This book was prepared primarily to describe existing buildings or places.

In preparing the guidebook, an initial list of approximately 350 historic sites was evaluated by the Associated Historical Societies of Los Angeles County at a meeting at California State University, Dominguez Hills. Few sites were deleted, many others were added. The list was then circulated to local historical societies, museums, libraries, other concerned agencies and institutions for additional appraisal. A final review board of local historians scrutinized the site descriptions for accuracy of content and general public interest.

A decision was made by the editors to exclude almost all sites of which the only physical evidence was a plaque. This was done both to conserve space (since the number of sites to be included was so voluminous) and to save the visitor from disappointment. A few such sites were included in order to relate the history of an area, if the location still conveys an historical mood to the visitor. In addition to buildings which no longer exist, most archeological sites have been deliberately omitted. When excavations have been completed and preservation safeguards put into effect, these will be listed in revised editions.

Admission fees, hours that sites are open, and telephone numbers listed were correct as of January 1978. However, fees may be subject to change as may times, and days of admission. If difficulty is encountered in reaching any of the telephone numbers listed at specific sites, an alternative solution would be to try the local City Hall, Chamber of Commerce or historial society.

A word to the wise: passage by California voters in June 1978 of a property tax limitation may have an effect upon the hours and fees of those buildings operated by public agencies. Visitors should phone ahead for current information.

All telephone numbers listed are in the Los Angeles area code 213 unless otherwise indicated.

Introduction

Los Angeles is and over time has been such a sprawling entity that its historic landmarks test the stamina of any walking or riding siteseer. On top of that, Los Angeles has gone through so many seachanges and fresh starts that it has myriad history makings to memorialize. Can a mere 400 selections, the ration for this book, make a dent in calling the roll of historic sites?

The answer is that the editors have made good representative choices, describing and assessing each, adding anecdotes, and mapping locations so that the curious can transport themselves back to the twenties or eighties or the days of the ranchos and the pueblo.

Inevitably the tilt is retrospective. Triumphs of modern technology such as the Los Angeles Airport, the Permanente hospitals, the Jet Propulsion Laboratory, and Systems Development Corporation, especially if currently operative, tend to be passed over in favor of the California Collection of the Los Angeles Public Library, Plummer Park, Casa de la Centinela, and Sojourner Truth House. After a decent interval, some artifacts of the present generation may have become historic.

Three years have passed since the History Team of the Los Angeles Bicentennial Committee determined to undertake a survey of historic sites—modeled on but more comprehensive than that of the Federal Writers' Project of the 30s—and enlisted the aid of the Associated Historical Societies of Los Angeles County in identifying appropriate candidates for inclusion in the guide. More than 100 individuals have contributed to the project since its inception.

Preparatory to the discourse on the sites the editors present a spritely and informative capsule history of Los Angeles. It opens with Indians and Mexicans, and moves on to From Rancho to Boomtown, 1849-89, From Boom to Depression in 1929, and finally, Big Time Growth and the Consequence of the Superlative. These were composed by William Mason, Judson Grenier, Abraham Hoffman, and Richard Lillard. The result is committee writing with a grace and unity that no one would have dared expect. The volume is a handy guide to nostalgic reminders. It also offers an epitome of the pulsating experience and ambience of life in Los Angeles.

John W. Caughey

LOS ANGELES: A SHORT HISTORY

CHAPTER 1

Indians and Mexicans: The Founding Years, 1769-1848

William Mason, Historian, Los Angeles County Museum of Natural History

The coastal plain which comprises much of Los Angeles county stretches forty miles from the mountains named San Gabriel to the hills of Palos Verdes. Its climate is mild, with temperatures seldom below freezing and averaging in the mid-60s. Rainfall is sparse and the land is dry, though cooled by coastal breezes and fog. Lifeblood of this semi-desert region is water, and until 1913 the irregular flow of the Los Angeles and San Gabriel rivers provided the only outside source. Prior to the arrival of the Spaniards, little activity stirred the peaceful aridity of the plain. Wild grasses, scrub brush, live oak and cottonwood trees grew near streams, birds clustered in the salt marshes near the coast, and animals came to drink in the dark pools of the brea pits.

The first inhabitants of Los Angeles County were Indians, members of the Uto-Aztecan linguistic family. Utes, Paiutes, some New Mexico Pueblo Indians, Yaqui of northern Mexico, and Aztecs of central Mexico are all distant kinsmen of Los Angeles' aboriginal inhabitants. Considerable cultural and linguistic uniformity existed among these native peoples, known today as Gabrielinos and Fernandeños. These are not the names of individual tribal units. Primarily, they reflect mission identification when the Indians were neophytes during the period of Spanish rule.

Blood-related villages sometimes fought one another, despite their shared language and culture. As a rule, three or four villages usually were allied with one another against other similar village alliances. Marriages were exchanged between villages because few Indians married persons from their own village. Probably these marriages resembled the martial alliance patterns. By conservative estimate, the total Indian population in what is now Los Angeles county was about 5,000 people, although some modern ethnologists place the figure at closer to 10,000.

Though the economy was primarily one of hunting and gathering, apparently there existed a fairly abundant food supply, acorns in the interior and shellfish along the coast being bountiful. Food was adequate except during unusually dry cycles. Indians utilized a wide variety of seeds and fruits by efficiently gathering and storing for the winter season. Hunting of antelope,

Gabrielino Indians near Malibu, c. 1750. County Museum diorama.

deer, rabbits, quail, ducks, geese, herons, cranes, other birds, smaller animals, such as opossums, gophers, wood rats and squirrels, several reptiles, and even insects, such as grasshoppers, characterized the Indian struggle to find sufficient protein to supplement the acorn staple. Coastal Indians had a diet abundant in protein, and evidently traded with inland peoples for acorns and other seeds in exchange for seafoods.

Most Indian villages were concentrated along the seacoast or near rivers, streams, lakes, and ponds. Southern California had more surface water available two centuries ago, prior to the construction of modern dams, cement channels, and pumps to tap the ground water supply. Indians made good use of the water available to them. The average size of a village was probably somewhere between 100 and 300 people, larger along the coast, but smaller in the more arid regions near the desert.

Although local Indians did not make pottery, they had fairly good dishes made of soapstone or steatite, and the basketry was excellent. Some baskets were watertight and could be used for cooking. Willow bows and flint-tipped arrows were the most common weapon used for hunting, along with throwing-sticks and nets made from grass fibers. Houses were made with willow stick frames, covered with grass and rushes woven together with switches and branches. These houses were circular and conical, rounded on the tops, standing seven to nine feet high. Other tools and artifacts were commonly made, such as fish-hooks, tobacco pipes, canoes of tules,

Gabrielino Indians constructing a Kish, c. 1750.
County Museum diorama.

steatite animal figurines, and stone scraping knives. Women usually wore skirts from waist to knee made of beaten reeds; men often wore nothing in good weather. Both sexes wore rabbit-skin capes or fox-tail garments in cold weather, while coastal people sometimes wore clothing made from seabird skins.

In 1769 the first Spanish effort to settle in California was undertaken. An expedition, under the command of Don Gaspar de Portolá, was well-received by the local Indians. When the party arrived at the banks of Los Angeles River, they were given presents of seeds and other food. The members of the expedition noted the area appreciatively, and two years later the religious portion of the occupying forces, members of the Franciscan Order, sent missionaries to the area. As a result, the first Spanish outpost in the Los Angeles region, Mission San Gabriel, was founded in September 1771, about five miles southeast of the present mission site.

The padres of San Gabriel had difficulty in curbing the outrages committed by the soldiers sent to protect them. The missionaries complained that the permissive corporal in charge permitted the soldiers to leave the mission area and take women by force from the surrounding villages. Their behavior provoked a series of Indian attacks against the mission. After the governor removed the corporal, the relationship between the mission and the Indians improved.

By 1775 the mission was relocated to its present site. The early mission buildings were simple constructions of willow poles and branches, chinked and plastered with clay or mud, thatched with reeds. They differed from the Indian huts primarily in their shape, which was rectangular instead of circular. The large tiled and plastered brick and adobe buildings associated with the California missions were built later.

By 1777 some 300 Indians had been baptized and were living near the mission in a village built for the converts. They were taught Hispano-Mexican agricultural techniques by the missionaries, in addition to several other skills, such as weaving wool and cotton, tanning cowhide and working with leather, tile and adobe-making, carpentry, animal husbandry, soap-making, and iron-working. Most of the converts, usually called neophytes, were involved in the agricultural pursuits of the mission, raising the staples of corn, wheat, and beans.

In 1781 another settlement, a civilian pueblo or town, was placed in Los Angeles County. It was founded as an agricultural colony, designed to feed the soldiers stationed in southern California. The two presidios or forts of northern California were supplied by the pueblo of San Jose, founded in 1777. As another fort was to be built in southern California at Santa Barbara, in addition to the one already at San Diego, California's Governor Don Felipe de Neve decided to found the pueblo of Los Angeles for the benefit of the southern Californian installations.

Part of the 1781 expedition came overland, while another part came across the Gulf of California and up the Baja California peninsula, arriving at San Gabriel during the summer. On September 4, 1781, *Alférez* (second lieutenant) José Darío Argüello assigned houselots and fields to the 44 people in eleven families who had arrived to build the new town of El Pueblo de la Reina de los Angeles. Some of the townsmen had possibly cleared the site earlier. The main irrigation ditch and temporary houses of willow poles, branches, and thatch, much like the early houses of San Gabriel, were built around a rectangular plaza. Fields were plowed and a crop was planted. The *pobladores* were largely of mixed racial origin—Indian, Negro, and Spanish. Much of California's colonial population was of multi-racial origin.

Typical sodao de cuera, mounted, in Los Angeles, c. 1790.

Woman colonist at the founding of Los Angeles, c. 1781.

Three of the families requested to leave the pueblo in 1782. Governor Neve judged them useless as farmers and permitted them to leave. Two of these families joined the group bound for the founding of the Santa Barbara presidio, while the third left California. The remaining families continued to farm and raise stock, and in 1785 Governor Pedro de Fages discontinued grain shipments to California since the province was self-sustaining in that respect.

A guard of four soldiers, under Acting Corporal Vicente Féliz, was placed in the pueblo for protection against possible trouble with the numerous, though friendly, Indians. In 1787 he was placed in charge of the pueblo, although a civilian mayor and two councilmen were elected yearly to govern. The governor had decided it would be more efficient that a military liason run the pueblo, as in San Jose. The officer, called a *comisionado,* was the most powerful man in Los Angeles. The office was retained without interruption until Mexico became independent from Spain.

In 1784 one family immigrated from San Jose. In 1787 and 1788 several families, the heads of household recently discharged from army service, were permitted to settle in the pueblo. The pueblo had 139 inhabitants by 1790. Newcomers outnumbered the original settlers roughly four to one, and there were more than thirty adobe buildings around the plaza and its environs.

By 1790 Los Angeles had settled into a pattern which would last with some variations for two to three decades. Retired soldiers from San Diego and Santa Barbara presidios continued to settle there with their slender monthly pensions of eight pesos, augmented by raising the usual crops of corn, beans, and wheat, as well as cattle and horses, for sale to the presidios. The supply ships that sailed from Mexico to California left their goods at the presidios. Spanish colonials were not permitted to trade with foreign ships; consequently the presidial storehouses, with their cloth, tools, household goods, and other articles, were the only place the people of Los Angeles could obtain such items.

In addition to the surplus grain and livestock, the settlers raised in their gardens pumpkins, chiles, squashes, melons, potatoes, and other vegetables. Small boys had the jobs of collecting firewood, frightening birds away from the crops, and as they grew older, helping their fathers in the fields. At age sixteen they could join the army if they so chose, and they often did, repeating the cycle their fathers had lived. Two or three generations came and went from presidio to pueblo in this manner. Daughters aided their mothers until they were old enough to marry and frequently became wives of soldiers. From the 1780s to the 1820s the shifts of families from presidio to pueblo and back again provided people throughout southern California with many friendship and kinship bonds.

Those who had accumulated enough livestock were able to petition the governor for a specific grazing permit to pasture their stock on a stipulated range. This was the beginning of the ranchos, famous in southern California history. Prior to 1822 ranchos were not outright grants of land. They could be revoked any time the governor deemed it convenient to do so. In Los Angeles County there were about ten or twelve such grazing permits given between 1784-1821, of which three were revoked. The first three ranchos in California were in Los Angeles County. They were granted to soldiers Juan José Domínguez, Manuel Nieto, and José María Verdugo in 1784. About 10 years later, Francisco Reyes received the San Fernando Valley, and shortly after 1800, Bartolo Tapía was granted Malibu, Miguel Ortega received Las Virgenes, and Vicente Féliz awarded Los Feliz.

Most farmers in the pueblo had their stock in the pueblo's common lands, taking their turn at herding cattle from time to time. Everyone in the pueblo took their turn in the communal duties of night-watch, maintenance of the irrigation system, guarding the fields against cattle or pests, and watching over the cattle, horses, and sheep.

San Fernando mission was founded in 1797 on the rancho of Francisco Reyes, who was displaced. He received another rancho elsewhere. Later, in 1809, as San Fernando mission expanded over the valley, the rancho of Mariano Verdugo at Cahuenga was absorbed. San Fernando, a successful mission, was not as large in population as San Gabriel, which was one of California's richest missions.

Governor Diego de Borica introduced the planting of grapevines and olive orchards in Los Angeles during the years 1795-98. Wine and olive oil became pueblo products in the ensuing decade; even brandy production was begun before 1809. To prevent cows from grazing in planted fields, farmers placed fences of willow poles around their fields. The fences took root and grew into willow hedges.

Another crop which was beneficial to Los Angeles for a short time was hemp. The government granted a subsidy for hemp crops, and Californians responded with vigor. From 1806 to 1810 Los Angeles settlers busied themselves in planting and harvesting this commodity, making a fair profit for a time. The unsettled conditions in Mexico after 1810, however, caused the hemp subsidy to be dropped as the Spanish government attempted to cope with Mexican patriots demanding independence from Spain. Los Angeles dropped from mild prosperity to occasional penury because of the uncertainty of supplies shipped from Mexico. In the winter of 1810-11 an Indian revolt at the mission of San Gabriel flared, aided by Indians living in villages far to the east around Riverside and San Bernardino. The reasons for the revolt are uncertain. Indians from such distant points as Corona and Cajon Pass assisted the rebels, possibly in reaction to missionization among these Indians in prior years. The Los Angeles artillery militia, organized in 1806, was called out to patrol the area east of San Gabriel on horseback and confront any hostile parties headed west. A detachment from San Diego and a squad under the famous Indian fighter Gabriel Moraga from the San Francisco district had the revolt controlled by June 1811.

From 1799 to 1811 the population of Los Angeles fluctuated between 300 and 400 people. After 1812 the population climbed steadily for four to five years, to between 500 and 600 people. Fewer men were joining the army, while more soldiers in the presidios requested discharge and moved to the pueblo.

California was isolated by the Hidalgo and Morelos rebellions in central Mexico. If the quality of life had suffered somewhat in Los Angeles because of the scarcity of manufactured goods and cloth, the situation at the presidios was much worse. The army payroll was cut, uniforms and clothing, guns, swords, saddles, and other military materials failed to arrive, while the garrisons had to depend on whatever food and crude woolens the missions could provide to sustain them. Some irregular supplies were available from occasional Spanish vessels from Peruvian and Mexican ports, exchanging various goods for Californian hides and tallow. People in the pueblos were in a better position to trade than the poverty-stricken soldiers. Trade with Russian, American, English, and other foreign ships, though still illegal, was finally tolerated because of the critical shortages.

Life in Los Angeles was fairly tranquil while Mexico churned in the caldron of rebellion. A San Gabriel padre was moved to complain that the farmers in that area had begun a vicious circle, hiring pagan Indians from the interior for work in their vineyards, whereupon they would make wine, trade it to christianized Indians in the missions for clothing, and barter the clothing for more Indian aid in planting more vineyards, thus making more wine. Los Angeles farmers had usually depended on Indian aid in planting, weeding, and harvesting. Indians often came from desert areas and from the mountains near San Diego to work. The padres of San Gabriel sometimes accused Los Angeles farmers of competing with the missions for unbaptized Indians. Several Indians, who spoke Spanish well, lived in and around the pueblo, but had never been inside the San Gabriel mission, which was still the parish church for Los Angeles as late as 1826.

In 1822 word came that Mexico was independent from Spain. After eleven years of neglect, Los Angeles inhabitants and most of California were not displeased, even though they had remained loyal to the Spanish Crown. The office of *comisionado* was abolished, then reinstated to govern all retired soldiers and militia members (which included most of the adult male population of Los Angeles) until 1825, when the power of elected government was expanded to include jurisdiction over military personnel. The pueblo was separated from Santa Barbara presidio, and Los Angeles was made directly responsible to the governor of California at Monterey. By the 1820s Los Angeles had a population in excess of 600 persons. It was the largest settlement in California, and had been for several years. A foreign visitor counted 82 adobe houses in the pueblo in 1828 and estimated the population at 800 people, in addition to some 200 Indian laborers living within there on a temporary basis.

Another aspect of Los Angeles' cattle industry changed rapidly during the 1820s. Private rancho growth, rather than communal grazing, was stimulated after trade with foreign vessels was legalized. Cattle became the means of acquiring material goods in a manner well-suited to Californian needs. Hides and tallow were shipped to other countries, where there was a demand. Land granted for ranchos under Mexican law was owned by the grantee. Many of the older Spanish permits were reconfirmed. The biggest cattle-raisers and hide-and-tallow businessmen involved in foreign trade were not rancheros, but the missions of San Gabriel and San Fernando. These missions had more cattle than the pueblo and the nearby ranchos combined, despite the sharp increase in the number of rancho grants around Los Angeles, 1821-28.

Foreigners were permitted to settle in California after 1822, but few came to Los Angeles to live. Some became successful merchants since there was little competition from the Mexican inhabitants. The lack of a merchant class in a region largely rural in character is not surprising. A few individuals from larger towns in central Mexico also came to Los Angeles and opened stores. The native-born population had little interest in such pursuits, with the exception of a few enterprising women, native to California, who opened small stores and taverns. Given the sophistication of those non-native merchants, for the most part from large cities and well-educated, it is not surprising that in time they came to own a major portion of the more desirable buildings in town and some of the best ranchos.

In 1822 the Los Angeles plaza church was completed after six years of effort on the part of parishoners, missions' donations, volunteer, and chain-gang labor. A priest was finally sent to reside permanently at the pueblo in 1826. The pueblo government was expanded about this time to add a secretary and a *síndico,* equivalent of a city attorney, to the mayor and two councilmen.

By 1830 the pattern of settlement in Los Angeles County was still not very extensive. About 1,400 Indians lived at San Gabriel mission, 800 at San Fernando. There were hundreds of gentile Indians, many of whom spoke Spanish well, living in or near the pueblo; they provided a ready pool of labor. A few Indian villages still existed in the northern part of the county, in the

Ruins of custom house erected late in the 18th Century at San Pedro by Padre Lausen, and visited by Richard Henry Dana in 1834-35. (Photo 1899.)

desert and mountain areas, but the Gabrielinos and Fernandeños had for the most part gravitated to the missions or to the pueblo and larger ranchos. The number of people on the ranchos varied from 50 or more persons living at Rancho Santa Gertrudes, near what is now Whittier, to a couple of cowboys living in a brush hut on a smaller rancho. Of about 1,100 *gente de razón* (non-Indians) living in the Los Angeles area, about 300 lived on ranchos. Most lived at the pueblo, with a few families at San Gabriel. The great drop in the Indian population is explained primarily by the deaths from disease between 1769 and 1830. Measles, dysentery, influenza, and several other diseases which were less catastrophic in Europe were deadly to the American Indians, who had been unexposed previously to these maladies.

Changes in the political structure of California affected Los Angeles between 1822 and 1831, when the political struggles became armed conflicts. The transition in 1822 from Spanish colony to Mexican Imperial province was a fairly smooth one, as was the transition from Empire to Republic in 1825. Increased self-government on a local level came with these changes, as did participation in the provincial government in a modest way. With the expansion of local political control came a desire for some self-government on a provincial level. Governors were still sent from Mexico to California, as they always had been. Between 1822 and 1825, however, a native of California, Luis Argüello, was governor. This was a precedent most Californians wanted to continue, but the central government, considering California a territory, did not permit the selection and election of local political aspirants.

The first tremor of revolt came in 1829 at Monterey, when a barracks coup was attempted. Southern California supported the legal governor, José María Echeandía, who resigned his position. In 1831, however, the political turmoil reached the outskirts of the pueblo. Opposition to the newly appointed and reactionary Governor Manuel Victoria had grown into open revolt in San Diego, and a rebel detachment from that town found a welcome in Los Angeles. The local *alcalde* (mayor), Vicente Sánchez, had made himself unpopular through his support of Victoria and the arrest of several dissidents. The governor came south with a small detachment still loyal to him and was defeated about half a mile west of the Los Angeles Plaza. (Some confusion among historians has made Cahuenga, several miles to the west, the site of the battle.)

Another dissident action came in 1836, when a vigilante group in Los Angeles executed Gervasio Alipás and his mistress, Rosario Villa, for the murder of Domingo Féliz, the woman's husband. This was the first such action in California. Although the governor investigated the execution, he could do little.

Until 1836 northern and southern Californians had not been at odds politically. A change came after 1835 when the Mexican government made Los Angeles the capital of California. With this appointment came the title of city, the first of the California hamlets to be so honored. Los Angeles had just over 1,000 *gente de razón* and about 300 Indian laborers living within the city limits. There were about 40 foreigners, all adult males, over half of them Americans. A few British, French, German, and other nationalities rounded out the foreign elements. There is a tendency on the part of local historians to exaggerate the role of the foreigners in most spheres of Californian endeavor, but it should be pointed out that two of the

Los Angeles plaza, 1847; sketch by William Rich Hutton is earliest complete depiction of the city.

wealthiest merchants, Abel Stearns and John Temple, were Americans. Stearns' role in some of the southern California political intrigue against Mexican governors is not precisely known, but suspected with good reason. Several governors were of the opinion that he was an unreliable element and had made efforts to curb his commercial activities. In 1836 conflict arose between Juan Bautista Alvarado, made governor by his clique in Monterey, and Carlos Carrillo, a Santa Barbaran, who was appointed governor by the central government in Mexico City. Alvarado was *de facto* governor, however, and sought to impose his rule on the south by force of arms, which he did successfully. Los Angeles was occupied by his soldiers in 1838 and Carrillo's tenure of office ended when Alvarado moved against San Diego.

The most important economic and social change for the decade of the 1830s was the secularization of the missions in 1834-36. Thousands of neophyte Indians were separated from their missions. Most sought work on the ranchos or in the pueblo itself. Between 1835 and 1846 land which had belonged to the missions was for the most part divided up into many private ranchos, few of the pieces going to the Indians themselves, despite legal provision awarding them half of all such property. Most of the better grazing land went to the *gente de razón* who already had some herds of cattle. Most of the missions' cattle was butchered for the hides by the missionaries in 1834, and what remained of the cattle was often taken by those who had recently acquired ranchos from the land formerly owned by the missions. Little of the material goods of the missions was left to the Indians who had lived in them. San Gabriel and San Fernando were secularized in 1834, and nearly all the land owned by these two missions was divided up into ranchos. Several of the ranchos were granted to the foreigners who were residents of the pueblo.

Secularization brought conflict with some of the recently missionized Indians. The Cahuilla, who lived about 70 miles to the east of the city, took up arms against the Mexicans, burned San Bernardino Asistencia, a chapel and village belonging to San Gabriel, and threatened San Gabriel itself. They were stopped by Los Angeles volunteers, but skirmishes with Indians continued for a few years.

By 1840 there were at least 35 ranchos in the Los Angeles district, where only seven or eight had existed around 1820. The age of the ranchero had truly begun in the 1830s. More ranchos were granted between 1840 and 1846. The missions were no longer competitors for the land, hide trade, or Indian labor. Hundreds of discharged Indian neophytes labored for the people of Los Angeles and its surrounding ranchos.

In 1845 with the ousting of another governor sent from Mexico, the post was again filled by a native Californian. Pío de Jesús Pico was elected governor by a junta, and Los Angeles was chosen capital of the territory. The capital city was a little town of around 1,250 *gente de razón* and perhaps 600 Indian laborers and domestics. Los Angeles was still the largest settlement in the territory, and served as the terminus of overland routes from New Mexico and Sonora. In July 1846 the conflict which had severed Texas from Mexico and had developed an appetite for expansion in the United States brought war to California. American troops landed at Monterey and San Francisco. They soon landed at San Pedro and marched inland to take the city in August. There was little organized resistance at first. Leaving a garrison in the city under the command of Archibald Gillespie, U.S.M.C., the bulk of the force was withdrawn for duty elsewhere. Resentment grew over Gillespie's restrictions against public gatherings, meetings, and movement in and out of the city. Sérvulo Varelas and several of his friends organized resistance to the occupying Americans in September. Armed confrontations near the plaza obliged the garrison to withdraw from Los Angeles to San Pedro, where they remained aboard ship. Commodore Robert F. Stockton landed with marines at San Pedro on October 23 and marched overland toward Los Angeles, when they were confronted by some 100 Californios near the Dominguez ranch. Using a salute cannon which had been buried and disinterred, the local force successfully halted Stockton and forced his retreat to San Pedro.

The people of Los Angeles, though they had little in the way of guns or powder, moved against other American garrisons in southern California with some success. Their most notable victory came on December 6, 1846, when a California column under General Andrés Pico defeated the troops of General Stephen W. Kearny at San Pascual, near San Diego. The Americans were extricated by a relief column from San Diego; the combined force moved north against Los Angeles. The Mexicans failed to halt the advance at the San Gabriel River or at La Mesa, just south of Los Angeles. On January 10, 1847, Los Angeles was permanently occupied by the Americans. General Pico capitulated to Lt. Col. John C. Frémont at Cahuenga Pass on January 13. The war was over for Los Angeles.

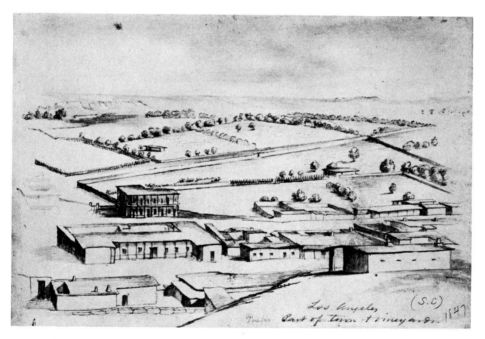

Another Hutton sketch of the city, showing a two story building known as Bell's Row which served as Col. Fremont's residence in the Pueblo.

CHAPTER 2

From Rancho to Boomtown:
The Transition Years, 1849-1889

Judson Grenier, Professor of History,
California State University, Dominguez Hills

Changes in the style and pace of life in Los Angeles came only gradually under the Stars and Stripes. The United States government had neither the resources nor the compulsion to treat southern California like an occupied country; it carried out no mass incarcerations, deportations, or confiscations of property. Inhabitants of the city went their way much as before. But surface impressions were deceptive; time and Yankee traditions of enterprise and politics would have their effect.

Units of the United States army exercised ultimate authority until the end of the war, coexisting with a military-backed civil government which, in Los Angeles, gradually was "Americanized." When news of the Treaty of Guadalupe Hidalgo arrived, local residents argued that the military no longer was needed. While the U.S. Congress debated the establishment of a state or territorial government for California, two Army officers, Col. Richard Mason and Gen. Bennet Riley, served as governor. Riley, sensing the increasingly restive mood of the people as to their ultimate future, called an election for delegates to meet in convention in

Los Angeles Plaza, 1869, showing church and brick reservoir.

Monterey in September 1849 to consider the prospect of self-government. Representing Los Angeles were José Antonio Carrillo, Manuel Domínguez, Stephen C. Foster, Hugo Reid, and Abel Stearns, some native Californios, some ''Mexicanized gringos.'' In a six-week session the convention drafted a concise constitution which laid the foundations for representative government and admission of California to the Union as a free state.

At home, Foster and José Lugo served as alcalde until replaced by the team of Abel Stearns and Juan Sepúlveda. The city was formally chartered in 1850 and a number of new offices created, which stimulated a host of applicants. Any interim period is a time of social tension; until a legal government is operating, uncertainties exacerbate normal civic problems such as maintaining public order and meeting basic human needs. It is difficult to judge whether the onset of the gold rush increased or mitigated those tensions, but it certainly diverted attention from them.

Los Angeles Plaza, 1869, with Lugo Adobe.

News of the discovery of gold on the American River reached Los Angeles about the same time as did news of the peace treaty. Actually, the city had experienced its own mini-rush a few years earlier. Gold or rumors of gold in the area had been known since the mission period. The mayordomo of Mission San Fernando, Pedro López, had introduced the mountainous area lying between the mission and the Antelope Valley to his nephew, Francisco López. One day in 1842 the younger López was hunting livestock in Placeritas Canyon when he discovered gold on the roots of wild onions he had unearthed. A sizeable amount of the metal was mined prior to the discovery of the larger vein in the Sierras. Adobe structures built by the López family endured into the twentieth century.

The Sierra gold rush affected Los Angeles in many ways. Young men abandoned their chief occupations and headed north, and the city experienced a momentary decline in population.

But the influx of immigrants into California more than compensated. An overflow from the mining areas brought many newcomers of various ethnic background, some of them refugees from the camps, some of shady reputation. New problems of crime, rowdy behavior, and racial tension were soon encountered. But the decade of the 1850s also was characterized by prosperity brought on by the demands of the miners for southern California beef, and, along with it, increased real estate exchange and construction. A few of the area's historic buildings date from this period.

The "cattle on a thousand hills" around Los Angeles brought sudden prosperity to their owners, and they, in turn, plunged into a round of land acquisition and ranch expansion, often borrowing large sums at high rates of interest to finance the venture. Representative buildings during this decade included purchase and reconstruction of the Rancho Las Tunas adobe by Judge V.E. Howard (1852); purchase of half-interest in Rancho San Fernando by Don Andrés Pico (1854); additions to Ranchos San Pedro, Los Cerritos and Los Alamitos; construction of the hacienda of Don Ricardo Véjar on Rancho San José near Diamond Bar (1850) and the Temple home on Rancho La Merced near Mission Vieja; the José Ramírez adobe on Rancho Santa Gertrudes (1855) and the López adobe at Elizabeth Lake.

Pico House (Hotel) and street railway, c. 1873.

Rancho prosperity coincided in time with increased expenditures for lawyers, title verification, patents, and suits. As Americans arrived in the area, they coveted land. Security in their property was guaranteed Californians by the Treaty of Guadalupe Hidalgo, but so many different grants had been made by different authorities that claims were clouded. Boundaries were vague and imprecisely defined. Taking advantage of these loopholes, squatters sometimes occupied plots on the fringes of land grants. For example, at El Monte a group of Texans established themselves on land belonging to the Workman-Rowland ranches, though they

Appleton Ranch, west San Fernando Valley, 1880s.

agreed to pay rent for so doing. And for a time part of the San Gabriel mission was turned into a saloon which catered to gamblers, including a justice of the peace who was reputed to make decisions in the midst of card games.

Faced by rising administrative costs and a depleted treasury in 1849, the Los Angeles city council *(ayuntamiento)* decided to take advantage of the interest in land by selling off its vacant lots. The pueblo's Spanish land grant involved four square leagues—eventually held to be 17,172 acres—centering on the Plaza Church, and a formal survey was a prerequisite to any sale. The council gave the job to Lieutenant E.O.C. Ord, a young West Point graduate. Ord offered to receive payment in both cash and land, but the council, aware of rapidly increasing land values, closed the deal at $3,000, cash only. Ord's official map is a historical milestone. From the foothills to about Pico Boulevard, named and unnamed streets were surveyed and plotted on the map. Ord provided both Spanish and English identification: Hill (Loma), Flower (Flores), Spring (Primavera), Main (Principal). When the first auction was held in November, it was clear that the city was moving south; lots in that part sold for more than those on older northern streets.

Outside the pueblo, landowners were forced to verify their claims according to provisions of the Land Law of 1851. Passed by the U.S. Congress, it established a three-man Board of Land Commissioners which sat in San Francisco from January 1852 to March 1856 to weigh claims stemming from old land grants. Rejected land reverted to the public domain and was fair game for squatters. The land law itself was not as troublesome to ranch owners as the long legal hassles often encountered. Ranch titles themselves brought little as collateral, and some owners whose claims eventually were substantiated lost their land through bankruptcy or inability to meet the exhorbitant interest on their debts. Weekly interest of 12 percent was not unusual. Property taxes also took their toll.

Los Angeles landowners fared better by the Land Commission than those in the north. Not as much pressure existed from squatters because of the generally arid climate. In 1852 local ranch owners petitioned the Commission to come south for a sitting. The event produced a fiesta hosted by Manuel Garfías and considerable rapport, after which most land decisions were rendered routinely, and, by and large, fairly. Thanks to the title confirmation and the "beef prosperity," and in spite of considerable mismanagement of resources, the rancheros as a whole weathered the 1850s. Of the 25 leading landholders in the county, most possessed a good part or all of their property in 1859.

The city of Los Angeles retained its Mexican character until after the Civil War period. Roads, vehicles, houses had a rural flavor; few people lived beyond hearing distance of the bell on the Plaza church. But shingles were replacing brea as roofing material, and the adobe architecture was embellished by decorative woodwork. The prosperous years of 1853-55 saw the owners of some town houses near the Plaza adding second stories, and the names del Valle, Coronel, Aguilar, Carrillo, Sanchez, Lugo, Olvera, Gallardo, and Avila were synonymous with gracious living and hospitality. North of the plaza, row adobes housing the poorer Mexicans clustered in "Sonoratown"; while to the west, square wooden buildings testified to the presence of Anglo-Americans. The Latin-American element, including neophyte Indians, outnumbered Yankees until 1870.

Entrepreneurs responded to the increased socio-economic needs of the population. John Lewis and E.G. Buffum launched the Los Angeles *Star* in 1851, and under the editing of an Englishman, Henry Hamilton, it grew into a thriving, regionally-oriented newspaper. The *Southern California* soon followed, and, in 1855, the first Spanish-language weekly, *El Clamor Público,* edited by an outspoken champion of the Californios, Francisco Ramírez. Many religious, social and political organizations formed during the decade which directly or indirect-

Mascarel ranch, Hollywood-Wilshire district, c. 1885.

ly promoted learning and the arts. The first English language school was opened on the corner of Second and Spring, and the first Protestant church established. Under the guidance of Catholic Bishop Tadeo Amat, a girls' orphanage and school, "Institución Caritativa de Los Angeles," was opened in January 1856 near the church. The girls and their mentors, the Sisters of Charity (who began operation of a charity hospital in 1859), were fixtures in religious festivals thereafter. Bishop Amat also established a boys' parochial school featuring bi-lingual education in January 1859. St. Vincent College opened on the Plaza in 1865 and was moved two years later to Sixth and Broadway. By the end of the decade, the city had a Masonic Lodge, a Hebrew Benevolent Society, a French Benevolent Society, and a Turnverein.

Though no bank opened in Los Angeles until 1865—Hellman's First City Bank—commercial building took place in the '50s, particularly at the end of the decade, when 35 brick structures appeared. Public attention centered on the two-story Arcadia Block constructed by Abel Stearns, and the courthouse built by Juan (Jonathan) Temple in 1858. After Don Juan's death in 1866, the property was acquired by his younger brother Francisco ("Templito"), who added the prosperous middle section of the "Temple Block," and then the last section, which housed the bank whose collapse would cost the Temples their fortune and drain the finances of the Workman and Sanchez families.

The 1850s also put Los Angeles on the map as a center of crime, violence, and vigilante action. Each week the *Star* reported new killings and shooting sprees. Homicides daily took place in the notorious Calle de los Negros, a 500-foot block of shacks, saloons and houses of ill repute, known as the "wickedest street on earth." Congregated there were refugees from the gold camps of various ethnic makeup, young immigrants from Mexico, the jobless, panderers, and prostitutes. Those who suffered most were descendants of the local Indians. Cut off from their land, their mission support and their cultural foundations, many Indians became addicted

Timm's Landing and Deadman's Island, San Pedro, 1876.

to a grape-based alcohol which only speeded their demise. Hundreds of Indians congregated in Los Angeles on weekends, sometimes battling in the hills behind the Plaza and being arrested for drunk or disorderly conduct. After 1850, Indian prisoners could be auctioned to private individuals for physical labor; chain gangs of those remaining were put to "public work." The resulting semi-slavery destroyed hundreds of people. One historian states that "Weekly auctions took place in Los Angeles until as late as 1869, but the shortage of workers, caused by the high death rate of Indians, resulted in abandoned vineyards, neglected fruit orchards, and a suffering municipal water system." By 1870 disease had nearly finished them.

To handle law enforcement a panoply of officialdom was created: a county board of supervisors, a court of sessions with three justices and a county judge, a grand jury, a city mayor and six councilmen, a district and city prosecutor, a city marshal and his deputies, the city police, 16 justices of the peace in outlying communities supported by 32 policemen, a sheriff, a sub-sheriff and a deputy sheriff and a deputy sheriff for the county, and 23 judges of the plains with police powers. Yet this large body of officials found it next to impossible to adjudicate the area's social relationships, complicated as they were by differing habits and traditions of justice.

Into this simmering brew was stirred the danger of organized banditry. In the 1850s some disaffected youths of Mexican-American descent took to gang thievery. More then 50 joined the band of a young Mexican, Juan Flores, who escaped incarceration and terrorized the area from Ventura to Capistrano. Flores ambushed and killed a number of law enforcement officers until his gang was hunted down and captured by a posse. Other bandits, from the semi-legendary Joaquín Murieta to the very real Tiburcio Vásquez, made citizens uneasy about travel or isolated residence until the mid-1870s.

The dominant political party in Los Angeles County in the 1850s was the Democratic party. Whigs were active, but generally unsuccessful. Democratic leaders wooed the dons, counting upon them to provide incentives to lure their families and workers to the polls. Whigs were depicted as anti-Mexican and anti-Catholic. Additionally, much of the population newly-arrived from the United States came from Southern or frontier states where the Democratic party maintained traditional strength. Local Democrats supported measures to divide the state of California in half, largely on the grounds that the southern counties were unfairly taxed. In 1859 Senator Andrés Pico put through both houses of the state legislature a resolution separating southern California into a new territory; the measure garnered three to one support in local plebiscite. But the Civil War was pending, and to many people in northern California, as well as members of Congress, pressures for division seemed pro-slavery agitation in disguise. Unquestionably, southern California was more sympathetic to the cause of the South than was the rest of the state.

The firing on Fort Sumter saw Confederate flags unfurled south of the Plaza and a portrait of Confederate General P.T.G. Beauregard hung at the Bella Union Hotel. The *Star* condemned President Lincoln for starting the war; eventually its editor was imprisoned and its mailing rights suspended. Southern recruits enlisted locally (some trained in El Monte), and a column left secretly for Texas by way of Yuma, Arizona. Among local men serving as Confederate officers were Generals Albert Sidney Johnston and Joseph L. Brent. But Los Angeles generally remained loyal to the Union. Its leading Democrat, John G. Downey, was a Unionist; Downey was elected lieutenant governor of California and succeeded to the war-time governorship of the state. The U.S. Army strengthened its headquarters at Drum Barracks at Wilmington. Its commandant, Winfield Scott Hancock, "showed the colors" to discourage secessionist sentiment and organized local militia into a company to maintain order. A few local men soldiered with the "California Column" and the Native California Cavalry into Arizona territory to prevent Confederate seizure of that area.

The Civil War years saw the collapse of dominance of the rancheros in Los Angeles county. Business speculation and lack of currency brought on a depression in the late 1850s, which in turn lowered land values and depressed cattle prices. Cattle could be bought at any price by the summer of 1861. That winter the economy was weakened by heavy rainstorms and flooding. Rampant water washed out the city's water works, mail deliveries were halted, and the city's merchants waded waist deep to attempt to save their goods. The San Gabriel River jumped its banks and altered its course, while destroying vineyards and orchards. But the final blows to agriculture came in the form of a scorching drought which lasted for two years, 1862-64, and when it had ended, the "cattle on a thousand hills" were largely gone. Many of the ranches were subdivided and sold in small plots to grain cultivators.

Collapse of the rancho system was by no means total. Some, like Don Manuel Domínguez, managed to adapt successfully to the new system. Domínguez completed his formal political career in 1857, stepping down as Los Angeles county supervisor, but was active behind the scenes until his death in 1882. His Rancho San Pedro was the first of the original grants in the county to receive a clear patent of title from the government. The land was retained by the Domínguez family, except for a northern tract sold to George Compton for a new town and 2,400 acres near the harbor sold to Phineas Banning for development of "New San Pedro," later named "Wilmington."

First load of lumber to Los Angeles on one of the country's two trains, railroad wharf, Wilmington, 1870.

Nor did construction of adobe ranch homes totally cease. The year 1865 produced at least a half-dozen, including three which stood nearly a century—Antonio Rocha's Rancho Rincón (Los Angeles) and the homes of Francisco Grazide in Puente and Martin Ruíz in Bouquet Canyon. More adobes appeared in the 1870s, particularly in the San Fernando Valley. They included homes of Andrés and Rómulo Pico (1873), George K. and B.F. Porter (1873), Valentín and Geronimo López (1878), and Rómulo Pico's Rancho La Liebre (1875).

In 1873 a United States survey revealed Rancho Ex-Mission de San Fernando to be the largest grant in California, 116,858 acres; by the end of the decade it had been split. The northern half was jointly acquired by the Porters for ranching and by Senator Charles Maclay for subdivision. Maclay set a style for real estate promotion. He drove to Los Angeles in 1874 to record the first real estate map of the valley, with street names, 25-foot town lots and 40-acre farm tracts. Maclay put on free barbecues to lure potential clients, and the Southern Pacific Railway offered them transportation at half-fare. The southern half of the valley by 1880 had been acquired by a new corporation, the Los Angeles Farm and Milling Company, which established wheat and barley farms. Dry farming in wheat was first successfully attempted in the eastern valley by Isaac Lankershim and Isaac N. Van Nuys in 1876.

Very close to the center of Los Angeles lay "Sonoratown," in which were concentrated many of the older and smaller adobe buildings which could be acquired cheaply, and there lived many Mexican-American residents. By the time of the Civil War the area had acquired characteristics of the classic "barrio" with a population somewhat culturally distinct—a working-class neighborhood with problems of poverty and crime and a degree of transiency, but affording the sense of belonging, of solidarity and brotherhood, which a parochial culture provides. Sonoratown expanded to the east during the 1870s, but as late as the land boom of the 80s, very few people of Mexican-American descent were living east of the Los Angeles river; some craftsmen and merchants had settled in Brooklyn and Boyle Heights.

Sonoratown, 1885.

Post-Civil War immigration into California and railroad building in the state were coincident with a rise in anti-Chinese sentiment, particularly in working-class neighborhoods. Los Angeles did not escape these tensions. The most serious violence occurred on October 24, 1871, in Chinatown, on Calle de los Negros. Chinatown, too, was culturally distinct, with its own forms of language, business and entertainment, and an obvious target for majority wrath. During disorders engendered by a tong war, a city policeman and two assistants were shot. A white mob quickly formed to seek retribution. In spite of attempts to prevent violence, the mob smashed windows, roofs and walls along the Calle and adjacent streets. At least 18 Chinese were killed. The incident caused international repercussions but locally provoked little sympathy. The coroner's jury identified only four of the killers, later acquitted, and suits of the Chinese against the city were thrown out by the California Supreme Court. But reaction to the affair did produce a Sunday-closing law in the city.

By the mid-1870s, gas lamps had been installed in the central city and four streets—Spring, Main, San Pedro and Aliso—displayed horse-drawn street cars. Main and San Pedro were the most prestigious residential streets, and the four main hotels were concentrated on Main between the Plaza and Market. Each hotel maintained a carriage or horse-drawn bus to meet tourists at the wharves at Wilmington or San Pedro and treat them to a long, hot ride into the city. Popular social centers were George Lehman's beer garden adjacent to a brewery between Spring and Main, and William Buffum's elegant new saloon. Many locations—from the Plaza to the harbor—sponsored commemorative ceremonies on Independence Day, 1876, but that at Lehman's Garden was reputed to be most festive of them all.

By the 1880s, Los Angeles had acquired such cultural attributes as a community orchestra and a truly professional theater, Childs Opera House, located on Main near First, which opened in 1884 and featured such players as Edwin Booth and Madame Helena Modjeska. Long-established newspapers were the *Express, Herald* and *Weekly Mirror*; like the population of the city, they usually leaned Democratic politically. On December 4, 1881, a Republican paper, the *Times,* made its appearance, but the owners sold out after only eight months to their printing company, which hired as editor Colonel Harrison Gray Otis, previously editor of the Santa Barbara *Press*. By 1886, Otis had assumed financial control of the *Times.* He was a man

Rancho San Pedro (Dominguez), 1888.

Third street, looking southeast from the hill, c. 1890.

with a flashy writing style and strong opinions, supporting free enterprise and opposing unionization. In 1885 Otis purchased the first lot in a new tract development laid out west of the central city by H. Gaylord Wilshire; his home later was deeded to the county for an art institute.

New public schools were built to serve the growing community. Compulsory grammar school attendance began in 1874. The first high school was constructed in 1873 on a hill at Temple and Broadway. Later it was moved across the street, and, in 1917, relocated in a strikingly-turreted building on Olympic Boulevard. In 1880 a group of Protestants, primarily Methodists, founded the University of Southern California, built and financed by donations of land from citizens of all religious denominations. Seven years later, local Presbyterians established Occidental College and Congregationalists founded Pomona College in communities east of the city. Pride of the public was the State Normal School, opened in 1882 at Fifth and Grand with three teachers and 61 students, and later (1914) moved to a 25-acre site on Vermont before its conversion to the University of California, Southern Branch.

The history of Los Angeles city and county is written in large part by transportation systems, both without and within. Each major development—building of the Southern Pacific and Santa Fe Railways, the local inter-urban lines, the electric transit systems, and shipping routes to the harbors—shaped the growth and character of the area. The first rail line was built by the county with funds raised through bond sales and ran from the central city to the harbor. Phineas Banning unloaded the first locomotive at Wilmington after the line was completed, and the operation proved immediately profitable. Another rail line was built to Santa Monica by John P. Jones. But eyes were focused mainly on the Southern Pacific system, headquartered in San Francisco, and building south through California with its goal a transcontinental network. Interested in profits and needing money to maintain construction prior to the time transportation fees would carry the road, the Southern Pacific solicited contributions from communities in its path. The price for Los Angeles was a right-of-way, 60 acres for the depot, a grant equal to five percent of the county's assessed valuation, and the local railroad to the harbor. After seven years' negotiations and a county-wide ballot, the agreement was signed. Construction of bridges, overpasses and tunnels through the Tehachapis was a prodigious endeavor. The final golden spike marking the opening of the line was driven by S.P. President Charles Crocker at a ceremony at Lang's Station in Soledad Pass on September 5, 1876. The Southern Pacific also built an extension to Anaheim.

But the great land boom of the 1880s did not begin until completion of the Santa Fe Railroad to Los Angeles in 1885. Its monopoly of less than a decade broken, the Southern Pacific responded by lowering prices for transporting both goods and people. A rate war then ensued, with prices for travel from the Missouri river to Los Angeles plummeting downward from $125 to $15, and, at the peak of the rivalry, reportedly only $1. Later it went up to $40 and there stabilized. The rivalry encouraged many Middlewesterners to seek a new life in southern California, lured by railroad advertising of opportunities in local business and agriculture.

The first wave of settlers largely intended to buy and work the land; the second wave included both investors and real estate promoters who sought to take advantage of the boom. Overloaded trains twice daily dumped their crowds into a Los Angeles which was bursting at the seams and in which housing was at a premium. Town lots shot up 300 percent in value. Ranches and orchards were subdivided into small plots. New townsites were laid out along the railroads' rights-of-way. Many lots were sold and resold by day and night. New cities were created with

Looking south from the hill, c. 1890.

Italian or Spanish names and Los Angeles County came to resemble land along the Mediterranean Sea. Many speculators became "millionaires of a day" in places called "Arcadia," "Avalon," "La Canada" or "Glendale."

But the land boom collapsed almost as quickly as it had begun. Too much optimism, too many false values, too much manic selling, an over-commitment of capital—all contributed to the bust. Land syndicates went bankrupt and much of the property reverted to original owners. For a decade the courts were filled with suits and countersuits, and banks were foreclosing on debts.

Los Angeles rode out the storm of the financial collapse. Few banks failed. Many of the newcomers stayed on. Most of the new cities and towns incorporated or consolidated and survived. But some disillusionment with local government was expressed regionally. When Los Angeles County was organized in 1850, it included all of San Bernardino and Orange Counties. Both of these adjacent areas were affected by the boom, and population growth meant increase in local problems. When Orange County was carved out of Los Angeles in 1889 and went its own way, residents professed a need for a center of government close to home. Nevertheless the city's optimism remained. Los Angeles businessmen in 1888 formed a chamber of commerce to help promote the area in lean times. Its promotional activities would later attract fresh waves of settlers determined to seek the good life in southern California.

Windermere Ranch, La Mirada, 1890s.

CHAPTER 3

From Boom to Depression:
Los Angeles Becomes a Major City, 1890-1929

Abraham Hoffman, Instructor of History, Los Angeles Valley College

In the wake of the boom of the 1880s, Los Angeles boosters hoped that development of the region would in the future be less chaotic. The city's population had peaked during the 1880s at 70,000, down to a more stable 50,000 in 1890. Speculation in real estate continued as an ever-constant preoccupation, but business leaders realized that without a solid economic base the city could never achieve major metropolitan status.

One major goal of Los Angeles businessmen was the development of a viable harbor. But in 1890 no such facility existed, although the Santa Fe Railroad ran its trains along a short wharf at Redondo and loaded ocean-going steamers with relative ease. By contrast, cargoes at San Pedro had to be loaded from freight cars to harbor lighters, which then met deep-draft ships in the outer harbor. The Southern Pacific Railroad, under the direction of Collis P. Huntington, had originally favored a San Pedro port; however, in 1891 Huntington pulled his railroad out of San Pedro and began construction of a huge pier at Santa Monica, outflanking the Santa Fe's Redondo facility.

Building the breakwater, Los Angeles harbor, c. 1890.

Oil wells west of Bunker hill (area of west Temple street), c. 1895.

Business center of Japanese section, 1900s.

Los Angeles street from First, looking toward the Plaza, c. 1900.

Fog buoy offshore at Point Fermin, with Palos Verdes in background, c. 1900.

The Southern Pacific's intentions to build a wharf at Santa Monica alarmed Angelenos who feared the railroad was acting, as it had done in the past, for selfish reasons. When a board of engineers submitted a report to Congress recommending federal appropriations for development of a harbor at San Pedro—reversing an earlier federal decision favoring Santa Monica—Huntington lobbied fiercely for the Santa Monica location. Which port would win the federal appropriation? Local newspapers, businessmen, and partisans for and against Huntington's railroad took sides. Supporters of the San Pedro port established a Free Harbor League, to the anger of Santa Monica citizens who felt that such a title clouded the issue.

In the United States Senate the contest was joined between Senator William Frye of Maine, a Huntington supporter, and Los Angeles' own Stephen M. White, serving his first senatorial term. As political maneuvering placed legislation approving the San Pedro site in peril—and at one point a bill appropriating $3 million for Santa Monica and nothing for San Pedro reached the Senate floor—White debated Frye, demanding another impartial engineering commission investigation. White won the point, the third federal report again favored San Pedro, and

Glass bottom boat, Catalina Island, c. 1905.

Pacific Electric tracks, Manhattan Beach, 1906.

Great White Fleet on its visit to Japan arrives in San Pedro, 1908.

First air meet in the West, Dominguez ranch, 1910.

Building the Los Angeles Aqueduct, c. 1911.

Angelenos were jubilant as construction began in 1899. Although problems with Southern Pacific ownership of San Pedro frontage would continue for years, Los Angeles had won a commitment from the federal government to improve its favored harbor location. The opening of the Panama Canal in 1914 contributed to the development and success of the harbor's commercial operation. By that time residents of the San Pedro area had voted their annexation to the city, making the connection through a mile-wide "shoestring strip."

Having secured the development of the city on the seaward side, supporters of continued growth for Los Angeles now considered the problem of water in another form—an adequate fresh-water supply for domestic use. Located in a semi-arid basin, Los Angeles had depended upon its river for domestic needs, but by 1900 the city had reached a new high of 100,000 people. And there was every indication that the population would continue to increase dramatically. Propagandizing the virtues of the region had become a full-time operation for the Los Angeles Chamber of Commerce, founded in 1888. The chamber sent a flood of promotional literature back east extolling the climate, the opportunities, and the attractions of southern California.

The influx of people combined with a long drought period to create a serious water shortage in southern California. As parks and lawns turned brown, concerned civic leaders investigated new methods and new sources for water. The alternative—an end to growth—was unacceptable to city boosters who based the success of their own enterprises on an ever-expanding population. In 1902, after several years of litigation, the City of Los Angeles acquired the operation of its own water company. Now all that was needed was water, more of it, and more for future needs as well as present use.

In 1905, with the estimated population of the city at 200,000, a controversial solution was presented that still provokes argument more than seven decades later. Fred Eaton, a former mayor of Los Angeles with ranching interests in the Owens Valley, approached his friend William Mulholland, city engineer for the municipally owned water bureau, with an unusual proposal. Eaton demonstrated the feasibility of bringing water from the Owens River across some 240 miles of desert and mountain regions through a gravity-flow aqueduct. Mulholland investigated the idea and found it could be done. Options of water rights were secretly obtained—to avoid a drastic rise in price—and on July 29 the grand scheme was announced.

Not everyone was pleased with the news. Cries of betrayal echoed from the Owens Valley, where Inyoites had expected approval of a proposed federal reclamation project; and not a few settlers had sold water options to Eaton in the mistaken belief he represented the U.S. Reclamation Service. Samuel T. Clover, editor of the Los Angeles *Evening News,* editorially opposed the proposed aqueduct; and questions were also raised about the secrecy under which the plans had been made. When it was revealed that a coterie of prominent businessmen had purchased land in the San Fernando Valley, and that those men had learned of the Eaton-Mulholland scheme through the cooperation of Moses Sherman, a member of the land syndicate who also happened to be serving on the Board of Water Commissioners at the same time, charges of conflict of interest were made.

Whatever the issues of morality, Los Angeles voters gave their approval to the aqueduct bonds, and construction soon began. Under Mulholland's leadership the aqueduct was constructed in a six-year period, 1907-13. On November 5, 1913, as Owens River water cascaded into the San Fernando Valley before the view of thousands who had come out to watch the spectacle, Mulholland delivered his famous cryptic message: "There it is. Take it."

"There it is. Take it." The water arrives at Owensmouth, 1913.

Although the new water supply promised to meet future needs for some time, the city had failed to construct an adequate storage reservoir in the Owens Valley itself. A decade later this oversight proved costly. During another drought period, in the 1920s, Los Angeles again began the extensive purchase of water rights, moving beyond this approach to buying up Owens Valley land as well. The fewer farms needing water in the Owens Valley, it was reasoned, the more water that would be available for the city's use. A policy of continuing annexation had made Los Angeles the largest city in the world in terms of area by the 1920s. This in turn left the city with little margin to spare in its water resources.

Even as Mulholland and his engineers began to look to the Colorado River as a new source for the thirsty city, angry Owens Valley settlers escalated their quarrel to the level of violence. Between 1924 and 1927 the aqueduct was repeatedly dynamited. Resistance to the city's will at last ended when Inyo County's leading bank failed as a result of embezzlement by the valley's leading defenders. Bitterness, however, long remained. A proper storage reservoir in the valley was not built until 1940. Today the City of Los Angeles remains the largest single landholder in the Owens Valley, and a second aqueduct—constructed in the 1960s—is the target for court injunctions and renewed protests. Defensive of its water needs, Los Angeles continues to obtain much of its water from the Owens Valley.

Assured of a major water supply after construction of the aqueduct, Los Angeles rapidly grew in the early decades of the 20th century. Demographic change altered the face of the city. From 1900 to 1910 the population of the city tripled, swelled in part by new arrivals, but also the result of annexations of surrounding areas. Some of these communities joined the city for economic reasons, some for political, but most to participate in the municipal water and power system. Thirteen square miles to the south and west were added just before 1900, and in the following decade 58 square miles, including the Hollywood area.

New waves of immigration after 1902 included Europeans from Italy, Austria, Hungary, and Russia. Fleeing Czarist persecution was a large Jewish contingent. Undergoing resurgence was immigration from Mexico (often via Texas). In 1900 about 3,000 Mexican-Americans lived in Los Angeles, of whom 817 were born in Mexico; by 1910 this number stood at 10,000, of whom over half were native Mexicans. The population of Japanese in the city rose from about 150 in 1900 to 4,238 by 1910. Many of these two groups, as well as Blacks from the South, came to Los Angeles to participate in construction of rapid transit systems in the city and its suburbs. The heart of the Japanese community in southern California, in the shadow of the City Hall today, was soon known as Lil' Tokyo.

From 1902 to 1908 the central city experienced a building boom; many landmarks were constructed then, including the Hibernian Building, tallest structure in Los Angeles until the City Hall was completed two decades later, and Hamburger's Department Store, predecessor of the May Company.

Construction and business activities slowed because of a recession in 1908. The unemployed walked the streets and ate free lunches at local settlement houses. But after 1910 the economy quickened, and annexations proceeded with seven square miles each of the Arroyo Seco and Palms areas. Except for Glendale, Burbank, and San Fernando, the entire San Fernando Valley was annexed by the city in 1915. Annexations continued until 1927, when the renewed threat of a water shortage ended the era of growth by geography. In the meantime, the far reaches of the county had become linked through a transportation system which old-time southern California residents recall with nostalgia—the big red cars of the Pacific Electric Railway.

In 1898 Henry E. Huntington, nephew of Collis Huntington of Southern Pacific notoriety, embarked on an enterprise that provided southern California with a modern rapid transit network. Beginning with the purchase of the Los Angeles Railway, in 1899 Huntington and his partners created the Pacific Electric Railway. He purchased existing companies, laid trackage to outlying areas, and bought new trolley cars. Huntington not only provided a major transit system for the City of Los Angeles, he also linked such communities as Riverside and Santa Monica by means of Pacific Electric trackage. In its heyday the system speedily sent its red trolley cars at 55 miles per hour from one end of the county to the other and beyond. They took commuters to and from work, provided easy access to beaches and mountains, and enabled developers to sell lots in Venice, Redondo Beach, Long Beach, and numerous other communities. For better or worse, the germ of an idea—suburban residence and city employment—was initially made possible by Huntington's "big red cars."

The idyll was not to last forever. In the 1920s the fixed transit system went into decline, in part the victim of its own success. As the city's population increased from 576,673 in 1920 to over 1,238,000 in 1930, patronage of the railway system failed to increase in the same degree. To take up the slack fares were raised, but profits continued to drop.

What had happened was a major change in the life style of southern California, a change so drastic that it spelled doom for the streetcars and permanently altered the character of the region. In short, Los Angeles met the automobile, and it was love at first sight. Even as passenger fares failed to hold their own for the transit system in the 1920s, automobile registrations increased 5 1/2 times between 1919 and 1929.

City planning in Los Angeles was then in its earliest stages, the city planning commission having been created only in 1920. Faced with major traffic jams in the downtown area—jams which also slowed streetcars—planners tried to create a comprehensive fixed-transit system that would help streetcars function more efficiently. A chief element in the plan was the construction of a downtown terminal. But the number of different plans suggested prompted a wait-and-see attitude that proved fatal to the streetcars.

Many planners in the 1920s believed rapid transit an obsolete concept. They favored reliance instead upon automobile transportation, calling for construction of paved highways in outlying areas. Developers who had advertised homes and lots strategically located near transit lines now boasted of paved roads and garages.

New residents to southern California demanded homes in suburban locations. Never a city of high population density, Los Angeles chose decentralization as a way of meeting the challenge of hundreds of thousands of new residents arriving in the 1920s. Indeed, the real estate boom of the 1920s dwarfed earlier periods of land speculation. Moreover, it was characterized by the sale of lots for single-family homes. And to move from one area of the county to another, the people overwhelmingly adopted the automobile. Within the space of a decade the pattern was set. By 1930 Los Angeles claimed two cars for every five people, as compared with one car for every four people in second-place Detroit.

No longer were people just coming to southern California for farms, retirement, or tourism, although these still were strong motives which lured many new residents. The city had acquired major metropolitan status, not only in terms of population—San Francisco was passed by in 1920—or transportation, but in the diversified industries and businesses that contributed impressively to the region's economic growth.

Southern California's industries themselves reflected the ambitions of a developing metropolis at the beginning of a new century. By 1900 Los Angeles had already experienced its first oil boom, with overnight fortunes being made from numerous discoveries within the city itself. Edward L. Doheny began his fortune near Second Street and Glendale Boulevard in 1892 by sinking a miner's shaft down to the black gold. From such crude beginnings the oil industry was born. A second boom period began after the World War with oil discoveries at Santa Fe Springs, Signal Hill, Huntington Beach, and other areas. Speculation in real estate found its match in the scramble for oil stocks. Eventually—and inevitably—fraudulent stock sales and overproduction marred the progress of the industry, as did poor methods of conserving oil-field pressure.

Considerably less speculative but no less dramatic than the petroleum industry, aviation development found colorful beginnings in southern California. The first air meet in the United States was held at Dominguez Field, built especially for the occasion. From January 10-20, 1910—a time of year not unnoticed by potential manufacturers and investors living in winter-bound portions of the country—a fascinating variety of aircraft flew over a crowd of 20,000 delighted spectators.

World War I proved that aviation could be a major industry rather than a diversion or indulgence. Glenn Martin had started his aircraft company before the war. In 1920 Donald Douglas, with support from Harry Chandler of the Los Angeles *Times* and other investors, began building airplanes in Santa Monica for the U.S. Navy. The Lockheed Aircraft Company traced its origins to 1916 when it was founded in Santa Barbara by Allan and Malcolm

The doughboys arrive home after World War I.

Loughead; it was revitalized in Burbank in the 1930s by Robert E. Gross. Other aircraft companies transferred operations to southern California or began operations there in the 1930s.

Southern California's mild climate has proven to be a major selling point for aviation, and the sunshine-filled days also contributed to the development of another important industry—motion pictures. Like aviation, the motion picture industry originated elsewhere; but southern California's climate, topography, and proximity to the Mexican border—in case of lawsuits—brought early moviemakers to the region. After the first rush to view anything on film, patrons became more discriminating. The quality of films improved after 1910 in response to public tastes as the fledgling industry produced westerns, comedies, and adventure stories set in all times and ages. Increasing cosmopolitanism is evinced by the popularity of stars of diverse background, such as Rudolph Valentino, Sussue Hayakawa, and Anna May Wong.

The first studios were generally located in Hollywood, although consolidations and mergers, plus the incredibly rapid expansion of the industry, caused the larger companies to build their studios in such areas as Burbank, Culver City, and the San Fernando Valley. As a major industry which was highly profitable, raised real estate values, and attracted new people to southern California, motion pictures joined aviation and petroleum as visible advertisements for the area's dynamism and growth.

Other industries also contributed to the region's economic development. Downtown real estate values shot up as old structures were torn down, to be replaced by modern buildings. Department stores, hotels, and business concerns ranging from textile manufacturing to merchandising found space in the many new buildings being constructed along Broadway, Hill Street, and other downtown thoroughfares. In 1926 the Los Angeles Public Library opened the doors of its new building to patrons, and the new Los Angeles City Hall was completed in 1928. By the end of the 1920s businesses were also branching out into new areas; the Miracle Mile, a stretch of Wilshire Boulevard once considered too remote for profitable enterprise, attracted such merchants as Desmond's and Silverwood's.

As a land of opportunity Los Angeles had proved a successful venture for many people. For many others, however, success had to be measured in the size of a paycheck and the quality of life made possible by the amount of wages earned. Many workers believed their wages and working conditions unequal to the labor they gave. Prominent Los Angeles businessmen, on the other hand, looked upon attempts by workers to organize into unions as threatening to their rights as employers. With the continuous arrival of new people seeking jobs, the union movement in Los Angeles found organizing work difficult.

Capital and labor soon polarized in the young metropolis. Under the leadership of Harrison Gray Otis and his son-in-law Harry Chandler, the Los Angeles *Times* led the fight against unionism. During the year 1910 union-backed strikes met active opposition from employers organized as the Merchants and Manufacturers Association. Scabs fought pickets; police vigorously enforced an anti-picketing ordinance and threw strikers in jail. Then, on October 1, 1910, an explosion rocked the Los Angeles *Times* building, killing twenty employees. Otis blamed union agitators. Several months later private detectives hired by Los Angeles County District Attorney John D. Fredericks apprehended three labor leaders. One of those captured implicated the other two in the *Times* bombing as well as dozens more in a country-wide conspiracy.

The trial of the McNamara brothers, accused of the *Times* bombing, became the contest by which the direction of the labor-capital struggle in Los Angeles would be determined. Many people looked upon the McNamara brothers as innocent martyrs, while supporters of business viewed them as calculating murderers. Socialists triumphed in the 1911 Los Angeles municipal election. Mayoral candidate Job Harriman, who was one of the lawyers defending the McNamaras, was favored to win the runoff. Shortly before the trial began, however, the defendants' chief attorney, famed lawyer Clarence Darrow, changed their plea to guilty in the belief the case could not be won.

The event proved traumatic to the labor movement in Los Angeles. Harriman lost his election, the American Federation of Labor abandoned its militant approach to union organization, and Los Angeles enjoyed a reputation as an "open shop" city that lasted for many years. Not until the mid-1930s would the labor movement in Los Angeles recapture its lost respectability.

Along with the economic struggles of the early twentieth century, the City of Los Angeles experienced problems in the political arena. Although Los Angeles did not suffer from the machine politics of other cities, occasional scandals did occur. The city also had to endure a succession of mediocre nonentities as mayor. On the positive side, a civic reform movement, led by Dr. John R. Haynes, contributed towards making local government more responsive to the will of the voters. Haynes' campaign forced the resignation of Mayor Arthur C. Harper in 1909 and helped end partisan politics in municipal elections. Reform was shortlived, however, and in the 1920s corruption seemed firmly entrenched in local government. Bootleg liquor, corrupt police officials, and organized crime flourished. Not until another major reform movement was launched in the late 1930s would city and county governments regain the public trust.

As the 1920s drew to a close southern Californians could well believe that not only the "Roaring 20s" decade but the entire preceding forty years had been a time of exuberant, uninhibited growth. From a mid-sized town not especially different from other ambitious municipalities, the City of Los Angeles had grown to dominate its county. It had acquired a major harbor, attracted a multitude of people, encouraged new and developing industries, and endorsed a unique life style stressing the blessings of suburban life and the automobile. Like a glorious bubble, the development of Los Angeles kept pace with its ambitions, growing ever larger. And like so many other bubbles in 1929, Los Angeles' schemes and dreams burst with the Great Crash and the start of the Great Depression.

Lick Pier, Ocean Park, c. 1920.

Olvera street, 1920s.

Old St. Paul's Cathedral (Olive between Fifth and Sixth) where Biltmore now stands, c. 1923.

CHAPTER 4

Big Time Growth and the Consequences of the Superlative, 1930-1978

Richard G. Lillard, Professor of English, Emeritus, California State University, Los Angeles

In January 1930 as Los Angeles County began the decades of change preceding the bicentennials of San Gabriel mission, 1971, the nation, 1976, and the metropolitan county seat, 1981, the expansive boom spirit of the 1920s carried on some of its momentum. The Great Depression, symbolically begun on Wall Street, had not fully made its destined impact on the subsidiary outpost, Spring Street, Los Angeles.

Construction was down and real estate quiet, but the population was growing at a rate of about 5 or 6% a year, the harbors at Long Beach and Los Angeles were handling a record volume of commerce, and the motion-picture studios kept busy promoting a new generation of stars who could talk and sing. The relatively small local industries, canning fish and fruit, generating electricity, and manufacturing iron and steel, airplanes, and tires were all doing well, though furniture was slackening. A new oil field had come in a Santa Fe Springs but oil production was falling off.

The county continued, as for half a century, to be an agriculture bonanza, a national leader in the production of oranges, walnuts, vegetables, livestock, dairy products, and assorted deciduous fruits. From the almond and pear orchards of the Mojave Desert uplands in Antelope Valley to the strawberry fields of Gardena, and from the truck gardens of Santa Monica to the citrus groves of Pomona and Claremont, the county was the cornucopia of edible products long touted by the Chamber of Commerce. Floriculture also has been a major product. Commercial flower growers were established along the entire coastline of the county long before W.W. II. Refrigerated railroad cars carried cut flowers throughout the nation.

Los Angeles had the future on its side. It had the modern ports and an oceanic potential for world trade. In the Mojave, the San Fernando Valley, and the 30 miles of flatlands between the mountains and the sea there was—or so there seemed—ample space for homes, factories, schools, airfields, highways and streets, and all other urban developments, including stores and office towers. The Pacific Electric system with its Big Red Cars was a superb rapid transit system that linked all parts of the county south of the mountains and tied tightly, too, into Orange county beaches and towns and the western cities of San Bernardino and Riverside counties. Though slowed down by increasing automobile traffic at grade crossings, the Pacific Electric trains with their broad rights-of-way hastened crowds to and from the city centers, to new outlying subdivisions, as in the San Fernando Valley, and they led people directly to famous novelties such as the cogwheel railway to Mount Lowe and the steamer for Avalon and Santa Catalina, the county's big island.

Los Angeles had a big, unspoiled share of the Mediterranean type of climate found in the

United States only in California. Above all was the spacious canopy of sun and blue sky that had led travelers to call southern California "America's Italy."

Some things worsened in 1930 and later. The number of business failures picked up; so did the number of unemployed, as tire, furniture, and meat packing companies lowered production. There was a shortage of single-family dwellings. But deflation helped as prices fell, including the price of gasoline to under ten cents a gallon. Between December 1930 and February 1932 the cost of living fell more than 8%. Important public works continued, such as street widening and new installation at the harbors. In September 1931 voters passed the bond issue for the Colorado River Aqueduct, assuring future water for the 13 cities of the Metropolitan Water District. Preparations for the Olympic Games of 1932 led to new sports facilities and much city grooming.

Olympic village, Baldwin Hills, 1932.

Compton policeman inspects damage after earthquake struck southern area, 1933.

At the same time, Los Angeles spawned one of the most flamboyant religious figures in southern California history, Aimee Semple McPherson. Sister Aimee's Four Square Gospel was preached to thousands of disciples gathered at her Angelus Temple on Echo Park and to a vast radio audience. Another radio personality was the outspoken minister-turned-politician, the Reverend Bob Shuler, who harangued his audience on corruption and politics and ran for governor in 1934.

The county, already supplying nation and world with news of movies and movie makers, furnished news, too, of natural disasters such as the deadly Long Beach earthquake of 1933, a flood at the very end of 1933 that wrecked homes at the foot of the mountains in Montrose and La Crescenta, and a series, not yet ended in 1978, of forest and brush fires in canyons and on mountainsides from one end of the country to the other.

Given time and national programs, the Depression terminated. Oil, shipping, motion pictures, and agricultural products, plus tourism and immigration brought in money and created jobs. New plants assembled cars. Aircraft plants expanded. By 1938 FHA loans were stimulating construction of new homes. Subdivisions began to chew into orchard and crop land in the San Fernando and San Gabriel valleys, at popular spots along the coast, and at Palmdale in the high desert.

During the 1930s, Los Angeles became increasingly politically conscious. In this area Upton Sinclair, Socialist-turned-Democrat, founded his End Poverty in California movement. Using EPIC as his political vehicle, he mounted a strong but losing bid for the governorship in 1934. A veteran of the campaign, Sheridan Downey, later was elected to the United States Senate. In 1938 a "clean government" ticket headed by Judge Fletcher Bowron, fought a victorious recall election against the incumbent city mayor, Frank Shaw. Mayor Bowron instituted a large number of reforms. Vice and corruption were rooted out, and the city's administrative personnel removed from the political arena and professionalized. Bowron served 15 years in office.

The Nazi thrust in Europe and the evident speeding up of U.S. war preparations stimulated activity in all of California. The European war of 1914-18 had depressed Los Angeles County, which then depended on immigration, real-estate activity, and building construction and could not share in the war-born industrial prosperity of the Middle West and East. But now, with a much changed economy the county was ready to participate in and even dominate portions of the national effort in a war both European and Asian, particularly in the South Pacific. During 1937-39, when most other American industrial areas showed a decline in production, Los Angeles County added a thousand new industrial concerns. The decade of preparation, war, and post-war adjustment was a turning point in local history.

Opening day, Los Angeles airport, March 9, 1931.

Los Angeles' gift to popular culture, the "drive-in" (Carpenter's, a chain), Western and Wilshire, c. 1938.

By 1940 the county bustled with activity. Douglas, Lockheed, Vega, Vultee, North American, and Northrop were making planes, for which a multitude of subcontractors supplied components. The U.S. Housing Authority was providing for a large residential building boom, especially on the grazing and agricultural flatlands near new factories. The plants needed employees, skilled or not, and the ports needed cargo space, and workers from other states began a great migration to the county, which in one year alone—1941—grew by 150,000 persons. By the middle of 1941 the county was undergoing what economists called "the most extensive industrial development in its history." Over half the industrial employment in California was in the county. Notable was an increase in clothing, style leadership, and

Santa Anita racetrack, temporary barracks to house Japanese before reconcentration, March, 1942.

women's wear. Clothing was employing more persons than any other industry, and only aircraft, oil and movies were making higher profits. As never before, women found work, everywhere, especially in clothing, textiles, and leather. In 1942 the county was second only to Wayne County (Detroit) among U.S. counties in the volume of war contracts received as federal money built steel mills, aluminum plants, aircraft facilities, and Army camps.

The spring of 1942 also saw the sudden mass evacuation of Japanese Americans throughout the area. Little effective opposition was voiced to newspaper columnists, nativist groups and politicians who denounced them as potential spies and saboteurs. No evidence was produced to document these allegations. By the summer of 42, Los Angeles' Japanese Americans, the largest concentration in the continental United States, were removed. Over 110,000 Japanese were placed in federal camps scattered throughout the nation. Although the majority were American citizens by birthright, they were condemned without due process; their forced evacuation by the U.S. Army was ordered without a declaration of martial law, yet lasted for the duration of the war.

The economic boom of 1940-41 did not end with overt war with Germany and Japan. War had irreversibly altered the face—and the faces—of the county. It became a center of steel and aluminum production, aircraft and ship building, military training and overseas embarkation. From 1941 to 47 the county moved up from 11th place among U.S. industrial centers to 7th or 6th. In the five years 1940-45 men and women built 193,000 dwelling units in the county. These remained full, even became overcrowded, and pressures for housing remained intense because in 1946 local industries began speedy conversion to peacetime or cold-war production. Aircraft turned to missles, to aerospace, to electronics. RAND and others think tanks appeared, attracting a formidable in-migration of Ph.D.'s in physics and mathematics, and the computer industry began to boom. G.I. loans enabled veterans to buy or build homes and the G.I. Bill enabled them to attend the variety of available colleges and universities. Wartime workers and

San Pedro, early in World War II.

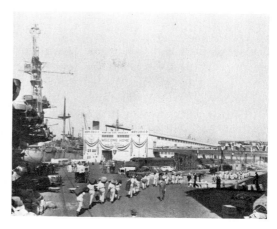

"The boys come home." Los Angeles harbor in November, 1945.

servicemen who had functioned briefly in Los Angeles communities during the war returned to settle or study. Native Californians of Japanese descent, exiled during the war, came back. Thousands of Blacks, replaced by machinery in Southern fields, moved in. Also, numerous corporations moved their national headquarters from the East or set up Pacific Coast branch offices.

All this swelling in population and housing put a strain on county and city services, which fell behind in providing new schools, streets, sewerage, water lines, police and fire protection. Taxes rose, bureaucracies bulged, and unplanned developments were the disorder of the day. Uncoordinated, undirected change foreboded crises in air, agriculture, and transportation.

Back on July 26, 1943, Los Angeles had had its first big "gas attack," an affliction soon called smog, and while citizens had accepted smog during the years devoted to the destruction called war, now in an era of peace, the Korean War excepted, they made a crusade of trying to clean up the air. Responding to crises and pressure, the Legislature created the Los Angeles County Air Pollution Control District, an entity novel in human history, and began a more than thirty years' war, far from ended now.

In 1946 and for a number of years the county remained first in the nation for value of agricultural products, but subdividers ever prized prime agricultural land as the flattest and easiest to develop, and the extent of the best land relentlessly shrank. During the ten years beginning in 1949 the county lost 43,000 acres in fruits and nuts, including three-fourths of the acreage in oranges. In 1960 bulldozers were tearing up 3,000 acres of orange trees per day. Olive, walnut, and apricot orchards vanished in San Fernando Valley, hayfields in the Antelope Valley, feedlots along the lower Los Angeles and San Gabriel rivers. On fields of prime land that temporarily remained devoted to intensive cultivation, smog from steam plants and the ever-increasing motor vehicle traffic blighted spinach, romaine, celery, and head lettuce (once called Los Angeles lettuce). Truck gardening ceased to contribute to the economy and to the scenery. Fresh produce had to come from afar. Generally it had less flavor, and always it cost more. Los Angeles lost its top ranking to Fresno County and steadily slipped downward. It remained importantly agricultural only in flowers, seeds, and bulbs. Even so compact an activity as dairying phased out more and more as dairies moved eastward or northwest to San Joaquin Valley counties.

Concomitant with other big changes that meant prosperity or disaster, or both, was the multiplication of private automobiles and the virtual disappearance of public transportation. The Pacific Electric lines lost patronage, died back, and finally stopped running. The new buses of the Rapid Transit District never anywhere near fully replaced the street cars of the 1930s. In 1946 Los Angeles County had 1,412,000 motor vehicles, 41% of the state total, and with retail customers and businessmen car minded, the number was bound to increase, especially when the state began to build a system of freeways to crisscross the county and handle traffic. In 1950 the county held a third more cars than the year before, 479 cars per thousand persons. In 1952 the county held more passenger cars than any other U.S. county—40% more than all New York City boroughs, 47% more than Cook County (Chicago). Only California and 6 other states registered more cars. The following year the county had 2,500,000 motor vehicles of all sorts, 515 per thousand persons. Plants in the county assembled more cars than any other center on earth except Detroit, made more tires than any center except Akron. By 1975 with the flowering of used-car lots, the two-car garage, and the business of renting and leasing cars the County claimed more than 3,900,000 registered automobiles.

By 1948 new car sales had helped the county to become third in the nation in bank deposits and Los Angeles City to become third in the dollar volume of business, but where electric car lines used to take people to a central downtown, motor cars took them just about anywhere but downtown, and the flight of customers from downtown Los Angeles began. The dominant department stores established branches in Beverly Hills, in Pasadena, in new shopping centers on recent cropland in the San Fernando Valley, in new industrial-residential complexes like Lakewood, and in other counties. The downtown banks hurried to establish dozens of branches wherever people shopped or special-interest groups clustered, as on the show-biz center on Sunset Boulevard in West Hollywood. The movement of customers to branches far from downtown paralleled the movement of families from house to house, from older sections of the towns to newer ones. In "normal" 1940 one-tenth of all county households changed residence; in 1946 one-sixth did; in 1953, one-third.

Not only did householders become residentially mobile. Newcomers kept pouring into the county, at the rate of about a thousand a day. Job opportunities or relative freedom from old restraints attracted workers from Mexico, Indians from the Southwest, Blacks from the rural South, and whites, often poor, from everywhere. The county came to contain the biggest Jewish community west of New York, a large American Indian group, more Blacks than in any Southern city or any other city west of Chicago, and the fourth largest Mexican community on earth. In addition to the long-established Chinese, Japanese, and Filipino communities, the relaxation of federal immigration quotas in the early 50s resulted in new arrivals from other parts of Asia and the Pacific. The largest population of Samoans and Guamanians on the continent resides in areas adjacent to L.A. harbor, while Koreans and Thais are two of the fastest growing Asian groups in the inner city.

While many of these newcomers merged into the general population, especially at the more affluent and professional levels, there were serious white-majority-ethnic minority problems in housing, employment, and schooling, and in time local and county authorities had to concern themselves with several hundred Mexican or Chicano, Black, and Caucasian youth gangs.

Schools in Pasadena and Los Angeles faced recurrent crises over integration and busing. By mid-1965 the black population of Los Angeles totaled 650,000, two-thirds of whom lived in Watts. The ghetto seethed with discontent, which flared into a bloody and devastating riot in August, 1965. After six days of rioting, 34 persons were dead, more than 1,000 wounded, and $40 million worth of property destroyed. Order was restored by 14,000 national guardsmen who were called to duty, but the scars of the riot were long remembered.

Problems or not, the data continued to make the county a statistical marvel. By the mid-1950s it was adding more factory workers each year than any other area in the country. In 1955 the home building rate was exceeded only by California and New York. More residential units were going up than in all of Texas, all of Illinois, all of Michigan, Pennsylvania, or Florida, though a shift was evident to building apartments and multiple-family structures, and the idea of the condominium was taking hold.

Spurred on by American participation in Asian wars and unending militarism in Washington, electronics continued to grow, along with electric machinery, instruments, ordnance, and electronic guidance, until in 1963 aerospace was the leading industry. While agriculture shriveled, internation trade by ship and plane boomed, as did exportation of machinery, motion pictures, taped television shows, and aircraft itself. In 1965 the county was second only to New York in international trade.

The Terminal Island—San Pedro Ferry in the 1940s.

With growth in population and the economy came parallel developments in education, culture, and recreation. The 8 junior colleges of 1930 became 21, with more campuses in the making. No other county had so many such two-year colleges. The University of Southern California, UCLA, and California Institute of Technology continued to grow and extend their offerings. These included a new medical school at UCLA and a great expansion of the USC medical facilities at the County General Hospital. New colleges appeared in the Claremont Colleges cluster, patterned after Oxford, new universities came into being, Pepperdine, for example, which developed a Los Angeles and a Malibu campus, and new institutions appeared, such as California Institute of the Arts in the wholly new community of Valencia. Within twenty years, beginning in 1947, the present State University and Colleges system founded 5 institutions in the county—in Los Angeles, Northridge, Long Beach, Dominguez Hills, and Pomona, which constituted more than a quarter of the system of 19 campuses.

With help from the county treasury the Hollywood Bowl continued as a summertime mecca for performing artists, and in downtown Los Angeles near the convergence of 5 freeways, again with county subsidy, a notable and impressive complex of 2 theaters and an auditorium rose to loom on the horizon, giving the region an extraordinary center for stellar musical and theatrical events. Motion picture production increasingly moved from Hollywood and Culver City to rustic Malibu or to foreign locations, but numerous urban studio complexes continued in Los Angeles and Burbank for the manufacture of television shows and the recording of popular music, which by the early 1970s was a large industry. Also, with help from donors, the county government created a new art museum on Wilshire Boulevard and continued to improve and ex-

John Kennedy is nominated to run for President, Sports Arena, 1960.

pand the museum devoted to history and science, in Exposition Park. The county government's Coliseum and Sports Arena, Pasadena's Rose Bowl, the sports pavilions on campuses, and private facilities provided space for notable university teams in football and basketball, for professionals in golf and tennis. Luxurious tracks in Arcadia and Inglewood provided for first-rate horse-racing seasons. Machine-dug marinas at Long Beach and Playa del Rey, crowded with watercraft, were among the world's largest. By 1976 the county was a world headquarters for resident talent in the sciences and arts, including architecture, in the professions, and in sports.

In historical retrospect the County had undergone amazing changes in a third of a century. Since 1940 alone it had multiplied by 14 times the value of retail sales, it had more than doubled world trade through Los Angeles Customs, with a shift from more exports to more imports, and it had increased by 20 times the number of passengers at the airports in Long Beach, Los Angeles, Burbank, and Lancaster. The economic maturity of Los Angeles made it the chief competitor with San Francisco as America's link to Asia. Trans-Pacific exchange was particularly dramatic in the heavy investment of Japanese firms in all sectors of the local economy, from banking and manufacturing enterprises to sales of autos and electronics. By the 70s, the County was 17th in agriculture, 2nd in cattle-slaughter, 1st nationally as a flower market, and

Newly-completed Harbor Freeway winds through a new urban area, Carson, 1962.

1st in the West as a trucking center. It had the largest district attorney's office, and the largest county fire department, ready with elaborate equipment to battle enormous brush fires in the San Gabriel and Santa Monica mountains.

In contrast to the increases, good in official eyes, there were other data. Los Angeles County had become the bankruptcy capital of the U.S. and a leader in auto-payment defaults. There were 10 divorces to every 12 marriages. Mortgages on homes were more common than stable unions, for 70% of families were paying off mortgages or trust deeds. The suicide rate was above the national average, especially for men. And—shocking to uncritical boosters—during the five years 1970-75, a time of little house construction, big layoffs in aircraft plants, and unemployment as high as 10%, the population of the county had apparently declined about 1%.

Since 1930 the number of incorporated cities in the county had grown from 43 to 78, a number of them being special-interest cities concerned with commerce alone, or country living with horses, or elegant residence, but despite efforts by cities and the county to plan for the future, the county remained in effect a glaring example of planlessness in the name of development and profit. Much of the county was a gigantic, continuous assemblage of subdivisions and local governments, including overlapping districts, connected by—or separated by—highways, freeways, transmission lines, and concrete-lined riverbeds.

During the 1960s the county had gained in influence in the state government when reapportionment, long delayed, gave the county 14 state senators in place of 1, but the county government itself, set up by charter in 1912, when the population was rural and small, was in trouble. It was ruled by 5 elected supervisors. In 1976 with the population, now urban, at around 7,240,000—the size of whole nations—each county supervisor was in charge of more than 1.4 million persons. No other local officers in the U.S. had such broad responsibilities. The supervisors had more personal, financial power than most counts or dukes, or most kings, in history. Yet the government was fragmented, remote, with no record of any supervisor who was a woman or member of an underprivileged ethnic minority. There were organized secession movements in outlying portions of the county, and there was also an effort to keep the county intact by altering and reforming its constitution. One careful plan called for a 9-member county legislature and an elected county executive. City government also considered proposals for reform.

In the postwar period, the Los Angeles area produced four political figures of national importance. A young Richard Nixon began his political career as a Congressman elected from the Whittier environs in 1946. Within four years he was a United States Senator; two years later he was Vice-President. Although defeated for the Presidency in 1960 and for Governor in 1962, he made a remarkable comeback, being elected President in 1968 and resoundingly re-elected in 1972, only to founder in the quagmire of Watergate. Former state legislator and Congressman Samuel L. Yorty served three terms as Los Angeles mayor (1961-73), second only to the Bowron record of years-in-office. Feisty in temperament and outspoken, Yorty's reputation as a political maverick carried him into the Presidential primaries in 1972. In 1973 Yorty was defeated in the mayoralty campaign by Thomas S. Bradley, a former policeman and city councilman, the first black to hold that office. Actor-turned-politician Ronald Reagan of Pacific Palisades won the Governor's office in 1966 and swept to an impressive second term victory in 1970. Retiring from that office, he launched a near-successful campaign to capture the Presidential nomination of the Republican party in 1976.

During the overall transition from the start of the Depression to the arrival of the Bicentennial, Los Angeles county had changed from rural to industrial, from open-spaced to crowded, from colonial to imperial, from an area dominated by whites to an area where large populations of ethnic minorities were voting, demanding, and getting more and more of their proper share of political and economic power. It had changed, too from a county largely concerned with material acquisition to an area increasingly preoccupied with the arts, education, ecological balance, and the quality of the environment. The new Music Center complex, which is a feast for the senses, exemplified the increasingly sophisticated taste of the citizenry. Throughout the county, new designs in office and residential structures and industrial plants testified to southern California's reputation as a mecca for architects.

With demand for housing surpassing construction, particularly of single-family homes, property values in the county rose rapidly in the 1970s. The county assessor instituted periodic (normally every three years) revaluation of property for tax assessment purposes. A groundswell of public concern about continued home ownership led to passage in June, 1978, of Proposition 13, a tax limitation initiative. Enactment of this amendment to the state constitution sent shock waves through city and county government and provoked considerable speculation about financing local government and the social, cultural and economic services it provides.

The once idyllic landscape with its "beckoning climate" and its bungalows, symbolized by sun-kissed oranges, had become a tumultuous and unending metropolis symbolized by high-rise apartments and an administrative center of massive buildings holding county, city, and federal offices—the largest, bulkiest civic center in the nation, an architectural concentration that stands astride cavernous subterranean parking levels and in height and volume far surpasses the famous forum of ancient Rome. The face of Los Angeles had changed, but as the city nostalgically contemplated its past, it also looked forward with confidence to the celebration of the 200th anniversary of its founding in 1981.

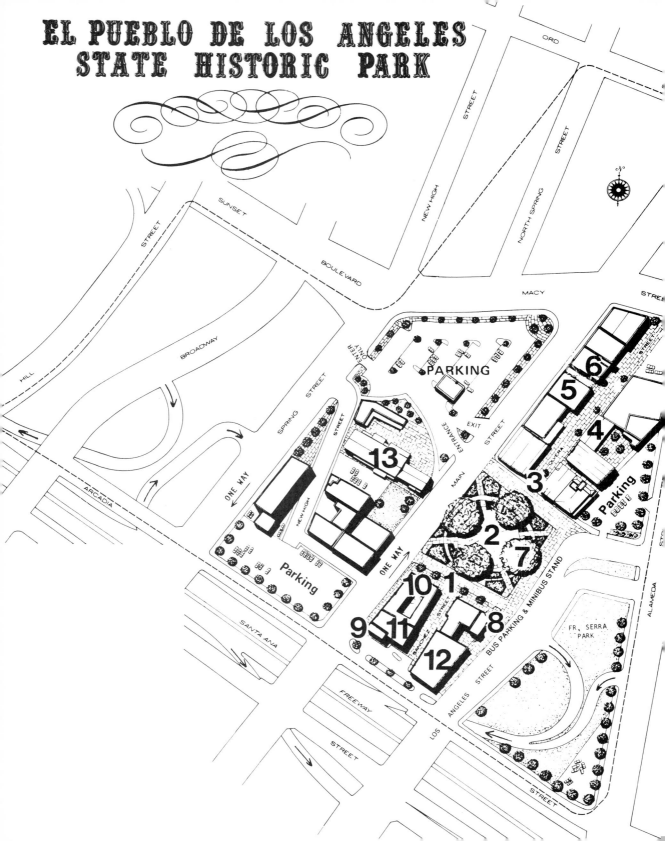

EL PUEBLO DE LOS ANGELES
STATE HISTORIC PARK

TWELVE ZONE MAPS AND SITE DESCRIPTIONS

SECTION AA

The Plaza Area

1. El Pueblo de Los Angeles State Historic Park
   420 N. Main Street
2. The Plaza
   Main Street and Sunset Blvd.
3. Olvera Street
   Paseo de la Plaza and Main Street
4. Avila Adobe
   10 Olvera Street
5. Sepulveda House
   Olvera Street
6. Pelanconi House
   W17 Olvera Street
7. Site of the Lugo Adobe
   El Pueblo de Los Angeles State Historic Park
8. Fire House No. 1
   Paseo de la Plaza
9. Masonic Temple
   416 N. Main Street
10. Pico House
    420 N. Main Street
11. Merced Theatre
    418 N. Main Street
12. Garnier Block
    Los Angeles Street at Arcadia
13. Church of Our Lady Queen of the Angels
    N. Main Street at the Plaza

Plaza with Cabrillo adobe, c. 1868.

El Pueblo de los Angeles State Historic Park, looking northwest.

El Pueblo State Historic Park, looking southwest.

AA 1. EL PUEBLO DE LOS ANGELES STATE HISTORIC PARK

The central core of Los Angeles history can be seen in the 42 acres surrounding the Old Plaza. It was here that the city was founded on September 4, 1781, by a group of 44 *pobladores*—eleven families recruited in Mexico to establish a *pueblo,* or town, near the river that gave the city its name of *el Pueblo de la Reina de los Angeles al margen del Rio de la Porciúncula*—the city of the Queen of the Angels by the bank of the Porciúncula River, long since shortened to Los Angeles.

With the growth and development of Los Angeles the Plaza area became neglected. Buildings dating to the Mexican period deteriorated, and the Plaza beckoned transients and vagrants. This situation changed gradually after 1928, the year that Mrs. Christine Sterling recognized the historic value of the area and launched a campaign to preserve it. Her efforts helped make Olvera Street an outstanding tourist attraction. Finally, in 1953, Mrs. Sterling persuaded three levels of government—the State, the County, and the City—to establish

El Pueblo de Los Angeles State Historic Park.

The Park includes the Plaza, Olvera Street, the Plaza Church, and a number of historically important buildings. It is easily reached through the city's freeways, and ample parking is available across Main Street at Sunset Blvd. Public transportation available to location.

Admission free
Pay Parking Available

El Pueblo de los Angeles State Historic
   Park
Visitors Information Center, Tour
   Information
420 N. Main Street
Los Angeles, Calif., 90012
628-1274

AA 2. THE PLAZA

Originally situated northwest of its present location, the Plaza was laid out in 1815 during construction of the Plaza Church. The Plaza attracted rancheros who constructed town houses around it during the 1830s and 1840s, the heyday of the rancho period. Bull fights—during which the bulls were rarely killed—were held on Sundays, the Plaza being fenced in for the occasion.

The Plaza was officially dedicated as a public park in 1869. It did not assume its familiar circular form until the 1870s, and through the years it had been redesigned and relandscaped. In 1931 the people of Chihuahua, Mexico, commemorating the 150th anniversary of the founding of Los Angeles, presented a statue of Felipe de Neve to the city, which was dedicated by the Native Daughters of the Golden West the following year. The Plaza was remodeled again in 1962. A kiosk was installed through the efforts of Olvera Street merchants and the city. Musical concerts are given at the kiosk, which also serves as the setting for the Christmas Creche. Landscaping the Plaza is a continuing project of El Pueblo de Los Angeles Historic Park. Declared an historic cultural monument by the Los Angeles Cultural Heritage Board in 1970, the Plaza is also a State Historical Landmark. Public transportation available to location.

Admission free

Main Street and Sunset Blvd.

The Plaza

Olvera Street by day

AA 3. OLVERA STREET

Originally known as Vine or Wine Street because of its location near vineyards and a winery, the street was renamed in honor of the first county judge of Los Angeles County, Agustín Olvera. Olvera had fought on the side of Mexico in the Mexican-American War of 1846-48 and was one of the signers of the Treaty of Cahuenga which ended the war in California.

After many years of neglect, Olvera Street was revitalized in a campaign led by Mrs. Christine Sterling to recreate the street as a "typical Mexican marketplace." Olvera Street was officially opened in April 1930 and serves as a major tourist attraction and entertainment center. For example, during the Christmas season Olvera Street is the site of the annual "las Posadas" celebration which attracts thousands of visitors from December 16-24.

Besides the appeal of the many shops and *puestos* (stalls), which feature hand-crafted leather goods, silver jewelry, and souvenir items, Olvera Street preserves essential features of Los Angeles history. The Avila Adobe, the oldest existing residence in Los Angeles, is located on Olvera Street, as are

Olvera street by night with city hall in background.

the Pelanconi House and Sepulveda House. Visitors to the street will also notice a triple row of bricks running diagonally across the street near the fountain. The bricks denote the course of the *Zanja Madre* (Mother Ditch), an early system of providing water from the Los Angeles River to the growing pueblo. Public transportation available to location.

Open daily, 10:00 A.M.-10:00 P.M.
Admission free

Paseo de la Plaza and Main Street
628-1274

AA 4. AVILA ADOBE

Constructed about 1818, the Avila Adobe is the oldest existing residence in Los Angeles. It was built by Francisco Avila, who served a term as *alcalde* (mayor) of the pueblo. The building, intended as a town house for the Avila family, is constructed of adobe brick, with the walls about three feet thick. Over the years portions of the building were modified and reconstructed. The original floors were simply packed earth, but planked flooring was later added. Door and window frames were shipped from Boston. Damaged by earthquakes in 1870 and again in 1971, the building has been completely restored.

During the Mexican-American War the Avila Adobe briefly served as the residence of Commodore Robert F. Stockton, commander of the U.S. Pacific Fleet. But for many decades the Avila building, along with other buildings in the area, suffered from neglect. By the late 1920s the City of Los

Avila adobe, 1926.

Avila adobe after restoration.

Angeles was making plans for the building's demolition. In 1928, however, Mrs. Christine Sterling began her campaign to restore the area. With the help of descendants of the Avila family and a successful drive for funds, the Avila Adobe was saved; it became the base for the larger effort to preserve and develop the Plaza and adjacent surroundings. The Avila Adobe is now part of El Pueblo de Los Angeles State Historic Park and is restored as an example of California lifestyle of the early 1840s. It has been designated a State Historical Landmark. Public transportation available to location.

Tuesday-Friday 10 A.M.-3 P.M.
Weekends 10 A.M.-4:30 P.M.
Admission free

10 Olvera Street
628-1274

Sepulveda house

AA 5. SEPULVEDA HOUSE

The Sepulveda House is a remarkable example of Victorian architecture in Los Angeles, one of the few such structures still found in the city. Built by 1887 as a combination residence, hotel, and boarding house, it was named for its owner, Eloisa Martinez de Sepulveda, married to an important pioneer family.

Today the Sepulveda House is one of the important buildings preserved in El Pueblo de Los Angeles State Historic Park. The interior of the building will be restored and open to the public shortly. Public transportation available to location.

Not open to the public

Olvera Street
628-1274

Pelanconi house in 1926

AA 6. PELANCONI HOUSE

One of the first brick buildings constructed in Los Angeles, the Pelanconi House dates back to around 1855. The builder, an Austro-Italian named Giuseppe Covacichi, intended the building to be a wine cellar below and residence above. Antonio Pelanconi, a gold miner originally from Italy, bought the building in 1865. The Pelanconi House was remodeled during the restoration of Olvera Street in 1929. Today the original wine cellar houses La Golon-

drina Cafe, a popular Mexican restaurant.
Public transportation available to location.

Opens daily at 11 A.M.
Closed Wednesday

W17 Olvera Street
628-4349

AA 7. SITE OF THE LUGO ADOBE

A plaque marking the site of the Lugo
Adobe on the east side of the Plaza is the
only evidence remaining of this home, one of
the very few two-story buildings dating back
to the Mexican period. It was built as a one-
story adobe by the in-laws of Vicente Lugo
in the 1830s. In 1867 the house was donated
to St. Vincent's College, now Loyola
University, the first college in southern
California.

As with many other historic places, the
Lugo Adobe failed to pass the test of time—
and urban renewal. Public transportation
available to location.

El Pueblo de Los Angeles State Historic
    Park

AA 8. FIRE HOUSE NO. 1

The first fire station in Los Angeles was
constructed in 1884 and used for that purpose from about 1885 to the late 1890s. Mrs.
Bigelow, the owner of the two-story brick
building, leased it to the Los Angeles Fire
Department's Chemical Company No. 1 for
$50.00 a month. After the fire station was
relocated the building was used as a hotel,
restaurant, and saloon.

Fire house number 1, c. 1885.

Fire house today, with city hall in
background.

Today the Fire House is a major feature of
El Pueblo de Los Angeles State Historic
Park. It has been completely restored, and it
features fire fighting equipment from the
1880s, including an original pumper and a
chemical wagon. The building has been

declared a State Historical Landmark. Public transportation available to location.

Open daily, 10:00 A.M.-3:00 P.M.
Weekends until 4:30 P.M.
Admission free

Paseo de la Plaza
628-1274

AA 9. MASONIC TEMPLE

This building was the second home of Los Angeles Lodge No. 42, and the first building built for lodge purposes in the city. Masonic Lodge No. 42, F. & A. M., was instituted in 1853, and is the second oldest founded in southern California. After meeting in temporary quarters, the Lodge decided to find a permanent site. When one was found the firm of Perry and Woodworth, contractors and builders, was chosen to handle the construction. Lacking the necessary funds to build the structure, the Lodge loaned the builders sufficient money at 1% per annum. By the end of 1856 the brick building was completed. The lodge moved into the second floor, renting the space for $20.00 a month, while the lower floor was rented out for commercial purposes.

Today, in the ante room of the building the Los Angeles Lodge has set up a museum which preserves the Lodge's history and that of the city as well.

Guided tours through Las Angelitas,
El Pueblo de Los Angeles State
Historic Park Office

416 N. Main Street
Los Angeles 90012
628-1274

AA 10. PICO HOUSE

The Pico House was the first major three-story hotel in Los Angeles. Named for Pio Pico, the last Mexican governor of California, the hotel was commissioned by him in 1869 and was finished on June 19, 1870. The architect was Ezra F. Kysor. Pico intended his hotel to be the finest in the city. Its strategic location at Main Street and the Plaza, as well as such luxurious features as gas lights and indoor plumbing, should have made the hotel a prosperous enterprise. However, it passed through a variety of owners and businesses, and suffered the general decay of the area. Today under process of restoration, the Pico House retains essentially its original exterior design, but many changes in its interior were done by the building's various owners. The building has been designated a State Historical Landmark. Public transportation available to location.

Tuesday-Saturday, 10:00 A.M.-2:00 P.M.
Admission: guided tours only (free)

420 N. Main Street
628-1274

Pico house

Pico house, Merced Theatre and Masonic Temple, 1876.

AA 11. MERCED THEATRE

The Merced Theatre was the first theatre building constructed in Los Angeles. It was built in 1870 by William Abbott, using the architect who had designed the Pico House, Ezra F. Kysor. The Merced Theatre was the tallest building in Los Angeles, topping its next-door neighbor, the Pico House, by four feet. Abbott named the theatre for his wife, Dona Merced Garcia.

The theatre, which seated 400, was on the building's second floor and was connected to the Pico House so that guests might easily attend performances. The stage was about 12′ × 18′, and the theatre provided two small dressing rooms. The Abbott family lived on the third floor; the ground floor and the basement were leased for other businesses, including a mortuary.

After other theatres caused business to decline, the building was rented out for a variety of purposes. For a time it was used as a saloon and also, by contrast, as a

Methodist church. It was even used as an armory. Today it is in process of restoration and has been declared a State Historical Landmark. Public transportation available to location.

Not open to public at this time

418 N. Main Street

AA 12. GARNIER BLOCK

The Garnier Block was constructed in 1890 by Phillipe Garnier, who intended to rent space in it to Chinese customers to use as businesses and apartments. The block, a two-story brick-and sandstone building, is important for the history of the city's Chinese residents. The importing firm of Sun Wing Wo, operated by the Lew family, conducted its business in the building from 1890-1948. From 1900-48 the Chinese Benevolent Society's headquarters were located on the second floor of the building.

The State of California acquired the building in 1953. The exterior of the Garnier Block has been restored and is included in El Pueblo de Los Angeles State Historic Park.

Garnier block

The building features such interesting details as both gas and electric systems on the same fixture. It has been included in the Historic American Buildings Survey. Public transportation available to location.

Guided tour only, free

Los Angeles Street at Arcadia
El Pueblo de Los Angeles State Historic
  Park
628-1274

Church of Our Lady Queen of the Angels

AA 13. CHURCH OF OUR LADY QUEEN OF THE ANGELS

The Plaza Church, as it is popularly called, is the oldest place of religious worship in the City of Los Angeles. Built by Franciscan fathers and Indian neophytes between 1818-1822, the Church of Our Lady of the Angels, as it was first known, was intended to serve worshipers in the pueblo who until then had to travel to Mission San Gabriel. The Plaza Church was not a part of the mission system begun by Father Junípero Serra, but functioned as a parish church. To raise the funds for its building, donations of cattle and brandy were sold.

After 1852, when the Franciscan padres left San Gabriel, the church continued as a parish church, the first and only place of Catholic worship in Los Angeles until 1876.

In 1859 the church became the episcopal residence of Bishop Thaddeus Amat. Ten years later the Plaza Church's name was altered to its present title, Our Lady Queen of the Angels. The Claretian Missionaries were given charge of the church's administration in 1910. Masses have been continuously offered since 1822.

Building alterations in the Plaza Church have taken place periodically since its original construction. The church bells are for decorative purposes only, and various changes have been made in the facade. The church is located across from the Plaza and is easily reached by freeway from all parts of southern California. It has been declared a State Historical Landmark. Public transportation available to location.

Open daily 24 hours throughout the year

N. Main Street at the Plaza

NOTES

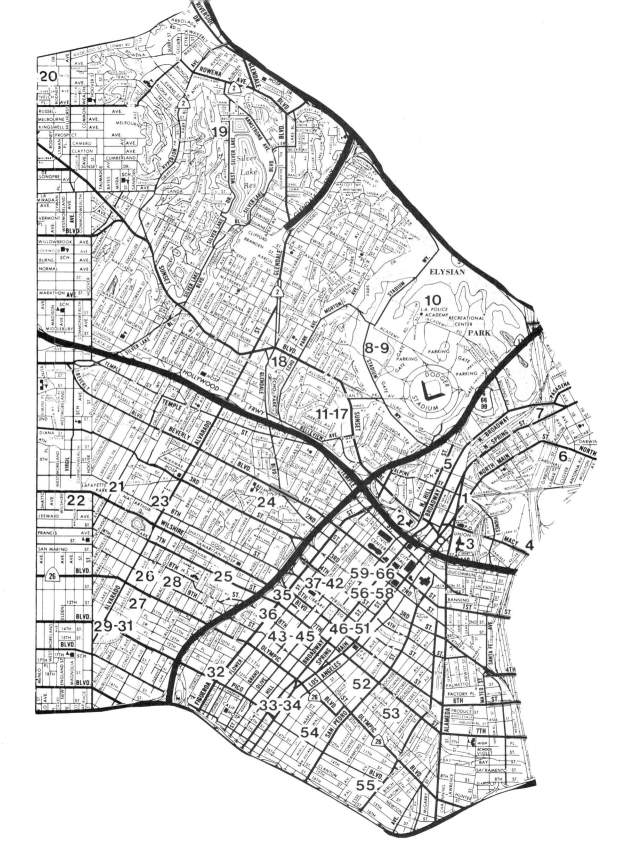

SECTION A

Los Angeles Central Area (Downtown)

1. Rochester House
   Alameda and San Bruno
2. Fort Moore Memorial
   Hill Street, between Temple and Ord Streets
3. Union Station
   800 N. Alameda Street
4. Macy Street Residence
   1030 Macy Street
5. Chinatown
   900 N. Broadway and adjacent area
6. San Antonio Winery
   737 Lamar Street
7. Southern Pacific Railroad River Station
   Between N. Broadway and N. Spring Street
8. Chavez Ravine Arboretum
   Elysian Park
9. Portola Trail Campsite
   Elysian Park
10. Los Angeles Police Academy
    1880 Academy Drive
11. Angelino Heights
    1300 Block of Carroll Avenue
12. Aaron Phillips House
    1300 Carroll Avenue
13. Ferdinand Heim House
    1320 Carroll Avenue
14. Daniel Innes House
    1329 Carroll Avenue
15. Charles Sessions House
    1330 Carroll Avenue
16. Charles Haskins House
    1344 Carroll Avenue
17. Henry Pinney House
    1355 Carroll Avenue
18. Foursquare Gospel Church (Angelus Temple)
    1100 Glendale Blvd.
19. Tierman House
    2323 Micheltorena Street
20. St. Mary of the Angels
    4510 Finley Avenue
21. Lafayette Park
    2830 W. 6th Street
22. Bullock's Wilshire
    3050 Wilshire Blvd.
23. MacArthur Park
    2230 W. 6th Street
24. S. J. Lewis House
    1425 Miramar Street
25. Foy House
    633 S. Witmer Street
26. Frederick M. Mooers House
    818 Bonnie Brae Street
27. Bonnie Brae Street Residence
    1036-38 S. Bonnie Brae Street
28. Chancery Archives, Los Angeles Diocese
    1531 W. 9th Street
29. People's Temple Christian Church (Formerly First Church of Christ, Scientist)
    1366 S. Alvarado Street
30. Alvarado Terrace
    1300 Block of Alvarado Terrace
31. Morris Cohn House
    1325 Alvarado Terrace
32. Trinity Methodist Church
    1201 S. Flower Street
33. Los Angeles *Examiner* Building
    1111 S. Broadway

34. St. Joseph's Catholic Church
    218 E. 12th Street
35. St. Paul's Cathedral
    615 S. Figueroa Street
36. Global Marine House
    811 W. 7th Street
37. California Club Building
    538 S. Flower Street
38. Los Angeles Public Library, Central Building
    630 W. 5th Street
39. California Collection, Los Angeles Public Library
    630 W. 5th Street
40. Biltmore Hotel
    515 S. Olive Street
41. Philharmonic Auditorium (Temple Baptist Church)
    427 W. 5th Street
42. Pershing Square
    W. 5th and Hill Streets
43. Los Angeles Athletic Club
    431 W. 7th Street
44. Garfield Building
    403 W. 8th Street
45. Clifton's Cafeteria
    648 S. Broadway
46. Finney's Cafeteria
    217 W. 6th Street
47. Palm Court, Alexandria Hotel
    501 S. Spring Street
48. Arcade Building
    541 S. Spring Street
49. Farmers and Merchants Bank Building
    401 S. Main Street

50. Coles P. E. Buffet
    118 E. 6th Street
51. Fire Station No. 23
    225 E. 5th Street
52. Cast-Iron Commercial Building
    740-748 S. San Pedro Street
53. Site of the First African Methodist Episcopal Church Building
    Eighth and Towne
54. Cohn-Goldwater Building
    525 E. 12th Street
55. Coca Cola Building
    1334 S. Central Avenue
56. Grand Central Public Market
    317 S. Broadway
57. Million Dollar Theatre
    307 South Broadway
58. Bradbury Building
    304 S. Broadway
59. Los Angeles *Times* Building
    202 W. 1st Street
60. Los Angeles County Record Center
    222 N. Hill Street
61. Los Angeles County Records Office
    227 N. Broadway
62. Los Angeles City Hall
    200 N. Spring Street
63. City of Los Angeles Archives
    200 N. Spring Street
64. Federal Building (U.S. Courthouse)
    312 N. Spring Street
65. St. Vibiana's Cathedral
    S. Main Street at 2nd Street
66. Little Tokyo
    200 E. 1st Street and adjacent area

Echo Park, c. 1940.

A 1. ROCHESTER HOUSE

Thousands of freeway motorists remember the Rochester House as the building with the sign asking that it be saved. Built in 1887 by Rufus Herrick Dorn for himself and his family, it received its name from a similar structure Dorn had seen in Rochester, New York. In 1897 the Van Nuys family purchased it and in 1919 divided the house into 15 apartments. It was variously known as the "Rochester Apartments" or the "West Temple Apartments" after its location on 1012 West Temple Street. Efforts to preserve the building, which had been vacant since 1963, were undertaken by the Historic Los Angeles Association, along with a federal grant given to the Pueblo Commission. In 1970 the building was moved to a temporary location at Alameda and San Bruno Streets, where it currently awaits a permanent site within the El Pueblo de Los Angeles State Historical Monument area. Public transportation available to location.

The Rochester house is built entirely of redwood and is in the style known as Mansard, or Second Empire style, with two stories and dormer attic. Few buildings in Los Angeles remain that were constructed with this arresting architectural design. The house was designated an historic cultural monument in 1963 and was recorded in the Historic American Building Survey the following year.

Not open to public at present

Alameda and San Bruno (temporary)

Rochester House

A 2. FORT MOORE MEMORIAL

The Fort Moore Memorial commemorates the construction of a fort during the Mexican-American War. A volunteer Mormon battalion obtained timber from the San Gabriel Mountains to build the fort on a hill with a commanding view of Los Angeles. It was named Fort Moore after Captain Benjamin Moore, who had been killed at the Battle of San Pascual on December 6, 1846. The fort was completed in the spring of 1847.

The fort has long since disappeared, and the hill now houses the administrative offices of the Los Angeles Unified School District. The memorial was constructed in 1957. It features a relief sculpture depicting the raising of the American flag on the hill. Other sculptures commemorate the ranchos, pioneers, and water and power development. Although the original construction featured a waterfall, energy priorities have caused its discontinuance. Public transportation to one block of location.

Hill Street, between Temple and Ord Streets

Union Station

A 3. UNION STATION

In 1933 the Southern Pacific, Union Pacific, and Santa Fe railroads pooled their funds for the construction of a railroad station under their joint ownership. John Parkinson and his son Donald B. Parkinson received the commission for the $11 million building, which was officially opened on May 7, 1939. Over 1 1/2 million people visited the station during its initial three days of operation. They viewed a main waiting room measuring 52 feet from the floor to the ceiling's highest point, marble floors, and arched windows. The building's exterior combines Spanish and Moorish architecture.

Ironically, Union Station was completed at the end of the era of rail travel. The hustle and bustle of passengers and well-wishers is now absent, transferred through technological change to the Los Angeles International Airport. But visitors to Union Station will find the terminal ideal for nostalgic reminiscences, or for an appreciation of how countless visitors had their first glimpse of Los Angeles. In 1972 Union Station was declared an historic cultural monument. Public transportation available to location.

800 N. Alameda Street
Los Angeles 90012
683-6873

A 4. MACY STREET RESIDENCE

Situated between Boyle Heights and the Los Angeles River is one of the few brick homes of the Victorian era still standing in Los Angeles. It dates from the 1880s or possibly even the late 1870s. Architectural historians find it unusual that a single-story residence should display such a broad floor plan and such a flourish of detail; perhaps the builder was forced to halt construction of a second story. Particularly noteworthy are the handsome bay window and elaborately decorated porch columns.

Private residence.
Not open to the public.

1030 Macy Street
Los Angeles 90033

A 5. CHINATOWN

The Chinese community in Los Angeles dates back to the gold rush period. Chinese residents often suffered from exploitation and discrimination, reaching a violent extreme in October 1871 when 19 Chinese were murdered. The original Chinese community was located in the Plaza area and along Alameda Street. The construction of the Union Station marked the end of the community in this location, and a large area known as New Chinatown came into existence in the 1930s. New Chinatown, located about a mile north of the original area, encompasses several blocks along North Broadway and Hill Street.

According to the 1970 Census, almost 41,000 Chinese and Chinese Americans live in the Los Angeles metropolitan area. Many of these who arrived since World War II are from northern China, whereas most of the

Los Angeles street, Chinatown (Calle de los Negros), c. 1880.

earlier influx was from the south around Canton. New Chinatown features over 40 restaurants, dozens of curio shops, and other tourist attractions, including a colorful celebration of the Chinese New Year. Public transportation available to location.

Open daily, 10:00 A.M.-midnight

900 N. Broadway
and adjacent area

A 6. SAN ANTONIO WINERY

The San Antonio Winery was founded by Santo Cambianica in 1917 in the Lincoln Heights area and is the oldest producing winery in Los Angeles. The original buildings, constructed from wooden boxcar

San Antonio Winery

sidings, remain intact. At first the winery obtained grapes from vineyards in Burbank, Sierra Madre, and other local areas, but the vineyards of southern California have long since passed into history, and the winery now purchases grapes from other areas in the state.

Although a relatively small operation, the San Antonio Winery stresses quality in production. The wine is aged in wooden casks, some of which are over 100 years old. Within the winery a museum features old bottles, corkpullers, and other artifacts. The building is located on three acres of land which includes an acre of picnic grounds. In 1966 the winery was designated an historic cultural monument. Public transportation available to one block of location.

Monday-Saturday, 8 A.M.-8 P.M.
Sundays, 9 A.M.-6 P.M.

737 Lamar Street
Los Angeles 90031
223-1401

A 7. SOUTHERN PACIFIC RAILROAD RIVER STATION

The Southern Pacific Railroad reached Los Angeles in 1876, and much of the subsequent construction may still be seen today at the River Station. Bounded by North Broadway on the west, North Spring Street on the east, the Los Angeles River to the north, and the Capitol Milling Company to the south—with a touch of Elysian Park to the northwest—the station's freight yards include tracks, warehouses, docks, and cobblestone pavements which date back to the nineteenth century. Still used today, the River Station symbolizes the importance of rail communication and transportation in the development of Los Angeles. The station was designated as an historic cultural monument in 1971. Public transportation available to station area.

A 8. CHAVEZ RAVINE ARBORETUM

Southern California's first botanic garden, Chavez Ravine Arboretum in Elysian Park, was established in 1893 when the Los Angeles Horticultural Society began to plant rare trees in the upper part of the Ravine. Most of the original trees are still standing, many being the largest of their kind in the area. Throughout southern California are generations of trees taken as seedlings from the 1893 plantings.

The Arboretum's double row of date palms on the east side of Stadium Way between Scott Avenue and Academy Way was planted in 1895. Rubber trees in the picnic grove were introduced to this region by the U.S. Department of Agriculture in 1900. Additional rare tree plantings continued until about 1930. Thanks to the labeling efforts of the Southern California Horticultural Society in 1965, visitors can learn such information as the fact that the Arboretum's Golden-leaf Baphia is perhaps the only one in cultivation in America.

The Arboretum is that portion of Elysian Park north of Scott Avenue to the intersection of Stadium Way and Elysian Park Drive, and west from Stadium Way to the park road just above Elysian Park Drive. A visit to the Arboretum may include a stop at the stadium which houses the Los Angeles Dodgers baseball team.

Arboretum open 24 hours daily.
No charge.

A 9. PORTOLA TRAIL CAMPSITE, ELYSIAN PARK

The expedition of Don Gaspar de Portolá from Mexico passed this way en route to Monterey to begin the Spanish colonization of California. With Captain Fernando Rivera y Moncada, Lieutenant Pedro Fages, Sergeant José Francisco Ortega, Portolá and his party camped near this spot on August 2, 1769. A plaque commemorates this historic site.

Elysian Park
Los Angeles

A 10. LOS ANGELES POLICE ACADEMY

The Los Angeles Police Academy dates back to 1925, when a pistol range was constructed on property leased from the city in Elysian Park. When Los Angeles hosted the Olympic Games in 1932, Revolver and Pistol matches were held at this facility. After the Games, the Olympic Committee donated the mess hall building used at the Olympic Village to the city police department. The structure was transported to Elysian Park and converted to a clubhouse.

The first class of recruits graduated from the Police Academy in 1936. Now about 600 new officers join the L.A.P.D. each year.

In 1935, the Board of Park Commissioners approved plans of the Los Angeles Police Revolver and Athletic Club for development of an athletic center which included an Olympic-sized pool and a rock garden and waterfall near the athletic field and drill ground. Two years later landscape architect Francois Scotti designed and built the picturesque rock garden, comprising a series of four pools, cascades, dining area and amphitheater. At night multi-colored

Los Angeles Police Academy, tropical forecourt

lights illuminate the garden. During the day one may follow foot trails from the garden to surrounding hills.

The main building houses classrooms, offices, gymnasium, a restaurant restricted to officers and guests, and a cafe which serves approximately 300,000 persons yearly.

Cafe open to the public 7:00 A.M. to
   3:00 P.M.
Outside facilities also open these hours.
Closed Saturdays and Sundays.
From the Pasadena Freeway, exit at
   Academy Rd.
From the Golden State, exit at Stadium
   Way.

1880 Academy Drive
Los Angeles 90012
221-3101

A 11. 1300 BLOCK OF
CARROLL AVENUE,
ANGELINO HEIGHTS

Angelino Heights exemplifies the phase of city building entered upon by Los Angeles as rail transportation, becoming cheap and well publicized, brought a four-fold increase in population within a decade. Developers Everett H. Hall and W. W. Stilson filed their tract map in 1886, and because the original plan respected the natural contours of the hill, Angelino Heights is distinguishable as an entity even today. Together with East Los Angeles (including Boyle Heights) and Lincoln Heights, Angelino Heights formed the first ring of satellites of the central city. Because of their remoteness and hilly terrain, all three of these tracts were developed as suburbs, with community grocery and service stores, and were built in conjunction with surface transportation. Hall and Stilson were associates in the Temple Street Cable Car Company and they laid out their 230-lot tract to front on Bellevue Avenue, route of the cable cars. The Hollywood Freeway now runs parallel to the old cable car route.

Within Angelino Heights, nine remaining houses in the 1300 block of Carroll Avenue represent the highest concentration of pre-1890 Victorian architecture within the city of Los Angeles. All front on an avenue located at the crest of a hill which overlooks downtown Los Angeles. Only one house, that of developer Stilson, has undergone drastic remodeling.

American Renaissance idioms, these two-story, wood-framed residences cost between $5,000 and $10,000 to build, and the lots sold for about $500 in the late 1880s. Many of the upper middle class residents were active in the social life of Los Angeles, their names being listed year after year in the *Blue Book*.

Cable cars operated from 1888 to 1902, when they were supplanted by "electrics" a street car line that circled the Heights on Edgeware Road. Streetcars, which passed Carroll Avenue at 10 minute intervals, made the run to Spring Street in 16 minutes. Yet, as the remaining barns and carriage houses show, residents relied mainly on horses and buggies for transportation.

Each of these Victorian houses is now in the hands of individuals dedicated to preservation, and a substantial effort is being devoted to restoration. One house is in its original condition; several have already been restored, and restoration is actively underway in most of the rest. In recent years, Carroll Avenue has become a popular site for artists and tourists alike.

Around some of the homes, the landscaping, garden arbors, retaining walls, and carriage houses have been preserved. The quiet tone of the street, with its turreted and gabled houses and stately palms, provides a dramatic contrast to new downtown office towers which are visible in the background.

All the houses on Carroll Avenue are private residences and are open to the public *only* through especially arranged group tours.

A 12. AARON PHILLIPS HOUSE

This 2 1/2-story house was built around 1887-88 for Aaron Putnam Phillips, a merchant who left a prosperous hardware business in Iowa in 1866 to resettle his family and start a new furniture business. He arrived in Los Angeles from New York during the boom of the 1880s. Phillips lived in the house until about 1901, when it was purchased by Isaac Newhall. Phillips' daughter, Grace, who married Newhall, lived in the home until 1942.

The house is an ornate, well maintained example of the Queen Anne—Eastlake style of architecture which was popular in the 1880s. Notable are the spindle work and turned posts at the entry, the stained-glass windows, the textures obtained by the use of

shingles, and the shadows cast by the ornamental millwork. Five original palms in the yard now reach heights of 60 feet.

Private residence
Not open to the public

1300 Carroll Avenue
Los Angeles 90026

A 13. FERDINAND HEIM HOUSE

This Queen Anne-styled house was built about 1888, and was occupied from 1890 until about 1930 by Ferdinand A. Heim, a native of Austria who came to Los Angeles in the late 1880s and became a local brewer. The house became a rooming house in the 1940s and today it is a single-family dwelling again.

Spindle and spool ornamentation and turned railings decorate the porch and second floor. A turret and tower extend from both sides of the front elevation, and a pediment tops the front entrance. Apart from a new foundation and porch steps, there have been no exterior structural alterations.

Private residence
Not open to public

1320 Carroll Avenue
Los Angeles 90026

A 14. DANIEL INNES HOUSE

Built in 1886 for Daniel Innes, Los Angeles councilman, real estate agent, and merchant, the 1 1/2-story, wood-framed house is designed in carpenter Gothic with

Eastlake details. Innes was a native of Scotland, and his family was one of the first to be listed in the Los Angeles *Blue Book*. The Inneses occupied the home until 1920.

Originally painted slate blue, the exterior is now white with red trim. Some wood ornamentation on the porches now exists, as does the original granite retaining wall. A large back room was added after 1900, and about 1950 the building became a rooming house.

Private residence
Not open to public

1329 Carroll Avenue
Los Angeles 90026

A 15. CHARLES SESSIONS HOUSE

In 1888 this 12-room home was built for dairyman Charles Sessions by J. Cather Newsom, one of several San Francisco architects attracted to Los Angeles in the boom of the 1880s. The house later was the residence of several other prominent Angelinos, but in the 1920s it was converted to multiple family use.

With a shingle and clapboard exterior, the house has considerable ornamentation, including a spindle-screened upper porch with a circular aperature, a main entrance arch with a Greek Revival pediment and Queen Anne lattice work framing, art glass windows and carved wooden scrolls terminating in lion's heads which guard the porch. An intriguing feature of the exterior is the use of elongated cyma brackets sweeping from the level of the second story window sills up to the eaves, creating interesting shadows and, to some extent, providing relief from the direct sunlight in the windows. Two other houses in the tract have similar brackets,

which may represent an early attempt to adapt the wood-framed house to the climate of California.

The front veranda has been enclosed to provide for a kitchen and two bathrooms, and an exterior stairway added, but otherwise few changes have been made.

Private residence
Not open to the public

1330 Carroll Avenue
Los Angeles 90026

A 16. CHARLES HASKINS HOUSE

A late addition to Angelino Heights, this house was built in 1895 for Los Angeles businessman Charles C. Haskins. It was sold after Haskins' death to another prominent local businessman, Emil Kirchner, whose *Blue Book* listing remained at this address through 1913. The house has fishscale shingling, a tall conical tower extending from the left side and a veranda extending from the rear. Especially noteworthy is the lightheartedness of the spindle and scroll ornamentation. A carriage barn in the rear was removed in 1965. Always a single family residence, this house is a favorite of Los Angeles film makers and tourists alike.

Private residence
Not open to the public

1344 Carroll Avenue
Los Angeles 90026

A 17. HENRY PINNEY HOUSE

Built in 1887 for Los Angeles businessman Henry L. Pinney, originally from Connecticut, this home is an example of the relatively unornamented, basic Eastlake style. It is one of the few houses on this street which has always been a single family dwelling. Pinney's son, Charles, who, at the time of this writing was 104 years old and still living in the house, was reported as one of the season's eligible bachelors listed in the Los Angeles *Blue Book* for 1894.

This residence is one of the few on Carroll Avenue in which there has been no structural alterations. There is a carriage house at the rear of the property.

Private residence
Not open to the public

1355 Carroll Avenue
Los Angeles 90026

A 18. FOURSQUARE GOSPEL CHURCH (ANGELUS TEMPLE)

The Angelus Temple, an enduring monument to the evangelical ministry of Aimee Semple McPherson, was constructed during 1922 and dedicated on January 1, 1923. Funds for the church were raised by Mrs. McPherson during evangelical campaigns from 1918-1922. The Temple is the headquarters church of the International Church of the Foursquare Gospel, founded by Mrs. McPherson and continued by her son, the Reverend Rolf K. McPherson. During the 1920s Aimee Semple McPherson personally conducted 21 services a week to capacity crowds in the main sanctuary, which seats over 5,000.

Angelus Temple (Foursquare Gospel)

The church also operates the L.I.F.E. Bible College in an adjacent building constructed in 1925, as well as radio station KFSG, one of the oldest stations in Los Angeles and the first to present religious programming. During the Great Depression the Angelus Temple Commissary fed and clothed people in need without regard for religion, race, or creed. The Angelus Temple is one of the largest Protestant church buildings in Los Angeles. Public transportation to one block of location.

Offices open Monday-Friday, 9 A.M.-5 P.M.
Sanctuary open Sunday, 9:30 A.M.-
    12:30 P.M.; 5 P.M.-8:30 P.M.
Tours may be arranged any time during
    office hours.

1100 Glendale Blvd.
Los Angeles 90026
484-1100

A 19. TIERMAN HOUSE

This house is a good example of the work of Gregory Ain, who designed it in 1939. Ain, whose work includes numerous private residences throughout Los Angeles, had a limited amount of floor space within which to work his design. The house features a central skylight; sliding glass doors open to a rear living porch. It indicates how well Ain's designs adapted to homes on a small scale.

Not open to public
Private residence

2323 Micheltorena Street
Los Angeles 90039

A 20. ST. MARY OF THE ANGELS

St. Mary of the Angels Episcopal Church was designed by Carlton Winslow, Sr., on land donated as a gift to the church. Opened in 1930, the church has long had a reputation as one of the most beautiful churches in Los Angeles. It has appeared as the setting for church scenes in numerous motion pictures and for celebrity weddings. Church decorations include wood carvings, Renaissance oil paintings, and statuary. The church also has an extensive archives of newspaper clippings and documents pertaining to its early history. Public transportation available to location, near Vermont Avenue and Los Feliz Boulevard.

Tours must be arranged during office
    hours:
Tuesday-Saturday, 10 A.M.-3 P.M.

4510 Finley Avenue
Los Angeles 90027
660-2700

A 21. LAFAYETTE PARK

Lafayette Park was acquired by the City of Los Angeles in 1895 as a gift from Mrs. Clara R. Shatto, who specified that the land was to be used only as a park. Until 1917 known as Sunset Park, the park's name was changed during World War I to honor Marquis de La Fayette, the French nobleman who fought in the American Revolution.

Lafayette Park is one of the oldest parks in the Los Angeles park system. Attractions include a recreation and senior citizens' center, a Shakespearean garden (adjacent to the Felipe de Neve branch library), tennis courts and other sports facilities, and a picnic area. A scent garden is maintained for the blind; it has numerous fragrant flowers. Public transportation available to location.

2830 W. 6th Street
Los Angeles 90057

A 22. BULLOCK'S WILSHIRE

Bullock's Department Store management made a major move in the late 1920s when it decided to open a specialty store featuring men's, women's, and children's clothing in what was then a suburb of Los Angeles. John and Donald Parkinson designed the building with each department planned as a separate unit. When the store opened on September 26, 1929, an estimated 300,000 people arrived—not only to inspect the merchandise but to admire the building's art and architecture. Its highest point is a six-story copper-crested tower, 241 feet high. A huge ceiling mural by Herman Sachs, depicting the history of transportation, is at the motor court entrance; this mural was restored in 1973. The entire building, with park landscaping, is a superb example of Art Deco design and commercial architecture. In 1968 Bullock's Wilshire was designated as an historic cultural monument. Public transportation available to location.

Hours open, Monday-Saturday, 9:30 A.M.-5:45 P.M.

3050 Wilshire Blvd.
Los Angeles 90010
382-6161

A 23. MACARTHUR PARK

In 1886 the City of Los Angeles received 32.15 acres of land for a park in exchange for other city land. The location was hardly promising; the lake was a swamp, cluttered with debris, and of no value. The following year Mayor William Workman secured $500 from Los Angeles citizens which he matched with city council funds to create a public park. By 1890 Westlake Park, as the park was named, was on its way to becoming a major attraction. The lake was enlarged and a pathway 40 feet wide built around it. The park's strategic location at the terminus of two streetcar lines attracted many visitors who enjoyed boating on the lake and listening to the Sunday afternoon concerts given at the bandstand, which was constructed in 1896.

In May 1942, in recognition of the services of General Douglas MacArthur during World War II, Westlake Park was renamed MacArthur Park. A statue honoring General MacArthur was placed there in 1955, with the general attending the dedication ceremony. The park's attractions include a bandshell constructed in 1957, a children's playground, a recreation center for senior citizens, and other conveniences in an area of high population density and commercial activity (Wilshire Boulevard bisects the park). However, boating was discontinued

in 1969. In 1972 MacArthur Park was designated an historic cultural monument. Public transportation available to location.

2230 W. 6th Street
Los Angeles 90057

MacArthur Park (Westlake) in the late 1930s.

A 24. S. J. LEWIS HOUSE

Reputedly, Joseph Cather Newsom, a San Francisco architect, challenged in 1890 to design a house to fit California's climate and landscape, created this home. He borrowed the best features of several architectural styles and combined them to create a uniquely California-style house, three stories in height, set in a wide lawn. The landscaping dates back to the house's construction. In 1966 the house was designated an historic cultural monument. Public transportation available to one block of location.

Private residence not open to the public

1425 Miramar Street
Los Angeles 90026

S.J. Lewis House

A 25. FOY HOUSE

The Foy House, constructed about 1873 on the present site of the Statler Hilton Hotel, was later moved to its present location. It was the longtime residence of Mary E. Foy, the city's third librarian and the first woman to hold that position. Miss Foy was vitally concerned with the history of California, and during her long life she helped to organize such groups as the First Century Families and the California Parlor of the Native Daughters of the Golden West. In 1962 the Foy House was marked by a plaque from the Los Angeles High School Alumni Association. That same year the house was also designated an historic cultural monument. Public transportation available to one block of location.

633 S. Witmer Street
Los Angeles 90017

A 26. FREDERICK M. MOOERS HOUSE

The Mooers house is one of a number of Victorian mansions still standing along Bonnie Brae Street between 8th and 10th Streets. Built in 1894, it was probably constructed by its first owner, Frank Lorin Wright, a building contractor. The home changed hands many times and was occupied from 1898 to 1900 by Frederick Mitchell Mooers, a wealthy miner who was a co-discoverer of the Yellow Aster gold mine in Kern county. Millionaire Mooers had once been a drug clerk and bookkeeper. The house was purchased by its present owner, Ralph Demmeler, in 1944 and has been restored since that time.

The 2 1/2-story, wood-frame structure has a side-board and shingle exterior. Distinctive features include a long front veranda, a side tower with a conical roof, a pediment above the arched entrance, a segmented pediment on the second floor, and an abundance of exquisite wood craftsmanship on the exterior. The outside color is light green with red trim. An extension to the rear was added in 1914.

Not open to the public.
Private residence.

818 Bonnie Brae Street
Los Angeles 90057

A 27. BONNIE BRAE STREET RESIDENCE

This unique building was constructed in a "chateau in wood" design and features a striking facade. Built in 1896, its architects were Merithew and Haley. Public transportation to within a block of location.

Not open to public
Private residences

1036-38 S. Bonnie Brae Street
Los Angeles 90006

Bonnie Brae Street Residence

A 28. CHANCERY ARCHIVES, LOS ANGELES DIOCESE

Although records concerning California Catholic history date back to 1842, not until 1963 was the Chancery Archives formally established. During the intervening years records of great historical value were continually shifted about from one location to another or left to the whims of untrained caretakers. The modern Chancery Archives follows an organized system of records management for its holdings. Among the materials available for use by qualified scholars are the files of *The Tidings,* correspondence and documents reaching back to the mission period, the microfilm copies of relevant materials obtained from other repositories. The Chancery Archives is not intended to serve the general public, but historians and scholars of any faith may make application for research in the archival holdings. The Chancery Archives continues to solicit materials which will provide information on California's Catholic heritage. Public transportation available to one and one-half blocks of location.

Winter: (September through May)
   Wednesday—9:00 A.M.-4:00 P.M.

Summer: (June through August)
   Daily—9:00 A.M.-4:30 P.M.
   and by appointment

1531 West 9th Street
Los Angeles 90015
388-8108

A 29. PEOPLE'S TEMPLE CHRISTIAN CHURCH (FORMERLY FIRST CHURCH OF CHRIST, SCIENTIST)

Architect Elmer Gray designed this Italian Romanesque style church edifice for the First Church of Christ, Scientist, and construction began in 1912. For six decades it served as the central church for this denomination locally. The building was sold in 1972 and converted to use by the Disciples of Christ congregation of People's Temple Christian Church.

1366 South Alvarado Street
Los Angeles 90006
384-3604

People's Temple Christian Church

A 30. ALVARADO TERRACE

Along the north side of Alvarado Terrace, a slightly curving street only one block long, are some of the city's finest surviving examples of exclusive residences constructed around the turn of the century. Each of these five houses was constructed circa 1902.

Perhaps the most historically significant residence is the house at 1345 Alvarado Terrace, built and lived in by Pomeroy Powers, president of the Los Angeles City Council from 1900 to 1904. As a real estate developer, Powers also constructed the house next door at 1333 Alvarado Terrace, a home with unusual utilization of oak and stone with excellent carving throughout. He was instrumental in the establishment of the adjacent Terrace Park. "Powers Place," the red brick strip of roadway which divides Terrace Park into two parts, was named in his honor by a city ordinance in 1911.

Two other houses at 1317 and 1353 Alvarado Terrace are both designed in the architectural style of English and German chateaux. The former home was built in 1905 for Calvin A. Boyle and purchased in 1908 by Edmund H. Barmore, president of the Los Angeles Transfer Company, and the latter residence was constructed about 1902 for R. H. Raphael, who was very prominent in the glass business in the early 1900s. The Barmore House was a private residence until 1971, when it was acquired by the Union Rescue Mission. Only slightly altered and in excellent condition, the house today is a Christian youth home known as Joel House.

Private residences
Not open to the public

1300 Block of Alvarado Terrace
Los Angeles 90012

A 31. MORRIS COHN HOUSE

Designed by two noted Los Angeles architects, Hudson and Munsell, this 2 1/2-story house was built in 1902 for Morris R. Cohn, prominent business man and probably founder of the sportswear-garment industry in Los Angeles. Cohn arrived in the city in 1887, and within two years he established his own firm and began to manufacture shoes and clothing. In 1893 he moved his business to 318-320 N. Los Angeles Street and began to produce overalls and shirts, thus becoming the first garment manufacturer in the city.

The wood-framed house has a brown shingle and stone exterior, with white trim. A semi-closed veranda dominates most of the front of the structure, and three sloped dormers adorn the roof. Only minor alterations have been made in this home, which is in excellent condition on a well-landscaped setting.

Private residence
Not open to the public

1325 Alvarado Terrace
Los Angeles 90012

A 32. TRINITY METHODIST CHURCH

The history of Trinity Methodist Church is traced back through a series of mergers and building locations to 1869. The location at 12th and Flower Streets, originally a Christ Episcopal Church building, was obtained in 1916 by the Trinity Methodist Church after the funding for another building proved unfeasible. From 1919 to 1973 the Trinity Church provided Methodist leadership in downtown Los Angeles. At

Trinity Methodist Church

Los Angeles Examiner Building

that time a merger was effected with the Wilshire United Methodist Church, and the congregation continued at the Wilshire Boulevard location.

For over 30 years (1920-1953) the minister of the Trinity Church was Dr. Robert P. Shuler, a controversial church leader who crusaded against crime and civic corruption in the 1930s, operating a radio station from the church property. Not until 1937 was the work of Shuler and other reformers vindicated with the recall of Mayor Frank Shaw and the election of Fletcher Bowron. Public transportation available to location.

No longer open to public

1201 S. Flower Street
Los Angeles 90015

A 33. LOS ANGELES *EXAMINER* BUILDING

In December 1903, William Randolph Hearst commenced publication of the Los Angeles *Examiner,* the latest in his chain of newspapers. He commissioned Julia

Morgan, who would be best known for her work on the San Simeon estate, and Los Angeles architects Henke and Dodd to design a building to serve as the newspaper's offices and production center. The building was completed in 1912. Over the years the Hearst Corporation acquired the *Herald* and the *Express,* merging the two in 1931, and in 1962 combining the afternoon paper with the morning one to make up today's *Herald-Examiner.* Public transportation available to location.

Not open to public

1111 S. Broadway
Los Angeles 90015
748-1212

A 34. ST. JOSEPH'S CATHOLIC CHURCH

St. Joseph's Church was constructed in 1901 and has been in continuous operation since then. Designed and engineered by Franciscan fathers working in collaboration, the Catholic church is a beautiful example of Gothic architecture. Thirty-five stained glass windows highlight the building, which contains seven altars. The church was designated an historic cultural monument in 1963. Public transportation available to location.

Daily, 6 A.M.-6 P.M.

218 E. 12th Street
Los Angeles 90015
748-5394

St. Joseph's Catholic Church

A 35. ST. PAUL'S CATHEDRAL

St. Paul's Cathedral, serving members of the Episcopal Church, traces its origins in Los Angeles to 1865, when it was known as the St. Athanasius Parish Church. In the 1880s the name was changed to St. Paul's Church, and the church's location was moved from its original spot on New High Street to South Olive Street, where the Biltmore Hotel is now located.

Construction of the present cathedral began in 1923, and the first service in the new building was held July 13, 1924. The architectural team that designed the building included Reginald Johnson, son of the Right Rev. Joseph H. Johnson, the first Episcopal Bishop of Los Angeles. The new cathedral was consecrated on November 12, 1924.

Among the cathedral's special features are a Great Cross hand-cut from California redwood, numerous relics from English churches, and marble quarried from Siena, Italy, and from the State of Alabama. St. Paul's Cathedral serves the largest diocese in the Episcopal Church. The building was designated an historic cultural monument in 1970. Public transportation available to location.

Services: 9 and 11 A.M. Sunday
September-May Office Hours:
  9-5 weekdays
June-August Office Hours: 8-4 weekdays

615 S. Figueroa Street
Los Angeles 90017
626-6721

A 36. GLOBAL MARINE HOUSE

In 1925 the architectural firm of Albert R. Walker and Percy Eisen designed the Fine Arts or Havenstrite building, distinguished for its combination of Gothic and Romanesque features and its terra cotta exterior. The Havenstrite Oil Company used the building until 1969 when it was sold to Global Marine Inc. It is now known as the Global Marine House. The lobby of the building features 17 bronze cases which exhibit oil paintings on all themes. The Global Marine firm periodically changes the displays. Public transportation available to a half block of location.

Monday-Friday, 8:00 A.M.-5:00 P.M.

811 W. 7th Street
Los Angeles 90017
680-9550

California Club Building

A 37. CALIFORNIA CLUB BUILDING

The California Club building was designed by one of its members, architect Robert David Farquhar, in 1929. The 8-story building was completed in August 1930. It features set-back terraces, large-scale design, and a facade of Roman-style bricks. In 1966 the club building was designated an historic cultural monument. Public transportation available to location.

Private club (not open to public)

538 S. Flower Street
Los Angeles 90017
622-1391

A 38. LOS ANGELES PUBLIC LIBRARY, CENTRAL BUILDING

After several locations since first being established in 1878, the Los Angeles Public Library found a home in a specially designed building. It was designed by Bertram G. Goodhue shortly before the architect's death and constructed during 1925-26. Goodhue's design was patterned on his earlier creation, the Nebraska State Capitol building at Lin-

coln. The building was dedicated on July 15, 1926.

For many years the library building featured numerous entrances, tile pools, and rolling expanses of grass. One by one these attractions were reduced or eliminated by pressures for parking places and storage needs. The building, at the head of a system which includes 61 branch libraries, contains far more than books. The rotunda murals by Dean Cornwall, historical murals by Albert Herter, and other murals and sculpture enhance the unusual architectural designs.

Named in 1964 for long-time library commissioner Rufus B. von KleinSmid, the library was designated as an historic cultural monument in 1967. The Southern California Chapter of the American Institute of Architects has declared it a distinctive Los Angeles landmark. Despite recent controversy over the building's future as a library, it continues to provide valuable reading and reference services to thousands of visitors daily. Public transportation available to location.

Monday-Thursday, 10 A.M.-9 P.M.
Friday and Saturday, 10 A.M.-5:30 P.M.
(Closed Sunday and Holidays)

630 W. 5th Street
Los Angeles 90017
626-7461

A 39. CALIFORNIA COLLECTION, LOS ANGELES PUBLIC LIBRARY

When the Los Angeles Public Library was completed in 1926, a portion of the History Department was set up as the California Collection. This collection is one of the world's most extensive holdings of material relating to California history, biography, and travel. It includes an extensive collection of pictures of historical value, including a portrait file of pioneers, and many early local scenes. Some of the most valuable California items have been transferred to a special bibliographers vault. Public transportation available directly to location.

Monday-Thursday, 10 A.M.-9 P.M.
Friday-Saturday, 10 A.M.-5:30 P.M.

630 W. 5th Street
Los Angeles 90017
626-7461

A 40. BILTMORE HOTEL

The Biltmore Hotel, built at a cost of $7 million, was opened in 1923, with 1,000 rooms. Three years later a wing was added with 500 more rooms, making the hotel the largest one in Los Angeles. The hotel was designed by the New York firm of Schultze and Weaver; its reddish brick, terra cotta roof tiles, and cream-colored stone make the building instantly recognizable, as does the suggestion of three towers on the facade. Its strategic location across from Pershing Square has made the hotel a major center for conventions and meetings. In 1960 the hotel served as headquarters for the Democratic National Convention at which John F. Kennedy was nominated for President.

Over the years the hotel has been periodically refurbished, with attention paid to preserving the ceiling and wall murals. These were done by Giovanni Battista Smeraldi, whose paintings are also in the Blue Room of the White House. Public transportation available to location; Harbor Freeway exits at 4th and 6th Streets, then east to hotel.

515 S. Olive Street
Los Angeles 90013
624-1011

A 41. PHILHARMONIC AUDITORIUM (TEMPLE BAPTIST CHURCH)

This eight-story building contains the offices of the Temple Baptist Church and the Philharmonic Auditorium. The building replaced a recreational center known as Hazard's Pavilion which was razed in 1905. Built of reinforced concrete and steel, at the time of its construction the combination auditorium and office building was the largest such building in the world. The building was dedicated on July 29, 1906. On Friday, November 8, 1906, the opera "Aida" was presented in the 2,700 seat Temple Auditorium, and on the following Sunday, Pastor Robert J. Burdette delivered the first sermon.

The church endorsed the use of Temple Auditorium as a center for Los Angeles musical culture for over 40 years. In 1920 it was leased to the Los Angeles Philharmonic Orchestra, and it then became known as the Philharmonic Auditorium. In 1947, when the church acquired all the stock of the auditorium company, it desired to restrict use of the building to religious purposes. Philharmonic concerts and artistic productions continued there, however, until the opening of the Music Center. Temple Baptist Church, deliberately located in the heart of downtown Los Angeles, considers all of the County as its congregation. Public transportation available to location.

427 W. 5th Street
Los Angeles 90013
624-8088—information office in building
628-7361—church

Pershing Square, showing Biltmore Hotel and Philharmonic Auditorium, c. 1925.

A 42. PERSHING SQUARE

Pershing Square dates back to 1866 when on December 11 of that year Mayor Cristobal Aguilar approved an ordinance providing for a public square. Over the years the square was known by several names, including Central Park, Sixth Street Park, Public Square, and other titles. On November 18, 1918, the city council renamed the park Pershing Square in honor of General John J. Pershing. Since then the park has been relandscaped several times; in the 1950s the multi-level Pershing Square Garage was constructed underneath the square-block park. Public transportation available to location.

W. 5th and Hill Streets

A 43. LOS ANGELES ATHLETIC CLUB

The history of the Los Angeles Athletic Club dates back to its founding in 1880. After the club had moved several times, the membership, including a number of promi- nent Los Angeles business and professional men, decided to construct the best and most modern athletic club possible. The club commissioned architects John Parkinson and Edwin Bergstrom to conduct a two-year study of notable club buildings in the United States. In 1912 the building was constructed; among its unusual features was the installation of a 100-foot-long swimming pool on the sixth floor of the building instead of the basement. The club's facilities include tennis courts, bar and restaurant, gymnasium, and a wide range of athletic programs. Athletic trophies, paintings and artifacts are on display. More than 75 club members have won medals in the Olympic Games. In 1970 the club was designated as an historic cultural monument. Public transportation available to location.

Private club, not open to public
(Tours arranged)

431 W. 7th Street
Los Angeles 90014
625-2211

A 44. GARFIELD BUILDING

The 1920s was an important period of construction of major buildings in Los Angeles. One of the outstanding examples of this era is the Garfield building, constructed in 1928 as a modern office building. Officially titled the International Office Building in 1971, the structure is still informally known by its original name. Of particular interest is the lobby, with walls and floors of imported marble, trimmed with German silver and gold leaf. Strategically located at Eighth and Hill Streets in downtown Los Angeles, the 12-story building was recently refurbished at a cost of $1 million. Public transportation available to location.

Open Monday-Friday, 7:45 A.M.-8 P.M.

403 W. 8th Street
Los Angeles 90014
627-5152

Garfield Building, 1920s rendition

A 45. CLIFTON'S CAFETERIA

This is the oldest of the cafeterias established by Clifford E. Clinton (1900-69). Clinton came from a family of restaurant operators in the San Francisco Bay area. Having successfully operated a half dozen cafeterias in San Francisco, Clinton sold them and in 1931 went to Los Angeles. In 1935 he commissioned the firm of Plummer, Wurdeman, and Becket to supervise the

remodeling of a cafeteria on Broadway near Seventh Street. He wanted a distinctive design utilizing a mountain theme; in fact, diners find themselves seated amid waterfalls and redwood trees on several levels. Clinton also purchased a mountain resort in the San Gabriel Mountains and ran buses from the cafeteria to the resort in the 1930s.

Clinton's "Clifton's Cafeterias" proved a tremendous success in Los Angeles. He provided "Food for Thot," a weekly bulletin of advice and philosophy, and insisted that dissatisfied customers have their money cheerfully refunded. Becoming involved in local politics, Clinton played an important role in the recall of Mayor Frank Shaw in 1938. He also experimented with providing low-cost meals for poor people. Today there are six public cafeterias and two others operated as concessions for private companies. The most recent cafeteria, Clifton's Silver Spoon at 515 West Seventh Street, has exhibits showing Clifton's history. Public transportation available to location.

Open daily, 6:00 A.M.-9:00 P.M.

648 S. Broadway
Los Angeles 90014
627-1673

A 46. FINNEY'S CAFETERIA

Around the time of the First World War, guests staying at the Alexandria Hotel expressed the desire for a convenient restaurant. Their wish was granted in 1914 with the establishment of the Chocolate Shoppe. The name was changed in 1936 when Sam Finney took over the restaurant; he also changed it to cafeteria style. Today the owner is Abe Orr, but he has retained the familiar name. Besides home-made pies and cakes, the cafeteria features murals and tiles designed by artist Ernest A. Batchelder. Public transportation available to location.

Daily, 6 A.M.-8 P.M.

217 W. 6th Street
Los Angeles 90014
626-2968

Arcade Building, interior.

A 47. PALM COURT, ALEXANDRIA HOTEL

A prime attraction of the Alexandria Hotel is its Palm Court, featuring a stained glass ceiling, rose mirrors, and gold-flecked wall panels. When the hotel opened in 1906, it was advertised as among the most luxurious in the West. Three United States Presidents—Theodore Roosevelt, William H. Taft, and Woodrow Wilson—were guests at the Alexandria, as well as many other famous people.

During World War II the glass ceiling was painted over as a blackout precaution. In 1969 the Alexandria began a renovation program and today is a major leader in the revitalization of downtown Los Angeles. The hotel lobby and many rooms feature framed photographs of many of the famous guests who have stayed at the Alexandria. Public transportation available to location.

Tours:
Groups of 35 or more: may arrange tours
    anytime;
Individuals: Last Wednesday of each
    month (reservations only)

501 S. Spring Street
Los Angeles 90013
626-7484

A 48. ARCADE BUILDING

In 1883 the Los Angeles Board of Education purchased the property of what is now 541 S. Spring Street for $12,500. Adolph Ramish, 36 years later, purchased the land for over $1.5 million, a clear indication of the huge rise in land values in downtown Los Angeles. Ramish commissioned architect Kenneth MacDonald, Jr., to create a replica of London's Burlington Arcade. Construction commenced on May 10, 1923, and the building was completed by February 1924. The building has space for 350 offices and 61 shops. Its distinctive glass roof makes it a notable landmark in downtown Los Angeles. Public transportation available to location.

Monday-Saturday, 7 A.M.-9:30 P.M.
Admission free

541 S. Spring Street
Los Angeles 90013

A 49. FARMERS AND MERCHANTS BANK BUILDING

In 1868 two Los Angeles banks were founded—Hayward and Company and Hellman, Temple and Company. Later in the same year the banks changed partners and names. John G. Downey, a former California governor and a partner in Hayward and Company, joined Isaias W. Hellman in creating the Farmers and Merchants Bank. F.P.F. Temple and William Workman opened the Temple and Workman Bank. Financial over-extension ruined the Temple and Workman Bank, but the F. & M. bank weathered the crisis and for many years was a leading Los Angeles bank. In 1956 the Farmers and Merchants Bank merged into the Security-First National Bank of Los Angeles, now Security Pacific National Bank. The Farmers and Merchants building at Fourth and Main Streets, built in 1904, still carries on the Hellman traditions. Public transportation available to location.

Monday-Friday, 10 A.M.-3 P.M.

401 S. Main Street
Los Angeles 90013
613-6211

Farmers and Merchants Bank, c. 1960.

A 50. COLES P. E. BUFFET

Coles P. E. Buffet has been in operation since 1908 and is the oldest restaurant and saloon in Los Angeles. Located in the Pacific Electric Terminal building, the restaurant was founded by Harry Cole, who also ran a check-cashing service for commuters. The facilities include a huge mahogany bar, Tiffany shades, and other decorations which recall Los Angeles in the heyday of the big red trolley cars. Pictures on the wall show the early transportation history of the city, from horse-drawn cars to freeways. Coles P. E. Buffet was designated an historic cultural monument in 1972. Public transportation available to location.

Monday-Friday, 7 A.M.-8 P.M.

118 E. 6th Street
Los Angeles 90014
622-4090

Pacific Electric Building, Sixth and Main, with Buffet in far left corner, c. 1910.

A 51. FIRE STATION NO. 23

This historic fire station was constructed in 1910 at a cost of $57,000. Three stories in height; the first floor housed the fire fighting equipment, the second floor was for the firemen's living quarters, and the third floor provided space for offices and for the residences of the chief engineer and his family. The building was recognized as advanced in its design of living and working quarters. In 1960, after answering almost 60,000 alarms, the station was retired from active service. It is still used as a training headquarters. The equipment includes a horse-drawn steam pumper, hose wagon, and a motorized Gorter Water Tower of almost unique design. In 1966 the building was declared an historic cultural monument. Public transportation available to location.

225 E. 5th Street
Los Angeles 90013

A 52. CAST-IRON COMMERCIAL BUILDING

This long two-story building was constructed in 1903 and is one of the last remaining partly cast-iron structures in the Los Angeles area. Its architecture has been described as late Queen Anne mixed with Italianate details, featuring oriel windows and interesting iron work craftsmanship from the turn of the century.

This building is used as a warehouse and is not open to the public.

740-748 S. San Pedro Street
Los Angeles 90021

A 53. SITE OF THE AFRICAN METHODIST EPISCOPAL CHURCH

In the Spring Street home of Mrs. Biddy Mason, a former slave, the First African Methodist Episcopal Church was organized in 1872. As the first Negro church in Los Angeles, with 12 charter members, it became the mother church for all other black churches subsequently established in the city. By purchasing a lot at the corner of 4th and Grand Avenue for $700, the congregation became the first Negro group in the city to buy land and build a church. The congregation later moved several times until in 1903 it completed construction of a beautiful Gothic edifice at 8th and Towne, modeled after an English cathedral designed by Sir Christopher Wren. An additional wing, used as a youth center, was designed in 1947 by Los Angeles architect Paul R. Williams.

After the church moved to a new location at 227 South Harvard Boulevard, the Towne Avenue structure was taken over by the Federation of Black History and Art. Plans for creating a community cultural center at this site were halted when a fire completely destroyed the edifice on July 4, 1972.

Marker at 801 S. Towne Avenue
Los Angeles 90026

First African Methodist Episcopal Church, c. 1940.

A 54. COHN-GOLDWATER BUILDING

The Cohn-Goldwater building was constructed in 1909 at a cost of $150,000. The first modern steel-reinforced concrete factory building in Los Angeles, it was built for the garment manufacturing firm of Morris Cohn and Lemuel Goldwater, who had formed their partnership in 1899. The building is still being used for the manufacture of clothing; in fact, the Cohn-Goldwater firm contributed to making Los Angeles a national leader in the apparel industry. In 1973 the Cohn-Goldwater building was designated an historic monument. Public transportation available to one block of location.

525 E. 12th Street
Los Angeles 90015

A 55. COCA COLA BUILDING

In 1935 architect Robert V. Derrah designed a highly unusual facade for the Coca Cola Company's Los Angeles bottling plant. The structure was completed in 1937. Actually covering five separate buildings, Derrah's facade looks like an ocean liner. The windows are shaped like portholes, and the doorways resemble entryways on a ship, even down to simulated rivets. A superstructure atop the facade adds to the illusion which, even though abstract, is clearly identifiable. For almost 40 years the unique design of the plant has appealed to visitors of all ages. Public transportation available to location.

Tours available on request

1334 S. Central Avenue
Los Angeles 90021

A 56. GRAND CENTRAL PUBLIC MARKET

The oldest of all concession-type markets on the Pacific Coast, the Grand Central Public Market was established in 1917 on the street level of the Homer Laughlin building. A six-story office and professional building constructed in 1897, the Laughlin building's first floor was originally leased as a department store. In 1917 the street level was made over into a food market with over fifty individually owned stalls, extending into a three-story annex that had been built in 1905 and which provided access from Broadway through to Hill Street. The Laughlin building was the first earthquake and fire-proof building in Los Angeles, with structural steel on the Broadway side and reinforced concrete on the Hill Street side. Public transportation available to location.

Monday-Saturday, 9 A.M.-6 P.M.
(Closed Sunday)

317 S. Broadway
Los Angeles 90013
624-2378

A 57. MILLION DOLLAR THEATRE

Downtown Los Angeles has numerous theatres which were built to feature the burgeoning motion picture industry of the "silent screen" era. Although they no longer reflect their past glory, these buildings are worth a visit, if only for the decorative embellishments on wall, ceiling hallway and marquee. South Broadway was a mecca for theatre-goers in the early '20s, and of the extant buildings in this area, the Million Dollar Theatre is perhaps most representative.

This theatre is part of an office building which originally housed the Edison Company and, later, the Metropolitan Water District. The theatre was designed by architect William Lee Woollett and opened on February 1, 1918, by Sid and D.J. Grauman. Both films and live entertainment have played its stage since the beginning. The auditorium and facade remain much as they were on opening day, though the lobby has been altered. Statuary, ceiling, and organ screens are particularly impressive. Today the theatre presents first-run films and productions from Mexico in the Spanish language.

307 South Broadway
Los Angeles, Calif. 90013

A 58. BRADBURY BUILDING

Conceded by architects and public alike as possibly the most architectually unique building in Los Angeles, the Bradbury building was commissioned in 1893 by a wealthy real estate developer and mining entrepreneur, Louis L. Bradbury. After rejecting a plan submitted by Sumner P. Hunt, Bradbury offered the assignment to a junior draftsman in the Hunt firm, George Herbert Wyman. The story is told that Wyman accepted the commission only after receiving a message on a planchette (ouija board) stating the building would make him famous.

Although the building's exterior is deliberately restrained, its interior features a dazzling light-filled open court illuminated by a glass roof, a careful marriage of marble and steel, and the gentle clicking of an hydraulic elevator. Rails and bannisters of iron, generous wood paneling, and open stairways and corridors make the building a delight to the eye. The building continues to serve its original function as an office

Bradbury Building interior.

building, attracting attorneys, architects, and other professional people. Many of the offices are furnished in the style of the era of its construction. The Way Back When Photo Salon offers visitors an opportunity to be photographed in an antique photo style. The Bradbury building was designated an historic cultural monument in 1962 and was included in the National Register of Historic Places in 1971. Public transportation available to location.

Weekdays, 7:00 A.M.-7:00 P.M.
Admission $1.00, tours from $2.00 to $10.00 can be arranged.

304 S. Broadway
Los Angeles 90013

A 59. LOS ANGELES *TIMES* BUILDING

The Los Angeles *Times* building, forming a major part of Times Mirror Square, is the

Los Angeles Times Building, c. 1950.

fourth home of the *Times.* Founded in December 1881, the paper has been published by the same family since August 1882, when Harrison Gray Otis became its editor and publisher. Constructed in 1935, the building is the corporate headquarters of the Times Mirror Company, including executive, editorial, business, and art departments. Deep within the building 12 newspaper presses print up to 60,000 copies per hour. Much of the newspaper producing process is automated. In 1948 an annex, the *Times* Building South, was constructed for production of the Los Angeles *Mirror,* which is no longer published. An additional new wing was added to headquarters building in 1974. Today Otis Chandler, great-grandson of Harrison Gray Otis, oversees the production of over a million copies of the *Times* daily, and over 1.2 million copies on Sundays. Public transportation available to location.

Public tours on Tuesdays and Fridays at
2:45 P.M. for groups of 6 or less;
Children must be over age 10. Other
group tours by arrangement.

202 W. 1st Street
Los Angeles 90053
625-2345

A 60. LOS ANGELES COUNTY RECORD CENTER

Included among the vast and partially indexed holdings formerly known as the County Archives are the first book of the County Board of Supervisors for 1852, some of the books of the Court of Sessions which preceded it, transcribed and translated records of the *pueblo alcalde* (town mayor) from 1825 to 1850 (the originals are in the Huntington Library), court cases from 1840-50 (recorded in Spanish), and grand jury reports going back to the 1890s. Most of the court cases are indexed, and there are hopes of indexing the other materials as soon as possible. Public transportation available to location.

Monday-Friday, 8 A.M.-5 P.M.

Room 110, Archives Record Center
222 N. Hill Street
Los Angeles 90012
974-1379

A 61. LOS ANGELES COUNTY RECORDS OFFICE

In the Hall of Records building are seven floors of materials relating to all forms of land and land transfer. There are records of leases, tax sales, deeds of trust, reconveyances, notices of completion, maps, and mining claims. Each floor has its own index. Public transportation available to location.

Monday-Friday, 8 A.M.-5 P.M.

227 N. Broadway
Los Angeles 90012
974-6616

Los Angeles City Hall (completed 1928)

A 62. LOS ANGELES CITY HALL

For many years the highest visible landmark on the city's urban horizon was the Los Angeles City Hall, 454 feet high. Since the city's early years as a pueblo the location of city government offices had been moved numerous times. To provide a central location for the various city departments and to provide services for Los Angeles citizens, construction on a modern city hall was begun in 1926, to be completed two years later, on April 26, 1928.

Besides municipal offices and departments, there are a number of items of general interest to City Hall visitors. The marble columns come from 27 different countries, and the building's architectural design includes many interesting features, including derivations from Grecian, Romanesque, and Modern American styles. The rotunda contains a domed ceiling with inlaid tile patterns illustrating municipal government services. Tour guides conduct visitors throughout the day, and the observation tower is open to the public. Public transportation available to location.

Monday-Friday, 10:00 A.M.-4:00 P.M.
Saturday-Sunday, 11:00 A.M.-5:00 P.M.
(Building open 24 hours)

200 N. Spring Street
Los Angeles 90012
485-2121

A 63. CITY OF LOS ANGELES ARCHIVES

The archives of the City of Los Angeles are kept in the City Clerk's Office, where all records are stored that pertain to the city's government. These include the City Seal, citizen petitions and communications, minutes of the City Council dating back to 1832, and indexes of all Council actions. Those records are housed in a large vault. Until May 5, 1854, the Council records were kept in Spanish. The archives also contains election records going back to 1828. Public transportation available to location.

Monday-Friday, 8:00 A.M.-5:00 P.M.

Room 395, City Hall
200 N. Spring Street
Los Angeles 90012
485-2121

A 64. FEDERAL BUILDING (U.S. COURTHOUSE)

The United States Federal building, which includes the courthouse and government offices, was constructed in 1937 as an enlargement of the original building. Visitors to the building will see several excellent works of sculpture. Two eagles in terra cotta relief on the facades of ths building were designed by Henry Lion. At the south end of the lobby of the Main Street entrance, an imposing sculpture titled "Law," created by Archibald Garner, stands eight feet high. At the north end of the lobby is James Lee Hansen's sculpture, "Young Lincoln." Public transportation available to location.

Monday-Friday, 8 A.M.-4:30 P.M.

312 N. Spring Street
Los Angeles 90012
688-3253

St. Vibiana's Cathedral

historic cultural monument in 1963. Public transportation available to location.

Open daily 7:00 A.M.-6:30 P.M.

S. Main Street at 2nd Street
Los Angeles 90012
624-3941

A 65. ST. VIBIANA'S CATHEDRAL

St. Vibiana's Cathedral was constructed between 1871 and 1876, its design derived from the Church of the Puerto de San Miguel in Barcelona, Spain, by architect Ezra F. Kysor. Kysor, a prominent Los Angeles architect of the period, also designed the Merced Theatre, Pico House, and other buildings. St. Vibiana's, named for an early Christian martyr, was the first cathedral church for the diocese of Monterey and Los Angeles.

From its construction until 1922 the building was virtually unchanged. In that year extensive renovations were done, including alteration of some ceilings, the installation of new painted glass panels in the windows, and removal of the original facade. The cathedral was again remodeled in 1975.

St. Vibiana's Cathedral has for over 100 years served the people of Los Angeles. In the sanctuary area relics of the martyr Vibiana are encased in a marble sarcophagus. The cathedral was designated an

A 66. LITTLE TOKYO

A very few people of Japanese origin were present in Los Angeles during the Mexican period but more followed after the lifting of travel restrictions by the Japanese government. Before World War II the Japanese community in southern California was primarily involved in agriculture and commercial fishing.

The evacuation of Japanese Americans from the Pacific Coast in 1942 stands as a shameful incident in American history. Although no act of sabotage was ever committed by Japanese Americans on the U.S. mainland, and although two-thirds of the people were Nisei—second generation Americans—all persons of Japanese ancestry were removed from their homes and businesses and taken to assembly centers such as the Santa Anita Race Track, and from there on to ten "relocation centers" mainly in desert areas. After the war the Japanese Americans returned to California—though a number chose to move elsewhere—to take up their lives again. But the heavy involvement in agriculture was permanently disrupted. Today Japanese Americans are active in a wide variety of occupations and professions.

About 100,000 Japanese Americans live in the Los Angeles area, but the cultural heart of the community remains Little Tokyo, located on East First Street beginning just east of Main Street. Here one finds restaurants, businesses, churches, temples, and cultural centers. Each August a Nisei Week is held, featuring a parade and demonstrations ranging from karate tournaments to tea ceremonies. Public transportation available to location.

Regular business hours

200 E. 1st Street
and adjacent area

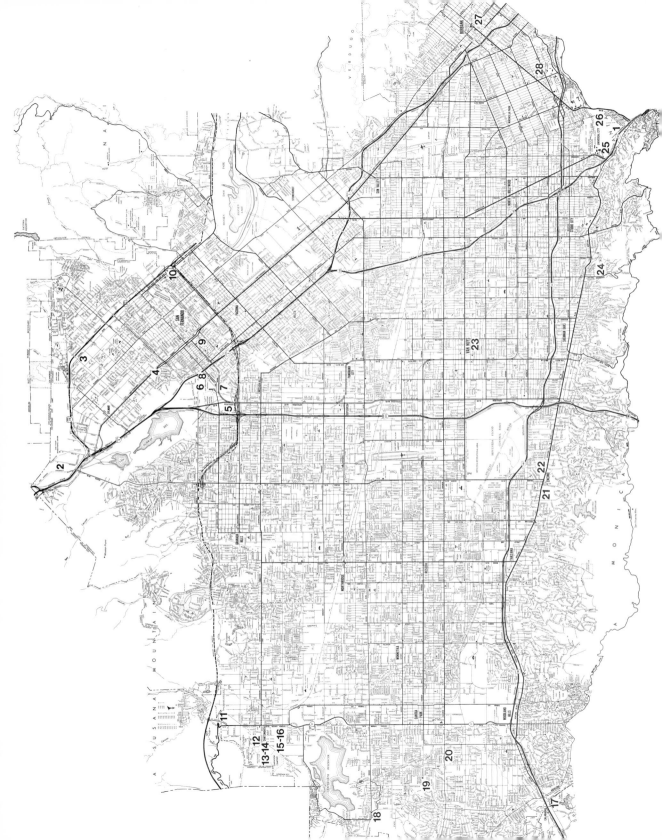

SECTION B

San Fernando Valley

1. El Camino Real
   Highway 101
2. Owens River Aqueduct Cascades
   Foothill Blvd., north of Interstate 5;
   San Fernando
3. Pioneer Cemetery (aka: Morningside
   Cemetery and Sylmar Cemetery)
   Foothill Blvd. at Bledsoe Street; Sylmar
4. Mission Wells and Settling Basin,
   Sylmar
   Bleeker and Havana Streets
5. Andres Pico Adobe
   10940 Sepulveda Blvd.; Mission Hills
6. San Fernando Mission
   15151 San Fernando Mission Blvd.;
   Mission Hills
7. Memory Garden, Brand Park
   15100 San Fernando Mission Blvd.;
   Mission Hills
8. Mission Dam, Mission Hills
   Between Laurel Canyon and Sepulveda
   Blvds., south of Golden State Freeway
   (on Renaldi)
9. Lopez Adobe
   1100 Pico Street; San Fernando
10. Griffith Ranch
    Foothill Blvd. and Vaughn Street; San
    Fernando Valley
11. Stoney Point Outcropping, Chatsworth
    East side of Topanga Canyon Blvd.,
    bisected by northern border of Los
    Angeles County-City
12. Palmer Residence, Chatsworth
    West end of Devonshire Street
13. Old Stagecoach Trail, Chatsworth
    South of Chatsworth Park, North of
    Oakwood Memorial Park, East of Los
    Angeles County Line, West end of
    Devonshire Street
14. Indian Pictographs
    Located on the Old Stagecoach Trail;
    Chatsworth
15. Oakwood Memorial Park, Chatsworth
    22601 Lassen Street
16. Chatsworth Community Church
    22601 Lassen Street
17. Leonis Adobe
    23537 Calabasas Road; Calabasas
18. Rancho Sombra del Robles—Orcutt
    Ranch Horticultural Center
    23600 Roscoe Blvd.; Canoga Park
19. Canoga Mission Gallery
    23120 Sherman Way; Canoga Park
20. Shadow Ranch House
    22633 Vanowen Street; Canoga Park
21. Oak Tree, Encino
    Louise Avenue, 210 feet south of
    Ventura Blvd.
22. Los Encinos State Historic Park
    16756 Moorpark Street; Encino
23. Van Nuys City Hall
    14410 Sylvan Street
24. St. Saviour's Chapel, Harvard School
    3700 Coldwater Canyon; Studio City
25. Campo de Cahuenga
    3919 Lankershim Blvd.; North
    Hollywood
26. Universal Studios
    Hollywood Freeway at Lankershim
    Blvd., 100 Universal City Plaza;
    Universal City
27. Warner Research Collection, Burbank
    Central Library
    110 North Glenoaks Blvd., at the corner
    of Olive Avenue
28. Walt Disney Archives
    500 S. Buena Vista Street; Burbank

Mission San Fernando, c. 1895.

El Camino Real Highway Marker

B 1. EL CAMINO REAL

California's El Camino Real, "The Royal Road," is actually the northernmost portion of a highway which historically ran as far south as Guatemala. The California section was established in the late eighteenth century as the connecting road between San Diego and Sonoma, established by Spanish soldiers and Franciscan missionaries.

Highway 101 follows this famous route, in some places quite closely. In 1906 several hundred mission-bell guideposts were set up to guide visitors to nearby towns and, of course, to the missions. Over the years these guideposts gradually disappeared. During the 1960s new mission-bell guideposts were installed. Motorists on the Hollywood and Ventura Freeways may observe the guideposts and know they are traveling on the historic King's Highway.

B 2. OWENS RIVER AQUEDUCT CASCADES

The Owens River Aqueduct Cascades marks the official terminus of the Owens Valley-Los Angeles Aqueduct. This aqueduct, 233 miles long, supplies water to Los Angeles from Inyo and Mono Counties. It was constructed under the supervision of William Mulholland from 1907-13 and was considered a major engineering achievement of its time. The cost of the aqueduct was $23,000,000.

The official opening date for the aqueduct was Wednesday, November 5, 1913. On this day over 40,000 people traveled by train, automobile, and carriage to San Fernando. After a round of speechmaking, the signal was given for the opening of the aqueduct. Mulholland unfurled an American flag, and the engineers at the top of the hill turned the wheels that would allow the water to flow down the cascade and on to the San Fernando Reservoir. Amid the sounds of a brass band, the cheering crowd, and the firing of cannons, the water rushed down the cascade. As the crowd ran towards the side of the cascade for a closer view, Mulholland made a famous five-word speech: "There it is, take it."

The cascade is still in operation and may easily be seen driving north on Interstate-5. It is on the north side of the freeway, a short distance beyond the Balboa Boulevard exit. For an even closer view, get off at Balboa and turn left at Foothill Boulevard, and proceed to site.

Los Angeles Aqueduct at Owensmouth, 1913.

B 3. PIONEER CEMETERY. AKA: MORNINGSIDE CEMETERY AND SYLMAR CEMETERY

The Pioneer Cemetery in Sylmar is the oldest nonsectarian cemetery in the San Fernando Valley. Established in the mid 1800s, it was utilized until 1939. After legal abandonment in 1959, the cemetery is now owned by Native Daughters of the Golden West, San Fernando Mission Parlor, and maintained as a pioneer memorial park. Public transportation available to six blocks of location.

Foothill Blvd. at Bledsoe Street
Sylmar 91345

Mission Wells, San Fernando

Andreas Pico Adobe, 1932.

B 4. MISSION WELLS AND SETTLING BASIN, SYLMAR

Built around 1800 by Indians from the San Fernando mission, the wells provided a source of water for the mission complex. Use of water from this source has been continuous, making it the oldest existing water supply source in the City of Los Angeles apart, of course, from the Los Angeles River. The wells were constructed of mission tiles and are still in good condition. In August 1919 the Department of Water and Power purchased the six-acre well site and replaced the five wells then in use with six newer ones. Water from this source provides over 2 1/2 million gallons daily to about 20,000 people. Part of the property has been developed by the DWP as a small park. Public transportation available to about six blocks from the park.

Open all day

Bleeker Street and Havana Avenue
Sylmar 91345

B 5. ANDRÉS PICO ADOBE

The main part of this historic abode was built approximately in 1834 by ex-Mission San Fernando Indians. It is the second oldest home in Los Angeles City. Eulogio de Celis, a Los Angeles merchant, purchased the Valley in 1846 from Governor Pío Pico and began adding rooms to the Adobe. Andrés Pico, brother of the ex-governor, purchased half of the Valley from de Celis in 1853, which included the Adobe. Pico and his son, Romulo, added the second story in 1873. Among the many visitors was Tiburcio Vasquez, once an overnight guest. Other owners and renters followed and during the early part of the 1900s the Adobe fell into neglect until 1930 when Dr. M. R. Harrington, curator of the Southwest Museum, purchased the ruin and 20 acres surrounding it. The restoration was completed in 1932.

The Adobe was purchased by the City of Los Angeles in 1967 and is now the headquarters of the San Fernando Valley Historical Society, which has a contract with the City. Public transportation available to location.

Saturday-Sunday, 1:00-4:00 P.M.
Group tours during the week, call 365-7810

10940 Sepulveda Blvd.
Mission Hills 91345
365-7810

B 6. SAN FERNANDO MISSION

San Fernando Rey de España was founded on September 8, 1797, with Father Fermín Lasuén in charge of ceremonies. The area was strategically located in its proximity to water, good land, and Indians, and was on the road between Missions San Buenaventura and San Gabriel. The number of Indian converts rapidly increased, and the mission complex soon included stables, granaries, workshops, and houses. In fact, for many years the mission contained a larger population and activities than the pueblo of Los Angeles.

The Franciscan administration of the mission came to an end in 1834 when the Mexican government secularized the California missions. During the Mexican-American War the mission acreage, covering much of the San Fernando Valley, was sold for $14,000. John C. Frémont used the mission as a headquarters for a time. Although the mission was returned to the Catholic Church

after California became a state, the buildings fell into disrepair. People took the roofing tiles away, the adobe walls crumbled in the rain, and vandalism periodically occurred as treasure seekers looked for a fortune supposedly hidden by the mission fathers.

In 1900 restoration commenced and in 1923 an extensive restoration was begun. The mission of today contains the convent buildings which dated back to the Spanish period. Following the disasterous 1971 Sylmar earthquake, the mission church was demolished and an exact replica rebuilt. A museum features a pictorial history of the mission and a display of Indian crafts. Public transportation available to location.

Open 7 days a week, 9:00 A.M.-5:00 P.M.
Tours: 75¢ adults, 25¢ ages 7-15.

15151 San Fernando Mission Blvd.
Mission Hills 91345
361-0186

Mission San Fernando Cloisters from Memory Garden, c. 1926.

B 7. MEMORY GARDEN, BRAND PARK

Located across from the San Fernando Mission, Brand Park features the Memory Garden, which contains plantings from

Santa Barbara Mission. Two fountains from the mission are in the park, as are the vats used for making tallow in the Spanish-Mexican period. Picnic and athletic grounds are available; many school groups picnic at the park before touring the mansion. Public transportation available to location.

Open daily, 6 A.M. to 10 P.M.
Admission free

15100 San Fernando Mission Blvd.
Mission Hills 91345
361-1377

B 8. MISSION DAM, MISSION HILLS

This masonry and boulder dam was built by Indians in December 1808 to store water from the Mission wells, located about two miles to the northwest, and to send the water on to the San Fernando Mission through tiled pipe. It was located high enough so that water could move by gravity flow to the mission. As the first dam in the San Fernando Valley, it supplied water to the crops, orchards, and vineyards of the mission. It is now in ruins, but a portion of the dam still remains, and the Los Angeles County Flood Control District has constructed a small view site. Public transportation available to area.

Between Laurel Canyon and Sepulveda Blvds., just south of Golden State Freeway on Rinaldi, on north side of street.

B 9. LOPEZ ADOBE

The Lopez Adobe was built in San Fernando in 1882 by Valentin Lopez, a longtime resident of the area who made the home available to his brother-in-law and sister,

Geronimo and Catalina Lopez. The walls are two feet thick. The upper and lower levels have porches with handcut wooden railings and a jig-saw-patterned balustrade. The building is a good example of the period of architecture following the mission era but prior to the heavy influx of Americans to the region.

In 1969 the Lopez House Committee was formed with the goal of raising funds to acquire and restore the Lopez Adobe. The 1971 Sylmar earthquake damaged the building but provided only a temporary setback for the committee. By 1973 enough funds had been raised to match a federal grant, and the money was used to purchase the home from the Lopez heirs and to restore it to its original floor plan. The City of San Fernando now owns the building which was opened to the public in March 1975.

Open Wednesday and Saturday,
  11:00 A.M.-3:00 P.M.
Sunday, 12:00 noon-3:00 P.M.
Groups may reserve a film on the history of
  the San Fernando Valley.

1100 Pico Street
San Fernando 91340
365-9990 (during hours of operation)

B 10. GRIFFITH RANCH

David W. Griffith, famous pioneer director in the motion picture industry, purchased a ranch in the northeastern part of the San Fernando Valley in 1912. *Birth of a Nation* was filmed on the ranch as were many western movies. A marker commemorating Griffith's contributions is located at Foothill Blvd. and Vaughn Street just east of the San Fernando City limits. Public transportation is available to about a dozen blocks of location.

B 11. STONEY POINT OUTCROPPING, CHATSWORTH

This famous landmark was the site of an ancient Indian village, was used as a marker by the Southern Pacific Railroad during construction of its line through the Santa Susana Mountains, and was said to be one of the hideout locations of 1870s outlaw Tiburcio Vasquez. Franciscan fathers on the trail from Mission San Fernando to Mission San Buenaventura noted it as they made their way. In recent times the rock formation is familiar as a recreation site near Chatsworth Park, a location for motion pictures, and as an area used by mountain climbing courses taught at Cal State Northridge. Not easily accessible by public transportation; automobiles can drive to the site.

East side of Topanga Canyon Blvd.,
bisected by northern border of Los Angeles County-City

B 12. PALMER RESIDENCE, CHATSWORTH

Now known as the Palmer home, this house was constructed by James David Hill, a pioneer Chatsworth resident. Hill homesteaded the property in 1886 and built a house. In 1913 he constructed a second home, now owned by a granddaughter, Minnie Hill Palmer. A typical rural home of the period, the Palmer house now stands on land owned by the Los Angeles Department of Recreation and Parks, with the provision that Mrs. Palmer be allowed to live there for the remainder of her life. Not easily accessible by public transportation.

Private residence
Not open to public

West end of Devonshire Street
Chatsworth 91311

B 13. OLD STAGECOACH TRAIL, CHATSWORTH

From the late 1850s until 1905 a stagecoach road provided a link between Los Angeles and San Francisco. The Coast Line, San Juan and Los Angeles Stage Company operated along the road for many years. The steepness of the Santa Susana Pass often caused passengers to get out and help the driver push the stagecoach up the incline. Although there was little construction as such, the road's existence may still be seen in the pick-axe marks at the summit of Santa Susana Pass, the foundations of the relay station, cisterns, and rock quarries utilized for the Los Angeles Harbor breakwater. Sites of Indian villages have been discovered in the area.

Periodic hike-ins arranged by Santa Susana Mountain Park Association, P.O. Box 831 Chatsworth 91311

South of Chatsworth Park,
North of Oakwood Memorial Park,
East of Los Angeles County Line,
West end of Devonshire Street

B 14. INDIAN PICTOGRAPHS

Located under a sandstone ledge along the Old Stagecoach Trail at Chatsworth, these pictographs are both monochrome and polychrome. Those nearest the Trail are done in black paint while others have black, red and white paint. The paintings represent squirrels, birds and geometric designs. The site is believed to have been a ceremonial site for the Chumash Indians whose boundaries were to the west. Other nearby groups included Allilik and Tougva. The area is known as Burro Flats and is now owned by Rocketdyne.

Private property, closed to public

Located on the Old Stagecoach Trail
Chatsworth

Pioneer Church, Oakwood Memorial Park, Chatsworth

B 15. OAKWOOD MEMORIAL PARK, CHATSWORTH

This cemetery dates back well into the nineteenth century when it was an Indian burial ground. Its use as a cemetery has been continuous, but the area has also experienced a number of historical activities. The Old Stagecoach Trail bisects the property, a relay station for the stagecoaches existed here, and rock was quarried in this location for the Los Angeles Harbor breakwater. Old cistern foundations remain, as does the only remaining adobe structure in the northwestern part of the San Fernando Valley. In 1965 the Chatsworth Community Church, a pioneer church in the valley, was moved to this location. Public transportation available to about one mile from the cemetery.

Open daily, 8:30 A.M.-6 P.M.

22601 Lassen Street
Chatsworth 91311
341-0344

B 16. CHATSWORTH COMMUNITY CHURCH

The Chatsworth First Methodist Church, as this church was originally known, was the second oldest Protestant church in the San Fernando Valley. Built on a Topanga Canyon Boulevard lot in 1903 by volunteer labor, the church served for over 40 years as a center of religious and social life in Chatsworth. It is reported to be the only church of New England-type architecture in the county.

In 1962 the congregation sold the church, and for a time it seemed the building might be demolished. However, the lot owner offered to donate it to the Chatsworth Historical Society if it could be moved to a new location. This was accomplished in January 1965, and the church is now located at Oakwood Memorial Park. In 1976, after 12 years of work, the refurbishing of the church was completed. One room of the church has been made into a museum displaying artifacts of Chatsworth history. Public transportation available to 1 1/2 miles of the location.

Not presently open to the public
(Office open daily, 8:30 A.M.-5 P.M.
Sunday, 9:30 A.M.-5 P.M.)

22601 Lassen Street
Chatsworth 91311
341-0344

B 17. LEONIS ADOBE

Although the original portion of this adobe house is believed to have been constructed in 1844, its most effective owner was Miguel Leonis, who acquired it at some point in the late 1850s or early 1860s. Leonis gained a reputation as a powerful local landholder and rancho owner. In about 1879 he extensively remodeled the adobe as a Monterey-style house. He walled in upstairs and downstairs porches to add on more rooms, paneled the living room walls, and added other features. After his death in 1889 his widow continued to live there until she passed away in 1906.

The Leonis Adobe Association, a non-profit corporation, acquired the property and in 1965 restored it to its circa 1879 condition. The grounds include the adobe with furniture and other items dating to the 1870s, a barn, windmill, blacksmith shop, and other ranch buildings. The Leonis

Leonis Adobe, Calabasas

Adobe is most easily reached by automobile: Ventura Freeway to Mulholland Drive/Valley Circle Blvd., offramp; a sharp right and a curve left to Valley Circle, left over bridge across freeway, then right on Calabasas Road to address.

Open Wednesday, Saturday, Sunday,
     1:00-4:00 P.M.
Admission free (donations accepted)

23537 Calabasas Road
Calabasas 91302
346-3683

B 18. RANCHO SOMBRA DEL ROBLES—ORCUTT RANCH HORTICULTURAL CENTER

Rancho Sombra del Robles ("Ranch of the Shaded Oak") was the private home, garden, and orchard for William and Mary Orcutt, who commissioned architect C. G. Knipe to design the house in 1920. Orcutt was a prominent geologist and engineer who discovered the prehistoric fossils in the La Brea tar pits. He later became a vice-president with the Union Oil Company. The Orcutt ranch encompassed 200 acres in the western part of the San Fernando Valley.

The Orcutt home contains an interesting blend of Indian and Mexican details, including arrows set into the bricks in the central garden area and extensive use of tile from Mexico. Citrus and walnut groves were planted on the property, along with many trees and shrubs from foreign lands. These thrive along with the area's native oak trees, one of which is estimated to be 700 years old. The gardens also include statuary and specially designed resting areas of stone and brick.

The Los Angeles City Recreation and Parks Department purchased the 24-acre heart of the Orcutt ranch in 1966. It is now used as a horticultural center, picnic area with nature trail, and location for meetings of garden clubs, historical societies, and other groups. The Save Orcutt Community Organization sponsors the horticultural center's operation. Transportation by automobile: Ventura Freeway to Valley Circle Blvd., north to address.

Grounds open weekdays, 7 A.M.-5 P.M.; weekends, 8 A.M.-5 P.M.
House tour 2-5 P.M., last Sunday of the month.
Admission free (donations accepted)

23600 Roscoe Blvd.
Canoga Park 91304
883-6641

B 19. CANOGA MISSION GALLERY

The Canoga Mission Gallery is an interesting example of a twentieth century building constructed in the mission style as a reminder rather than an imitation of an earlier era. Actor Francis Lederer constructed the building 1934-1936 as a stable on his ranch. With the urbanization of the San Fernando Valley, the Lederer family gave a new definition to the structure. Mrs. Lederer and Mr. and Mrs. Obdulio Galeana remodeled the building and in 1967 opened it as a nonprofit art gallery and cultural center. The gallery features the work of noted artists and has on permanent exhibition decorative arts and paintings from Taxco, Mexico, Canoga Park's sister city in the People to People Program. Public transportation available directly to location.

Open Wednesday-Sunday, 11:00 A.M.-5:00 P.M.
Admission free

23130 Sherman Way
Canoga Park 91307
883-1085

B 20. SHADOW RANCH HOUSE

This city park with its huge eucalyptus trees was originally part of the landholdings of the Los Angeles Farm and Milling Company, owned by Isaac Lankershim and I. N. Van Nuys in the latter part of the nineteenth century. The 60,000 acre ranch was used for the cultivation of wheat. The ranch's superintendent, Albert Workman, obtained 13,000 acres of the property and constructed a ranch house between 1869-72. A native of Australia, Workman imported eucalyptus trees and planted them on his ranch. These trees are said to be the parent stand of the eucalyptus trees which are now an important part of southern California's scenery.

After a number of changes of ownership the ranch was purchased by Florence and Colin Clements in 1932. They restored the ranch house, using original wood and materials wherever possible. Mrs. Clements renamed the Workman property "Shadow Ranch." In 1957 the City of Los Angeles purchased 9.1 acres for a park, including the house, and remodeled its interior to create a community center. Over 100 recreational and cultural programs for persons of all ages are conducted at the park, and many community clubs also meet there. Public transportation available directly to the park site.

Open daily, 9 A.M.-5 P.M.
Sundays, 2 P.M.-5 P.M.
Free tours by appointment
Admission free

22633 Vanowen Street
Canoga Park 91307
347-9126

B 21. OAK TREE, ENCINO

This huge oak tree was old when it was first seen by Father Juan Crespí on the 1769 Portolá expedition. Its branches spread over 150 feet and its trunk is eight feet in diameter. The tree, estimated to be 1,000 years old, is known as "Live Oak" or "Holly Oak." Public transportation is available to within a short distance of this magnificent tree.

Louise Avenue
210 feet south of Ventura Blvd.
Encino

B 22. LOS ENCINOS STATE HISTORIC PARK

The five acres of Los Encinos State Historic Park constitute the heart of what at

Los Encinos State Historic Park showing de la Osa Adobe and Garnier Building

one time was a 4,460-acre cattle and sheep ranch, the Rancho Encino. The area was first noted by the 1769 Portolá expedition. For a time the acreage was operated by Franciscan fathers. In 1845 Governor Pío Pico granted the rancho to Don Vicente de la Osa, who effectively established the rancho. He constructed a 9-room adobe house in 1849 and raised 15 children there. During the 1860s and 1870s the rancho served as a stagecoach station. De la Osa sold the rancho in 1867 to James Thompson, who three years later sold it to Eugene Garnier. He constructed a two-story limestone house designed in the style of his native France. After several more changes of ownership the rancho came into the possession of the Amestoy family, who operated it until 1945.

In 1949, following subdivision of the rancho, the present five acres and buildings were acquired by the State Department of Parks and Recreation. The De la Osa Adobe, the Garnier House and other buildings illustrate the 200-year history of the park. The rooms have been furnished and restored in the style of the various owners of the Rancho Encino and include many artifacts and antiques from each phase of the rancho's history. Public transportation to within a block of the park.

Hours: Wednesday-Sunday 1:00-4:00 P.M.;
    other hours by special arrangement
Park grounds open Wednesday-Sunday,
    8 A.M.-5 P.M.
House tour: 50¢ adults over 17, 25¢ ages
    6-17. Picnic fee 10¢ for children over 12.

16756 Moorpark Street
Encino 91436
784-4849

B 23. VAN NUYS CITY HALL

Van Nuys was named for pioneer developer Isaac N. Van Nuys, who commenced large-scale farming operations in the San Fernando Valley in 1876. After the completion of the Owens Valley-Los Angeles Aqueduct in 1913, San Fernando Valley residents came to recognize that Los Angeles would market its surplus water only to city residents. In 1915 an overwhelming majority of valley residents voted to annex their communities to the City of Los Angeles. This annexation doubled the size of the city from 107.62 to 284.81 square miles and marked the beginning of a great annexation movement. The subsequent growth of the San Fernando Valley's population necessitated a local office to provide city services. The Van Nuys City Hall was constructed in 1932 to meet these needs for valley residents. Peter K. Schabarum was the architect. Public transportation available to location.

Open Monday-Friday, 8:00 A.M.-5:00 P.M.

14410 Sylvan Street
Van Nuys 91401
782-6125

B 24. ST. SAVIOUR'S CHAPEL, HARVARD SCHOOL

St. Saviour's Chapel provides an interesting example of an historic site that has served two locations. Designed by Reginald Johnson, son of Los Angeles' first Episcopal Bishop, for the Harvard School, the chapel was constructed in 1914 at Venice Blvd. and Western Avenue. In 1937 when Harvard School moved to a new campus in the San Fernando Valley, it was decided to move the chapel rather than demolish it. The building was cut up into 16 sections, brought over Sepulveda Blvd. to the new campus, and reassembled.

The chapel features a large rood cross made by students in the school's wood shop. In 1964 a dozen stained glass memorial windows, designed by Reverend John S. Gill, the school's chaplain, were installed. The chapel is an excellent example of the collegiate chapel style, with pews arranged choir-wise, facing the center aisle. Its design is based on the chapel at Rugby School in England. Public transportation to two blocks of location.

September-May, open
Monday-Friday, 8 A.M.-4 P.M.
June-August, open
Monday-Friday, 9 A.M.-3 P.M.
Sunday afternoons by appointment

3700 Coldwater Canyon
Studio City 91604
980-6692

B 25. CAMPO DE CAHUENGA

Campo de Cahuenga was the location of an event of major historic importance in California. On the veranda of a six-room

Cahuenga adobe, c. 1910.

3919 Lankershim Blvd.
North Hollywood 91602
769-8853

B 26. UNIVERSAL STUDIOS

Universal Studios was founded in 1915 by Carl Laemmle who purchased a chicken ranch in the San Fernando Valley and converted it into a film studio. Since that time Universal has produced an average of 55 feature films annually, including many Academy Award-winning motion pictures. Universal also produces numerous television series.

adobe house built by Tomás Feliz in 1845, representatives of the United States Army and the Californians met to end hostilities in the province of California during the Mexican-American War. On January 13, 1847, Lt. Col. John C. Frémont and General Andrés Pico signed the Treaty of Cahuenga, putting an end to the war within California.

Despite the historic significance of the location, the adobe house was allowed to disintegrate, until it was finally demolished in 1900. The City of Los Angeles purchased the property in 1923 and established the Frémont-Pico Memorial Park. A replica of the original adobe house was constructed; it serves as a meeting place for many recreational and historical groups. The main room features copies of documents relating to the signing of the treaty, portraits of Frémont and Pico, and other items of historical interest. Public transportation available to the location.

Monday-Friday, 8:00 A.M.-4:00 P.M.;
7:00 P.M.-10:00 P.M.
by appointment only.

Universal Studios, c. 1930.

In 1964 Universal began offering public tours of its facilities. Since then many special effects attractions have been designed for the tours, which take two hours and include the entire 420 acres of Universal City. Public transportation available to studio area, trams to location.

Hours:
June 8-September 6, 8 A.M.-6 P.M.
September 7-June 7, 10 A.M.-3:30 P.M.
Admission: Adults (17 and over) $6.25
Juniors (12-16) $5.25
Children (5-11) $4.25
under 5 with adult free
Parking 50¢
(Prices subject to change)

Hollywood Freeway at Lankershim Blvd.
100 Universal City Plaza
Universal City 91608
877-1311 (recorded message)
877-2121 (further information)

B 27. WARNER RESEARCH COLLECTION, BURBANK CENTRAL LIBRARY

One of the most unusual library collections in the world is a small research facility housed within the Burbank Central Library. Accumulated over a period of 39 years at Warner Brothers Studio for use in authenticating motion picture costuming and interior decoration, it consists of more than 20,000 volumes dealing with art, architecture, travel and history, over a million newspaper clippings which are added to daily, and a myriad of photographs. Warner Brothers donated these materials, which are mostly pictorial, to the Burbank Library, but the service to the motion picture and television industries has continued.

Especially unique is the large collection of automobile license plates which includes plates from every state in America from 1936 to the present. Special arrangements with each state's department of motor vehicles were necessary so that no license number used in a movie or on TV would duplicate that of a bonafide and duly licensed driver.

The Warner Research Collection in the Burbank Central Library is open 1:00 to 4:00 P.M. every day except Saturday and Holidays. No one is allowed access to the materials, except research librarians, who charge $17.50 an hour ($8.50 minimum) for use of their time. Special tours can occasionally be arranged. Please telephone in advance for an appointment.

Monday-Friday, 9 A.M.-6 P.M. by appointment only

110 North Glenoaks Blvd., at the corner of
Olive Avenue
Burbank 91503
847-9743

B 28. WALT DISNEY ARCHIVES

Created in 1970, this limited access library is devoted exclusively to the history of Walt Disney Productions (the company dates from 1923), Disneyland, Walt Disney World, and the Disney family. The archives include letters, photographs, business records, toys, blueprints, posters, books, comics, and original art.

Open to serious scholars Monday-Friday, 8 A.M.-5 P.M., by appointment only

500 S. Buena Vista Street
Burbank 91521
845-3141, ext. 2425

NOTES

SECTION C

Western Area (Malibu to Los Angeles Airport)

1. Malibu Lagoon
   Malibu Lagoon State Park; Malibu
2. J. Paul Getty Museum
   17985 Pacific Coast Highway; Malibu
3. Founder's Oak
   Haverford Avenue between Sunset Blvd. and Antioch Street; Pacific Palisades
4. Eames House
   203 Chautauqua Blvd.; Pacific Palisades
5. Old Santa Monica Forestry Station, Rustic Canyon
   701 Latimer Road
6. Will Rogers State Historic Park
   14253 Sunset Blvd.; Pacific Palisades
7. University of California, Los Angeles
   405 Hilgard
8. UCLA Special Collections
   405 Hilgard
9. Mormon Temple and Archives
   10741 and 10777 Santa Monica Blvd.; Los Angeles
10. Sawtelle Veterans' Center
    Wilshire and Sawtelle Blvds.; Los Angeles
11. Serra Springs
    University High School, 11800 Texas Avenue; Los Angeles
12. Santa Monica Pier
    End of Colorado Avenue at Ocean Avenue
13. Santa Monica Public Library
    1343 Sixth Street
14. Club Del Mar (Synanon Foundation)
    1910 Ocean Front Walk; Santa Monica
15. Horatio West Court
    140 Hollister Avenue; Santa Monica
16. Venice's Canals
    Venice Blvd. east to Dell Avenue; Venice
17. M-G-M Studio
    10202 W. Washington Blvd.; Culver City
18. Rancho La Cienega o Pasa de la Tijera
    3725 Don Felipe Drive; Los Angeles
19. Loyola-Marymount University
    7101 West 80th Street; Los Angeles
20. La Casa de la Centinela Adobe
    7634 Midfield Avenue; Los Angeles
21. Centinela Springs
    Centinela Park, 700 Warren Lane; Inglewood
22. Aviation Library and Museum, Northrop University
    1155 West Arbor Vitae; Inglewood
23. Citizens Savings Athletic Museum Hall of Fame
    9800 S. Sepulveda Blvd.; Los Angeles
24. Hangar No. 1 Building
    5701 West Imperial Highway; Los Angeles

Venice Pier on a Sunday, c. 1910.

C 1. MALIBU LAGOON

One of the oldest historic sites in Los Angeles County is the Malibu area. Malibu Creek flows to the coast in rainy weather and near the point forms a natural lagoon, at which is located Malibu Lagoon State Park. At the mouth of the creek is an archaeological excavation (not open to tourists) at the site of the Humaliwo Indian settlement and prehistoric cemetery. Fishing boats put out to sea from the cove until well into the Spanish period. The name Malibu probably is of Chumash (Indian) origin; it was part of the Topanga-Malibu-Sequit Rancheria land grant of 1805. Nearby is Malibu Beach and Surf Riders State Beach, where the sport of surfing was popularized and a dozen motion pictures of the 1950s were filmed.

C 2. J. PAUL GETTY MUSEUM

The history of the J. Paul Getty Museum began when the millionaire oilman purchased a large ranch-style home on 65 acres of land in Malibu. He remodeled the two-story house completely and created a zoo on the grounds. In 1954, after adding two wings to the house, Getty opened a museum to display the art objects he had been collecting. Accessibility was limited to two afternoons a week, by appointment only.

In the late 1960s Getty decided to construct an entire new museum, as his collection had outgrown his home. The museum was constructed—not a modern building, but a reconstruction of a Roman seaside villa buried in an eruption of Mt. Vesuvius in 79 A.D. This new museum, completed in 1974, contains 38 galleries and occupies ten acres of the Getty property. The works of art include antiquities from Greece and Rome,

Renaissance and Baroque paintings from Western Europe, and eighteenth century French decorative arts, all approved or personally purchased by Getty in the course of his travels.

Because of limited parking, it is advisable to make reservations at the telephone number indicated below, or else use public transportation, which is available to the museum location.

Open April-September, Monday-Friday,
    10:00 A.M.-5:00 P.M.
October-March, Tuesday-Saturday,
    10:00 A.M.-5:00 P.M.
No fees. Parking reservations
    recommended—call 454-6541.

17985 Pacific Coast Highway
Malibu 90265
459-2306

C 3. FOUNDER'S OAK

Founder's Oak received its name from the men and women of the Methodist Association of Southern California who planned the town of Pacific Palisades. First recognized in 1920 as an ideal location, Pacific Palisades differed from the usual real estate subdivisions because of its religious sponsorship. On January 14, 1922, the Association conducted dedication ceremonies under the shade of the big oak tree. By the summer of 1922 the new community's first home was under construction and the first stores in the shopping district had opened for business. By 1925 the community consisted of over 100 homes. For more than fifty years the Founder's Oak has served as a focal point marking the progress of Pacific Palisades. In 1966 the oak tree and its immediate area were designated as an historic cultural monument. Public transportation available to one block of location.

Haverford Avenue between Sunset Blvd. and Antioch Street

C 4. EAMES HOUSE

Charles Eames, internationally known architect, designed his own residence in 1949 as a part of the Case Study Program of experimental houses created by local architects. Its striking use of steel framing and glass profoundly affected architectural styles in Europe and the United States, especially in the design of commercial buildings. Public transportation available to location.

Private residence
Not open to public

203 Chautauqua Blvd.
Pacific Palisades 90272

C 5. OLD SANTA MONICA FORESTRY STATION, RUSTIC CANYON

The Santa Monica Forestry Station was established December 20, 1887, by the State Board of Forestry. Rustic Canyon was the first experimental forest site in California as well as in the entire nation. Pioneer studies were made of exotic trees, especially eucalyptus trees. The Board of Forestry operated the station until 1893, when it was taken over by the University of California. In 1921 the Uplifters Club purchased the area and used it for a country home until 1947. The original buildings were destroyed by fire in 1904; the buildings which replaced the original ones were themselves torn down when the area was subdivided. In 1953 the acreage was added to Rustic Canyon Park.

The historical value of the area has been noted with a plaque marking the site as a state historical landmark, dedicated in 1971 under the sponsorship of the State Board of Forestry, the State Department of Parks and Recreation, and county and city (Los Angeles) agencies. Public transportation to Sunset Blvd.; then a 15-minute walk to location.

Rustic Canyon Park office open:
Monday-Thursday, 9 A.M.-10 P.M.
Friday, 9 A.M.-8 P.M.
Saturday, 9 A.M.-5:30 P.M.
Sunday, 10 A.M.-5:30 P.M.

701 Latimer Road
Santa Monica 90402
454-5734

C 6. WILL ROGERS STATE HISTORIC PARK

Famed cowboy humorist Will Rogers supervised the construction of his ranch in Pacific Palisades in the early 1920s. He lived there from 1924 until his untimely death in a plane crash in 1935. His widow continued to live on the ranch until her death in 1944, at which time the grounds were presented to the State of California for use as an historic park.

The park is maintained in the same manner as when the Rogers family lived there. Attractions include a golf course, riding and hiking trails, stables, and roping arena. The ranch house contains artifacts and memorabilia on Will Roger's career. Public transportation to park entrance; then 1/2 mile walk.

Open daily, 8:00 A.M.-5:00 P.M.
Admission $1 per car

14253 Sunset Blvd.
Pacific Palisades 90272
454-8212

Will Rogers Ranch House

Polo Field, Will Rogers Ranch

C 7. UNIVERSITY OF CALIFORNIA, LOS ANGELES

UCLA was originally known as the Southern Branch of the University of California. It was established in 1919 and was located for the first ten years on Vermont Avenue, at what is now Los Angeles City College. In 1927 the school's name was changed to University of California at Los Angeles (the "at" was dropped in 1953). Two years after the name change UCLA moved to its present 411-acre Westwood location.

The campus' main quadrangle consists of a central core of Italian Romanesque-Byzantine buildings: Royce Hall, Kinsey Hall, Haines Hall, and Powell Library. More recent buildings have been constructed with a more contemporary design, but the coloring and atmosphere of the four original buildings has been preserved. Current campus enrollment exceeds 33,000.

UCLA offers an astonishing variety of facilities and attractions to visitors that make the school one of the world's great universities, a feat accomplished within the last 40 years. In fact, while 14 campus buildings were constructed prior to World War II, 74 were built after the war. The library holdings total 3.5 million volumes. The campus includes a major medical center, botanical gardens, sculpture garden, art gallery, planetarium, and many other buildings and exhibits. In 1970 the American Council on Education ranked UCLA among

Royce Hall, UCLA, c. 1935

the top ten schools in the nation for its graduate programs and faculty in the arts and sciences.

UCLA has several tours of its campus, either by automobile or by foot. Maps and brochures are available at Murphy Hall, the administration building. Public transportation available to location; from the San Diego Freeway, autos may exit at either Sunset Blvd. or Wilshire Blvd., and east to campus.

Monday-Friday 8:00 A.M.-5:00 P.M.
Most exhibits and displays open; other attractions as scheduled.
July 7-August 8—tours: Thursday, 1:30.

405 Hilgard
Los Angeles 90024
825-4338 (Visitor's Center)

C 8. UCLA SPECIAL COLLECTIONS

The Department of Special Collections at the University of California, Los Angeles, was created in 1946. The Department is responsible for the acquisition and care of rare books, pamphlets, manuscripts, newspapers, and other materials considered to be of historical and literary value. Special strengths are in Californiana and Western Americana, children's books dating back to the eighteenth century, and manuscript materials on the political and cultural history of southern California. The Department also houses copies of the interviews conducted by the Regional Oral History Project on the Berkeley campus. These contain the reminiscences of people involved in a wide variety of occupations, businesses and political affairs.

For many years the Department of Special Collections was located in the old Powell

Research Library, UCLA

Library. After the University Research Library was expanded in 1970, the Department moved into these modern quarters. Researchers use a spacious reading room looking out to the Library's garden; provision is made for audiovisuals, microfilms, and typewriter use. The growth of the Special Collections Department is reflected in its holdings: over 120,000 volumes and 1.2 million manuscripts and other special materials. Public transportation available to the UCLA campus, which is easily reached from the San Diego Freeway, east on Sunset Blvd. to location.

Monday-Saturday 9:00 A.M.-5:00 P.M.

405 Hilgard
Los Angeles 90024
825-4879

C 9. MORMON TEMPLE AND ARCHIVES

The Church of Jesus Christ of Latter-Day Saints constructed its Mormon Temple in West Los Angeles during the 1950s. Designed by Edward Anderson of Salt Lake City, this is the largest temple ever built by the Mormon Church. At the crest of its 257-foot tower is a 15-foot statue of the Angel

Moroni, cast in aluminum and covered with gold leaf. Excavation of the building site began in August of 1952; the building was completed in October 1955, with its dedication taking place on March 11, 1956. The Temple itself is open only to Church members; however, a Visitors' Center has displays and exhibits depicting the Mormon faith, plus four rooms in which films detailing historical and church activities are shown. The Mormons have an active historical presence in southern California dating back to the War with Mexico.

The Mormon Temple Genealogical Library, located in the basement of the Visitors' Center, was created in 1964. This research facility contains the complete manuscript censuses from 1790-1880 on microfilm, as well as major military pension indexes, major east coast and gulf state passenger lists, and vital records for England and Wales. The library is a major center for genealogical research. Public transportation available to location; also easily reached by freeway, east of San Diego Freeway from Santa Monica Blvd. offramp.

Visitors' Center open daily 9:00 A.M.-10:00 P.M., last tour at 9:00 P.M. Genealogical Library open Monday *and* Friday, 9:00 A.M.-5:00 P.M. Tuesday-Thursday, 9:00 A.M.-9:00 P.M., Saturday 9:00 A.M.-3:00 P.M.

10741 Santa Monica Blvd. (Visitors' Center)
10777 Santa Monica Blvd. (Temple)
Los Angeles 90025
474-1549 (Visitors' Center)
474-9990 (Library)

Mormon Temple

Sawtelle Veterans Home, 1890s.

C 10. SAWTELLE VETERANS' CENTER

The Veterans' Administration Center in West Los Angeles was originally known as the Pacific branch of the National Home for Disabled Volunteer Soldiers. Several of the buildings date back to the nineteenth century; the chapel was built in 1900 and a dormitory shortly before that. The dormitory, three stories in height, is an outstanding example of the Queen Anne style of architecture and is one of the very few buildings of that type still to be found in Los Angeles. Public transportation to location.

Wilshire and Sawtelle Blvds.
Los Angeles 90073

C 11. SERRA SPRINGS

Considerable legend surrounds Serra Springs, named for Father Junípero Serra, which still flow in the horticulture area of the campus of University High School in West Los Angeles. Although the springs are named for the pioneer Franciscan padre, these may have been the same springs found by the Portolá expedition in 1769. Father Juan Crespi said mass near a spring and named it *las lagrimas de Santa Monica*—"the tears of Saint Monica." The name was later given to the City of Santa Monica when it was founded in 1875. However, no documentation exists to verify that Serra Springs and Las Lagrimas de Santa Monica were one and the same. Public transportation to one block of school.

Open Monday-Friday, 8:15 A.M.-3:15 P.M.

University High School
11800 Texas Avenue
Los Angeles 90025
478-9833

C 12. SANTA MONICA PIER

Santa Monica Pier was originally constructed in 1907 to carry the city's sewage line into the ocean. A city bond issue in 1919 to rebuild the pier resulted in its revitalization in 1921 as a municipal pier for public recreation. The pier features fishing and a wide variety of shops and attractions. In 1917 an adjoining pier known as Loof Pier was built under private ownership; when sold in 1942, its name was changed to Newcomb Pier. Eventually this pier was acquired by the city.

Despite extensive remodeling of the municipal pier in 1957, it was declared un-

Santa Monica Pier and Palisades, 1975.

safe in 1964. Santa Monica considered demolishing the pier but at last elected to save it. In 1974 the city council passed a $1.6 million repair project for both piers, to be completed over a two-year period. Santa Monica pier continues as a prime recreational facility. Public transportation available to location.

Many businesses open weekends until
    10 P.M.

End of Colorado Avenue at Ocean Avenue

C 13. SANTA MONICA
PUBLIC LIBRARY

Although the main building of the public library of the City of Santa Monica has stood for only a decade, the library itself is nearing its centennial celebration. A group of citizens formed the Santa Monica Library Association in 1879 (c.), and a modest collection of books were housed in a room adjoining a drug store. In 1890 the books were placed in rented rooms in the Bank of Santa Monica building. In 1903 the city purchased a lot at Arizona Avenue and Fifth Street,

and the first library building was completed the following year, courtesy of a Carnegie grant. Carnegie also provided funds for constructing the oldest extant library in Santa Monica, the Ocean Park Branch, completed during World War I (1918), and located at 2601 Main Street. The main branch has an extensive collection of historical photographs of the environs, and prints may be ordered at the reference desk.

Monday-Friday, 10:00 A.M.-9:00 P.M.
Saturday, 10:00 A.M.-5:30 P.M.
September-June, also open Sunday,
   1-5 P.M.

1343 Sixth Street
Santa Monica 90401
451-5751

C 14. CLUB DEL MAR
(SYNANON FOUNDATION)

Once the most luxurious beach club in Santa Monica, the Club Del Mar now serves an entirely different purpose. It was opened in 1926 and until World War II was famous for its big band entertainment, gymnasium and health club, and banquet facilities. During the Second World War the Navy used the Del Mar as an enlisted men's club. In the postwar period the club went into decline. The Synanon Foundation purchased the club in 1967 and converted the facilities for use by the Synanon Foundation. Synanon extends its services to drug abusers, juvenile delinquents, alcoholics, and other criminal delinquents who take part in a cooperative life style. Founded in 1958, it is the oldest program for reeducation of drug abusers in the United States and has served as a model for thousands of other programs. Public transportation available to one block of location.

Always open.

1910 Ocean Front Walk
Santa Monica 90405
399-9241 or 870-1649

C 15. HORATIO WEST COURT

The Horatio West Court apartments, designed in 1919, is a good example of the work of architect Irving Gill (1870-1936). As such, it shows the development of Gill's thoughts in moving from an Hispanic influence to modernism. The two-story apartments feature living rooms with windows on three sides with views of the mountains and the ocean. Public transportation available to location.

Private residences
Not open to public

140 Hollister Avenue
Santa Monica 90405

C 16. VENICE'S CANALS

In 1904 a successful businessman, Abbot Kinney, took advantage of the publicity about southern California being an "American Italy" with a "Mediterranean climate" to develop an oceanside community he named Venice. The town was supposed to be a replica of Venice, Italy, complete with an elaborate system of canals and Italian-style bungalows. Kinney even imported gondolas and gondoliers. Although the real estate project was successful, Kinney's hopes for Venice to become an artistic and cultural center met with failure. Instead, Venice assumed a Coney Island atmosphere with roller coasters and side-shows. As time passed the canals were neglected; after Los Angeles annexed Venice in 1925, most of the canals were filled in and converted to streets.

Today only four canals remain as links to Abbot Kinney's dream. Dell Avenue crosses these canals with the only remaining Venice-style bridges. Motorists take Venice Blvd. eastbound from Pacific Avenue to Dell Avenue and turn right onto Dell.

Venice's Canals, c. 1905

C 17. M-G-M STUDIO

The studios that evolved into Metro-Goldwyn-Mayer Inc., were constructed in Culver City between 1918-1936. In 1924, after a series of mergers, M-G-M was formed. It has been a major producer of motion pictures and television programs throughout the history of the industry. Public transportation available to location.

Not open to the public

10202 W. Washington Blvd.
Culver City 90230
836-3000

C 18. RANCHO LA CIENEGA O PASO DE LA TIJERA

At one time ranked among the city's better known historic sites, Rancho La Cienega is no longer featured on the "mission-rancho" circuit, victim of commercial development and changing ethnic patterns. This lapse is unfortunate, for the old adobe building still stands, and its view of Los Angeles is spectacular.

A plaque provided by the Native Daughters states that it was constructed between 1790 and 1795, and the present occupants believe the central section was built in 1794. These dates are questionable. Squatters probably arrived on the land about this time, and some structure may have been erected, but not of adobe. More likely it dates from the period after the ranch was granted Francisco Avila in 1823 and before its acquisition by Vicente Sanchez, Alcalde of Los Angeles in 1843. It was later inherited by Los Angeles sheriff, Tomás A. Sanchez.

From its hillside vista, most travelers from the central city to the seacoast could be

Rancho La Cienega (Sanchez adobe), c. 1900

Loyola University, c. 1939.

spotted. The ranch itself served as head-quarters for directing a wide variety of agricultural activities to the west and south. Much of the area was later acquired by E. J. "Lucky" Baldwin, and named Baldwin Hills. Prior to World War II its rural character was preserved by its use as a golf course, Sunset Fields; the adobe structures served as the clubhouse. After the war, the area was subdivided and pioneering Crenshaw Shopping Center built nearby. Asphalt and concrete covered the rolling land, and the adobes now overlook an expanse of parking lots. They serve as the offices of Consolidated Realty company.

From Crenshaw Blvd., drive west on Stocker Street for half a mile, turn north on Don Felipe for about half a block, use the driveway to the realty office.

Monday-Saturday, 9:00 A.M.-5:00 P.M.
Other hours by appointment

3725 Don Felipe Drive
Los Angeles
299-5570

C 19. LOYOLA-MARYMOUNT UNIVERSITY

Loyola-Marymount is the successor of the oldest college in southern California, St. Vincent's. Bishop Amat opened St. Vincent's in the Lugo House on the Plaza in 1865; the college existed for 46 years. In 1911 Jesuit fathers opened high school classes in Highland Park, with the college division of the then-named Los Angeles College (later renamed St. Vincent's), resumed in 1914. It was incorporated as Loyola College of Los Angeles in 1918 at a site on Venice Boulevard. The Westchester campus was donated by Harry Culver in 1927, and classes began there two years later. In 1968, Marymount college moved to Loyola's Westchester campus and the two unified under a single board of trustees in 1973. The library contains some materials concerning the early history of the city. Additionally, the university is currently constructing a room which will serve as an archives to house institutional historical records. The campus is west of the San Diego Freeway, Manchester offramp.

Library hours:
Open Saturday, 9 A.M.-5 P.M.; Sunday, 1 P.M.-11 P.M.

Winter (September-June): Monday-Friday,
    8 A.M.-5 P.M.
Summer (June-August): Monday-Thursday,
    8 A.M.-10 P.M.; Friday, 8 A.M.-5 P.M.

7101 West 80th Street
Los Angeles 90045
642-2700

C 20. LA CASA DE LA CENTINELA ADOBE

This adobe house is considered to be one
of the most beautifully preserved in Los
Angeles. It was built in the early 1800s and is
the oldest structure in the area, having
served as the main house on the Rancho

Rancho Centinela

Aguaje de Centinela. Modest in size, it has
been furnished with furniture from the Victorian era. The Centinela Adobe serves as
the headquarters of the Historical Society of
the Centinela Valley and is open for tours.

Open Sunday and Wednesday,
    2:00-4:00 P.M.
Donations accepted

7634 Midfield Avenue
Los Angeles 90045
649-6272
(for tours, call 677-7916)

C 21. CENTINELA SPRINGS

Centinela Springs, located in Inglewood's
Centinela Park, has been known as a principal water supply for the area since Indian
times. The springs, a source of artesian
water, are estimated to date back to the
Pleistocene Era. A drinking fountain in the
park commemorates the historical use of the
springs. Public transportation available to
location.

Open daily, 6 A.M.-11 P.M.

Centinela Park
700 Warren Lane
Inglewood
649-7407

C 22. AVIATION LIBRARY AND MUSEUM, NORTHROP UNIVERSITY

In 1931 Professor David D. Hatfield, a
prominent aviation historian, began collecting photographs, books, magazines, and
documents pertaining to aviation history. He
kept the growing collection in his home until
1967, at which time he presented his collection to the Northrop Institute of Technology
(now Northrop University) for the school's
Aviation History Library.

The importance of the Hatfield collection
was recognized when Northrop University
established the American Hall of Aviation
History in a building adjacent to the cam-

pus. The Hall, operational in 1976, includes exhibits dealing with all areas of aviation history, from autogyros to gliders. The collection includes some 250,000 photo negatives and over 150,000 magazines. Professor Hatfield, as director of the Hall, is continuing the life-long project. Public transportation available to two blocks of location.

Monday-Saturday, 8:30 A.M.-4:30 P.M.

1155 West Arbor Vitae
Inglewood 90306
670-6339

C 23. CITIZENS SAVINGS ATHLETIC MUSEUM HALL OF FAME

In 1936 the late Paul Helms, Sr., created the Helms Athletic Foundation, with W. R. Schroeder as managing director. The purpose of the foundation was to establish a sports museum and library to bring together materials and exhibits relating to all types of amateur, college and professional sports activities. From a modest beginning in an office building in downtown Los Angeles, the museum expanded until it was moved into its own building on Venice Boulevard in 1948.

In 1970 the Foundation came under the sponsorship of United Savings and Loan Association, which merged in 1973 with Citizens Savings and Loan Association, giving the Foundation its new name. The museum's history, however, is a continuous one. Exhibits include trophies, photographs, one of the most complete sports libraries in

the world, and a major collection of Olympic Games materials. Items of special interest include one of Joe Louis' boxing gloves, bats used by Babe Ruth and other baseball players, and football championship game balls. The research library on the second floor, available by permission, is valuable for the history of sports. Public transportation available to location.

Monday-Friday, 9:00 A.M.-5:00 P.M.
Saturday, 9:00 A.M.-3:00 P.M.
Admission free

9800 S. Sepulveda Blvd.
Los Angeles 90045
670-7550

C 24. HANGAR NO. 1 BUILDING

Los Angeles International Airport was originally known as Mines Field, which in October 1928 was leased by the City of Los Angeles for use as a municipal airport. The Curtiss Flying Service—now Curtiss-Wright—constructed Hangar No. 1 in 1929, designed as a Spanish-style building. Los Angeles purchased title to the airport property in 1937. Since October 11, 1949 it has been known as Los Angeles International Airport. Hangar No. 1 continues in service as a hangar for the executive planes of Rockwell International.

5701 West Imperial Highway
Los Angeles 90045

SECTION D

West Central Area (Includes Hollywood and Beverly Hills)

1. Mulholland Drive
   (Santa Monica Mountains)
2. Beverly Hills Hotel
   9641 W. Sunset Blvd.; Beverly Hills
3. Beverly Hills Electric Fountain
   Intersection of Wilshire and Santa
   Monica Blvds.
4. Greystone Mansion
   501 N. Doheny Road; Beverly Hills
5. Fowler Museum
   9215 Wilshire Blvd.; Beverly Hills
6. Portola Trail Campsite No. 2,
   La Cienega
   La Cienega Blvd. between Olympic
   Blvd. and Gregory Way; Beverly Hills
7. Schindler House
   833 N. Kings Road; Los Angeles
8. Storer House
   8161 Hollywood Blvd.; Los Angeles
9. Plummer Park, with oldest surviving
   house in Hollywood
   7377 Santa Monica Blvd.
10. Chaplin Studio
    1416 N. La Brea Avenue; Los Angeles
11. Grauman's Chinese Theatre
    6925 Hollywood Blvd.; Los Angeles
12. Crossroads of the World
    6671 Sunset Blvd.; Los Angeles
13. Hollywood and Vine
    Hollywood Blvd. and Vine Street;
    Hollywood
14. Hollywood Palladium
    6215 W. Sunset Blvd.; Los Angeles
15. Radio Station KNX and Columbia
    Square
    6121 Sunset Blvd.; Los Angeles
16. DeMille Studio Barn
    Paramount Studios, 5451 Marathon
    Street; Los Angeles
17. Radio Station KHJ
    5515 Melrose Avenue; Los Angeles
18. Freeman House
    1962 Glencoe Way; Los Angeles
19. Hollywood Bowl
    2301 N. Highland Avenue; Los Angeles
20. Pilgrimage Play Theatre
    2850 Cahuenga Blvd.; Los Angeles
21. Hollywoodland Stone Gates
    At intersection of Beachwood, West-
    shire, and Belden Drives; Hollywood
22. Hollywood Sign, Mt. Lee
    Visible from Griffith Park Observatory
    and many other locations; Hollywood
23. Novarro House
    5699 Valley Oak Drive; Los Angeles
24. Sowden House
    5121 Franklin Avenue; Los Angeles
25. Fern Dell Nature Museum and Site of
    Gabrielino Indian Village
    5373 Red Oak Drive; Los Angeles
26. Griffith Park, Planetarium, and Zoo
    Los Feliz Blvd. and Riverside Drive;
    Los Angeles
27. Lovell House
    4616 Dundee Drive; Los Angeles
28. Ennis House
    2607 Glendower Avenue; Los Angeles
29. Barnsdall Park and Hollyhock House
    Hollywood Blvd. at Vermont Avenue;
    Los Angeles
30. Rocha House
    2400 Shenandoah Street; Los Angeles

31. Farmers Market
    6333 W. 3rd Street; Los Angeles
32. La Brea Pits
    650 S. Ogden Drive, or Wilshire Blvd.
    at Curson; Hancock Park
33. Buck House
    805 S. Genessee Avenue; Los Angeles
34. Memorial Branch Library
    4625 W. Olympic Blvd.; Los Angeles
35. Wilshire United Methodist Church
    4350 Wilshire Blvd.; Los Angeles
36. Evans House
    419 S. Lorraine Blvd.; Los Angeles

37. Wilshire Boulevard Temple
    3663 Wilshire Boulevard; Los Angeles
38. Ambassador Hotel
    3400 Wilshire Blvd.; Los Angeles
39. Korean Royal Church (Temple Sinai East)
    407 S. New Hampshire; Los Angeles
40. St. Sophia Cathedral
    1324 S. Normandie Avenue;
    Los Angeles

Hollywood Boulevard in the 1920s.

Mulholland Drive in the 1920s.

D 2. BEVERLY HILLS HOTEL

Constructed in 1911-1912, the Beverly Hills Hotel preceded the official founding of the City of Beverly Hills by two years. The unique architectural style of the hotel complex was done by architect Elmer Grey, who designed a Mission-style resort hotel on 16 acres of grounds. The hotel, consisting of 325 rooms and bungalows, was built at a cost of $500,000. It has been added to and remodeled a number of times since its original construction. One example of a continuing motif is the palm trees on the hotel grounds which are repeated on wallpaper patterns in the hotel corridors.

Beverly Hills Hotel

D 1. MULHOLLAND DRIVE

This scenic highway was constructed in 1923-24, along the crest of the Santa Monica Mountains. It was officially opened in December 1924. Named for William Mulholland, the city engineer who built the Owens Valley-Los Angeles Aqueduct, Mulholland Drive stretches from Cahuenga Pass at the Hollywood Freeway west to the Pacific Ocean at Leo Carrillo State Beach. The highway is about 40 miles long, including some unpaved sections. It offers spectacular views of mountain canyons, the San Fernando Valley, and the Pacific Ocean. Despite increasing urban development over the past five decades, much of the highway is in a natural setting, and the signs warning to watch for deer should be taken literally. Turnouts along the route allow views of the San Fernando Valley on one side and of Hollywood and west Los Angeles on the other. Automobile transportation recommended.

The proximity of the hotel to the rapidly expanding motion picture industry contributed to a life style that has made the hotel internationally famous. Celebrities ranging from billionaire Howard Hughes to film star Elizabeth Taylor have stayed at the hotel's bungalows, enjoying the lush gardens and the attractions of pool, tennis courts, and restaurants, including the Persian Room and Polo Lounge. Throughout its existence the hotel has attracted attention by the flambuoyant behavior of some of the celebrity guests. Nevertheless, the hotel has also established a tradition of service catering to the needs of businessmen and tourists. Public transportation available to location.

PR office open 9 A.M.-5 P.M. M-F

9641 W. Sunset Blvd.
Beverly Hills 90213
276-2251

Greystone Mansion courtyard

D 3. BEVERLY HILLS ELECTRIC FOUNTAIN

The Beverly Hills Electric Fountain was designed by architect Ralph Flewelling, and artist Merrell Gage composed the frieze around the base, depicting the history of California. General Electric engineers plotted the lighting effects. The fountain began operation in 1931, its water jets and color effects combining to give 60 different combinations of color and water effects every eight minutes.

Over the years the fountain was misnamed the "Pocahontas" fountain after the figure at its top, who is not Pocahontas at all but the figure of a prospector. Recently the fountain fell victim to the energy crisis, and its electrical display was curtailed. The fountain, nonetheless, has remained an important and entertaining landmark for over forty years. Public transportation available to location.

Intersection of Wilshire and Santa Monica Blvds.

Greystone Mansion reflecting pool

a gift, his present took three years to construct. Greystone Mansion was built 1925-28 and was constructed of steel-framed, reinforced concrete. Architect Gordon B. Kaufman designed the 46,054 square foot, 55-room house on the site of a 410 acre ranch purchased by Doheny. Kaufman's use of a variety of European architectural styles resulted in a building on the scale of a castle, with hand-carved oak bannisters, marble floors, and huge rooms. The grounds include riding stables, tennis courts, and kennels. Built at a cost of $4 million, Greystone Mansion, if built today, would cost $20 million.

In 1957 Greystone was sold to the Park-Gray Corporation, which in turn sold it in 1964 to the City of Beverly Hills. After con-

D 4. GREYSTONE MANSION

When the millionaire oilman Edward L. Doheny decided to present his only son, Edward Jr., and his five grandchildren with

siderable debate over whether to tear down the mansion, the city decided to find a non-commercial tenant who might lease the estate. The American Film Institute found Greystone ideal as a location for both preserving the heritage of film-making and advancing its art. $500,000 was spent by the Institute in refurbishing the interior. The grounds are now a public park. Greystone has served as the setting for numerous motion pictures and television programs. Accessible by car or tour bus.

Tours by appointment only on Saturday-
   Sunday at 11:00 A.M., 1:00 P.M.,
   3:00 P.M.
Adults $2, children 50¢. For tickets call
   271-8174.
Park open daily 10:00 A.M.-6:00 P.M.

501 N. Doheny Road
Beverly Hills 90213
550-4769

D 5. FOWLER MUSEUM

The Fowler Museum, established in 1953, was named for Francis E. Fowler, Jr., who endowed a foundation in his name. The museum contains an outstanding collection of decorative arts from America, Europe, and Asia, in 20 different categories. This includes carved ivories, unusual firearms, silver vessels, and other objects. The Rasputin Chalice, a gift from the Tsarina Alexandra to Rasputin, is on display. The museum is especially strong in silver items from the fifteenth to eighteenth centuries with one of the best American silver collections on the west coast. Public transportation available to location.

Hours; Monday-Saturday 1:00-5:00 P.M.
Closed Sundays and major holidays
Admission free

9215 Wilshire Blvd.
Beverly Hills 90210
278-8010

D 6. PORTOLÁ TRAIL CAMPSITE NO. 2, LA CIENEGA

On August 3, 1769, the colonizing expedition led by Gasper de Portolá camped at a choice location where several springs were surrounded by sycamore trees. The site was commemorated 190 years later when the California State Park Commission, the City of Beverly Hills, and Los Fiesteros de Los Angeles cooperated in the placing of a plaque marking the location of the campsite, the second place where Portolá stopped in southern California as his party headed northward. The location has been designated a state historical site. Public transportation available to location.

Located on La Cienega Blvd. between
Olympic Blvd. and Gregory Way
Beverly Hills

Fowler Museum on Wilshire

D 7. SCHINDLER HOUSE

The designer of numerous residences and apartment complexes in southern California, architect Rudolph M. Schindler (1887-1953) created this home in 1921 for his private residence. He used his own house as a sounding board for various ideas, including tilt slab concrete walls with glass in the space between each slab, and sliding doors in every room opening to private courtyards. The end result was an unusual house in the Modern style.

Private residence
Not open to the public

833 N. Kings Road
Los Angeles 90069

D 8. STORER HOUSE

The Storer house was designed in 1923 by noted architect Frank Lloyd Wright (1869-1959). Its interesting design features a two-story living room that opens out onto front and rear terraces. Public transportation available to location.

Private residence
Not open to the public

8161 Hollywood Blvd.
Los Angeles 90069

D 9. PLUMMER PARK, WITH OLDEST SURVIVING HOUSE IN HOLLYWOOD

In 1877 the Plummer family purchased a part of the Rancho La Brea and in the following year built a home there. Cecelia Plummer's husband was a seaman who was seldom at home; she operated Plummer Ranch herself, successfully enough so that she also bought and operated several others. Plummer Ranch became a social center for such visitors as Helen Hunt Jackson, author of *Ramona*. The family raised vegetables, fruits, flowers, and dairy products for sale to Los Angeles residents.

Eugene Plummer, heir to the estate, received title to a portion of the Plummer holdings and lived in the home until his death at age 90 in 1943. A generous man, his co-signing of notes for friends cost him almost all of his ranch property. The last three acres, including the Plummer home, was purchased by Los Angeles County and made a park, with the Plummer family being allowed to remain there. The county made continuous improvements to the park, including recreational facilities and an auditorium, named Fiesta Hall.

The original Plummer home has been used as the headquarters of the Los Angeles Audubon Society since 1937 and is now known as the Audubon House. A few interior modifications have been made, but otherwise it remains substantially the same as it was almost a hundred years ago. Public transportation available to location.

Audubon House hours,
Monday-Saturday, 10:00 A.M.-3:00 P.M.
(Closed Sundays and major holidays)

7377 Santa Monica Blvd.
Los Angeles 90046
876-0202

D 10. CHAPLIN STUDIO

The Charlie Chaplin Studio, constructed in 1918 as one of Hollywood's first complete motion picture studios, continued into the

Charlie Chaplin Studios, 1928.

1970s as an important center of entertainment production. The original buildings included Chaplin's home as well as studio and offices. Many of Chaplin's film classics, including "The Gold Rush," were made here in the 1920s and into the 1930s. Chaplin also put his footprints in cement in front of one of the sound stages.

In 1942 the property was sold to Safeway Markets, which built a market on the northeast corner of the property. The rest of the property was sold for $600,000 and the new owners continued in theatrical productions. Red Skelton bought the complex in 1958 and after putting in $2 million in improvements sold it to CBS in 1962. The "Perry Mason" television series was filmed at the studios. In 1966 the A & M Record Company purchased the property, which to date consists of 2.2 acres and includes three sound stages and full production facilities. Public transportation available to location.

Not open to the public

1416 N. La Brea Avenue
Los Angeles 90028
469-2411

D 11. GRAUMAN'S CHINESE THEATRE

The glamour of the motion picture industry is preserved in the architecture of the Grauman's Chinese Theatre and in the inscriptions in cement of over 150 film personalities. Hollywood realtor C. E. Toberman built and financed the theatre for Sid Grauman, who had earlier opened the Million Dollar, Egyptian, and other theatres. The Chinese opened for business on May 18, 1927, with Cecil B. deMille's "King of Kings."

The theatre's Oriental decor has attracted millions of tourists to view the architecture as well as the film show in the theatre. The courtyard features the handprints, footprints, and signatures of film stars since the 1920s (estimates are that enough space remains to include future film stars for the next 40 years). The theatre was designated as an historic cultural monument in 1968. Public transportation available to location.

No fee to view Forecourt of the Stars

6925 Hollywood Blvd.
Los Angeles 90028
464-8111

Grauman's Chinese Theater in the 1920s.

D 12. CROSSROADS OF THE WORLD

This unusual complex was designed in 1936 by Robert V. Derrah who also created the Coca Cola plant and the Farmers' Market. Derrah captured the idea of an automobile-oriented society by designing structures that paid homage to mobility. A master of the Streamline Moderne style, Derrah created a shopping center that featured two themes: a ship, repeating his earlier idea with the Coca Cola plant, and a European Village, with Spanish, medieval English, and French motifs. The ship design featured a large tower topped by a lighted turning ball which represented the world. The European village also included a lighthouse. Originally a shopping center, the Crossroads complex is now mainly offices and wholesale stores. Public transportation available to location.

6671 Sunset Boulevard
Los Angeles 90028
463-5611

D 13. HOLLYWOOD AND VINE

This famous intersection is the focus of the Hollywood legend, a state of mind rather than geography—the place where star-struck tourists were, and possibly still do go, always hoping to see film stars and celebrities. Such a point in time never existed, but the legend has persisted—even though the only stars a visitor may see are those implanted in the sidewalk along Hollywood Boulevard, commemorating people involved in all phases of the entertainment industry.

Hollywood Boulevard was originally named Prospect Avenue, and in 1900 it ran past orchards and farmhouses. The Jesse L. Lasky Feature Play Company came to the Hollywood area in 1913 to film "The Squaw Man," the first feature-length film made in Los Angeles. Film studios and actors were at first not welcomed by the Hollywood community, but by the 1900s motion picture production had become a major industry. The growth of Los Angeles spilled over into Hollywood and made Hollywood Boulevard into a commercial area.

Although none of the film studios are now located at Hollywood and Vine—indeed, most studios are miles away from the intersection—the area does offer a wide variety of department stores, specialty shops, and movie theatres. The area is easily reached by public transportation.

Hollywood Blvd. and Vine Street
Hollywood 90028

D 14. HOLLYWOOD PALLADIUM

On October 31, 1940, the Hollywood Palladium opened its doors as the world's largest dining and dancing emporium. Independent film producers Maurice M. Cohen and Edward Small formed Southern California Enterprises, and with other Hollywood businessmen and film celebrities raised the money for its construction. Built at a cost of $1.6 million, the Palladium has been host to over 38,000,000 people, including five Presidents and celebrities from all phases of the entertainment industry, as well as tourists from all over the world.

The Palladium has served as headquarters for Lawrence Welk, television's Emmy awards, and for sales meetings, exhibitions, and other events. Throughout the years the Palladium has been constantly refurbished and continues its existence as an active Hollywood landmark. Public transportation available to location.

Open hours when functions held.
(Office open weekdays, 9 A.M.-5:30 P.M.)

6215 W. Sunset Blvd.
Los Angeles 90028
466-4311

D 15. RADIO STATION KNX AND COLUMBIA SQUARE

Radio Station KNX traces its beginnings to September 1920, when Fred Christian assembled a 5-watt transmitter with the call letters 6ADZ. He borrowed records from music stores in exchange for free advertising. In November 1921, Christian received a license to operate as KGC; and in March 1922 he was assigned the letters KNX for his new 50-watt transmitter. In 1923 KNX began operating on 500 watts. No less than 22 stations shared the same wave length in 1922, and intense competition for choice hours occurred. In 1924 Christian sold KNX to Guy Earl, owner of the Los Angeles *Evening Express*. As the years passed KNX's broadcast power increased, and in 1936 the station became a CBS affiliate.

The KNX/CBS studios on Sunset Boulevard were built in 1937, and the building was dedicated on April 30, 1938. Designed by William Lescaze and E. T. Heitschmidt, the building is considered a classic example of the new architectural style of the 1930s. Because of Fred Christian's 5-watt transmitter, KNX claims the title of being the oldest radio station in Los Angeles. Public transportation available to location.

Not open to the public

6121 Sunset Blvd.
Los Angeles 90028
469-1212

D 16. DEMILLE STUDIO BARN

The deMille Studio Barn, constructed some time prior to 1913 as a horsebarn and storehouse for feed and hay, achieved fame as Hollywood's first major film company studio. Originally located at the intersection of Selma and Vine Streets, it was transferred to the Paramount Studios address in 1927. Cecil B. deMille rented half of the barn for use as a studio when he made "The Squaw Man" in 1913-14, Hollywood's first feature-length motion picture. In 1956 the California State Park Commission and the Historical Landmarks Committee of Los Angeles County declared the barn a state historical landmark. Public transportation available to location.

Not open to the public

Paramount Studios
5451 Marathon Street
Los Angeles 90028
463-0100

DeMille Studio Barn (where the Squaw Man was filmed in 1913), Paramount Studios

D 17. RADIO STATION KHJ

Radio Station KHJ originated in a small studio on the roof of the old Los Angeles *Times* building at First and Broadway in April 1922. The *Times* sold the station to Don Lee, Inc., in 1927, and the following year it was moved to the Don Lee building at 7th and Bixel. In December 1940 the station was moved to 5515 Melrose, from there to 1313 N. Vine Street in May 1948, and back to the Melrose address in 1962, where it continues at the present time as one of the oldest radio stations in Los Angeles. Public transportation available to location.

Not open to the public

5515 Melrose Avenue
Los Angeles 90038
462-2133

D 18. FREEMAN HOUSE

Located in the Hollywood Hills, the Freeman house represents Frank Lloyd Wright's most successful effort at designing pre-cast concrete block homes. He designed the home in 1924. Built into the hill, the home features living, dining, and kitchen space at street level, and the bedrooms below. Automobile transportation recommended.

Private residence
Not open to the public

1962 Glencoe Way
Los Angeles 90068

D 19. HOLLYWOOD BOWL

The history of the Hollywood Bowl began with a search for a natural outdoor amphitheatre to stage concerts and plays "under the stars." H. Ellis Reed, in looking for such a location, found a likely spot while hiking along the hills near Cahuenga Pass. His father called out from the center of the bowl-shaped depression as Reed listened from the hilltop. The area, originally named Daisy Dell, soon became known as the Hollywood Bowl. People found the first Bowl accommodations rather primitive. Worshipers at the Easter Sunrise Service or concertgoers at the Symphonies Under the Stars sat on the grassy slope and witnessed performers using a barn door for a platform. The first season as such occurred in 1922. Through the efforts of Mrs. Artie Mason Carter funds were raised for equipment, buildings, seats, and other necessities. A permanent organization, the Hollywood Bowl Association, was established.

During the past five decades the Bowl has seen a huge roster compiled of the world's greatest conductors and artists. Occasional financial crises threatened the Bowl, such as in 1933 during the Depression and in 1951 when the Bowl was threatened with bankruptcy. Since then, however, the Bowl season has grown as has the size of the audience. From time to time improvements were installed, including a modern sound system, concessions, and additional parking space. The Bowl's seating capacity exceeds 17,000.

For all its fame as a summertime entertainment attraction, the Bowl remains essentially a 116-acre park featuring over 2,000 trees, hundreds of shrubs, picnic spots, and fountains. Public transportation available to location; the Bowl is by the Hollywood Freeway at the Highland Avenue exit.

Grounds open June-August daily,
   9:00 A.M.-5:00 P.M., concerts as
   scheduled.

2301 N. Highland Avenue
Los Angeles 90068
876-8742

Hollywood Bowl

D 20. PILGRIMAGE PLAY THEATRE

The idea of an outdoor theatre to present the life of Jesus achieved reality when Christine Wetherill Stevenson and Mrs. Chauncey D. Clarke founded the Pilgrimage Play Association. A theatre was constructed in Cahuenga Pass in 1920, and on June 27th of that year the first of the Pilgrimage Play was presented. Nine years later a brushfire destroyed the wooden theatre. To replace it a concrete outdoor theatre was built on the original site in 1931. From that time until 1954 annual summer performances of the Pilgrimage Play were given. In 1943 the property was deeded to the County of Los Angeles, subject to a 99-year lease to the Hollywood Bowl Association. The play was to be given on a non-profit basis. Improvements were made by the county in 1946 when two 40-foot lighting towers were built.

The last Pilgrimage Play production occurred in 1954. Protests had been made against county funds subsidizing religious programs. The theatre was revitalized in 1973 when the Los Angeles Shakespeare Festival found the theatre ideal for its presentation of Shakespearean drama at no cost to theatregoers. More recently it has offered during the summer a brief season of chamber music by members of the Los Angeles Philharmonic Orchestra. Public transportation available to location.

2850 Cahuenga Blvd.
Los Angeles 90028
469-3974

D 21. HOLLYWOODLAND STONE GATES

These two stone gates, built in the early 1920s, marked the official entrance to the Hollywoodland real estate development. European stone masons were brought in to build the gates. They quarried and dressed the stone, living in tents up the canyon while they worked at their task. They also built a series of graceful stairways connecting street levels down the hillsides. The homes were exclusive; at one time a guard at the gates required telephoned permission from a visitor's hosts after 6:30 P.M. before admitting guests to the area. The stone masonry was designated as an historic cultural monument in 1963. Not accessible by public transportation.

At intersection of Beachwood, Westshire, and Beldon Drives.

D 22. HOLLYWOOD SIGN, MT. LEE

In the fall of 1923 real estate developers promoting a subdivision at the top of Beachwood Canyon erected a huge sign near the summit of Mt. Lee, on the perimeter of Griffith Park. "HOLLYWOODLAND" became a familiar symbol to residents, tourists and pilots. At night the sign was lighted by over 4,000 20-watt light bulbs; by day it could be see from the harbor area a full 25 miles away. The sign was maintained

Hollywood Sign, Mt. Lee, c. 1930.

until 1939 by a caretaker who lived in a small cabin behind the first "L."

Long after the last subdivision lot had been sold the sign still remained, neglected and a victim of vandalism. In 1945 the sign and adjoining acreage were deeded to the Los Angeles Department of Recreation and Parks. The Hollywood Chamber of Commerce repaired HOLLYWOOD but cut down LAND, so that the sign became a civic announcement rather than an advertisement. Various public service organizations have kept the sign repaired, although much still needs to be done. The letters of the sign are 50 feet high, and the length of the sign is 450 feet. Telephone poles sunk into the mountain, along with spikes and steel cables, support the letters. The letters are made from sheet metal, painted white. In 1973 the sign was designated an historical cultural monument.

Visible from Griffith Park Observatory and many other locations.

D 23. NOVARRO HOUSE

Located in the fashionable Griffith Park district, the Novarro house was designed by architect Lloyd Wright in 1928. Wright, son of Frank Lloyd Wright, earned his own reputation through his designs of homes, commercial buildings, and churches. The Novarro house was one of a number designed by Wright primarily for people in the movie industry.

Private residence
Not open to the public

5699 Valley Oak Drive
Los Angeles 90068

D 24. SOWDEN HOUSE

The Sowden house is another example of the architectural talents of Frank Lloyd Wright. Designed by him in 1926, the house was built around an inner court which contained an elaborate fountain. Visitors to the home entered through a striking cave-like opening. Public transportation available to location.

Private residence
Not open to the public

5121 Franklin Avenue
Los Angeles 90028

D 25. FERN DELL NATURE MUSEUM AND SITE OF GABRIELINO INDIAN VILLAGE

Archeological surveys done at the mouth of Fern Dell Canyon in Griffith Park reveal that fairly large settlements of Gabrielino Indians lived in the area. The 1769 Portolá expedition recorded their presence, but no exact map can be made of all the village locations. Gabrielinos first came to this area at least 10,000 years ago. With the creation of the mission system, the Gabrielinos became neophytes at the San Gabriel Archangel Mission, with the eventual loss of their culture and tribal identity.

Today Griffith Park's Fern Dell Nature Museum is located on the approximate site of a Gabrielino village. A plaque at the Los Feliz Boulevard entrance to the park states that the Gabrielinos named the area Mocohuenga Canyon. In 1973 the area was designated as an historic cultural monument. The boundaries of the site are Los Feliz Blvd. to the south, the museum to the north, Fern Dell Place on the west, and Los Feliz Estates on the east. Public transportation available to park area.

Museum hours,
Wednesday-Sunday, 1:00-5:00 P.M.

5373 Red Oak Drive
Los Angeles 90068

D 26. GRIFFITH PARK, PLANETARIUM, AND ZOO

On December 16, 1896, Colonel Griffith J. Griffith presented the City of Los Angeles with a gift of 3,015 acres of land for a park. During the first years of the park's existence, however, Griffith's personal life caused Los Angeles citizens to resent his philanthropy. The park gift was alleged to have been a way to avoid paying taxes, and Griffith's having served two years in prison for the attempted murder of his wife made his motives and generosity suspect. Another Griffith gift of $100,000 for an observatory was refused. When he died in 1919 he willed $700,000 to the city for the observatory and a Greek Theatre. This time his gift was not seen as a scheme for bribing his way into community leadership or respectability, and it was accepted.

Observatory, Griffith Park

Additions to the Griffith Park acreage now make the park, at over 4,000 acres, the largest city park in the United States. Golf courses, 35 picnic areas, athletic fields and bridle trails are among the park's attractions. The Los Angeles Zoo and Children's Zoo cover 110 acres in a natural setting. The Griffith Observatory and Planetarium include Hall of Science exhibits, programs, and use of the twin refracting telescope. Public transportation available to location.

Observatory open Monday-Friday
1:00 P.M.-10:00 P.M.;
    Saturday, 11:30 A.M.-10:00 P.M.;
    Sunday, 1:00-10:00 P.M.
Zoo: 10:00 A.M.-5:00 P.M. daily
    (Zoo open 'til 6 P.M. June-August)
Admission to main zoo $1.25 adults,
    children 12 to 15 50¢, under 12 free

Los Feliz Blvd. and Riverside Drive
Los Angeles
665-5188 Park
664-1192 Planetarium
666-4650 Zoo
664-1982 Office

D 27. LOVELL HOUSE

In 1929 architect Richard Neutra designed the Lovell house in the Griffith Park district. The house, designed in the international style, helped establish Neutra's reputation as an outstanding architect. Neutra utilized a free-flowing plan and modern materials. The Lovell house, however, represents more than architectural innovation. The original project was under the responsibility of architect Rudolph M. Schindler, who had earlier designed the Lovell beach house in Newport Beach. The commission, however, went to Neutra, with long-lasting bitterness resulting between the two men. Both men, however, are remembered as important figures in southern California architectural history. Automobile transportation recommended.

Private residence
Not open to the public

4616 Dundee Drive
Los Angeles 90027

D 28. ENNIS HOUSE

Another example of the architectural style of Frank Lloyd Wright, the Ennis house was designed in 1924. Wright's concept included the use of concrete blocks, resulting in what admirers called a palace and critics labeled a mausoleum. Automobile transportation recommended.

Private residence
Not open to the public

2607 Glendower Avenue
Los Angeles 90027

D 29. BARNSDALL PARK AND HOLLYHOCK HOUSE

In 1918 oil heiress Alice Barnsdall purchased 36 acres of land with the intention of building both a residence for herself and a

Barnsdall Home

theatre complex which would develop cultural activities for the city. She commissioned noted architect Frank Lloyd Wright to design the home, a theatre, a director's house and a guest house. The buildings were completed in the early 1920s, and in 1927 Miss Barnsdall deeded 11 acres, including the residence and director's house to the City of Los Angeles. She stipulated that the land be used for a park and playground and that the buildings be used for art purposes.

Nothing was done by the city for a number of years, and the Barnsdall home, named "Hollyhock House" for Wright's use of Miss Barnsdall's favorite flower, suffered from neglect and vandalism. Wright designed a Municipal Art Gallery for the park in 1954, which was an instant success. In the 1960s major redesigning occurred in Barnsdall Park. A new Municipal Art Gallery was constructed in 1971, Hollyhock House was extensively renovated, and the director's house was established as an arts and crafts building. Hollyhock House and Director's House are outstanding examples of Wright's "California Romanza" period, blending architecture with the environment. Both buildings are included in the Historic American Buildings Survey. In 1963 Hollyhock House was designated as an historic cultural monument, an honor extended to the entire Barnsdall Park complex in 1965. Public transportation available to location.

Hollyhock House open Tuesdays,
    Thursdays, and first Saturday of each
    month 10:00 A.M.-2:00 P.M.
Tours on the hour.

Hollywood Blvd. at Vermont Avenue
Los Angeles 90027
662-7272

D 30. ROCHA HOUSE

This 1 1/2-story ranch house was constructed in 1865 as a residence for Antonio Jose Rocha II, on a part of the Rancho Rincon de Los Bueyes. Rocha, who was of Portuguese ancestry, served as a local justice of the peace. The walls of the first floor of the house are of adobe bricks and are almost two feet thick. The second floor has walls of redwood siding. Much of the house retains its original construction, including covered porches on three sides of the building. The historical value of the Rocha home, which is still occupied by a family descendant, has been recognized by several organizations. In 1953 the Native Daughters of the Golden West marked the site, and the Historic American Buildings Survey recorded it in 1958. In 1963 the Los Angeles Cultural Heritage Board designated the Rocha house as an historic cultural monument. Public transportation available to two blocks of location.

Private residence
Not open to the public

2400 Shenandoah Street
Los Angeles 90034

D 31. FARMERS MARKET

The famous Farmers Market, located at Third and Fairfax, was originally a big field that was part of the Earl B. Gilmore property. Gilmore was a successful oil man who was involved in a succession of enterprises on his portion of what once had been Rancho La Brea. An adobe building still on the property dates back to rancho days.

In 1933 a man named Roger Dahlhjelm suggested to Gilmore that the field be used as a place for farmers to gather and market their fruits and vegetables and other farm products. Gilmore approved the idea; the local farmers took some persuading, but in July 1934 the Farmers Market opened with 18 stalls. In that same year Gilmore built Gilmore Stadium, a baseball field which in 1950 became the home of CBS Television City.

Today Farmers Market has over 160 stalls, salons, shops, restaurants, and stores of almost every description from bakeries to shoe repair. At least 20,000 people visit Farmers Market daily. The market is owned by the A F. Gilmore Company, and the area including Television City and Farmers Market is known as "Gilmore Island." Public transportation available to location.

Open June-September 9:00 A.M.-8:00 P.M.
October-May 9:00 A.M.-6:30 P.M.
(Closed Sundays)

6333 W. 3rd Street
Los Angeles 90036
933-9211

D 32. LA BREA PITS

When the Portola' expedition passed through southern California in 1769, its members observed springs of tar in the area

La Brea Pits before development, c. 1910

now known as Hancock Park. However, the value of the tar pits as a window to the prehistoric past was not recognized until the beginning of the twentieth century. Between 1906-1915, thousands of Ice Age fossils were recovered from the pits, including over 200 different kinds of mammals, plants, birds, reptiles, and insects. To date over 500,000 specimens have been recovered. Many of these can be seen at the Museum of Natural History in Exposition Park.

Currently the Rancho La Brea Project, begun in 1969, is yielding additional fossils and more precise data than was possible to obtain from earlier excavations. A new museum, the George C. Page Museum of La Brea Discoveries, in now open in Hancock Park. Plans are also under way to create a "Pleistocene Meadow" with life-like replicas of animals and birds from the Ice Age, along with plants and trees that may have grown in the area during that time. Public transportation available to location.

Tuesday-Sunday, 10:00 A.M.-5:00 P.M.
  Closed Monday, Thanksgiving, and
  Christmas
Guided tours Thursday at 1 P.M.,
  June-August
Admission free
Page tours: Tuesday-Friday at 2 P.M.,
  June-August

650 S. Ogden Drive, or Wilshire Blvd. at
  Curson
931-8082
933-7451 George C. Page Museum

D 33. BUCK HOUSE

Designed by noted architect Rudolph M. Schindler (1887-1953) in 1934, the Buck house serves as an example of Schindler's international style, with his concern for space and volume. Although he made little impression nationally, Schindler influenced a number of younger Los Angeles architects in the 1930s, and the Buck house is one of several homes designed by Schindler that received wide attention in architectural and popular magazines. Public transportation available to two blocks of location.

Private residence
Not open to the public

805 S. Genessee Avenue
Los Angeles 90036

D 34. MEMORIAL BRANCH LIBRARY

The Memorial Branch Library, directly across from Los Angeles High School, was constructed as a branch of the Los Angeles Public Library system in 1929. Its name is taken from its location in Memorial Park, deeded to the city in 1923 as a memorial to the graduates of Los Angeles High School who died in World War I. The building was dedicated on April 29, 1930.

Architects John C. Austin and Frederic M. Ashley designed the library as an English manor, paralleling the style of the high school. A special Memorial Window commemorates the alumni who died in the service. The library's collection emphasizes black, Jewish and Oriental culture. In 1971 the building was designated as an historic cultural monument. Public transportation available to location.

Monday-Thursday, 1:00 P.M.-9:00 P.M.
Friday, 10:00 A.M.-5:30 P.M.
Saturday, 9:00 A.M.-1:00 P.M.

4625 W. Olympic Blvd.
Los Angeles 90019
934-0855

D 35. WILSHIRE UNITED METHODIST CHURCH

The Wilshire United Methodist Church at Wilshire and Plymouth Blvds., represents the merging of four Methodist church congregations over a span of 90 years. The Hobart Methodist Church was founded in 1908, its name being changed in 1919 to the Wilshire Methodist Church. The Simpson Methodist Episcopal Church, founded in 1887, merged in 1910 with the Westlake Methodist Church, which had been organized in 1899. In 1927 the Westlake and Wilshire churches merged to form the Wilshire Methodist Church. The final merger occurred in 1973 when the congregations of the Trinity Methodist Church of 12th and Flower Streets in downtown Los Angeles merged with the Wilshire Church, the new name being the Wilshire United Methodist Church. This capped a long era of Methodist participation in the growth and development of Los Angeles.

Dating from 1924, the Wilshire United Methodist Church features elements of Romanesque and Gothic architecture and beautiful stained glass windows. Public transportation available to location.

Sunday Services: 9:30 and 11 A.M.
(Office: Weekdays, 8 A.M.-3:30 P.M.)

4350 Wilshire Blvd.
Los Angeles 90010
931-1085

D 36. EVANS HOUSE

This house was built to an architectural design unusual even for southern California. Architect I. Eisner based his creation on the classic revival occurring in the East at the turn of the century, with a Roman temple portico and Ionic columns dominating the exterior, and paneling and cornices inside in the same vein. Eisner designed the home around 1910 for Mrs. Jeanette Donovan, who named it "Sunshine Hall." The home, and others nearby, serves as an interesting example of the palatial homes built by well-to-do residents at the turn of the century. In 1973 the residence was designated an historic cultural monument. Public transportation to three blocks of location.

Private residence
Not open to the public

419 S. Lorraine Blvd.
Los Angeles 90020

D 37. WILSHIRE BOULEVARD TEMPLE

After several earlier sites had been used Congregation B'nai B'rith, the oldest Jewish congregation in Los Angeles, constructed the Wilshire Boulevard Temple at Wilshire and Hobart Boulevards. The building was dedicated June 7, 1929, with Rabbi Edgar F. Magnin officiating, along with other clerics and laymen of several faiths. The building is dominated by a 135-foot dome inlaid with mosaic. Murals by Hugo Ballin depict the history of the Jewish people; other decorations include Byzantine columns of black Belgian marble, a huge rose window, and bronze chandeliers. The Wilshire Boulevard Temple is one of the largest and most influential Reform congregations in Los Angeles. In 1973 the Temple was designated as an historic cultural monument. Public transportation available to location.

Open weekdays 9:00 A.M.-5:00 P.M.
Services on weekends

3663 Wilshire Boulevard
Los Angeles 90010
388-2401

Wilshire Boulevard Temple, c. 1930

Ambassador Hotel

D 38. AMBASSADOR HOTEL

The Ambassador Hotel was constructed from 1919-21 at a cost of $5 million. Located on a 23-acre site facing Wilshire Boulevard—then a dirt road—the hotel itself covered eleven of the acres. The rest of the area was landscaped with gardens, lawns and fountains. Nearly 3,000 guests occupied the hotel on its opening day, January 19, 1921.

The hotel's presence on Wilshire Boulevard helped make the street a main traffic artery. In its 50 years of operation the hotel has accommodated five U.S. presidents, numerous leaders of other nations, and countless celebrities. The hotel served as the setting for the Academy Awards presentations half a dozen times, and weddings, proms, birthday parties and movie premieres have utilized the hotel's facilities. The hotel also features the Cocoanut Grove, an entertainment center that has spotlighted innumerable singers and bands from the 1920s to the present. As is well known, tragedy marred the hotel's setting for Robert Kennedy's 1968 California primary campaign.

Facilities at the hotel have been continually updated. At one time a miniature zoo was featured as an attraction; its location is now used for parking. Recent additions include 13 lighted tennis courts and a complete health club. The hotel continues to serve as a major attraction for tourists, businessmen, and convention groups. Public transportation available to location.

3400 Wilshire Blvd.
Los Angeles 90010
387-7011

D 39. KOREAN ROYAL CHURCH (TEMPLE SINAI EAST)

Built in 1925, this building was the second synagogue of the Sinai Congregation, a Reform Jewish congregation founded about twenty years earlier. The architectural style has been described as eclectic, including Romanesque and Moorish elements. Its designer was S. Tilden Norton, who also designed the congregation's first building at 12th and Valencia Streets. An intricate inlaid brick design enhances the exterior face of the building, while the interior features leaded glass windows and exquisite carvings. After the Sinai Congregation moved to new quarters, the building was sold in 1973 to the Korean Royal Church. In 1971 the building was declared an historic cultural monument. Public transportation available to two blocks of location.

407 S. New Hampshire
Los Angeles 90020

D 40. ST. SOPHIA CATHEDRAL

The need for a cathedral for members of the Greek Orthodox religion in Los Angeles resulted in the construction of what many architectural experts consider to be one of the most beautiful churches in the world. Constructed between 1948-52, the church was designed along traditional Byzantine lines, with no exterior architectural decoration. The interior contains numerous murals, icons, and rich bronze furnishings. The Apostles and the Three Hierarchs are depicted in brilliant colors in stained glass. The interior dome, measuring 90 feet from floor to top and 30 feet across, has 24 windows around it. In the nave, which seats 850, there are 21 massive crystal chandeliers. One major departure from Byzantine architectural tradition, the elimination of columns provides unobstructed vision for the worshipers. Dedicated in September 1952, St. Sophia's has attracted people of all faiths to admire this triumph of church architecture. In 1973 St. Sophia's Cathedral was designated an historic cultural monument. Public transportation available to location.

Open daily, 10:00 A.M.-3 P.M.
Closed Thursday

1324 S. Normandie Avenue
Los Angeles 90006
737-2424

NOTES

SECTION E

South Central Los Angeles

1. William Andrews Clark Memorial Library
2520 Cimarron Street (at W. Adams Blvd.); Los Angeles
2. Golden State Mutual Life Insurance
1999 W. Adams Blvd.; Los Angeles
3. Wesley W. Beckett House
2218 S. Harvard Blvd.; Los Angeles
4. Rindge House
2263 S. Harvard Blvd.; Los Angeles
5. Second Church of Christ, Scientist
948 W. Adams Blvd.; Los Angeles
6. W. J. Davis House
2 Chester Place; Los Angeles
7. The Doheny Mansion
8 Chester Place; Los Angeles
8. Automobile Club of Southern California
2601 S. Figueroa Street; Los Angeles
9. St. Vincent de Paul Church
621 W. Adams Blvd.; Los Angeles
10. Stimson House
2421 S. Figueroa Street; Los Angeles
11. West Adams
300 to 500 block of W. Adams Blvd.; Los Angeles
12. John A. Forthmann House
629 W. 18th Street; Los Angeles
13. Patriotic Hall
1816 S. Figueroa Street; Los Angeles
14. Shrine Auditorium
3228 Royal Street; Los Angeles
15. University of Southern California
University Park, Figueroa Street and Exposition Blvd.; Los Angeles
16. Exposition Park
Bounded by Exposition Blvd., Figueroa Street, S. Park Drive, and Menlo Avenue
17. Exposition Club House
3990 Menlo Avenue; Los Angeles
18. California Museum of Science and Industry
700 State Drive; Los Angeles
19. Armory, Exposition Park
700 State Drive; Los Angeles
20. Museum of Natural History
900 Exposition Blvd.; Los Angeles
21. Los Angeles Memorial Coliseum
3911 S. Figueroa Street; Los Angeles
22. Site of the Birthplace of Adlai E. Stevenson
2639 Monmouth Avenue; Los Angeles
23. Second Baptist Church
2412 Griffith Avenue (corner 24th Street); Los Angeles
24. Sojourner Truth Home
1119 E. Adams Blvd.; Los Angeles
25. Biddy Mason Center
1152 E. Adams Blvd.; Los Angeles
26. Lincoln Theatre
2300 S. Central Avenue; Los Angeles
27. 28th Street YMCA
100 E. 28th Street; Los Angeles
28. Ralph Bunche Residence
1221-1223 E. 40th Place; Los Angeles
29. The Dunbar Hotel
4225 S. Central Avenue; Los Angeles
30. La Mesa Battlefield
4500 Downey Road; Vernon
31. Farmer John Pig Murals
3049 E. Vernon Avenue; Vernon

32. Central Avenue, Watts
    Central Avenue (from Alondra Blvd. on
    the south to Firestone on north) Watts
33. The Watts Station
    1686 E. 103rd Street; Los Angeles
34. The Watts Towers
    1765 E. 107th Street; Watts

35. Lynwood Pacific Electric Depot
    Fernwood and Long Beach Blvd.
36. The "Eagle Tree"
    Poppy and Short Streets; Compton
37. Heritage House
    205 Willowbrook; Compton
38. Angeles Abbey
    Compton Blvd. near Long Beach Blvd.

Memorial Coliseum after construction.

E 1. WILLIAM ANDREWS CLARK MEMORIAL LIBRARY

The Library was founded by William Andrews Clark, Jr., and bequeathed in 1934 to UCLA as a memorial to his father, Senator William A. Clark, Montana magnate. The younger Clark was also a founder and early patron of the Los Angeles Philharmonic Orchestra. The collections are housed in a stately brick building of Italian Renaissance style designed by Robert D. Farquhar and constructed between 1924 and 1926. The entrance vestibule is Italian Baroque, with floor and walls of varicolored marble in geometrical designs and with a curved ceiling painted by the American artist Allyn Cox. Elsewhere are English oak paneled walls, intricately carved ceilings, bronze bookcases, paintings dating from the seventeenth century, alabaster chandeliers, oriental carpets, and elegant furniture from the eighteenth and nineteenth centuries.

The volumes in the Library are principally representative of English culture of the seventeenth and eighteenth centuries, certain aspects of nineteenth century literature, and fine printing of the nineteenth and twentieth centuries.

When the Library became the charge of UCLA, it contained approximately 18,000 books and manuscripts. Since 1935 the collections have grown continuously, so that there are now on the shelves some 74,000 volumes and 12,000 manuscripts.

The Library is open to readers and visitors Monday through Saturday, except on University holidays, from 8:00 A.M. to 5:00 P.M. Please telephone in advance to arrange a tour; the Clark Library is not a museum but primarily a research library.

2520 Cimarron Street (at W. Adams Blvd)
Los Angeles 90018
731-8529

E 2. GOLDEN STATE MUTUAL LIFE INSURANCE

The Golden State Mutual Life Insurance Company was organized in a small one-room office at 1435 Central Avenue in 1925. A two-story brick home office building was erected at 4111 South Central Avenue in 1928. It is still standing but no longer used for company business. The founders of this insurance business were William Nickerson, Jr., Norman O. Houston, and George A. Beavers, Jr. The present home office building was dedicated in 1949, and is notable because it houses two large murals depicting the history of the Negro in California and an Afro-American Art Collection. Today,

Golden State Mutual Life Building

GSM operates in a number of states and ranks with the largest Negro businesses in the nation.

Offices are open for business Monday through Thursday 8:00 A.M.-4:45 P.M. Friday, 8:00 A.M.-12 noon.

1999 W. Adams Blvd.
Los Angeles 90007

Alston panel on the Negro in California history, Golden State Mutual Life

E 3. WESLEY W. BECKETT HOUSE

This interesting home, built in 1905, was built in the American Colonial Revival style popular at the turn of the century. In 1973 the house was designated an historic cultural monument. Public transportation available to three blocks of location.

Private residence
Not open to the public

2218 S. Harvard Blvd.
Los Angeles 90018

E 4. RINDGE HOUSE

The Rindge house was commissioned by Frederick H. Rindge, a prominent financier and land developer. Ironically, Rindge, who died in 1905, did not live to see the building's completion the following year. His widow lived in the house until her death in 1941. The house, which has recently served as a convent and a maternity home, is notable for its use of beautiful glass, wood, and marble. Its designer, architect Frederick L. Roehrig, created an unusual and beautiful residence. In 1972 the Rindge house was designated on historic cultural monument. Public transportation available to three blocks of location.

Private residence
Not open to the public

2263 S. Harvard Blvd.
Los Angeles 90018

E 5. SECOND CHURCH OF CHRIST, SCIENTIST

Designed by architect Alfred F. Rosenheim of New York, this imposing church edifice was constructed between 1907 and 1910 at a cost of $318,500. The church was formally dedicated (free of all debt) in September 1910 and has been in continuous use ever since. It was reinforced with steel following the 1933 Long Beach earthquake and refurbished during the late 1950s and early 1960s.

The style is modified Italian Renaissance, with six lofty Corinthian columns supporting the entrance portico. The magnificent concrete dome is sheathed in copper and has an interior diameter of nearly 70 feet. The 93 × 106 foot main auditorium accommodates more than 1,100 persons, while the Sunday school room seats approximately 750. Marble walls and door jambs and detailed balustrades decorate the church interior. The leaded glass window at the

Second Church of Christ, Scientist (Adams Blvd.)

west staircase was adjudged architecturally "perfect" in 1924 by a prominent architect.

Sunday service is from 11 A.M. to noon; Wednesday evening testimony meetings are from 6 to 7, and the church is open approximately a half hour before services.

Meeting room open:
Monday-Friday, 10 A.M.-3 P.M.
Saturday, 11 A.M.-1 P.M.

948 W. Adams Blvd.
P.O. Box 18831
Los Angeles 90007
749-3761

E 6. W. J. DAVIS HOUSE

Located in what once was the most luxurious residential area in Los Angeles, this 2-story Swiss Chalet-style mansion was designed by architects Eisen and Wyman for Dr. William J. Davis and completed in 1902. The construction displays excellent interior and exterior craftsmanship, with leaded glass windows, interior fresco friezes, and notable cabinet work. The exterior dormers have oriental details.

Los Angeles general contractor Carl Leonardt and his family lived in the house from 1912 to 1928. Leonardt's contributions to southern California include construction of the Los Angeles Hall of Records, the Los Angeles County Hospital, and the Hotel Green in Pasadena.

Beginning in 1928, Superior Court Judge Dr. Charles Wellborn occupied the home for many years.

The Davis house is one of ten mansions still remaining in what was once a private residential park. Chester Place was developed in the 1890s by Judge Charles Silent, and at one time it contained 13 homes. The entire complex of 15 acres was eventually acquired by Estelle and Edward Doheny, after whose deaths the property passed to the Catholic Church. Today the structure is known as Medaille Hall and is used as a library for the downtown campus of Mount St. Mary's College.

Library hours are 9:00 A.M. to 5:30 P.M. during which time the public may visit Medaille Hall.

2 Chester Place
Los Angeles 90007

Davis residence, Chester Place

Doheny Mansion

E 7. THE DOHENY MANSION

The Doheny Mansion is one of the best preserved and most impressive late Victorian residences remaining in the West Adams district of Los Angeles. It is the "master house" in the 15-acre exclusive residential park known as Chester Place. Designed by architects Theodore A. Eisen and Sumner P. Hunt, it was built in 1899-1900 for Mr. and Mrs. Oliver P. Posey. In 1901 the home was sold to Edward L. Doheny, pioneer Los Angeles oil magnate and philanthropist. Over the years the Dohenys made many changes in the house and in the grounds. The famous Pompeian Room which was built in 1906 to enclose an open court, added new elegance and splendor to the mansion and became the scene of many elaborate dinners and festive parties.

Following damage by earthquake in 1933, the brick red and plaster house was extensively altered in the French Rococo style. Steel beams and columns replaced the original timber construction. In the great hall downstairs, Siena marble veneered columns replaced the original ones of oak, and a Siena marble fireplace was installed. The general exterior architectural character resembles a French Gothic chateau. The formal gardens and spacious lawns are surrounded by brick walls surmounted by ornamental iron work with arched iron gateways.

The Doheny occupancy covered more than half a century, since Estelle Doheny continued to live there until her death in 1958, when the property passed to the Catholic Church. The Sisters of St. Joseph of Carondolet, who operate the Doheny campus of Mount St. Mary's College, located within Chester Place, use the mansion as a residence.

Tours may be arranged by telephone

8 Chester Place
Los Angeles 90007
746-0450

E 8. AUTOMOBILE CLUB OF SOUTHERN CALIFORNIA

For more than three-quarters of a century the Automobile Club has successfully championed the growing influence of the automobile upon southern California. When founded in 1900, Los Angeles was changing from a small city to a metropolis, going from the days of the horse-car into the automotive age. By encouraging construction and maintenance of good roads, the Club has been largely responsible for the development of suburbs and the decentralization of southern California.

Besides providing insurance and towing service, the Auto Club publishes *Westways* magazine. Known as *Touring Topics* from 1909 until 1933, when it became *Westways,* the popular monthly magazine has regularly included articles about southern California

Automobile Club of Southern California, c. 1920.

Open Monday-Friday 8:45 A.M.-5:00 P.M.
Saturdays 8:45 A.M.-1:00 P.M.

2601 S. Figueroa Street
Los Angeles 90007
741-3111

history and culture. The familiar Automobile Club symbol, a spoked tire wheel and a mission bell, effectively represents *Westways'* effort to pay homage to California's colorful heritage while simultaneously extolling the benefits of modern progress.

In its initial years, the Club occupied a series of small offices in the downtown area. In 1914 headquarters were transferred to Figueroa Street, about a dozen blocks north of its present location. By 1923 the growth which has made it the largest motor club in the United States enabled the Club to move into new permanent headquarters. A three-story Spanish Colonial building designed by architects Hunt and Burns was constructed with reinforced concrete. This headquarters complex was more than doubled in size by 1931, when additional structures were added in the rear. More recently additional expansion and extensive modernization has provided more floor space. But despite subsequent enlargements and modifications, the original edifice remains substantially intact.

The Automobile Club is at the corner of Adams and Figueroa, both of which are served by RTD buses. From the Harbor Freeway exit at Adams and go west one block.

E 9. ST. VINCENT DE PAUL CHURCH

St. Vincent's Church is unique both in its architecture and its location. The axis of the church is at a 45-degree angle to the intersection of Adams Boulevard and Figueroa Street. The donors of the church, Mr. and Mrs. Edward L. Doheny, requested the unusual placement so that commercial buildings would not detract from the visual beauty of the church.

The church was designed by Albert C. Martin, and groundbreaking took place on October 13, 1923. It was consecrated in October 1930. The church is notable for its furnishings and embellishments, based on the style of the Spanish Renaissance and California mission architecture. The seating capacity of the church is 1,200.

In 1939 the Southern California Chapter of the American Institute of Architects awarded St. Vincent's a certificate of merit for its interior design. The church was

St. Vincent de Paul Church

designated an historic cultural monument in 1971. Public transportation available to location.

Open every day, 6:00 A.M.-6:00 P.M.

621 W. Adams Blvd.
Los Angeles 90007
749-8950

Stimson House

Interior, St. Vincent de Paul

E 10. STIMSON HOUSE

Architect Carrol A. Brown designed this 30-room mansion for Thomas Douglas Stimson, a wealthy lumberman who moved to Los Angeles in 1890 from Chicago to live out his declining years. The house combines Richardson neo-Gothic and Romanesque forms, and its turreted stone exterior presents the imposing appearance of a fortress or castle. However, its most extraordinary feature is its magnificent interior paneling and wood carving. Each of the downstairs rooms is finished in a different kind of wood, including ash, birch, sycamore, mahogany, walnut, and oak. Some of the doors are made of two kinds of wood, to match the room on either side.

Lumberman Stimson lived in the house from 1891 until his death in 1898. His family continued to occupy the residence until 1907, when it was sold to Alfred Solano, a civil engineer. The Solano family lived there until about 1918, when the house was purchased by Edward R. Maier, president of the Maier Brewing Company. For several years after Maier's death in the early 1940s, the lovely mansion served as a USC fraternity house. In 1948 the building was bought by Mrs. Carrie Estelle Doheny, widow of oil magnate E. L. Doheny, whose property at 8 Chester Place adjoined the Stimson house at the rear. Mrs. Doheny donated the property to the Sisters of St. Joseph of Carondelet, who, after making extensive renovations, have occupied the premises since 1949.

During its earlier years, especially in the 1920s after Maier moved in, the Stimson house was the scene of many social gatherings. On such occasions, music was provided by a player-piano-type organ, the console of which was in the front hall at the foot of the stairs, with pipes below a grated floor in what is now the sacristy. Also below the first floor, in a maze of rooms and arched doorways, Maier stored wines and rare liquors.

The original parlor has been converted into a chapel, and the large mirror in that room has been covered with a painting of St. Joseph. The arch which connected the chapel with the present parlor (formerly library) has been enclosed with paneling varnished to match the adjoining wood.

The Stimson house is now called the Convent of the Infant of Prague. Although *never open to the public,* the interior has often been photographed as the backdrop for commercial advertisements.

Not open to the public.

2421 S. Figueroa Street
Los Angeles 90049

E 11. WEST ADAMS

Along West Adams Boulevard between Grand Avenue and Figueroa Street were built some of the finest and most exclusive houses in Los Angeles around the turn of the century. Many of the affluent residents who enjoyed the luxury of living in this area had grown wealthy primarily by being here among the first in southern California with money enough to buy the right parcel of land. The West Adams district contained the homes of such notables as Hancock, Banning, W. F. Cline, and General Longstreet. Although many of the old houses have been torn down, a number remain, in varying degrees of preservation.

Private residences
Not open to the public

300 to 500 block of W. Adams Blvd.
Los Angeles

E 12. JOHN A. FORTHMANN HOUSE

Situated near a freeway on-ramp, this large, two-story house is one of the most elegantly detailed Victorian buildings remaining in Los Angeles. As with most such elaborate structures of the 1880s, it is difficult to place stylistically for it represents an eclectic freedom uniquely Californian. Its angularity based on strong vertical and horizontal lines suggests its debt to the Eastlake style, as do the verge-boards on the eaves of the gables. But the classical ornament around the bay windows, on the porch and high on the tower and the heavily bracketed cornices associate it with the late Italianate style where French touches, such as the mansard roof on the tower, give great enrichment to an originally simple style.

The house was built in 1889 by John A. Forthmann, president of the Los Angeles

Forthmann House

Soap Company. It has had several additions on the second floor, but it is otherwise in a remarkable state of preservation, even to the survival of nineteenth century planting around it.

Private residence
Not open to the public

629 W. 18th Street
Los Angeles 90015

E 13. PATRIOTIC HALL

Patriotic Hall was constructed in 1924-25 as a meeting place for veterans' organizations and activities. Opened in 1926, it replaced an inadequate hall which had proved too small to handle the numbers of people attending meetings. In the last half-century the hall has provided banquet facilities, assembly rooms, a library, and office space for veterans' organizations which date back to the Spanish-American War. Over 200 organizations utilize the hall. Youth programs are sponsored and information of interest is provided to veterans. Meeting rooms are named for war-time leaders; military memorabilia are on display in the main lobby and in the meeting rooms. Patriotic Hall is considered by its users as a living memorial, the veterans' organizations maintaining a liason with Los Angeles County and with the Veterans' Administration. Public transportation available to location.

Monday-Friday, 8:00 A.M.-10:30 P.M.
First and fourth Saturdays,
    4:00 P.M.-10:30 P.M.

1816 S. Figueroa Street
Los Angeles 90015
747-5361

Patriotic Hall

E 14. SHRINE AUDITORIUM

The Shrine Auditorium, built in 1925 by the Al Malikah Temple, was for many years the largest theatre in the country. Its Spanish Colonial style of architecture, with a Moorish tinge, dubbed "neo-penal Bagdad" by Los Angeles *Times* music critic Martin Bernheimer, combines large Moorish domes, high narrow arches, and an elaborate Arabesque filigree. Inside is an immense stage, 186 feet wide and 72 feet deep, whose 13,400 square feet make it four times larger than any other stage in Los Angeles. There are 6,489 seats and three levels of foyers. The Moehler Pipe Organ is the world's largest theatre pipe organ. For such a large auditorium (the enormous tent-like interior with canopied ceiling has been a favorite with circuses visiting Los Angeles), the acoustics are remarkably sensitive. The

Shrine Auditorium

56,000 square foot Exposition Hall also serves trade shows, conventions, banquets, (up to 4,000 people), and, in recent years, folk and rock concerts.

For many years the Shrine housed the city's only grand opera, including the Metropolitan, Chicago, and San Francisco companies. Large-scale foreign ballet companies, renowned symphonies, jazz bands, and Broadway musicals regularly attracted large and appreciative audiences. For seven years the motion picture "Oscars" were awarded on stage at the Shrine. Notable performers who have appeared at the Shrine include Rudolf Nureyev, Duke Ellington, Maria Callas, Arturo Rubinstein, Fred Waring, and the Harlem Globetrotters.

With the advent of the Music Center in 1964, the Shrine suffered an inevitable decline. The last Broadway musical, "Hello Dolly," was presented in 1972. However, a multimillion dollar Hoover development project to rehabilitate the neighborhood with extensions of the USC campus, new office buildings, and apartment complexes has encouraged the Shriners to implement a face-lifting program of their own. Hopefully, the "dear old Shrine" will be able to continue its long community service.

The Shrine is open only during performances. Other access is by appointment.

3228 Royal Street
Los Angeles 90007
748-5116 (Variety Concerts, Inc., managers of the Shrine)

E 15. UNIVERSITY OF SOUTHERN CALIFORNIA

Founded in 1879 by the Methodist Church, the University of Southern California spreads over an attractive 98 acre campus between Jefferson and Exposition Blvd., in south-central Los Angeles. Architectural harmony between the older Romanesque-style buildings and more recent modern construction has been achieved by architect Durrel Stone, by use of the same surface material, red brick with cream-colored trim. Most interesting in terms of architectural or historical significance are Widney Hall, Mudd Hall, and Hancock Museum.

Once situated in the midst of a mustard field to which students made their way by horse-drawn streetcars, Widney Hall is the oldest university building in southern California. The two-story frame building, distinguished by "mansion" proportions and green shutters, has been in continuous use for educational purposes since its doors were first opened to USC students in October of 1880. Architects E. F. Kysor and Octavius Morgan furnished plans and specifications without charge, and lumber and other materials were supplied at cost—thus enabling completion of the structure for only $5,000. In the almost ten decades since its erection, Widney Hall has occupied three different locations, but has been altered only slightly in its appearance. Its last move and

Mudd Memorial Hall, USC, 1929

Widney Hall, USC

renovation cost USC nine times the original cost of construction.

In 1955 the structure was formally re-dedicated as Widney Hall, in honor of the principal founder of the University, Judge Robert Maclay Widney. Since the recent completion of the Performing Arts Complex, Widney Hall—formerly the administrative center for the school of music—has housed the General Alumni Association as a fitting retirement from the daily tromp of students, teachers, and administrators. It has been completely restored and renovated by Alumni gifts in 1976. It is both a state and cultural heritage monument.

Mudd Hall, named for mining engineer-philanthropist Colonel Seeley Wintersmith

Mudd, was designed by Beverly Hills architect Ralph Flewelling and was acclaimed the nation's most beautiful college building of the year in 1933. Located at 37th Street and University Avenue, the structure is easily distinguished by its square, slender clock tower.

Allan Hancock Memorial Museum, University Avenue at Childs Way, includes four formal rooms and a foyer which were part of the old 23-room Hancock Palladian-style mansion which stood at the northeast corner of Wilshire and Vermont since before the turn of the century. In 1936 the mansion was dismantled and the aforementioned rooms were taken to the campus, where they were rebuilt and installed on the ground floor of what was to become Hancock Hall. Steel girders were added to support additional floors above, and the four-floor edifice was completed and dedicated in 1940. The rooms in the Hancock Museum range from High Italian Renaissance through Louis XV French Rococo to English Georgian periods, all beautifully furnished, styled, and proportioned.

Campus open throughout the year
Buildings mentioned open daily,
    9:00 A.M.-5:00 P.M.

University Park
Figueroa Street and Exposition Blvd.
Los Angeles 90007

E 16. EXPOSITION PARK

Almost a century ago, the principal use of this site now occupied by the 114-acre Exposition Park, was as a track for horse racing and a place to exhibit farm products. In 1872 the property was deeded by James Thompson to the Southern District Agri-

Exposition Park, looking toward Space Museum (then the Armory), c. 1925.

cultural Society for California, which in 1885 became the 6th Agricultural District. Public spirited members of this organization converted the property into a fair grounds, but their venture ended in failure in 1892. Subsequently, Judge William M. Bowen, the "Father of Exposition Park," became worried that the area was contributing to juvenile delinquency, and in 1898 he undertook to redeem the park from its dilapidated condition. After considerable litigation to clear the title of legal encumbrances, the park was opened with public funds in 1910. Since then, with construction of a complex of museums, and athletic stadiums, a club house, and a seven-acre rose garden, Exposition Park has become a vital cultural and entertainment center for all of southern California. The park is operated jointly by the state, county, and city, and is bounded by Exposition Boulevard, Figueroa Street, S. Park Drive, and Menlo Avenue. Visitors may stroll through the park free of charge at any time. Public transportation available to location.

E 17. EXPOSITION CLUB HOUSE

Since its construction in 1928, this single-story club house in Exposition Park designed in the style of the Spanish Colonial Revival,

has been an integral part of the community and used continuously for many activities sponsored by the City Department of Parks and Recreation. Public transportation available to location.

Weekdays, 9 A.M.-6 P.M.
Saturday, 11 A.M.-5 P.M.
Sunday, 1-5 P.M.

3990 Menlo Avenue
Los Angeles 90037
749-5884

E 18. CALIFORNIA MUSEUM OF SCIENCE AND INDUSTRY

The edifice known today as the Museum of Science and Industry was constructed by the State of California as a display building for agricultural products grown in the area. For thirty-eight years it was called the "Sixth District Agricultural Association." In 1950 the building was transformed into a museum whose purpose is to relate contemporary science and technology to individuals of all ages.

During the past quarter century, attendance has risen from 400,000 per year to 3.3 million. The museum now houses some twenty-six permanent exhibits sponsored by such firms as General Motors and IBM. It presents over sixty temporary exhibits annually and also operates an in-depth educational program.

Open every day 9:30 A.M.-5:00 P.M., except
  Thanksgiving and Christmas
Admission free

700 State Drive
Exposition Park
Los Angeles 90037
749-0101

E 19. ARMORY, EXPOSITION PARK

Of the three principal buildings erected in Exposition Park by 1913, only the Armory remains unchanged in its exterior appearance—a curious circumstance since its architecture is not particularly interesting or noteworthy. It was constructed originally in 1913 as the headquarters for the California National Guard. During World War II it became headquarters for the State Guard Reserve. The military subsequently abandoned the building, which in 1965 was taken over by the nearby State Museum of Science and Industry, to be used for storage, educational programs, and science classes. Recently remodeled inside, it is now officially known as the Space Museum. The second floor houses offices of the California State Museum, and the ground floor contains exhibits of space probes, missiles, as well as various temporary displays.

Space Museum open every day,
  9:30 A.M.-5:00 P.M., except Thanksgiving and Christmas.

700 State Drive
Los Angeles 90037
749-0101

E 20. MUSEUM OF NATURAL HISTORY

When Exposition Park opened in 1910, the original plans included three large structures—a museum and an exposition building, both begun in 1910, and an armory, whose cornerstone was laid in 1913. The Museum of History, Science, and Art, designed in the style of the Spanish Renaissance and in the shape of a cross, cost an estimated quarter million dollars. Since opening in 1913, it has progressively been

County Museum of Natural History

enlarged to an area five times the size of the original structure. Part of the original architecture may still be viewed at the east end of the building facing the rose garden. The museum is the largest of its kind in the West. With completion in 1964 of a New County Museum of Art in Hancock Park, the old museum adopted its present name and function as the Los Angeles County Museum of Natural History. Currently construction is underway on a north wing which will give the museum additional facilities and a new Exposition Blvd. entrance and esplanade.

As one gathers from the name, this is a museum of nature and history. Exhibits of prehistoric fossils, mammals, birds, insects, and minerals have been assembled from southern California and from all over the globe. Special rooms are devoted to American history and American Indians. The California room is under reorganization. A research library houses books relating to the museum's collections. The limited-access archives contain considerable material on southern California, including a large collection of photographs, newspapers, pamphlets, and a few documents and manuscripts. The research library is open to the public from 10:00 A.M. to 4:00 P.M., Tuesday through Friday. The archives are open to serious researchers on Wednesdays and

Thursdays, 1:30 to 4:30 P.M., by appointment *only*.

Open Tuesday-Sunday 10:00 A.M.-5:00 P.M.
Closed Thanksgiving and Christmas
Admission free

900 Exposition Boulevard
Los Angeles 90007
746-0410

Los Angeles Memorial Coliseum, Olympic Games, 1932.

E 21. LOS ANGELES MEMORIAL COLISEUM

A prime factor leading to the construction of the Los Angeles Coliseum was the assurance that if a stadium was built in Exposition Park, the USC football team would play its home games there. Dr. George F. Bovard, president of the University's Board of Trustees, made this promise to his friend Judge William M. Bowen, known as the "Father of Exposition Park." Others whose efforts greatly encouraged the project were *Times* publisher Harry Chandler and William M. Garland, later instrumental in attracting the Olympic Games to Los Angeles in 1932.

During sixteen months, from 1921 to 1923, the firm of Edwards, Wildey and Dixon (now L. E. Dixon Co.) constructed the Coliseum according to plans of architects John and Donald Parkinson. To save excavation costs, the Stadium was built over a large gravel pit, around which a racetrack had formerly circled. The original 75,000 seat Stadium was enlarged in 1930-31 to accommodate the Olympics at an expense of $950,000, almost the same as the cost of the original structure. A capacity crowd of 101,022 witnessed the Opening Ceremonies to the Xth Olympiad in 1932.

The presence of the Coliseum has contributed to the growth of professional sports in Los Angeles. The Cleveland Rams arrived in 1946, the Brooklyn Dodgers in 1958. The 1959 World Series between the Dodgers and the Chicago White Sox was played in the Coliseum. One of the largest crowds ever to see a professional baseball game, 93,103, witnessed a pre-season contest between the Dodgers and the New York Yankees on May 7, 1959, to benefit former Dodger catcher Roy Campanella. Today USC, UCLA, and the Los Angeles Rams football teams use the Coliseum as their home field.

A display of Coliseum memorabilia is on exhibit at the nearby Sports Arena (built in 1959) at the corner of Figueroa Street and Santa Barbara Avenue. At the Coliseum Memorial Court of Honor at the peristyle end of the stadium, one can view bronze plaques commemorating individuals and events that have an historical bearing on the Coliseum.

The Coliseum is open only during events. Entrance fees vary considerably.

3911 South Figueroa Street
Los Angeles 90037
747-7111

E 22. SITE OF THE BIRTHPLACE OF ADLAI E. STEVENSON

When Adlai Ewing Stevenson was about six years old, around 1906, his family moved from California to Illinois. Stevenson subsequently distinguished himself for organizational and diplomatic service during and after World War II, was elected Governor of Illinois in 1948, and was twice nominated as Democratic candidate for the U.S. presidency. He served as Ambassador to the United Nations from 1961 until his death from a heart attack on a London street in 1965.

Today, Adlai Stevenson is widely regarded for his public service, eloquence, and wit, but few people are aware of the fact that he was born in the City of Los Angeles on February 5, 1900, where his father, Lewis Green Stevenson, was assistant general manager of the Los Angeles *Examiner*.

The Stevenson birthplace, built around 1892, originally had ten rooms. Today it is an 18-room, white-colored rooming house for university students, with a stucco-covered, wood-shingled exterior.

Private residence
Not open to the public

2639 Monmouth Avenue
Los Angeles 90007

E 23. SECOND BAPTIST CHURCH

The Second Baptist Church (the first black Baptist church in southern California) was established in a little upper room on Requina Street in downtown Los Angeles in 1885, eleven years after the founding of the (all white) First Baptist Church. Under the dynamic and spirited leadership of Reverend C. H. Anderson, the second pastor

Second Baptist Church

(1887-1907), Second Baptist became the largest and best equipped black church on the Pacific Coast. Notwithstanding this spiritual and financial vitality, there were disagreements and division within the 500-member congregation. Among those Los Angeles churches which left to form their own missions are Mount Zion, Tabernacle, and New Hope Baptist Churches.

The present Second Baptist Church edifice, designed by the renowned black architect, Paul R. Williams, was opened for worship in 1926. Many members of the congregation in the early 1920s helped to construct the impressive new building. John Session, reputed to be one of the finest carpenters in the Los Angeles area, was given special praise for his contribution.

For many years this church was the headquarters for numerous black conventions and mass meetings. The site still serves as a community center, with a social services building at the rear of the church and, across the street, Henderson Youth Center, named for a recent pastor.

Weekdays, 9 A.M.-5 P.M.
Sunday Services: 7:30-9 A.M. and
    11 A.M.-1 P.M.

2412 Griffith Avenue (corner 24th Street)
Los Angeles 90011
748-0318

E 24. SOJOURNER TRUTH HOME

The Sojourner Truth Industrial Club was formed in 1904 in the First African Methodist Episcopal Church of Los Angeles. The organization was named after a former slave named Isabella Baumfree, who, when she was freed, took the new name Sojourner Truth, and devoted her life to bettering conditions for all youth as she "sojourned for truth." The objectives of the club were to establish a home for self- supporting girls and young women on a non-profit basis, and to serve as a much-needed community center for Negro people. For these purposes a 15-room frame structure was built in 1913, where for half a century girls were trained in domestic work and other methods of making a livelihood and supervised until they were accustomed to city life. In addition the club extended courtesies to soldiers during World War I before there was a USO, entertained Negro leaders such as Booker T. Washington when they visited the city, presented prominent speakers, and emphasized black history and culture at their regular meetings.

The Sojourner Truth Industrial Club also acquired club houses with dormitories on Harvard, West Adams, and Crenshaw Boulevard, but only the latter is now in operation. The club's original 1913 structure was sold in 1965 to the Tabernacle of Faith Unity Church.

Worship services are conducted on Sundays from 12 noon to 2:00 P.M.

1119 E. Adams Boulevard
Los Angeles 90011
234-2037

E 25. BIDDY MASON CENTER

The Federation of Black History and Art is planning to convert the former residence of Mrs. Jessie L. Terry, which was built by her husband, Woodford H. Terry, pioneer black contractor, into a museum and community center for black history and culture. No date has been set for the opening.

1152 E. Adams Blvd.
Los Angeles 90011

E 26. LINCOLN THEATER

Lincoln Theater was built as a movie house in 1924 by the Metropolitan Theater Guild of Southern California. In the late 1920s and early 1930s it became the home of the Lafayette Players, a group of Negro actors. In later years it again served as a popular motion picture theater. Eventually, about 1956, Lincoln Theater was occupied by Crouch Temple, Church of God in Christ.

Sunday Service: 11 A.M.

2300 S. Central Avenue
Los Angeles 90021
232-7785

Lincoln Theatre

28th Street YMCA

E 27. 28TH STREET YMCA

For half a century the impressive 28th Street YMCA facility has served the youth and adults of Los Angeles' black community. Involvement of the YMCA with black people in California dates back to 1900, when the Ministerial Alliance, under the leadership of Reverend G. R. Bryant, organized the first YMCA for Negro youth on the Pacific Coast. Thomas Augustus Greene was elected Executive Secretary, and immediately assumed control of the "Y" in Los Angeles. Greene operated three years without a building, and almost two decades elapsed before the "Y" had a facility to match the ambition of its leadership.

Appropriately enough, the 28th Street YMCA building was designed by nationally known Negro architect, Paul R. Williams, a member of the Los Angeles "Y" since his youth. The four-story structure incorporated elements of Spanish design, and its cost was nearly $200,000. Albert Baumann, a prominent Negro druggist in Los Angeles, led the fund-raising drive beginning in 1924, and by 1926 construction was already completed. Philanthropist Julius Rosenwald, president of Sears-Roebuck of Chicago, topped the list with a check for $25,000. a photostatic copy of which has been preserved in the building's archives. Leaders of both racial groups participated in the dedication service in 1926.

More than anything else, however, the 28th Street YMCA building resulted from the patience, sacrifice, and persistent dreaming of Executive Greene. Known as "Professor" to a legion of boys and men, and endeared to the hearts of innumerable friends of both races as "T.A." or "Secretary Greene," he retired in 1932 after 26 years of active service.

Use of athletic and other facilities is limited to members, but the public is welcome to visit any day from 9:00 A.M. to 5:00 P.M. There are also residential quarters, so that part of the building is always open and in use.

Daily, 9 A.M.-5 P.M.

100 E. 28th St.
232-7193

E 28. RALPH BUNCHE RESIDENCE

Ralph Johnson Bunche—Under Secretary, United Nations; recipient of the Nobel Peace Prize, 1950; Citizen of the World—lived here from 1919 to 1927 while he attended John Adams High, Jefferson High, and the University of California at Los Angeles (then known as the Southern Branch). He left Los Angeles to study at Harvard University in 1927, earning his M.A. and Ph.D. in Political Science from that institution.

In the wartime winter of 1917, a 12-year-old Ralph Bunche was traveling around the country with his family. While in Albuquer-

Ralph Bunche Residence

que, New Mexico, his mother, Olive, died. Thomas L. Johnson, Ralph's uncle, came to California the following summer, rented a house on East 32nd Street, and a month later the family arrived in Los Angeles from New Mexico. The house on 32nd Street was too small for the family group which included Ralph's maternal grandmother, Mrs. Thomas Nelson (Lucy) Johnson, his two aunts, Misses Ethel and Nelle Johnson, and his sister, Grace, so the family soon moved to another rented house on Griffith Avenue. In 1919 Ralph's grandmother purchased a home on East 37th Street which was built in 1908. East 37th Street was later changed to East 40th Place by the city in order to reconcile the streets on the east side with those on the west side of the town. The house where young Ralph Bunche used to conjugate French verbs was later converted into a duplex, and two apartments and several garages were constructed on the rear of the property. The Bunche residence was occupied by members of the family until the death of Nelle Johnson, surviving aunt and an author in her own right, in 1975. Four first cousins of Ralph Bunche now own the property.

A memorial plaque will soon be placed in the sidewalk in front of the house.

Private residence
Not open to the public

1221-1223 E. 40th Place
Los Angeles 90011

E 29. THE DUNBAR HOTEL

Originally named the Hotel Somerville by its builder, Dr. John Alexander Somerville, this historic hotel hosted the first national convention of the National Association for the Advancement of Colored People as soon as it opened in June 1928. Dr. Somerville was a pioneer black Los Angeles businessman, professional and cultural leader who had worked his way through the University of Southern California and in 1907 became the first black graduate of the USC School of Dentistry. His wife, Dr. Vada Jetmore Somerville, also graduated from USC's School of Dentistry. According to Somerville's autobiography, the hotel was the first built in America specifically for Negroes and was a direct result of his inability to find hotel or room space when he came to San Francisco from the British West Indies in 1902.

The Dunbar Hotel, 1928

The Somervilles also built the La Vada Apartments in 1927, and the combination of these two new, modern buildings resulted in a new era of building and development on the city's east side.

In the early 1930s, the hotel was renamed the Dunbar when it was purchased by another prominent black community leader, Lucius Lomax. During the hotel's early years almost every prominent black entertainer and athlete who visited Los Angeles is said to have stayed there. There are plans to make the Dunbar Hotel into a museum as an historic-cultural center for the black community.

At present the hotel is not open to visitors.

4225 S. Central Avenue
Los Angeles

E 30. LA MESA BATTLEFIELD

La Mesa Battlefield served as a campsite for the California forces under General José Castro in the summer of 1846, during the United States' occupation of California in the Mexican War. The battle of La Mesa, the last military encounter of the war on the California front, was fought here January 9, 1847. As American forces under Commodore Robert F. Stockton marched toward Los Angeles, they were approached by the Californians under General José María Flores. The ensuing artillery duel at long range lasted several hours. On one or two occasions, the California cavalry charged upon the compact square of the advancing American Army, coming within a hundred yards or less, but did not succeed in breaking it, and were repulsed by musketry. There were some losses, chiefly of animals, on both sides. Flores lost one man killed, and an unknown number wounded; five of Stockton's forces were wounded. The site has been designated a California State Historical Landmark, and is commemorated by a plaque.

4500 Downey Road
Vernon 90058

E 31. FARMER JOHN PIG MURALS

Where else but in Los Angeles would one expect to find enormous and ever expanding murals, thousands of feet in length, devoted exclusively to pigs? Perhaps the question is unfair to the City of the Angels, but few will deny that the "splendidly outrageous" murals surrounding the Farmer John Brand Clougherty Meat Packing Company, conceived and begun about 1957 by Les Grimes, a scenic artist who had worked for local movie studios, have become a notable historical and cultural landmark. Without ignoring the factual mechanics inherent in creating a prodigious billboard on a variety of surfaces up to three stories high, the murals display humanity of workmanship, a blend of innocent and worldly humor, and even an element of surrealism. For example, pigs peer into windows both invented and actual, and packing house hardware and conduits are incorporated into the pastoral panorama.

Les Grimes worked alone and continuously on the murals until 1968, when he fell fifty feet from a scaffold to his death. Since then Arno Jordan, as Austrian immigrant, has been hired to freshen and continue the everlasting pastorale with pigs.

Safety precautions preclude allowing visitors inside the packing house, but the murals can easily be viewed from the street at any time.

3049 E. Vernon Avenue
Vernon 90008
583-4621

E 32. CENTRAL AVENUE, WATTS

During six never-to-be-forgotten days in August 1965, Los Angeles experienced the greatest outburst of frustration and violence in its history. What started with an arrest for a traffic violation at the corner of Avalon and 116th Place spread out roughly along the axis of Central Avenue, eventually affecting an area of 50 square miles, almost the entire black ghetto, with added flare ups in Venice and the Harbor area. Before it was over, the Watts Riot turned into a six-day shootout with snipers on one side and police and national guardsmen on the other. At least 34 persons were killed (31 were black), 1,032 injured, 3,952 arrested, and 3,411 charged with felony or misdemeanor. Fires and looting caused an estimate $40 million property damage. Many who had never stolen or looted before did so with the rationalization that they were collecting something white society had owed them for a long time.

Central Avenue (from Alondra Blvd. on
   the south to Vernon Avenue on the
   north)
Watts

E 33. WATTS STATION

One of the last remaining Pacific Electric stations in Los Angeles, Watts Station was built in 1904 and was the model for other PE stations at Glendora, Covina, and La Habra. Recently the building has been converted to commercial use, but originally it served as a combination freight depot and passenger waiting room and featured a broad portico, Doric columns, and wrought iron ticket window. The Station was Watts' first important building, and it was a community focal point until inter-urban railway service ended in 1958. The big red Watts local was a familiar sight in the downtown area and continued to run long after other PE lines had ceased operations.

1686 E. 103rd Street
Los Angeles 90002

E 34. THE WATTS TOWER

The Watts Towers are perhaps southern California's most remarkable piece of folk art. Working alone from 1921 to 1954, Italian immigrant Simon Rodia erected three immense concrete towers, the center being 104 feet high, surrounded by a wall. Construction material consisted of steel reinforcing rods, wire mesh, and waterproof cement, embedded with broken bottles, sea shells, fragmented china, wood, and imprints of tools and hands, all worked into colorful patterns by Rodia, who left the area after completing his project.

International attention was focused on the Towers in 1959 when the city Building and Safety Department urged their demolition as a safety hazard. Art lovers at home and abroad mounted a campaign to save the Towers, and stress tests verified their stability. Rodia died in July, 1965, in Martinez, California, knowing that his creation had become an important community landmark.

The Watts Towers are owned by a non-profit corporation, The Committee for

The Watts Towers

Simon Rodia's Towers in Watts. Nearby is the Watts Towers Community Art Center, which holds classes in art, music and drama.

Open daily, 9 A.M.-dark
Donation: adults 50¢, children 10¢

1765 E. 107th Street
Watts 90002
564-5169

E 35. LYNWOOD PACIFIC ELECTRIC DEPOT

The Lynwood Pacific Electric Depot was originally a shed-type shelter and bench adjacent to sugar beet fields. In 1917 the old shelter was replaced with a larger station for passenger operation, including a lunch room, at the intersection of Fernwood Avenue and Long Beach Boulevard. The station was built by the Lynwood Company for the Southern Pacific, owners of the Pacific Electric since founder Henry E. Huntington sold out in 1910 in return for other improvements to the intersection by the railroad, which included landfill, site grading, installation of drainage culverts, and relocation of a new cattle yard.

The architecture of the Lynwood Depot is a rare blend of Classical Revival, Mediterranean, and California bungalow styles which were all popular in 1917 but seldom combined in one building. The depot was so solidly built that it survived the 1933 Long Beach earthquake without even a crack in its tile roof. The station was abandoned in 1958 when the Pacific Electric went out of business.

In 1974 it appeared that the Lynwood depot was to be demolished because it stood in the path of the proposed Century (I-105) Freeway. However, in the same year the depot was placed in the National Register of Historic Places. Negotiations are currently underway between the city, state, and local chamber of commerce to have the depot relocated (at state expense) to another site, but it currently still belongs to the Southern Pacific Railroad Company. After the depot is relocated, it may become the home of the Lynwood Chamber of Commerce.

Fernwood and Long Beach Blvd.
Southern Pacific Railroad Company:
  629-6161
Lynwood Chamber of Commerce:
  537-6484

E 36. THE "EAGLE TREE"

One of the oldest landmarks in California, this ancient sycamore tree has for almost two centuries, marked the northern boundary of Rancho San Pedro. For many years it was known as the Eagle Tree because eagles once nested in its huge branches. When Manuel Dominguez received title to his rancho from the United States government in 1857, the Eagle Tree simplified the task of surveyors.

A plaque dedicated by the Compton Parlor of the Native Daughters of the Golden West was placed on this site in 1947. The Eagle Tree stands in a residential section of Compton on a Standard Oil easement, at the corner of Poppy and Short Streets.

E 37. HERITAGE HOUSE

Heritage House is one of the most unfortunate examples in the county of historical preservation gone astray. Identified in 1955 as the "oldest house in Compton," built in 1896 by A. R. Loomis, it was to have been restored "as a tribute to early settlers of the community." Heritage House was marked with a plaque officially designating it as State Historical Landmark No. 664, furnished by local residents, and docent tours established.

Regrettably, Heritage House in its current condition is deteriorating, sitting at the rear of the parking lot adjacent to the Compton City Hall. Its doors and windows are boarded over with plywood, and its paint is almost wholly peeled off, exposing its already badly warped and weather-beaten redwood frame to the elements. Although there are plans to restore Heritage House in the future, quick action appears necessary to preserve the structure.

205 Willowbrook
Compton
Compton City Hall: 537-8000

Angeles Abbey

E 38. ANGELES ABBEY

Out of the Arabian nights comes a piece of architectural imagination. The Angeles Abbey Mausoleum displays columns, domes, turrets, minarets, and decorative grill work in a spacious memorial park. The central chapel is a pure white building a la the Taj Mahal, with a triple-arched entrance. The main building was completed in 1928, and additional structures continue to be erected. The chapel contains a stained glass rendition of Millet's painting "The Angelus." The mausoleum claims to be the "largest of all," and it surely is an oasis of color in an urban environment.

Park open 8:00 A.M. to 5 P.M. daily.
Office hours: 9 A.M. to 4:30 P.M. daily.
Group tours by appointment.

Compton Boulevard just east of Long
   Beach Boulevard
636-6950

NOTES

SECTION F

Southwestern Area (Includes South Bay)

1. Standard Oil Refinery
   324 W. El Segundo Boulevard
   El Segundo
2. Manhattan Beach Pier
   Manhattan Beach
3. Hermosa Beach Strand
   Hermosa Beach
4. Redondo Beach Harbor
   Redondo Beach
5. Old Salt Lake
   North end of Redondo Beach between
   Pacific and Francesca
6. Torrance Historical Society, Post
   Avenue Library
   1345 Post Avenue
   Torrance
7. Southern Pacific Railway Station
   1200 Cabrillo Avenue
   Torrance
8. Lomita Railroad Museum
   250th St. and Woodward Ave.
   Lomita
9. Site of Indian Village of Suang-Na (1)
   Anaheim Street between Gaffey St. and
   Harbor Freeway
10. José Dolores Sepulveda Homesite
    Walteria
11. South Coast Botanic Garden
    26300 Crenshaw Blvd.
    Palos Verdes Peninsula
12. Wayfarer's Chapel
    5755 Palos Verdes Drive South
    Rancho Palos Verdes
13. Portugese Bend
    Palos Verdes
14. Point Fermin Lighthouse
    Point Fermin Park
    San Pedro

15. Cabrillo Marine Museum
    3720 Stephen White Drive
    San Pedro
16. Fort MacArthur
    San Pedro
17. Harbor View Memorial Park and Saint
    Peters Episcopal Church
    24th St. and Grand Ave.
    San Pedro
18. Peck House
    380 W. 15th St.
    San Pedro
19. Dodson House
    859 W. 13th St.
    San Pedro
20. Danish Castle
    324 W. 10th St.
    San Pedro
21. Timms' Landing
    San Pedro
22. Ferry Building
    San Pedro
23. Casino Building
    Avalon
24. Mt. Ada (Wrigley Mansion)
    Avalon
25. Zane Grey Pueblo
    199 Chimes Tower Rd.
    Avalon
26. Eagle's Nest
    Catalina
27. Banning House at Two Harbors
    Catalina
(Sites 23-27 are found on Catalina Island)

San Pedro, 1903.

Construction of wharf, Standard Oil Refinery, El Segundo, 1900s.

F 1. STANDARD OIL REFINERY, EL SEGUNDO

Standard Oil's El Segundo refinery was built by veteran oilman Richard J. Hanna, who selected the 842-acre site, and who became the refinery's first manager and later company treasurer. Hanna's wife chose the name, "El Segundo," and the 1 1/3 square miles of sand dunes and a little farm land became the second town in California which Standard Oil founded as a refining center. Storms destroyed the company's wharf at El Segundo even before it was finished (no land for a refinery was then available at San Pedro), and though the pier was rebuilt it was never safe in rough weather. Today it exists primarily to receive oil imports, for southern California has not been able to supply its own petroleum needs since the 1950s.

When El Segundo began production in 1911, it was a small and simple affair, with fifteen crude oil stills to furnish southern California with gasoline and kerosene. Constructed even before the company acquired substantial oil holdings in the region, it has grown into one of the largest refineries in the West, with giant tanks, towers, and a maze of pipes which has been called "a plumber's nightmare."

Smudge for heating orange groves on frosty nights was first produced in 1913, a natural gas plant installed in 1916, and a company hospital opened in 1918. In 1919 Standard Oil's El Segundo and Richmond refineries produced 1/5 of the oil lubricants used in the United States. That year El Segundo exported 3.6 million barrels of kerosene, an all-time record, but the company's future was clearly in gasoline for automobiles.

Tours of the refinery may be arranged by contacting the company's department of public relations.

324 West El Segundo Boulevard
El Segundo 90245
322-3450

F 2. MANHATTAN BEACH PIER

The community of Manhattan Beach began as a cluster of beach cottages lying between the Santa Fe and Pacific Electric Railways shortly after the turn-of-the-century. Two wooden piers were constructed in 1902, one later demolished by storms. The pier at Center Street (now Manhattan Beach Boulevard) supported a wave generator to produce electric power from the surf of Santa Monica Bay; for a brief time it lit the Strand.

Manhattan Beach Pier with extension, 1930s.

The city incorporated in 1912. Between 1916 and 1919 three bond issues were passed to raise $140,000 for a new pier. Lack of materials during World War I delayed construction, but eventually timbers were unloaded offshore, floated in along the beach, and dragged by mules to the construction site. The pier extends a thousand feet from shore; at its seaward end it supports an octagon building familiar to generations of South Bayans. A wooden extension added in 1927 was used by commercial fishermen and some pleasure boats; the locale is aptly described in one of Raymond Chandler's short stories. The extension was battered by storms in 1938 and destroyed in 1940.

In the winter of 1952 pier facilities were temporarily roped off after another storm tore out one of the pilings. When the state renovated the pier in 1959-60, the $300,000. cost was more than twice that originally spent to build the pier.

North from the pier stretches a flat right-of-way which originally was leveled for the P. E. Red Cars running along the beach from Playa del Rey to Redondo. Now it supports a segment of the Santa Monica to Palos Verdes bicycle path. One mile north of the pier are located remnants of sand dunes which served as the locale for filming many desert movies of the silent screen era.

Strand, Hermosa Beach with an undeveloped Palos Verdes in background, c. 1930.

lished this scenic walkway in 1908, it covered just three blocks, from 11th to 13th Streets. The name officially was changed from *Esplanado* to the Strand in 1909, and in 1922 all of the shoreline walkway excepting 10th and 15th Streets was zoned for residential use only. The city prohibited construction of churches, schools, or sanitariums along the Strand in 1941.

In the immediate postwar period, Pier Avenue west from the Strand established Hermosa Beach as a well-known center of jazz music, particularly of the "cool" variety. In the 1950s, poetry read to music, bookstores and coffeehouses attracted large numbers of young people to the area.

To reach the Strand from the San Diego Freeway, exit at Artesia, drive west to Pier Avenue, and follow it about two miles to the municipal pier.

F 3. HERMOSA BEACH STRAND

For almost two miles along the Pacific shoreline, the Hermosa Beach Strand stretches from one end of the city to the other, a typical concrete boardwalk which attracts both residents and tourists for bicycling, jogging, volleyball, and social activities. Southern California's "beach culture" can be observed here.

When the city of Hermosa Beach estab-

F 4. REDONDO BEACH HARBOR

The harbor at Redondo Beach is one of history's "might-have-beens." In the 1890s it appeared that the harbor might become Los Angeles' commercial outlet to the sea. Ocean-going vessels anchored off-shore, goods from Asia and the Pacific slope were unloaded on its wharves, a luxury hotel

Redondo Beach Hotel and Bath House, 1890s.

stood on the hill to welcome visitors, and railroad tracks ran from Los Angeles through Redondo out onto its docks. It was one of three harbors in the region (along with Santa Monica and San Pedro) considered by Congress for federal funds for harbor dredging and improvement. But San Pedro received the harbor and Redondo became a resort community, terminus of three railroad lines, including the Pacific Electric. An amusement park and massive indoor salt-water plunge entertained generations of Angelenos. During prohibition, entertainment boats frequented waters of the Bay beyond the three-mile limit.

By the time of World War II, the Red Cars were gone and the amusement park declined and became somewhat seedy. City officials determined to undertake a harbor development. With some federal aid garnered by Congressman Cecil King, but mostly through efforts of local businessmen, the entire harbor area was renovated. In the 1960s there were added pleasure boating facilities, hotels and restaurants. King Harbor today bears little resemblance to the bustling commercial port of the 90s, but the city of Redondo Beach, founded in 1892, remains the largest and most important of the communities along the South Bay.

F 5. OLD SALT LAKE

Indians from this area used to obtain salt from this lake. Sometime in the 1850s, Johnson and Allanson erected the necessary works to manufacture salt by artificial as well as solar evaporation. The peak salt yield was achieved in 1879, when 450 tons were produced. This site has been declared a state historic landmark and is commemorated by a plaque.

North end of Redondo Beach between Pacific Avenue and Francesca Avenue

Area of the Old Salt Lake as it is today

F 6. TORRANCE HISTORICAL SOCIETY, POST AVENUE LIBRARY

The City of Torrance was founded in 1913 by developer Jared S. Torrance, who purchased 3,500 acres from Rancho San Pedro to construct a model industrial-residential town. A group of civic buildings were constructed in the 1930s by the W. P. A.; two of these remain: the old City Hall, which is now a bank, and the original library on Post Avenue.

The Post Avenue library houses the collection of the local historical society, which consists primarily of photos, some books, and a few documents and manuscripts, but has ambitious plans for expansion

Library hours
Monday-Thursday, 11 A.M.-3 P.M.
Friday 11 A.M.-2 P.M.

1345 Post Avenue
Torrance
328-5392

F 7. SOUTHERN PACIFIC RAILWAY STATION, TORRANCE

In 1913 Olmsted and Olmsted, sons of Frederick Law Olmsted, famous park planner, were commissioned to lay out the town of Torrance as a model industrial community. Several companies, including Pacific Electric, had received a franchise from the Dominguez Land Corporation to use 700 acres on which to build a civic center, a railway station, shops, and houses for their employees. Architect Irving Gill moved his office from San Diego to Los Angeles, and within a year designed a bridge into the city, A Pacific Electric Station, two office buildings, and hundreds of cottages. The larger structures were constructed, but only ten of the cottages were completed because of labor difficulties and public hostility to Gill's pioneering use of concrete, with its

extreme simplicity and economy. Work on Gill's concrete houses ceased, and traditional wood houses were erected.

Gill's graceful three-arched bridge still carries freight into Torrance, and the long, low Pacific Electric station has become a Southern Pacific freight office. No trains are visible from the street, for the tracks are behind the station and below street level.

1200 Cabrillo Avenue
Torrance 91320
328-6322

F 8. LOMITA RAILROAD MUSEUM

The Lomita Railroad Museum was built by Irene Lewis for the City of Lomita. It was constructed in 1966 by John Gallareto on land donated by Mrs. Lewis, and modeled after the Greenwood Station in Wakefield, Massachusetts. Adjacent to the museum are a full-sized steam locomotive and tender purchased by the City of Lomita and a caboose donated by the Union Pacific Railroad. Mrs. Lewis and the City of Lomita split the cost of a lot on the corner of Woodward and 250th Street, put in brick walks and a fountain, and installed a box car where audio-visual railroad films will be shown.

Southern Pacific Railway Station Torrance

Lomita Railroad Museum

The museum exhibits equipment used in the age of steam railroading.

From the Harbor Freeway take Pacific Coast Highway offramp west three miles to Narbonne Avenue; go north to 250th Street and east one block to the N.E. corner of Woodward and 250th Street.

Museum open Wednesday-Sunday
  10:00 A.M.-5:00 P.M.
Admission 50¢

250th Street and Woodward Avenue
Lomita 90717
326-6255

F 9. SITE OF INDIAN VILLAGE OF SUANG-NA

Overlooking Lake Machado, now called Bixby Slough, where the Union Oil Refinery now stands, the populous Indian village of Suang-na is believed to have stood for hundreds of years. Suang-na, which meant "Place of the Rushes," a large and important rancheria, was one of a half-dozen Gabrielino Indian villages clustered around San Pedro Bay. Individual families lived in circular dwellings constructed of a willow framework and thatched with tule or grass. When Juan Sepulveda, one of the original owners of Rancho Palos Verdes, built his home in the 1850s on a nearby hill overlooking the lake, the Indian village was still there. With the advent of Americanization, the Gabrielinos eventually became extinct. On the site today are located the huge, round tanks of Union Oil, one of which has become a landmark, painted orange as a huge Halloween pumpkin.

The Suang-na plaque is located on the northeast slope of hills above what is now Anaheim Street between Gaffey Street and the Harbor Freeway.

F 10. JOSÉ DOLORES SEPÚLVEDA HOMESITE

By 1810, Juan José Sepúlveda, father of José Dolores, had obtained permission to graze cattle off that part of Rancho San Pedro which eventually was to belong to the Sepúlvedas. José Dolores Sepúlveda built his adobe home in 1818, more than a decade before the land officially was granted to his family. In an attempt to secure title, he journeyed to Monterey in 1824; on his return he stopped at Mission La Purísima, where he was shot fatally by an arrow during a neophyte-Indian uprising.

Don José's death did not diminish the family's ardour to acquire the land, and despite several notices served by government officials to vacate Palos Verdes, and the hostility of the Dominguez family, the Sepúlvedas refused to leave. Finally in 1834, ten years after José's death, his sons were granted Rancho Palos Verdes by Governor Figueroa on the basis of a quarter century of continued use.

Palos Verdes literally translated means "green sticks," freely translated, "green trees." In terms of contemporary landmarks, the Ranch was bounded by Sepulveda Blvd. on the north, Figueroa Street and the harbor on the east, and Pacific Ocean on the south and west. (The hill is believed to have been an island when water covered the Los Angeles basin.) The grant included the future cities of Lomita and Harbor City, part of Torrance, and all of the Palos Verdes Peninsula, including San Pedro.

The exact location of the 1818 adobe is not verified, but published authorities place it at the foot of the Palos Verdes hill near Walteria, just off Crenshaw Boulevard. The adobe is long gone, but a stand of gnarled old pepper trees at the mouth of a canyon into which Madison street runs is the supposed spot.

A visit to the site alone probably is not worth the effort, but it could be combined with a stop at the botanic garden and a drive west on Palos Verdes Drive to two locations which very nearly qualify as historic places: Malaga Cove Plaza, built in the 1920s and featuring a Fountain of Neptune that is a copy of a famous bronze fontana in Bologna, Italy, and which itself stood for 100 years in a courtyard near Venice before being transplanted to Palos Verdes in 1929; and venerable La Venta Inn, built in 1921-23 by architect Walter Davis, and a favorite luncheon spot (reservations: 378-5258) which has stood high on a hill overlooking the Plaza and the bay for a half-century.

F 11. SOUTH COAST BOTANIC GARDEN

A quarter-century ago this site was nothing more than a dump for trash. Planting by the Los Angeles County Department of Arboreta and Botanic Gardens began in 1961 on the east side of this site four years after trash was dumped there. At this time the Garden was developed to approximately three-fifths of its present size. As refuse dumping moved west, garden planting followed.

Ornamental trees and shrubs from every continent except Antarctica can be viewed in the Botanic Garden. It also includes a collection of cactus and succulents, and many plants from South Africa and Australia. Originally an experiment in landfill, it has become a model for how to reclaim lands used for refuse cut and fill dumping.

South Coast Botanic Garden is twenty-one miles southwest of downtown Los Angeles. Take the Harbor Freeway south to Pacific Coast Highway offramp; go west on PCH four miles from the intersection of PCH to Crenshaw Boulevard and turn south. The entrance is one mile from the intersection of PCH and Crenshaw. At present there is no public transportation closer than one mile.

The Garden is open daily
9:00 A.M.-5:00 P.M., except Christmas.

26300 Crenshaw Blvd.
Palos Verdes Peninsula 90274
377-0468

F 12. WAYFARER'S CHAPEL

The Wayfarer's Chapel was built in 1949-51 by the Swedenborgian Church as a national memorial to Emanuel Swedenborg, to serve as a chapel for meditation and prayer for wayfarers. Architect Lloyd Wright designed the chapel which is built of glass, redwood, and local stone.

Wayfarer's Chapel

The Chapel, often referred to as the "glass church," is a popular location for weddings because of the spectacular beauty of the site overlooking the ocean on the Palos Verdes Peninsula. Gardens tastefully landscaped with flowering shrubs and evergreen trees enhance the magnificence of the setting.

A Visitors' Center connected to the Chapel by a colonnade houses a large Bible diorama designed by Lloyd Wright, and exhibits of Swedenborg's contributions to religious thought, and a library of Swedenborgian literature.

The RTD runs a bus from Long Beach to Marineland, with a stop at the Wayfarers' Chapel. There is no entrance fee, and the Chapel is open every day of the year from 11:00 A.M. to 4:00 P.M.

5755 Palos Verdes Drive South
Rancho Palos Verdes 90274
377-1650

F 13. PORTUGUESE BEND

Whaling was pursued by enterprising New Englanders in the Pacific long before the acquisition of California. The dangerous but lucrative business of shore whaling developed in 1851, and eventually there was a string of whaling stations along the coast from Half Moon Bay to Baja California. One of these was Portuguese Bend, so named because most of the hardy whalers were Portuguese. The area was abandoned in the 1880s, not because of any lack of gray whales but because of a shortage of fuel with which to render blubber into oil.

The mile-long strip of Portuguese Bend is one of the most geologically unstable areas in southern California. A period of renewed movement beginning in 1956 destroyed approximately 100 homes, a symbolic testimonial to the lack of planning which has characterized most of southern California's growth. The rate of land movement reached a peak in 1957 of slightly over an inch a day, but slippage has slowed subsequently to several inches a year.

Half a mile west of Portuguese Bend is Abalone Cove, reputedly the rendezvous for Yankee smugglers for many years during the decades preceeding the American conquest.

The site of the old whaling station is commemorated by an historic plaque, located along the Palos Verdes Drive 2.5 east of Point San Vicente. Take Harbor Freeway south to Gaffey, Gaffey to the ocean and drive west.

F 14. POINT FERMIN LIGHTHOUSE

Four thousand dollars were appropriated as early as 1858 to build a government lighthouse at the southern tip of San Pedro Harbor. Not until 1874, however, did construction actually begin, when lumber and bricks were brought around Cape Horn by sailing ship. For its time the lighthouse was a palatial structure, replete with gimcrackery and surmounted with a cupola fitted with a 2,100 candlepower light. Miss Mary L. Smith, the first lighthouse keeper, lived with her sister, but they gave up the lonely occupation because there were no other settlers nearer than Wilmington. In the 1880s when Captain George Shaw was keeper, the lighthouse was the scene of many parties.

Oil lamps were used to signal approaching ships until 1925, when they were replaced with a new electric light which projected a 6,000 candlepower beam 18 miles out to sea. During World War II, the Coast Guard, for security purposes, turned off the light and painted the gleaming white building "war-

Point Fermin Lighthouse

time green.'' After the war the light remained off, and radar and direction finders took over sentry and signaling duties. The structure fell into disuse, eventually becoming a fixture of a 28-acre park, an expanse of tree shaded lawns, sheltered pergolas, a prominade along the edge of the palisade, and a picnic ground. The park bears the name of Point Fermin, which was named in 1793 by English Captain George Vancouver in honor of Fermín Francisco de Lasuén, *padre presidente* of the Franciscan missions. This vantage point atop the rugged bluffs affords a magnificent view of the ocean.

The lighthouse is in Point Fermin Park at the extreme southern end of Gaffey Street. From the end of the Harbor Freeway continue south on Highway 11 (Gaffey Street) for about three miles. By bus take Pacific Avenue south to the end of the line at Shepherd Street, get off and walk three blocks west.

Although the lighthouse has long been closed to the public, it is hoped that in the near future it may be reopened as a museum. The original cupola has been reconstructed, and a search is being made for the original lantern.

Point Fermin Park
Gaffey Street and Paseo del Mar
San Pedro

F 15. CABRILLO MARINE MUSEUM

In 1934 local beach lifeguards established a small collection of marine specimens in one room of the Venice Beach Bath House. Dr. William Lloyd, a W. P. A. worker and a retired dentist, was hired to curate the collection. He moved it to the central room of the Cabrillo Beach Bath House (built in 1928-29) which became the Cabrillo Beach Marine Museum. Low budget exhibits were displayed, dried specimens in shoe boxes, pickled ones in mayonnaise jars.

Cabrillo Marine Museum

Cabrillo Museum, interior

The outside arcade immediately south of the Spanish-style Cabrillo Bath House was enclosed in 1939 and transformed into the Fish Hall of the Museum. John Olguin, captain of the Cabrillo Beach Lifeguards, was appointed acting director upon Dr. Lloyd's retirement in 1949, and began to give impromptu talks to visiting school groups. Two years later the Bath House's second floor, a dance hall, was converted into the Maritime Hall, in which numerous displays collected largely through the efforts of San Pedro's Thirty Year Club are exhibited.

The tidepool area immediately south and west of Cabrillo Beach was established in 1969 as the Point Fermin Marine Life Refuge by the California legislature. John Olguin began the Whalewatch Program in 1972, co-sponsored by the American Cetacean Society, which takes groups to sea in boats to observe the winter migration of the California Gray Whales.

Marine biological exhibits include a sea water aquaria, with local fishes and invertebrates, models of local fishes, including sharks, whales, dolphin, porpoise and shore bird dioramas, marine fossils, and over 15,000 foreign and local sea shells. Maritime exhibits include nautical instruments, marine artifacts, ship models, ship tools, and historical photographs of San Pedro. Indian artifacts discovered at Malaga Cove are included in the archaeological exhibits. Paintings tracing the history of San Pedro decorate the walls. More than 150,000 visit the museum each year.

Take the Harbor Freeway to Pacific Avenue, south three miles to Stephen M. White Drive. RTD buses run from 6th Street and Harbor Boulevard in San Pedro to Pacific and 36th Street, one block west of the museum.

The Los Angeles City Department of Parks and Recreation operates the Cabrillo Beach Museum.

Monday-Saturday, 9 A.M.-5 P.M.
Sunday, 12 noon-4 P.M.
Closed Thanksgiving and Christmas
Schoolday mornings reserved for school groups.

3720 Stephen White Drive
San Pedro 90731
831-3207

F 16. FORT MACARTHUR

Fort MacArthur occupies three separate parcels of land totaling several hundred acres stretching from Western Avenue on the west almost to 22nd Street on the east. Toward the end of the Mexican era, when Governor Figueroa and Alvarado established the boundaries between Ranchos Palos Verdes and San Pedro, they decreed that a substantial amount of land along the beach of San Pedro and inland be left open for common pasturage and commercial transportation. Their decrees later proved to be the legal cornerstone for President Cleveland's 1888 executive order placing this area under government jurisdiction for future use as a military reservation. A small portion of this property had already become the site of a customs warehouse in 1880; not until shortly before World War I, however, did the U.S. War Department begin development of the area for military purposes. In 1914 the post was officially named in honor of Lt. Gen. Arthur MacArthur, father of Douglas MacArthur, who later commanded American forces in the Pacific during World War II.

In the summer of 1976 the Republic of Korea erected on the south slope an Asian-style belfry to house a "Friendship Bell," commemorating the bicentennial of the United States.

The so-called Upper Reservation of the Fort on the upper slopes of the Palos Verdes Hills behind Paseo del Mar and Gaffey Street, contains the Osgood Farley gun emplacement, constructed in 1917, which has been designated an historic monument and is to be preserved within a 20-acre site set aside for this purpose.

At sea level, east of the Upper Reservation, is the Lower Reservation, developed during World War II as a reception center but subsequently used as a training center for amphibious landing troops and military engineers. This section of the fort was also of major importance to America's coastal defense, overlooking the West Channel, bristling with anti-aircraft artillery, railroad guns with 40 foot barrels, and the derricks used to feed them heavy shells.

At present Fort MacArthur is still owned by the federal government but part of the land has been donated for future use as an historic and recreational park.

Fort MacArthur
San Pedro 90731
831-7211

F 17. HARBOR VIEW MEMORIAL PARK AND SAINT PETER'S EPISCOPAL CHURCH

Many local pioneers are buried in this old cemetery. August Timms deeded the property to the City of San Pedro for a cemetery in 1883, but there is record of an earlier burial dated 1879. Timms himself is buried here. The Sepúlveda family reserved a corner on which stands the Rudecinda Mausoleum.

St. Peter's Episcopal Church, the oldest church in San Pedro, was moved here in 1958, deconsecrated, and rededicated as a memorial chapel. Constructed originally in 1883 on Nob Hill between 2nd and 3rd Streets the church edifice was later moved to 10th and Mesa Street before finally being located at its present site. Bus transportation runs along Pacific Avenue a block east of the cemetery.

Weekly Sunday concerts are held in St. Peter's Memorial Church. They are provided free of charge by the Department of Recreation and Parks. Both church and cemetery are closed at night.

24th Street and Grand Avenue
San Pedro 90731

F 18. PECK HOUSE

This residence was built in 1887 for George Peck, a leading developer and benefactor of San Pedro. For many years it was the scene of important business and social events. It stood originally in a block of fine houses in the Nahah Settlement overlooking Timms' Landing. Much of this area was cut away in the twentieth century as part of the Standard Oil development of the Outer Harbor just east of 15th Street and Crescent Drive. The Peck House was moved to its present location in 1915, and has subsequently been altered and used for income rentals. Bus transportation on Pacific Avenue runs within 1 1/2 blocks of the Peck House.

Private residence
Not open to the public

380 W. 15th Street
San Pedro 90731

San Pedro, 1903.

F 19. DODSON HOUSE

This house was built in 1888 by the Sepúlveda family of Rancho Palo Verdes as a wedding present for their daughter Rudecinda. Her husband, James Dodson, was a merchant and one-time postmaster. Rudecinda Dodson dwelled in the home for the duration of her long life, becoming a notable local figure in San Pedro. She donated the clubhouse for the San Pedro Women's Club that stood at the corner of 11th and Gaffey Streets until recently, when it burned and had to be demolished.

One of San Pedro's best examples of Victorian architecture, the Dodson house was originally located at the corner of 7th and Beacon Streets; since then it has been moved twice, and is currently undergoing restoration.

Private residence
Not open to the public

859 W. 13th Street
San Pedro 90731

F 20. DANISH CASTLE

This striking example of the diversity of southern California's architectural heritage was modeled after a Danish prototype and

Danish Castle

constructed for a Danish sea captain named Jensen in the 1880s. Sailors nicknamed it the Danish Castle, and many colorful stories are associated with it. Bus transportation is available along Pacific Avenue, 2 1/2 blocks to the west.

Private residence
Not open to the public

324 W. 10th Street
San Pedro 90731

F 21. TIMMS' LANDING (SEPÚLVEDA LANDING)

The town of San Pedro traces its origin to a crude dock and landing built in 1835 by the Sepúlveda brothers, José Loreto, and Juan, in order to trade hides and tallow for the wondrous goods brought by Yankee sailing ships. In *Two Years Before the Mast* (1840) Richard Henry Dana described his efforts at San Pedro to get the hides up and over the nearby cliffs, across several hundred feet of shallow, rocky surf, and out to his ship anchored far offshore.

The Sepúlveda brothers later started a stagecoach line which ran from the "har-

Timm's Landing from Terminal Island, c. 1895

bor" to the pueblo of Los Angeles, and they sold the landing to August Timms in 1852. Timms gave his name to the landing, as well as nearby Timms' Point, formerly known as San Pedro Point. In 1881 the Southern Pacific extended the Los Angeles and San Pedro Railroad on pilings from Wilmington across the lagoon to Timms' Point and for the first time freight and passenger trains could reach deep water.

With the construction of Los Angeles Harbor in the twentieth century, the coastline was altered beyond recognition. A plaque at the corner of 14th and Beacon Streets at the base of the old cliffs marks the site of the original wharf.

F 22. FERRY BUILDING, SAN PEDRO

From 1941 until a decade ago, an auto ferry crossed the channel from San Pedro to Terminal Island at frequent intervals. It served navy personnel, fishing industry employees, and people who wished to avoid the long circuitous route through Wilmington and industrial Long Beach. Before construction of the ferry, in the nineteenth and early twentieth centuries, small skiffs made the crossing to Terminal Island.

The Ferry Building is at the foot of 6th Street and the Los Angeles Main Chan-

nel in San Pedro, just north of Ports of Call. From the Harbor Freeway, exit at Pacific Avenue, go south to 6th, turn left (east), and proceed a half-mile. Ports of Call is accessible by bus from most parts of Long Beach and San Pedro. At present the Ferry Building is closed, but efforts are being made to convert it into a Maritime Museum, with a fine view of the harbor as an added bonus for tourists and sightseers.

F 23. CASINO BUILDING

In a setting so rustic and beautiful as Catalina Island it is remarkable to encounter a massive architectural landmark as strikingly daring as the Casino building. Conspicuously ensconced on the jutting northwest promontory of Avalon Bay, the Casino is said to be the first completely circular edifice erected in modern times. Los Angeles architects Weber and Spaulding utilized cantilevered construction, ornamented in a modern adaptation of the Mediterranean style. The Casino was built from 1927 to 1929 under the supervision of D. M. Renton at a cost of $2 million—a stupendous sum of money at that time, especially when one con-

Avalon Harbor with Casino Building

siders that the entire island was valued in 1934 at less than $6 million. The Southern California chapter of the American Institute for Architects awarded the Casino building its Honor Award for "exceptional merit" in 1930.

Though it has but two floors, with a mezzanine in between, the Casino is equal in height to a 12-story building, formerly the skyscraper limit for the city of Los Angeles. The upper floor has a diameter of 158 feet, with a capacity of nearly 3,000 dancers, and the 20,000 square foot dance floor is inlaid in seven hardwoods. The big-name bands of the 1930s, featuring Benny Goodman, Bob Crosby, Ray Noble, Kay Kyser, Jan Garber, and Ben Bernie, broadcast from the Casino ballroom over coast-to-coast networks.

The auditorium on the main floor of the Casino seated 1,200 and was the first theater acoustically engineered for the showing of motion pictures. Movie tycoons Cecil B. de Mille, Louis B. Mayer, Samuel Goldwyn, and Joseph Schenck crossed the channel in their palatial yachts to preview their new talking-picture epics.

In the lobby are nine vividly colorful futuristic mural panels, each 10 × 25 feet which depicts the denizens of the forest, mountain crag, and undersea world. The interior decoration utilized 22,000 square feet of silver leaf, 500 square feet of 22-karat gold leaf, and 4,500 square feet of black walnut paneling. The 105,000 roofing tiles, as well as the patio floor tiles and glazed wall tiles, were all made on Catalina Island, as was the wrought iron of the balconies.

Since 1953 the main floor of the Casino has been devoted to the Catalina Island Museum Society, which preserves and displays pictures and photographs, specimens of flora and fauna, semiprecious stones found on the island, marine specimens, and an Indian room with relics of the extinct Channel Indians.

Museum open daily in summer months
   1:00-4:00 P.M. and 8:00-10:00 P.M.;
   rest of year, weekends 2:00-4:00 P.M.

F 24. MT. ADA (WRIGLEY MANSION)

Mt. Ada was formerly the Avalon residence of Mr. and Mrs. William Wrigley, Jr., of Chicago, who acquired ownership of most of Catalina Island in 1919. Wrigley personally selected the location because it provided maximum sunshine, an excellent view of Avalon, protection from the wind, and ease of access. He named the site for his wife, Ada.

Before construction began in 1921, it was necessary to level off the mountain peak, which is approximately 350 feet above sea level, and bring in much top soil for landscaping. Black powder was used to blast out the rock, and mules pulling fresnos (scrapers) graded the site, together with much hand labor. A concrete retaining wall, nearly one-half mile in length and in some cases over 10 feet high, was built around the

Wrigley Mansion

perimeter of the roadway leading to Mt. Ada, at a cost nearly equal to that of the residence itself.

The colonial architecture of the house presents the appearance of a two-story square structure but actually is L-shaped with a patio and circle driveway in the rear leading to the main entrance. There are 22 rooms and 7 baths in the main residence with 11 rooms in the former servants quarters adjacent to the rear. For therapeutic reasons, and partly due to the lack of fresh water, the baths had both hot and cold salt water from the ocean, as well as fresh water. The house contains valuable antiques which once furnished the Banning house in Two Harbors.

Wrigley died in 1932, but his wife continued to use Mt. Ada until she became ill while at her Pasadena residence (now headquarters for the Tournament of Roses Association) where she was confined until her death in 1958. In 1975 the Santa Catalina Island Company, a non-profit operating foundation, acquired title to about 86 percent of the island's 76 square miles.

The house has not been available for viewing because Mr. Philip Wrigley felt that it did not look as it did when the family occupied it and that it should not be opened to the general public until it was properly restored. The grounds of Mt. Ada, however, which originally were landscaped by Albert Conrad, Wrigley's head gardener at his Pasadena residence, are visited daily on the 50 minute Scenic Terrace Drive from Avalon.

F 25. ZANE GREY PUEBLO

Six years after moving to California, Western writer Zane Grey and his family built a summer home on Catalina Island. Completed in 1924, the "pueblo" adapted the style of a Hopi Indian compound, com-

Zane Grey Pueblo (two views)

prising three units—a main house, an adjoining house, and a garage with an upstairs apartment. Here, along with Grey's wife and children, lived his eldest brother Ellsworth and wife, his younger brother Homer C. Grey, and his sister, Ada. The famous author of Western stories had his study in the big house which had a long hall dividing the bedrooms overlooking the ocean and those overlooking the hills. A large living and dining room was graced by a fireplace with a long mantle, open beam ceilings, a hewn plank door, and an oak dining table with heavy benches. The teak beams were brought by Grey from Tahiti on one of his fishing trips. Workmen from the time of construction reported that goat's milk was added to the mortar.

Grey spent much of his later life in his Avalon home, writing and fishing until his death in 1939 at the age of 67.

The Zane Grey Pueblo is now a hotel. Guest rooms and a pool have been added between the big houses and the adjoining Homer Grey dwelling.

199 Chimes Tower Road
Avalon 90704
510-0966

F 26. EAGLE'S NEST

Eagle's Nest Lodge, located on Catalina Island beneath a clump of cottonwoods at the old Indian campsite of Eagle's Nest, was built some time before the turn of the century to lodge sheep herders. With construction of the stage coach line in 1897 and 1898, horses were changed here on the way from Avalon to the Isthmus, meals served, and, at times, overnight lodging quarters were made available. Even before automobiles replaced the stages in 1914, the Eagle's Nest had become a favorite headquarters for goat hunters. Today it is a stop-over on the Inland Tour on the road between Huddle Ranch and Little Harbor.

Eagle's Nest Stage Station

The 3 hour and 45 minute Inland Motor Tour leaves Avalon daily at 9 A.M. the year round, with additional departures during the summer months.

F 27. BANNING HOUSE AT TWO HARBORS

Judge Joseph Brent Banning was one of three brothers who owned Santa Catalina Island from 1892 until 1919, when it became the property of the Wrigley family. About 1909, Banning built a rambling hacienda on a knoll overlooking Two Harbors at the isthmus. Until 1914, the house served as the terminus of the stagecoach from Avalon. For many years the hacienda was the scene of brilliant social affairs, with guests from the mainland brought across the channel aboard the Banning steam yacht *Campanero*.

Judge Banning's brother, Captain William Banning, who also lived in the house, collected antique furniture which included four-poster beds, beautifully carved settees, chairs, and a captain's desk, all of which were brought around Cape Horn in the nineteenth century. Several decades ago, these furnishings were removed from the Banning house to the Wrigley mansion atop Mt. Ada.

Today modern cottages have been added to the former Banning home, which is now a popular guest house during the summer and a rendezvous for hunters of wild boar, goat, and quail, during the hunting season.

September-May: open daily, 8 A.M.-5 P.M.
June-August: daily, 8 A.M.-8 P.M.

For information regarding regularly scheduled 5 hour and 40 minute boat trips from Avalon to Two Harbors, contact:

Visitors' Information and Services Center,
302 Crescent Avenue
Avalon 90704
Phone: 510-2500

NOTES

SECTION G

Southern Area (Includes Long Beach)

1. Manuel Dominguez Home, Rancho San Pedro
   18127 S. Alameda St.
   Compton
2. Domingez Air Meet Site
   1000 E. Victoria St.
   Carson
3. Site of Suang-na Indian Village (2)
   Watson Industrial Park
4. Vincent Thomas Bridge
   430 N. Seaside Ave.
   Terminal Island
5. Fish Harbor
   Terminal Island
6. Wilmington-San Pedro-Long Beach Shipyards
   Harbor area
7. General Phineas Banning Residence
   401 E. "M" St.
   Wilmington
8. Wilmington Cemetery
   605 E. "O" St.
   Wilmington
9. St. John's Episcopal Church
   1537 Neptune Ave.
   Wilmington
10. Calvary Presbyterian Church
    1160 N. Marine Ave.
    Wilmington
11. Drum Barracks Officers Quarters
    1053 Cary Ave.
    Wilmington
12. Drum Barracks Powder Magazine
    561 Opp St.
    Wilmington
13. Rancho Los Cerritos
    4600 Virginia Rd.
    Long Beach
14. Long Beach and Sunnyside Cemeteries
    1095 E. Willow St.
    Long Beach
15. Alamitos No. 1
    Signal Hill
16. The Bembridge House
    953 Park Circle Dr.
    Long Beach
17. First Congregational Church
    3rd St. and Cedar Ave.
    Long Beach
18. Long Beach Public Library
    Pacific and Ocean Blvds.
    Long Beach
19. Queen's Pike Amusement Park
    444 W. Ocean Blvd.
    Long Beach
20. The Queen Mary
    Pier J
    Long Beach
21. Villa Riviera Apartments
    800 E. Ocean Blvd.
    Long Beach
22. Pacific Coast Club
    850 E. Ocean Blvd.
    Long Beach
23. Long Beach Museum of Art
    2300 Ocean Blvd.
    Long Beach
24. Rancho Los Alamitos
    6400 Bixby Hill Rd.
    Long Beach
25. Puvunga Indian Village Sites
    6400 Bixby Hill Rd. and
    California State University, Long Beach
26. Marine Stadium
    Long Beach
27. Naples (Long Beach)

Rainbow Pier, Long Beach, 1936.

G 1. MANUEL DOMINGUEZ HOME, RANCHO SAN PEDRO

First among all the Spanish land grants in California was 76,000 acres given by Governor Pedro de Fages to Juan José Dominguez in 1784. Nearly a dozen cities were eventually carved out of Rancho San Pedro, as the Dominguez grant was known, including parts of Los Angeles and Long Beach, as well as Compton, Gardena, Torrance, Redondo Beach, Hermosa Beach, and Carson. The original grant also included the Palos Verdes Peninsula and what later became Los Angeles Harbor.

Juan Dominguez was a bachelor and retired soldier who had been with Portolá in 1769. Despite his frequent and extended absences from Rancho San Pedro, the property was not neglected. At the time of his death in 1809, several thousand head of livestock roamed over the nearly 120-square mile land grant, and grain was crudely tilled on about 2,000 acres of rich river land east of Dominguez Hills in present-day Compton. The old soldier willed the rancho to his nephew, Sergeant Cristobal Dominguez, who commanded the guard at Mission San Juan Capistrano. Military duties prevented the new owner from residing at Rancho San Pedro. In the interval after Juan José's death, his *major domo* and executor, Manuel Gutíerrez, stepped in and for many years controlled the rancho. It was during this period that Gutíerrez granted grazing privileges on the Palos Verdes Peninsula to José Dolores Sepúlveda, whose heirs later successfully claimed title to this land on the basis of long occupancy. Pío Pico was governor at the time, and more than 31,000 acres, about 40% of the original rancho, was involved.

Following the death of Cristobal Dominguez, his eldest son, Manuel, assumed control of the rancho and about 1827 he built a home on the eastern slopes of Dominguez Hill. Despite his keen business sense, only 24,000 acres—about one-third of the original grant—remained in 1885 when the rancho was partitioned among his six daughters.

All but one of the Dominguez daughters married and the unions brought a list of names—Carson, Watson, and Del Amo—all familiar in the current development of the Dominguez area. For example Watson Industrial Properties, a leading developer of plant sites in the area, bears the name of descendants of James A. Watson and Dominguez sister María Dolores Simona. Because of the marriage of George Henry Carson to another sister, Maria Victoria, a city and a street were eventually designated by the name of Carson, while Victoria was the appellation given to the street upon which California State University at Dominguez Hills is located.

Dr. Gregorio Del Amo y Gonzales, a young Spanish physician, wed another of the sisters, María Susana Delfina, and it was on the Del Amo portion of the former rancho that oil was discovered in 1920. Located near downtown Torrance, the oil well sparked a boom that spread east to Dominguez Hill.

Manuel Dominguez Home, Rancho San Pedro

During the Boom of the 1880s in southern California, individual sales by the Dominguez sisters provided the foundation for the city of Redondo Beach and the later development of Terminal Island, then still known as Rattlesnake Island. The Dominguez Estate Company, formed to administer the collective interests of the Dominguez sisters, was eventually liquidated in 1967 in the largest single offering of real estate in southern California history. Almost 1,605 acres and $58.5 million were involved. In 1924 Dominguez heirs gave the home originally built by Manuel Dominguez and land surrounding it to the Claretian Fathers. They founded the Dominguez Memorial Seminary and have maintained the sprawling family home above Alameda Street as a museum.

The original adobe half of the Dominguez home contains elegant furnishings, paintings, and photographs relating to the history of Rancho San Pedro in the nineteenth century. The later lath and plaster half of the structure is being restored and will soon contain rooms furnished with artifacts of the Del Amo, Carson, and Watson families, as well as the 1910 Air Meet. A bronze plaque on the facade of the west entrance commemorates the 1846 Battle of Dominguez Ranch.

The Dominguez Home is located on Alameda Street just south of the Artesia Freeway.

Tuesdays and Wednesdays 1:00-4:00 P.M. free guided tours. Also second Sunday each month except holidays.

18127 S. Alameda Street
Compton 90220
631-5981 or 636-6030

G 2. DOMINGUEZ AIR MEET SITE AND NATIVE DAUGHTERS OF THE GOLDEN WEST PLAQUE

During ten days in 1910 more than 175,000 people gathered at Dominguez Field to witness the first air meet held in the United States. The event was so popular that the mayor of Los Angeles declared a holiday and shops and offices were closed so people could attend the historic occasion. A grandstand seated 20,000 but as many as 30,000 came in a single day. Several world records were set at the meet which spawned the huge aerospace complex in southern California today.

With the exception of the Wright brothers, all of the early aviators were at the meet. They included Glen H. Curtiss, Charles Willard and Glenn L. Martin, and Frenchman Louis Paulhan. Paulhan carried off the top prize money of $50,000. and made the first flight above the Pacific. He also became the first to fly above 4,000 feet as his plane reached an altitude of 4,600 feet. Curtiss was the first to fly at the meet, thus making the first recorded flight of an airplane west of the Great Plains. Records for speed, distance, and endurance were also set, including the first time an airplane reached the speed of 70 miles an hour.

The Native Daughters of the Golden West, Compton Parlors, originally placed a bronze plate on the actual site of the meet in 1941. The plaque, however, was stolen three times, usually by vagrants hoping to trade in the metal for a few bottles of wine. Luckily each time the Native Daughters were able to retrieve it. Due to industrial development of the area, the marker in 1974 was relocated on the campus of Cal-State Dominguez Hills, about a mile northwest of the original site, where it would be more secure and accessible to the public. Two bronze plaques mounted in a concrete block are located at

Air Meet Marker, California State University, Dominguez Hills

Dominguez Junction, with Ranch in center and Air Meet Site at left, 1941.

the front of the mall near the Victoria Street entrance to the college. The CSDH history department is collecting photographs and artifacts connected to the event. The campus is on Victoria Street a half-mile east of Avalon Boulevard.

Accessible daily 8:00 A.M.-10:00 P.M.

Cal-State Dominguez Hills
1000 E. Victoria Street
Carson 90747
515-3300

G 3. SITE OF SUANG-NA INDIAN VILLAGE (2)

This archaeological site was part of a large village complex occupying the inner harbor area prior to the advent of the Spanish. Its Indian inhabitants lived peacefully and subsisted mainly on shellfish, wild game and acorns. In 1784, Suang-na became part of the Rancho San Pedro landgrant. Indians worked at the ranch as vaqueros. Gradually, disease and an alien culture took their toll and the village was abandoned. The site has been partially excavated by local colleges. An historic marker was erected in 1972 by the city of Carson Indian Historical Committee and Watson Industrial Properties.

Leave the San Diego freeway at the Wilmington Avenue offramp, drive south on Wilmington to 230th, drive west on 230th for two blocks. The site is in an industrial park.

G 4. VINCENT THOMAS BRIDGE

Built at a cost of $21 million, the Vincent Thomas Bridge spans the Los Angeles Main Channel from San Pedro to Terminal Island. It is the only suspension bridge to be named after a living man, the state assemblyman who still represents the district of San Pedro. Construction began in May 1961, and the bridge opened for traffic in November 1963. An average of 20,000 cars crossed daily in 1973.

On a clear day this aesthetically pleasing landmark is visible for many miles and passengers crossing the bridge are afforded a spectacular view of the harbor. The main suspension span, 1,500 feet long, clears the water by 185 feet, more than enough space for military aircraft to fly safely underneath, and the two bridge towers extend another

Vincent Thomas Bridge

Fish Harbor in the 1930s.

180 feet skyward. With its approaches and two 500-foot side suspension spans, it is 6,060 feet long and weighs an estimated 120,370 tons, making it the third largest bridge in California.

The Vincent Thomas Bridge is at the southern terminus of the Harbor Freeway. Bus transportation crosses the bridge between Harbor Boulevard in San Pedro and Seaside Avenue on Terminal Island.

430 N. Seaside Avenue
Terminal Island 90731
831-0641

G 5. FISH HARBOR

A generation ago Fish Harbor bustled with canneries, boatyards, gasoline filling stations for tuna clippers, and producers of fish by-products such as fertilizer, pet food, and vitamins. The artificial inlet on the south side of Terminal Island was home port for many of the boats which comprised a fleet of more than 700 fishing vessels, operated by Japanese, Yugoslavians, Italians, Portuguese, and others. Nearly 500 million pounds of fish were caught by the nearly 5,000 fishermen from Los Angeles Harbor, sufficient to support nineteen packing plants, with more than 4,000 employees in the harbor district.

Overfishing by local boats as well as foreign trawlers has crippled and all but destroyed the once flourishing multimillion dollar local industry. Sardines disappeared entirely from southern California coastal waters by the early 1960s, and tuna, yellowtail, mackerel, and other fishes are found in greatly reduced numbers. The old purse seiners, sturdy boats from which nets were placed around schools of fish and drawn together like an enormous purse, have ceased their picturesque operations. A decreasing number of tuna boats venture into South American waters, where they are harassed by foreign governments who claim the Americans are trespassing in their territorial fisheries.

G 6. WILMINGTON-SAN PEDRO-LONG BEACH SHIPYARDS

Shipbuilding began as a major industry in southern California around the turn of the century, when the federal government undertook development of Los Angeles Harbor. Fellows & Stewart, funded in 1896, was one of several companies which began by

Harbor Area Shipyards, World War II

building wooden vessels. During World War I the industry expanded and shifted to steel construction, and the navy opened a shipyard on Terminal Island. Craig Shipbuilding, the first to build steel ships at this time, has been in business since 1907. Its first vessel was a tug of 170 tons, followed by two dredges used in the excavation and dredging of channels in the newly planned Long Beach Harbor.

With the coming of World War II, the army and navy took over much of the waterfront area; huge naval installations were constructed on Terminal Island. The shipyards hummed around the clock, building and repairing hundreds of vessels. Among the companies which constructed ships for both world wars was Los Angeles Shipbuilding & Dry Dock (later Todd Shipyard), which still makes naval and maritime vessels of all sizes, including supertankers of 250,000 tons deadweight.

Many ship-builders which contributed so much to the war effort no longer exist, e.g., Western Pipe and Steel, which made ice breakers for the Coast Guard. Others, such as Craig Shipbuilding, shifted to repair and conversion after the war. California Shipbuilding, one of the oldest, dating back to 1904, was purchased in 1947 by National Metal & Steel Corporation and converted to scrap processing and dismantling. Metal

processed here is used in autos, appliances, tin cans, buildings, toys, and many other steel and metal products. National Metals calls itself a "mine above the ground." The annual yield from the scrap processing industry is said to equal all the iron ore mined in one year, plus all the coal and limestone used to make the steel.

The Naval Shipyard on Terminal Island is the largest facility on the West Coast to service large vessels. Neither the naval yards in Oregon or San Diego can accommodate the largest ships, which are sent to Todd Shipyard, which recently installed a 175-ton capacity crane which stands 200 feet tall. On the premises of the Naval Shipyard is another crane, once considered one of the two largest in the world, taken as bounty from the Germans during World War I.

Offices open weekdays, 8 A.M.-4 P.M.

Long Beach Naval Shipyard
Terminal Island 90822
547-6146

Todd Shipyard Corporation
(formerly Los Angeles Shipbuilding &
    Drydock)
710 North Front Street
San Pedro 90731
832-3361

California Shipbuilding & Drydock
    Company
(formerly Craig Shipbuilding)
160 Water Street
Long Beach 90802
437-0481

Harbor Marine Industries
(formerly Fellows & Stewart Shipyard)
258 Cannery Street
East San Pedro (Terminal Island) 90731

National Metal & Steel Corporation
(formerly California Shipbuilding)
691 New Dock on Terminal Island
East San Pedro 90731
833-5281

G 7. GENERAL PHINEAS BANNING
RESIDENCE MUSEUM

Banning Home

One of the county's most important historic landmarks is the former home of Phineas Banning, who arrived in 1851, age 21 and virtually penniless. He established himself as the region's "transportation king," with freight lines extending throughout the Southwest, owner of a railroad and a fleet of ocean-going vessels. In 1858, with B. D. Wilson, he founded the town of New San Pedro, which the state legislature renamed Wilmington in 1863 after Banning's birthplace in Delaware. Banning's title of "general" stems from his service in the state militia during the Civil War. He later served as a state senator, and his efforts were largely responsible for bringing the Southern Pacific railroad to Los Angeles in 1876. Banning also is remembered as the "father of Los Angeles harbor," even though he died from a freak accident in 1885, more than a decade before a deep-water port actually was developed.

The Banning mansion was built in 1864. It has 24 rooms, although originally there may have been as many as 30, with three barns in the rear. The architecture has been praised as "the finest extant example of Greek Revival style in Southern California," with its stately columns and wide verandas. Three stories are topped with a cupola from which Banning scanned the horizon in search of ships entering his port. Construction materials came from throughout the world, including exquisitely colored glass and delicately veined Belgian marble. Lumber was brought from the Mendicino Coast, and labor was supplied by local Indians, seamen, and shipwrights.

The Banning hospitality was legendary, particularly the "regales" attended by leaders of civic, governmental, business and military affairs.

Twenty-acre Banning Park, in which the mansion is located, was created by a bond issue voted by the people of Wilmington in 1927, two years after the last of the Bannings moved from the house. Restoration of the house, gardens, and barn has been the work of the Friends of Banning Park, recently supplemented by financial assistance from the state. Some of General Banning's own furniture has been preserved, and many of the rooms have been restored with elegant furnishings from the 19th Century. An interpretive program has been developed by the Junior League of Los Angeles and community volunteers. From the "widow's walk," visitors still enjoy a fine view of the harbor area. Each April, Banning Park serves as site of an annual wisteria festival.

A facility of the Los Angeles Recreation
and Parks Department, open
Wednesdays, Saturdays and Sundays at

1, 2, 3, and 4 P.M.; group tours by appointment on Tuesday and Thursday mornings.

Admission free; donations accepted.

401 East "M" street
Wilmington 90744
549-2920

G 8. WILMINGTON CEMETERY

Phineas Banning donated land and constructed this cemetery for the burial of the first Banning baby at the time of its death in 1857. During the Civil War most burials were at the Drum Barracks military encampment. After the war the cemetery again came into general use. Among those interred there are the first baby born in San Pedro, and members of the Banning and Narbonne families. The area is also believed to contain old Indian gravesites. The present cemetery has approximately doubled in size since it was originally opened. Bus transportation along Pacific Coast Highway runs within several hundred yards of the cemetery.

Open 7:00 A.M. to 4:00 P.M. daily

605 E. "O" Street
Wilmington 90744
834-4442

G 9. ST. JOHN'S EPISCOPAL CHURCH

Wilmington's first Episcopal services were held in 1876 in the basement of the Banning mansion. Seven years later, on the urging of Mrs. Mary Hollister Banning, construction of a stave-type church was begun at 422 North Avalon Boulevard (then named Canal Street). The Rev. C. S. Linsley provided most of the carpentry work, with the Banning family paying for the materials. Christmas services were held in 1883 in the still unfinished church. During the four years the church stood without a roof, religious services were conducted in a building formerly housing a saloon.

The Banning family's contributions to St. John's are evident in the church's bell and altar. In 1882, General Banning donated the bell from the *S.S. Amelia*, one of his harbor channel boats. In 1925, Banning's heirs donated the Catalina marble altar, originally intended for use in the Banning home as a buffet. St. John's altar cross and rail, gifts from a navy chaplain in 1926, were made at Pearl Harbor from brass taken from a World War I German submarine.

In 1943 the church building was moved from its original site to its present location. With the exception of a small parish hall added at the rear in 1950 and some buckling of the stained-glasswindows, St. John's looks much as it did at the time of erection.

Open by appointment.
Sunday services at 10:00 A.M.

1537 Neptune Avenue
Wilmington 90744
835-7870

G 10. CALVARY PRESBYTERIAN CHURCH

Presbyterians in Wilmington began gathering together for worship in 1869. The church which they erected the following year is still standing, although it has twice been moved from the original site at the corner of Fries Avenue and G Street on property donated by Benjamin D. Wilson, the famous "Don Benito" for whom Mt. Wilson was

Calvary Presbyterian Church

named. This was not the first Presbyterian body established in the Los Angeles area; a church was chartered in Los Angeles about 1855, but it failed in 1869. Hence the Wilmington church is the oldest continually operating body in the county, known as the "Mother Church of the Los Angeles Presbytery." Charter members included Mr. and Mrs. Jotham Bixby, who resided at Rancho Los Cerritos in Long Beach.

Calvary Church blossomed for a decade, but hard times during the 1880s and 1890s reduced the congregation to a single member. No pastor was retained, and, finally a committee from Los Angeles Presbytery was sent to dissolve the church. When the committee reached Wilmington, the one remaining member refused to be dissolved, and continued to hold Sunday school with a few children and an occasional preaching service. When after the turn of the century San Pedro and Wilmington became Los Angeles Harbor, Calvary Church was revitalized.

The original church edifice, known today as Memory Chapel, has been used for religious services at three different locations. In 1908 a much larger building was built to house the growing congregation. Rather than raze the original structure, it was

moved to East Wilmington to become the home of Wilmington Park Presbyterian Church. The Wilmington Church was never a strong one, and was dissolved and abandoned during the Depression. The original building was again saved from destruction and moved in 1937 to its present site, two blocks south of Pacific Coast Highway and one block west of Avalon Boulevard. It still contains the original pews constructed in 1870.

Phone the church office to determine when the Memory Chapel is open; not used regularly.

1160 N. Marine Avenue
Wilmington 90744
835-8333

G 11. DRUM BARRACKS OFFICERS' QUARTERS

Drum Barracks is the only major Civil War landmark in California. From 1862 to 1866 the original complex of more than 20 buildings was the focal point for men and materials of the Union army destined for all parts of the Southwest. Today only two structures remain: one of the officers' quarters, known simply as "Drum Barracks"; and the powder magazine, located two blocks away.

Drum Barracks, c. 1863.

Camp Drum, named for Adjutant-General R. C. Drum, head of the Department of the West, served initially as the base for the California Volunteers. After the "California Column" left for Arizona and New Mexico to hold these territories for the Union, the post served as depot from which supplies were sent throughout the Southwest. One of the first telegraph lines in this area linked Drum Barracks with other federal fortifications. The post also served as a base for operations against Indians. During 1862 and 1863, the famous Army Camel Corps carried freight between Fort Tejon, Los Angeles, and Drum Barracks. Presence of federal troops at Drum Barracks served as warning to secessionist sympathizers in southern California who otherwise might have menaced the Union cause. During the war the number of soldiers stationed here varied from 2,000 to 7,000. Among the notable officers who served here were Generals Philip Sheridan, W. S. Hancock, George Stoneman, and Phineas Banning, and Colonel C. J. Couts.

The two-story colonial style officers' quarters was one of the first prefabricated structures assembled on the Pacific Coast. All its lumber, hardware, marble and bricks were shipped around Cape Horn from the Portsmouth Navy Yard in New Hampshire. The front section is large and rectangular, with two smaller wings extending toward the rear. Inside are 16 rooms, including a high-ceilinged central hall and a stairway with polished mahogany balustrade. Originally there were four marble fireplaces with U.S. Eagles on the mantels and andirons. An entranceway porch and second-story balcony stood at the front and rear.

In the twentieth century, Thomas Keaveney preserved the building by converting it into a residence.

Notwithstanding widespread recognition as a major historic monument, Drum Barracks officers' quarters was marked for demolition in February, 1965. Protests by the Cultural Heritage Board gained time for the Society for the Preservation of Drum Barracks to organize and raise money to purchase the building. In 1968 the Society sold the quarters to the Los Angeles Department of Parks and Recreation for $30,000. Later that year the Department relinquished the property to the State and was reimbursed the purchase price. The state allocated $95,000 to acquire adjacent property, restore the officers quarters, and develop the site as a State Historical Park Civil War Museum. However, only about $20,000 of the allocation has been spent during the last decade; the adjacent lots have not been purchased, and prospects of a park-museum seem fluid. Leaking water pipes severely undermined the brick foundation and cracked the interior plaster. The bricks from the foundation, fireplaces, and chimneys have been removed and stacked outside, but no plans currently exist to incorporate them into the eventual restoration. (Plans call for dummy fireplaces and chimneys.) A new foundation has been constructed, and the interior plaster has been replaced with drywall. Large timber supports are now bolted within the old walls, but most of the windows are broken and the rear porch and balcony have disappeared.

County historical societies have assigned a high priority to restoration of Drum Barracks.

Presently closed for refurbishment,
    although the exterior may be observed.

1053 Cary Avenue
Wilmington 90744

G 12. DRUM BARRACKS POWDER MAGAZINE

Two years before the Civil War, Lieutenant W. S. Hancock visited Los Angeles to acquire land upon which to construct a post for the Army Quartermaster's Department of the Southwest. For a $1 fee, Phineas Banning and B. D. Wilson donated sixty acres of land. Banning's generosity was repaid, for the government awarded him all construction contracts for the fort and hired him to build a flume from the San Gabriel River eight miles distant. Construction of the post lasted from 1860 to 1862. The headquarters site covered about 30 acres and included officers' quarters, adjutant's office, five soldiers' barracks, bakery, granary, hay barn, blacksmith and wheelright shops, hospital, four laundry buildings, guard house and powder magazine. Commissary buildings occupied seven acres near Banning's Landing at Wilmington. After the Civil War, the post was abandoned.

Existence of the Drum Barracks powder magazine today is not widely known because it has long been incorporated into the structure of a residential dwelling. In recent years this house has been rented to a Spanish-speaking family. Very few historically-minded persons have seen the powder magazine, and the wood-frame house which conceals it from public view was constructed in the 1920s or earlier. Sometime later, according to the resident caretaker of the nearby officers' quarters, the stone blocks which encased the interior of the powder magazine's three-feet thick walls were removed to make room for storage. According to this source, the State Legislature once allocated $18,000 to acquire the property, but the money was never spent.

Private residence
Not open to the public

561 Opp Street
Wilmington 90744

G 13. RANCHO LOS CERRITOS

In 1784, 200,000 acres were granted to Manuel Nieto by Governor Pedro Fages. This grant was later divided into five ranchos, one of which was Rancho Los Cerritos. In 1804 the rancho became the property of Manuela Nieto de Cota and her husband Guillermo through inheritance. In 1830, a "Yanqui," Jonathan Temple, married Dona Rafaela Cota, a second cousin to Guillermo. Temple acquired Mexican citizenship and became known as Don Juan Temple. In 1843 he purchased the remaining 27,000 acres of the rancho from the remaining heirs. Temple built the house now known as La Casa de Rancho de Los Cerritos in 1844. The adobe and redwood house was located at its present site on a bluff overlooking the Los Angeles River. From here Temple operated his ranch, pasturing 15,000 cattle, 7,000 sheep, and 3,000 horses.

Rancho Los Cerritos, c. 1875

After Commodore Robert F. Stockton seized control of Los Angeles, in August 1846, Don Juan Temple was appointed American *alcalde* of Los Angeles, California insurgents, angered by the American seizure, attacked the garrisons at Los Angeles and at Chino. The U.S. troops were forced to retreat to San Pedro; some were captured and held prisoner, along with Temple and his family, at Rancho Los Cerritos. During October 1846, the Rancho remained the headquarters for the Californians.

In 1866 Don Juan Temple sold the rancho to Flint, Bixby, and Company. The great drought of 1863-64 had all but ruined Temple's cattle business, and he was forced to abandon his ranch of 27,000 acres for $20,000. Jotham Bixby was engaged by the company as manager and took up his residence in the adobe. By 1869 Bixby had acquired one half interest in the ranch for $10,000 and adopted the firm name of J. Bixby and Co. From 1866 until 1881 the rancho was a major sheep-raising venture. In 1881 the Bixby family left the rancho, and for a quarter of a century the Los Cerritos rancho remained vacant except for the presence of a caretaker.

Eventually Llewellyn Bixby, a nephew of Jotham Bixby, purchased the rancho, and in 1930 he restored the adobe. The City of Long Beach purchased the property in 1955.

A research library of several thousand volumes of Californiana is located in the adobe. Archival holdings include documents, diaries, photographs, maps, and manuscripts from the Temple and Bixby periods. The museum houses artifacts from nearby Indian archaeological sites and historical artifacts including furniture and costumes from the period 1866-81.

To reach Rancho Los Cerritos, take the Long Beach Freeway to Del Amo Boulevard, go east to Long Beach Boulevard, south to San Antonio Drive, and north on Virginia Road which runs through the Virginia Country Club. Bus transportation runs along Long Beach Boulevard; get off at S. Antonio, walk east one block and north on Virginia Road about a half-mile through the golf course to the rancho.

Wednesday-Sunday 1:00-5:00 P.M.
  Admission free

4600 Virginia Road
Long Beach 90807
424-9423

Rancho Los Cerritos (two views)

Sunnyside Cemetery

G 14. LONG BEACH AND SUNNYSIDE CEMETERIES

The Long Beach Municipal Cemetery at various times has been called Signal Hill Cemetery and Long Beach Cemetery. It was part of the American Colony tract in the days when Long Beach was called Willmore City and Jotham Bixby Company began subdividing their huge Rancho Los Cerritos acreage. Between 1882 and 1900 about 35 persons were buried here. In the first few years it was customary for family or friends to prepare the grave. After burial of the deceased, a family member usually filled out the record book, which still exists, though the variety of handwriting makes it difficult to read. The cemetery was deeded to the City of Long Beach some time around 1910.

Sunnyside Cemetery, begun by T. W. Decker in 1913, is located at the corner of Willow Street and Orange Avenue, next to Long Beach Municipal Cemetery; some of its land is in fact part of the original Long Beach Cemetery. The Long Beach Cemetery Association originally owned both, but Sunnyside is now a privately owned corporation. Many old-timers who contributed to the beginnings of Long Beach are buried in both cemeteries.

Daylight hours every day

1095 E. Willow Street
Long Beach 90806
424-2639

G 15. ALAMITOS NO. 1, SIGNAL HILL

On the night of June 23, 1921, Royal Dutch Shell Company's Alamitos No. 1 shot crude oil 80 feet into the air, and over the top of the 114 foot derrick the following day. Within just two years, more than a thousand greasy wooden derrick, dotted the area of little more than two square miles surrounding Signal Hill. By 1950 Alamitos No. 1 had yielded more than 700,000 barrels of oil, and other Signal Hill wells had each pumped well over two million barrels. In terms of oil per acre, Signal Hill has been the most productive oil field in America. Peak production levels were attained in 1923, with 68 million barrels for the year, or almost 250,000 a day, and the output for the first decade exceeded 400 million barrels.

As "liquid gold" was piped to nearby wharves and refineries, the population of Long Beach tripled during the first decade of Signal Hill oil production. By 1953, nine refineries and twenty-four natural gas plants were operating in the Long Beach area, and the city treasury had been enriched by more than $11 million in royalties.

Before the oil discovery, several attractive homes had been built on Signal Hill. Various pioneer families had productive lemon orchards on the hill, but shipping costs at the time made lemon growing unprofitable.

Signal Hill, 1932

Later, large vegetable gardens, chiefly cultivated by Japanese, covered many acres.

Signal Hill's name has been attributed by some to signal fires built by Indians centuries ago, but a less romantic explanation is that the United States Coast and Geodetic Survey constructed a signal station there in 1853.

The City of Signal Hill, incorporated in 1924, contains only 2 1/4 square miles in area, bounded on all sides by Long Beach. Records of oil development, including photographs, are at Signal Hill City Hall, 2175 S. Cherry Avenue, half a mile north of Pacific Coast Highway and about a mile south of the San Diego Freeway.

Alamitos No. 1 is at the corner of Hill Street and Temple Avenue. From the San Diego Freeway, exit at Cherry, go south to 23rd Street, turn left, drive half a mile and turn left on Temple. Bus travelers should take Pacific Coast Highway, get off at Temple, and walk north half a mile.

G 16. THE BEMBRIDGE HOUSE

The Bembridge House, also known as the Green House and Rankin House, was built by Stephen and Josephine Green between 1904 and 1906. Green designed the two-storied redwood home with a master bed-

room occupying the tower section, four bathrooms, and a large dining room which became a showplace for her hand-painted china. A slightly raised platform was built into the tower of the attic, but its purpose is unknown. Roofing shingles were soaked nine times to make them fire resistant. Sixty years later this precaution saved the house from destruction when a processed log sent a shower of resinous sparks up the chimney and set numerous fires on the roof.

Stephen Green died in 1912, and the house had several owners before Thomas Rankin (father of the present occupant) and his family purchased it in 1918. Preoccupied with music, the Rankins considered the large kitchen sheer waste. So they added a smaller kitchen and breakfast room on the east and made an apartment out of the old kitchen, pantries, and smaller rooms. The softwood floors make an excellent soundboard, as does the circular tower which amplifies sound and resonance. The raised section of the attic became a stage for children's plays as well as a playhouse.

Today Dorothy Rankin Bembridge, who taught music and English in the public schools, entertains musical and educational groups in the house. The original hand-rubbed woodwork still gleams though it has

Bembridge House

never been refinished. The building went through the 1933 earthquake with nothing more than a toppled chimney.

The Bembridge house faces the 1.9 acre Drake Park (also called Knoll Park) given to the city in 1904 by the Seaside Water Company. Colonel Charles R. Drake, the president, was also a major investor in the company which was then building the lavish Hotel Virginia on Ocean Blvd. Drake Park is east of the Long Beach Freeway and Los Angeles River, south of Pacific Coast Highway, west of Daisy Avenue, and north of Anaheim. Get off the Anaheim or PCH bus at Daisy and walk about a quarter of a mile.

Private residence
Not open to the public

953 Park Circle Drive
Long Beach 90813

G 17. FIRST CONGREGATIONAL CHURCH, LONG BEACH

With an original congregation of 16 members, the First Congregational Church began holding religious services in 1887 at

First Congregational Church

Cerritos Hall, built by Jotham Bixby, owner of Rancho Los Cerritos. The first church edifice was erected in 1902 at the corner of 3rd and Cedar, and the present building was dedicated on the same site in 1914. Its architecture consists of red brick masonry, decorative tiles, a large tower on the corner, and three large red rose windows.

Office open weekdays, 9 A.M.-5 P.M.;
Saturday, 9 A.M.-noon
Sunday, 8:30 A.M.-noon

Corner of 3rd Street and Cedar Avenue
Long Beach 90812
436-2256

G 18. LONG BEACH PUBLIC LIBRARY

Long Beach's first library was a small reading room opened in 1896 on Ocean Boulevard. Andrew Carnegie contributed $30,000. for the library building that opened in 1909. The earthquake of 1933 caused no great structural damage, but the fire wall had to be rebuilt. The great increase in population following World War II rendered the libary's facilities overcrowded and inadequate. A new building at the same site of 135,000 square feet was completed in October 1976.

Special collections include the Marilyn Horne Archives (spanning her youth in Long Beach, graduation from Poly High School, and rise to the New York Metropolitan Opera), the California Historical Petroleum Collection, Popular Sheet Music, the Bertrand L. Smith Rare Books Collection, the Earl Burns and Lorraine Miller Fine Arts Collection, and Long Beach History (including some oral history).

The Library is in Lincoln Park (also known as the Civic Center Superblock) at the corner of Pacific and Ocean Boulevards, readily accessible by numerous bus routes.

Hours Monday through Thursday
   10:00 A.M. to 9:00 P.M.
Friday and Saturday 10:00 A.M.-5:30 P.M.
Sunday 1:30-5:00 P.M.

Pacific and Ocean Blvds.
Long Beach 90802
436-9225

G 19. QUEEN'S PIKE AMUSEMENT PARK

Some time around the turn of the century a few small food booths and gift stands near the foot of Pine Avenue in Long Beach formed the nucleus of what was to become for almost six decades the most popular amusement park on the Pacific Coast. The first Pine Avenue Pier, built in 1893, was also the first municipal pier in California. Concession stands later were built around the pier and to the west of it. On July 4, 1902, the Pike, as later generations grew to know it and love it, officially came into existence. On that date the first Pacific Electric street cars arrived in Long Beach, the Bath House (later known as The Plunge) opened for business, and foundations were laid for the "Walk of a Thousand Lights." Thousands came that day, and many who could not get rooms for the night slept on the beach. Colonel Charles A. Drake, president of the Long Beach Bath House & Amusement Association, constructed the first board walk along the beach.

The amusement zone extended along Seaside Boulevard from Pine Avenue to Chestnut Place, including the Silvery Spray Pleasure Pier, and was later extended west for about four blocks. The Pike eventually included three ballrooms, a roller coaster and many other rides, skating rink, fun houses, booths for games and fortune telling, some fair restaurants, and numerous gift shops.

Much of the old Pike no longer exists, including the pier, the Plunge, and the "Cyclone Racer" roller coaster, which was torn down in the 1960s. It has been replaced by a new, family-oriented fun zone. Many of the rides, however, such as the Ferris Wheel and bumper cars, are just as thrilling as ever. Especially notable are the merry-go-round horses lovingly hand carved by Charles Lauff in the 1920s.

Queen's Pike is just south of Ocean Boulevard between Pine and Cedar, and is easily accessible by bus from almost anywhere in Long Beach. From the Long Beach Freeway, exit at Ocean and drive east.

An admission charge of $3.50 for adults
   and $2.50 for children 12 and under
   covers all rides; $1.50 gets small children
   into kiddieland. All fees subject
   to change. Summer hours are
   12:00-11:00 P.M. daily.
Rest of year, Friday 6:00-11:00 P.M.
weekends 12:00-11:00P.M.

444 W. Ocean Blvd.
Long Beach 90802
435-1334

G 20. THE QUEEN MARY

The *Queen Mary* is the largest passenger ship ever built. It was constructed between 1930 and 1934 by John Brown's Clydebank Shipyard, Scotland, for White Star Lines. More than 1,000 feet long, almost 50 yards high above the water line, and weighing some 50,000 tons, the ship cruised at a normal speed of 28 1/2 knots (35 miles per hour). Up to 1,970 passengers were served by a crew of 1,000 to 1,200.

For more than three decades the *Queen Mary* sailed the North Atlantic between England and the United States, but not always as a luxurious ocean liner. Only three years after the ship's maiden voyage in 1936, Great Britain became involved in World War II. From 1940 to 1947, the *Queen Mary* served as a troopship. After the war the ship resumed regular passenger service for two decades until, after considerable decline in revenue, it was sold to the City of Long Beach in 1964. The *Queen Mary* completed its final voyage from Southampton to Long Beach in 1967.

Tens of millions of dollars have been invested by the City of Long Beach to convert the *Queen Mary* into a first-class tourist attraction, and in 1971 the ship was opened to the public.

During conversion of the ship, selected pieces of furniture, china, silver, and art were collected and preserved for the Museum of the Sea aboard the *Queen Mary*. Also on display are souvenirs and memorabilia donated by passengers and troops, photos and models of the ship from its construction to the present, celebrity photos, newspapers published on board for GI's during the war, and original menus. Museum files contain more than twenty cabinet drawers relating to design and construction, and more than 150 lineal feet of reports, logs and papers pertinent to the operation of the ship. The Jacques Cousteau's "Living Sea" portion of the museum deals with man and his relation to the sea.

Four hundred of the original 998 passenger rooms have been converted into hotel suites. Among the new additions are several restaurants and a variety of shops, a wedding chapel, and the Josephine Tussaud Wax Museum.

The *Queen Mary* is located at the southern-most end of the Long Beach Freeway. It is served by the Long Beach Public Transportation System. There is no boarding charge and the ship is open every day of the year. The Museum of the Sea charge is $4.00 for adults (12 and older) and $1.75 for children 5-11, which includes a tour of the upper decks and power train (engine room), as well as Cousteau's "Living Sea."
Museum hours:
Winter: 10:00 A.M. to 3:30 P.M. weekdays,
    10:00 A.M. to 4:30 P.M. weekends.
Summer: 10:00 A.M. to 4:30 P.M. daily.
Pier J
Long Beach 90802
435-4733 Tour information
435-3511 Hotel reservations

G 21. VILLA RIVIERA APARTMENTS

For a half-century the ocean front in Long Beach has been dominated by the 16-story Villa Riviera apartment building. The U-

Villa Riviera Apartments

shaped structure displays terracotta balconies, bay windows, decorated gables, and an central spire. At the time of construction in 1928, it was the second tallest building in southern California. It is one of very few buildings designed by Los Angeles architects (Richard D. King) which survived the 1933 earthquake in Long Beach.

Villa Riviera was built to be a cooperative luxury apartment; it has been well-maintained and still operates as a condominium, with luxury of design evident in its ballroom, garage, stained glass windows, and roof gardens.

Drive south on the Long Beach Freeway to Shoreline Drive and follow that highway to its intersection with Ocean Blvd.

800 East Ocean Boulevard
Long Beach

G 22. PACIFIC COAST CLUB

Rising to a height equivalent to 14 stories on the ocean side, the half-century old Pacific Coast Club looms as a spectacular monument to southern California's quest for the "good life." Five orchestras played to celebrate the grand opening in 1926. For decades the membership numbered in the thousands and included many of Long Beach's most prominent and wealthy citizens. Facilities included a gymnasium, wrestling room, handball courts, and a Natatorium with tiled Olympic-sized swimming pool. On the main floor were four huge rooms built around a central courtyard: the Main Lounge with an arched ceiling; the massive Grand Hall with gigantic chandeliers; the East Terrace with painted beam ceiling; and the Sunset Dining Room. The second floor contained the women's facili-

Pacific Coast Club

ties, a "separate club within a club," with its own private entrance and elevator. (For many years women were not admitted to full membership, but had a separate dining area and access to the pool on certain days.) The PCC also had its own barber shop and beauty salon, haberdashery, and tobacco stand. Upstairs a huge tower housed five floors of dormitory rooms for members and guests.

Architects C. T. Weber and Sons designed the 8.5-story structure to resemble a massive Norman castle, with lofty towers, battlements and iron gateways. The interior design carried out this theme with carved gargoyles and decorative niches for pewter goblets or statues. The women's area was furnished in the style of Louis XIV.

The Los Angeles Athletic Club took over management in 1928. Athletic endeavors always were emphasized, and the Pacific Coast Club became noted for its swim teams and later for its sponsorship of championship track and field teams.

In 1964 the Pacific Coast Club, Inc., purchased the property and broke ties with the Los Angeles Athletic Club; seven months later the new owners announced bankruptcy. In 1966 the new owner, E. L. "Ted" Fraser completely refurbished the club for its 40th Anniversary Ball. In 1970 the lending company foreclosed on the mortgage; the following year the doors were closed, tenants evicted, and the elegant furnishings sold at auction.

Attempts to condemn the building as an earthquake hazard have failed, and recent owners have thus far managed to save the club from demolition. The interior has suffered terribly from vandalism and the corrosive effect of ocean breezes wafting through broken windows. Notwithstanding enormous financial obstacles, optimism exists that the Pacific Club will "live again," and in 1977 future tenants such as shopkeepers and restaurants were being sought to lease space contingent upon projected restoration.

Not open at present.

850 East Ocean Boulevard
Long Beach 90802
437-2818

G 23. LONG BEACH MUSEUM OF ART

This building was originally constructed for Mrs. Elizabeth Milbank Anderson of New York. She used this 15-room mansion as a summer home, where she housed her collection of notable paintings and Chinese porcelain. Her husband, Abriam A. Anderson, was a portrait painter. Her granddaughter, Elizabeth Tanner, fabled as "the richest little girl in the world," played in the mansion as a child.

A "Mr. Roth" designed the building in 1912, with jutting brick and lava stone walls, today covered with masses of tightly clinging ivy. The garage, called the "Carriage House," has a five room apartment on the upper floor, used as a home for the caretaker and his family.

In 1926 the building opened as the "Club California Casa Real," the first athletic, social, and beach club in Long Beach, preceding the rival Pacific Coast Club, located just down the street, by three months. The club considered its investment at the time to be $500,000, though membership cost only $10 for one year. Despite having its own orchestra, horse-shoe dining room, dance floor, and art gallery, the Club closed after three years.

Oilman Thomas A. O'Donnell acquired the property in 1929; he spent his summers here, his winters in Palm Springs. The family lived here until the beginning of World War II, when guns and the Navy were brought to the bluff. The building served during the war as a club for petty officers stationed at Long Beach.

In 1950 the City of Long Beach purchased the property for $100,000 for use as an art center. The building was renovated, the elevator removed, and the upstairs windows filled in. In 1957 the Art Center was advanced to the status of a museum, its name officially changed to Long Beach Museum of Art, and new rooms and a reception center added. It currently displays an ever-changing variety of paintings, sculpture, and/or audio-visual works of art, but none of its exhibits are permanent.

In 1978 museum operations will be transferred into new facilities in the Long Beach Civic Center presently under construction. The City plans to retain the original building, but for what purpose is not yet certain.

Open Wednesday-Sunday 12:00-5 P.M.
Admission free

2300 Ocean Blvd.
Long Beach 90803
439-2119

Rancho Los Alamitos (two views)

G 24. RANCHO LOS ALAMITOS

Following the death of Manuel Nieto, a retired soldier who had accompanied Portolá in 1769, Los Nietos land grant was divided in 1834 among the heirs into five ranchos. Shortly thereafter Juan José Nieto sold the 26,000 acre Rancho Los Alamitos ("Ranch of the Little Cottonwoods") to Governor José Figueroa. In 1835 Figueroa died and his brother managed the rancho but let the structure fall into ruin.

Abel Stearns purchased the rancho in 1842 as a summer home for his bride of 12 months, the 15-year-old Arcadia Bandini. Stearns renovated the main adobe originally built by Juan José Nieto in the early 1800s on the hill by the spring. A long wooden wing, consisting of several rooms, was added

on to the west side of the house, which today is located on the north side of the patio. These rooms were used as a bunk house by the vaqueros.

Stearns mortgaged the Rancho in 1861 to Michael Reese, a money lender from San Francisco, for $20,000, with interest at 1 1/2% per month. Years of drought in 1863-64 devastated cattle ranching in southern California, and Stearns was not excepted. When Reese foreclosed on the mortgage in 1866, he leased the land and the house stood vacant.

John W. Bixby with his wife Susan and son Fred rented the property in 1878. The house was almost in ruin, and a small eucalyptus tree and a fair-sized pepper tree were all that remained of Stearn's fine gardens. Bixby constructed a fireplace, laid a wood floor, and plastered newspaper over the adobe which he later covered with wallpaper.

Rancho Los Alamitos was purchased for $125,000 from the estate of Michael Reese in 1881 by a partnership of I. W. Hellman, Jotham Bixby, and John Bixby, who was to manage the property. John Bixby died in 1884 at the age of 39. In 1888 the Rancho was divided three ways. The middle section which went to John Bixby's heirs, included the old adobe headquarters and retained the name Rancho Los Alamitos.

In 1898 Fred H. Bixby began operating Rancho Los Alamitos. Susan Bixby, widow of John, died in 1906, and Fred Bixby moved his family into the adobe ranch house which was to be his home for the next six decades. Structural additions in 1878 and 1906 of a hall, bathroom, and music room with floor-to-ceiling windows left the rooms inside the original adobe dark, so Florence Bixby had a skylight installed over the parlor, which soon became the library. Stearn's old bunk house was converted and used as a kitchen, men's dining room and two bedrooms for the cook and her helper. The westerly end became Fred Bixby's office. With the erection of a wooden wing on the south side of the house, enclosing the patio between the wings, the structure as it now stands was completed.

Following Fred Bixby's death, the City of Long Beach in 1968 acquired by gift the remaining 7 1/2 acres. The ranch house contains the original Bixby furnishings including a collection of glassware. On the grounds are a barn, a working blacksmith's shop, original farm equipment, gardens, some Indian artifacts, and an abandoned tennis court.

To get to Rancho Los Alamitos, take the San Diego Freeway to Palo Verde Avenue, go south to the entrance of Bixby Knolls and tell the gatekeeper you wish to visit the Rancho.

Wednesday-Sunday 1:00-5:00 P.M.
Guided tours only
Admission free

6400 Bixby Hill Road
Long Beach 90815
431-2511

G 25. PUVUNGA INDIAN VILLAGE SITES

The Gabrielino Indian village of Puvunga is the legendary place of origin for the famous religion of Chinichnich, which spread widely to other southern California Indian groups, even among those who spoke different languages. The name, Puvunga, probably means "the place in the crowd," and it is supposed to have been the place where legendary deities first appeared. Historical references to Puvunga can be found in baptismal records at the missions of San Gabriel and San Juan Capistrano, and the name is listed in Hugo Reid's compila-

tion of Indian villages. As such, Puvunga is one of the extremely rare instances of a specifically named village of extinct Gabrielino Indians which can be reasonably identified with a known archaeological site.

Puvunga occupied a low hill in eastern Long Beach, overlooking swamps and marshes that provided abundant wild food sources. At the base of the hill was the major fresh-water spring of this region. Although much of the evidence of the village site has been destroyed by construction and other recent activities, archaeological work has shown that remnants of the living areas still exist in at least nine places in an area of approximately 500 acres. Sections where living areas and burials are still preserved can best be seen at Rancho Los Alamitos and California State University, Long Beach.

At Rancho Los Alamitos, plans are being formulated to reconstruct a village including large domed houses, ceremonial structures, a cemetery, an altar, and other features that would have characterized a typical village. All would be constructed using native materials. Activity areas would be shown, such as food preparation and tool making, using artifacts that have already been found at the site and at other sites in the vicinity. Landscaping would use native plants and emphasize the aboriginal use of local resources. At the present time, however, visitors to the Puvunga site at Rancho Los Alamitos will see only a reconstructed conical Indian hut and a small exhibit case.

The Puvunga site at Cal-State Long Beach is located near the area of the organic garden and recycling center north of State College Drive near the Bellflower entrance to the campus.

Wednesday-Sunday 1:00-5:00 P.M.
Admission free

Rancho Los Alamitos
6400 Bixby Hill Road
Long Beach 90815
431-2511

California State University, Long Beach
1250 Bellflower Boulevard
Long Beach 90840
498-4111

G 26. MARINE STADIUM

As early as 1907, Alamitos Bay was the site of the first rowing regatta ever held in the Long Beach area; four-man crews from Stanford University defeated San Diego Rowing Club crews in two races. Until the 1920s, however, that portion of the bay which is today Marine Stadium was unimproved salt marsh and slough. As part of an agreement in 1923 with the San Gabriel River Improvement Company, the City of Long Beach dredged out an 800-foot wide strip which produced both the Marine Stadium channel and the Colorado Lagoon, and deposited the fill material on the company's remaining lands to the north. The city constructed extensive wooden bleachers along the shore. Marine Stadium was the site of the 1932 Olympic rowing events.

In 1964 Long Beach received approval from the State Lands Commission to expend $1.8 million from the Tideland Oil Revenue Fund for improving Marine Stadium. The project, completed the following year, included removal of the old bleachers, extensive site beautification, off-street parking facilities, boat launching ramps, a building to house shells used in crew races, 4,000 new permanent bleacher seats, and 7,000 temporary (portable) bleacher seats.

The new stadium, further remodeled and improved in 1966-67 with a rock-lined shore to reduce wave effect, hosted the 1968 U.S. Olympic Trials for rowing, canoes, and kayaks. Drag boat and circle races are conducted at the stadium, with boats reaching speeds of over 200 mph.

Marine Stadium houses a Rowing Center which is home port for the crews of Cal-State Long Beach and the Long Beach Rowing Association. Considered one of the finest crew facilities on the Pacific Coast, the Rowing Center frequently serves 80 to 150 oarsmen a day.

To reach Marine Stadium, take the Bellflower Boulevard exit off the San Diego Freeway and go south to the end of the road; turn right (west) on Colorado Street and go one mile. From downtown Long Beach, take the 7th Street bus east to Park Avenue, walk three blocks to Appian Way and southeast 3/8 mile to the main entrance at the junction of Appian, Colorado, and Nieto. The small boat ramp is accessible only from the east end of Marina Drive off 2nd Street. The Rowing Center is at Colorado and Santiago Avenue.

Marine Stadium is open daily 8:00 A.M. to sunset for public water skiing and boating. Boat-launching fees are $2.00; spectator fees for power-boat and rowing events vary from no admission to $5.00.

Mailing address:
155 Queens Way Landing
Long Beach 90802
432-5931

G 27. NAPLES

The idea of creating a small community with canals, bridges, and gondolas on the partially submerged mud flats within Alamitos Bay was envisioned by Arthur M. Parsons in 1903. Parsons and his son organized the Naples Land Company to acquire the marshy slough from the Bixby Alamitos Land Company, and soon forty salesmen were selling lots. The first houses were built in 1906, but the financial panic of 1907 forced Parsons to sell out to Henry E. Huntington, under whose ownership all development of Naples ceased. The firm of Warren McGrath and Samuel A. Selover acquired the land in 1923, renewed development, and completed the canals and bridges.

During the years when Parsons still controlled the Naples property, Miss Almira Parker Hershey, of the famous chocolate family, erected the Hotel Naples. She instructed her architect to duplicate the old Hollywood Hotel, which she had also built. Despite its then substantial cost of $87,000, the Hotel Naples stood vacant at 103 Ravenna Drive for a quarter of a century.

With the reopening of the Naples development in the 1920s, prospective buyers arrived via Pacific Electric Railway at the McGrath & Selover sales pavilion at Second Street and Bay Shore (where the Branch Library is now located), took a side-wheeler for a boat trip around the bay and received lunch and a sales talk while a band played on the steps of the Hotel Naples. The long-vacant hotel finally opened in 1929 and subsequently served as a rest home, again as a hotel as NYA housing for boys, and it was eventually remodeled into an apartment hotel.

After the earthquake of 1933 the Naples canal walls remained in ruins for about four years. Finally at a cost of more than a half-million dollars, the canal walls and arched bridges were rebuilt in 1938-39 with assistance from the county, city, the Works Progress Administration, and an assessment of $138,056 in the district. The celebration held upon completion of the work had as its guest of honor Arthur M. Parsons, the "founder of Naples," who was then 81 years old.

When the narrow arched bridges were demolished recently and replaced with higher ones to permit access of fire department boats, the task of demolition was complicated by the old bridges' unusually sturdy steel and concrete construction.

NOTES

SECTION H

Southeastern Area

1. Heritage Square
   3800 N. Homer Street; Highland Park
2. Hale House
   Heritage Square, 3800 N. Homer Street;
   Highland Park
3. Valley Knudsen Garden-Residence
   Heritage Square, 3800 N. Homer Street;
   Highland Park
4. Beaudry House
   Heritage Square, 3800 N. Homer Street;
   Highland Park
5. Mt. Pleasant House
   Heritage Square, 3800 N. Homer Street;
   Highland Park
6. Palms Railroad Depot
   Heritage Square, 3800 N. Homer Street;
   Highland Park
7. Los Angeles County Central Hospital
   State Street; Los Angeles
8. Hollenbeck Home for the Aged
   573 S. Boyle Avenue; Los Angeles
9. Old Jewish Home
   325 S. Boyle Avenue; Los Angeles
10. St. Ann's Home
    2700 E. First Street; Los Angeles
11. Estrada Courts Murals
    Estrada Courts Office, bounded by
    Olympic Blvd., Lorena Street, 8th
    Street, and Grande Vista Avenue; Los
    Angeles.
12. Farmdale School
    2839 N. Eastern Avenue; Los Angeles
13. Site of Mission Vieja
    Lincoln Avenue and San Gabriel Blvd;
    Montebello
14. Soto-Sanchez Adobe
    946-1000 Adobe Avenue; Montebello
15. Rio San Gabriel Battlefield
    Washington Blvd. and Bluff Road;
    Montebello

16. First Baptist Church of Rivera
    9141 E. Burke Street; Pico-Rivera
17. Vicente Lugo Adobe
    6360 E. Gage Avenue (at Garfield
    Blvd.); Bell Gardens
18. Gage Home
    7000 E. Gage Avenue
    Bell Gardens
19. Rancho Los Amigos (Originally County
    Poor Farm)
    7601 E. Imperial Highway; Downey
20. Pio Pico Mansion
    6003 S. Pioneer Blvd.; Whittier
21. Grave of "Greek George"
    Founders Memorial Park, Broadway
    and Citrus Avenue; Whittier
22. Fred C. Nelles School for Boys
    11850 E. Whittier Blvd.; Whittier
23. Southern Pacific RR Station,
    11825 Bailey Street (off Hadley);
    Whittier
24. Paradox Hybrid Walnut Tree
    12300 E. Whittier Blvd.; Whittier
25. Whittier College
    13406 E. Philadelphia Avenue; Whittier
26. Bailey House
    13421 E. Camilla Street; Whittier
27. Paddison House
    11951 Imperial Highway; Norwalk
28. Metropolitan State Hospital
    11400 S. Norwalk Blvd.; Norwalk
29. Gilbert Sproul Museum
    12237 Sproul Street; Norwalk Park
30. Hargitt House
    12450 Maple Dale Avenue; Norwalk
31. Neff Home
    San Cristobal and San Esteban Streets;
    La Mirada

Olympic Boulevard in 1927.

H 1. HERITAGE SQUARE

On a thin strip of land paralleling the Pasadena Freeway, Heritage Square occupies a parklike setting made available by the Los Angeles Department of Parks and Recreation to serve as a haven for historic buildings which can not be preserved in their original location. Since 1968, the Cultural Heritage Foundation has acquired a number of historic buildings and moved them to this site which eventually will accommodate a dozen or more structures. The Hale House was moved to Heritage Square in 1970, the Valley Knudsen Garden-Residence in 1971, the Beaudry Street Residence in 1974, and the Palms Railroad Depot in 1976.

When in the 1960s the Bunker Hill Redevelopment Project threatened two old Victorian houses known as the "Salt Box" and "The Castle," the last reminders of this once elegant residential area, the buildings were saved from demolition and removed to Heritage Square in 1968. On October 9, 1969, both structures were completely destroyed by fire attributed to vandals. Despite this terrible setback, the Foundation moved the Hale House to Heritage Square the following year, and the City constructed fencing in order to prevent recurrence of vandalism.

The private, non-profit Cultural Heritage Foundation serves as an adjunct to the Los Angeles Cultural Heritage Board. It maintains a board of 25 directors, with an unlimited general membership.

Guided tours:
2nd Sunday and 3rd Wednesday of each
    month, 11 A.M.-3 P.M.
Special tours of 10 or more may be arranged by calling the Municipal Arts
    Department of L.A. City Hall, 485-2433.

Heritage Square
3800 N. Homer Street
Highland Park 90031
222-3150

H 2. HALE HOUSE

This flamboyantly ornamented Victorian residence is one of the few remaining examples of Queen Anne-Eastlake style in Southern California. Its exterior displays a clapboard siding with wood carving and plaster ornaments, fish scale shingles, wrought iron, stained glass, two ornate brick chimneys and a turrent crowned with a copper fleur-de-lis. Inside are ten rooms with high ceilings, decorative wood carving, and original gaslight fixtures.

Hale House, Heritage Square

This superbly crafted redwood frame house was built around 1888 in the once fashionable Mount Washington district of Highland Park. James and Bessie Hale owned the home from 1901 until Bessie's death in 1966. Subsequently, the Los Angeles Cultural Heritage Foundation acquired the building for one dollar and moved it to Heritage Square in 1970. The Foundation owns some of the original furniture and plans to restore the interior in the style of the period in which the house was built. Les Dames de Champagne gave money in 1972 to restore the dining room, and in 1973 the federal government awarded $42,400 in Historic Preservation funds for exterior restoration.

In 1974 Heritage Square gained considerable publicity when Ameritone Paint Corporation painted Hale House in 39 colors for advertisements in *Sunset* and *Arts and Architecture.* Later that year Ameritone repainted the house in nine original colors designated by the Heritage Square Committee. Thus far the dining room and second parlor have been restored and are open to visitors approximately eight days each month.

For group reservations and information contact the Cultural Heritage Foundation, Room 1500, City Hall, Los Angeles 90012 (485-2121)

Heritage Square
3800 North Homer Street
Highland Park 90031
222-3150

H 3. VALLEY KNUDSEN GARDEN-RESIDENCE

Built between 1877 and 1885, this relic of the Victorian era is one of the few remaining examples of 19th Century Mansard style architecture in Los Angeles. Its exterior wood craftsmanship and decorative detail are distinctive.

When demolition threatened in 1971, the Cultural Heritage Foundation moved the building from 1926 Johnston Street, west of Lincoln Park, to Heritage Square. A rare coral tree at the Johnston Street site was rescued through the efforts of the Bel Air Garden Club. Building and tree subsequently were dedicated in honor of Mrs. Valley Knudsen, civic worker and founder of Los Angeles Beautiful, the urban beautification program promoted by the city Chamber of Commerce. '

At present the house is surrounded by scaffolding and being repainted. Restoration plans include replacement of a cupola which apparently was removed in the late 1920s.

For information on future opening of this residence, contact the Cultural Heritage Foundation, Room 1500, Los Angeles 90012 (485-2121).

Heritage Square
3800 North Homer Street
Highland Park 90031
222-3150

H 4. BEAUDRY HOUSE

The architecture of this unique residence has been described by Dr. Robert Winter as Italianate, Eastlake, and Queen Anne, "an unusual combination which I have never before witnessed in such a tiny house." Beaudry House is believed to have been built in the early 1880s, and was located at 140-142 North Beaudry Avenue in downtown Los Angeles just west of the Harbor Freeway. In 1974 the building was moved to Heritage Square, where it was recently placed on a permanent foundation. Funds for relocation work have been provided by the Bank of America Foundation.

For information regarding future restoration of the Beaudry House and its eventual opening to the public,

Contact the Cultural Heritage Foundation, Room 1500, City Hall, Los Angeles 90012 (485-2121).

Heritage Square
3800 N. Homer Street
Highland Park 90031
222-3150

H 5. MT. PLEASANT HOUSE

This historic Victorian mansion was built in 1876 for lumber dealer William Hayes Perry, a self-made man who had come to Los Angeles from Ohio 20 years earlier and risen to responsible managerial positions in his own business and a host of other companies. (He is the great grandfather of Actor Robert Stack.) It was located on Pleasant Avenue in Boyle Heights.

Architects Kysor and Mathews designed the residence in the Italianate style with six bedrooms and a parlor, each with a bath and dressing room. Interior paneling is black walnut, with bird's eye maple in the dining room. "Mt. Pleasant" is carved in stone curb steps of one riser, and the name "Hubbell" in another set of steps. Judge Steven C. Hubbell, second owner of the property, also was a civic leader and developer of local public utilities. One of the organizers of the University of Southern California, Judge Hubbell was the school's first treasurer and a member of its first board of directors.

Thanks to the Los Angeles-Pasadena chapter of the Colonial Dames of America, stucco coating applied in more recent years was removed in 1975 prior to relocating the building in Heritage Square. The future of "Mt. Pleasant" is dependent upon raising the necessary funds.

Heritage Square
3800 N. Homer Street
Highland Park 90031
222-3150

H 6. PALMS RAILROAD DEPOT

This small railway depot in 1976 became the latest addition to the impressive assemblage of historic buildings at Heritage Square. Built in 1886, it was used by the Southern Pacific Railroad until about 1941, when it was abandoned.

Typical of many supposedly "mission style" railway stations throughout California, this and other similar depots were actually patterned after H. H. Richardson's Romanesque models in Massachusetts, which in no way were adapted from California's Franciscan missions.

Heritage Square
3800 N. Homer Street
Highland Park 90031
222-3150

Mt. Pleasant House

H 7. LOS ANGELES COUNTY GENERAL HOSPITAL

Originally in 1878 this site was called the Los Angeles County Hospital and Poor Farm. The County Farm was part of the hospital in the early days to raise food for the inmates, thereby reducing costs. The name was later changed to the Los Angeles County General Hospital and in 1968 it became known as the Los Angeles County-University of Southern California Medical Center.

Beginning in 1858 the first County medical patients were cared for in the adobe of Augustin Aguilar by the Daughters of Charity. In 1869 new facilities were opened at Ann and Naud Streets, near the present railroad yards. The Los Angeles Infirmary, also operated by the Daughters of Charity, was the hospital from which 49 patients were moved in 1878 to the new County Hospital on Mission Road.

Contractor George F. Leonard constructed the original wood frame buildings for the county at a cost of $8,000. The property at 1100 Mission Road was owned by John S. Griffin, M.D. (for whom Griffin Avenue was named). None of the original buildings remain, but the old Administration Building on Mission Road was built in 1909.

Over the years the County Hospital has expanded from 35 to 89 acres and from 100 patients to almost 79,000 in-patient visits. The twenty-story white granite structure on State Street, completed in 1934, houses the largest general acute hospital in the country.

Visiting hours of patients are from noon to 8:00 P.M. For tours of the hospital call 226-2622

H 8. HOLLENBECK HOME FOR THE AGED

California's oldest retirement home appropriately bears the name of its founder and benefactor, the widow, Mrs. J. Edward Hollenbeck. Her late husband had been a prominent real estate investor, philanthropist, and banker who helped organize the First National Bank of Los Angeles and served as its first president. His more than 6,700 acres of land investments included a large holding on the east side of Los Angeles River, then known as Boyle Heights (in 1926 the name was changed to Hollenbeck Heights). Here on Boyle Avenue at the present site of the Home for the Aged, the Hollenbecks established their residence in 1876. In 1890, five years after the death of her husband, Elizabeth Hollenbeck donated the property and established a trust which included the Hollenbeck Hotel on 2nd and Spring Streets (razed in 1933) and property later occupied by Bullock's Wilshire.

In 1896 Hollenbeck Home admitted its first forty-three residents. The original three-story edifice was constructed of brick with a stucco finish, and was one of the first buildings in Los Angeles with a concrete foundation. Architects Morgan and Walls

Hollenbeck Home for the Aged

use of the "mission" style made Hollenbeck Home one of the earliest in southern California to incorporate this design. Various enlargements were constructed in 1907-08 and 1922-23 which blended harmoniously with the spirit of the original architecture.

Hollenbeck Home for the Aged is on Boyle Avenue between the Santa Ana and Golden State Freeways. From the Santa Ana Freeway exit on 4th Street, go east to Boyle and turn left (south).

Business hours are Monday-Friday
9:00 A.M.-5:00 P.M.

573 S. Boyle Avenue
Los Angeles 90033
263-6195

H 9. OLD JEWISH HOME

Until quite recently, this complex of tile-roofed, brick and stone buildings, begun in 1912, was one of several homes in Boyle Heights for the aged and blind of the Jewish community. During the years between the two world wars, with the addition of a synagogue and auditorium, this site became a center of many activities for the pre-dominantly Jewish ethnic neighborhood in this area. When the Jewish home for the aged moved to new facilities in Reseda in 1975, the Boyle Heights property was acquired by the Japanese community at large for a Japanese retirement home.

Monday-Friday, 8:30 A.M.-5 P.M.

325 S. Boyle Avenue
Los Angeles 90012
263-9651

H 10. ST. ANN'S HOME

St. Ann's Home for the aged is operated by the Little Sisters of the Poor, a mendicant order of 4,700 nuns who dedicate their lives solely to the care of the elderly poor. One of the nuns, Sister Antoinette, who was 95 years old on Christmas of 1975, has been caring for old people without family or funds since the home first opened its doors in Boyle Heights in 1906. Unfortunately, the four-story, stately red brick edifice no longer meets the rigid state fire code, and the building had to be vacated by January 1, 1978. By that time, hopefully, the sisters will have raised the necessary $3 million for a new home.

Not open to the public

2700 E. First Street
Los Angeles 90033
269-7435

Old Jewish Home

H 11. ESTRADA COURTS MURALS

One of the most exciting and culturally significant developments in Los Angeles has been the painting of literally scores of murals, some as high as ten feet, on the sides of the two-story apartment buildings at Estrada Courts. This splendid creative endeavor was initiated in 1973 to furnish a medium of expression for the Chicano artists of the community. Approximately three-fourths of the projected 80 murals have been completed to date. Brightly colored and varying in style from abstract to realistic, they represent historical and socio-philosophical themes related to the Chicano Community. The city housing authority furnished the paint, rollers, and brushes, and scaffolds were supplied by the fire department. Estrada Courts are in East Los Angeles, bounded by Olympic Boulevard, Lorena Street, 8th Street and Grande Vista Avenue.

Open to the public at all times
No charge

Estrada Courts Office
Los Angeles 90023
268-7295

H 12. FARMDALE SCHOOL

Thanks to the efforts of the Los Angeles School Board, the Education Department at Cal-State Los Angeles, and the El Sereno Bicentennial Committee, the oldest school building in the city has been restored to serve as a teaching station and museum. Farmdale Elementary School was built in 1889, but by 1935 the one-room schoolhouse no longer could accommodate the area's growing population; a series of bungalows called Farmdale School was built on the one-acre site and the old schoolhouse sat empty nearby. In 1936 a high school was constructed there, called Woodrow Wilson High School. It became El Sereno Junior High School in 1970 when Wilson was relocated.

Restoration was first proposed in 1960, but plans were not approved until 1974. The charming Victorian woodframe Farmdale schoolhouse contains a pot-bellied stove, kerosene lamps, individual desks with ink wells and slates, maps, and a U.S. flag of the era, old musical instruments, books of the period, and enlarged pictures of early Farmdale students, several of whom were present at the opening of the restored classroom in 1976. The school's original bell still hangs in the bell tower.

Open to the public during school hours.
September-May:
    Monday-Friday, 7:30 A.M.-2:30 P.M.
June-August:
    Monday-Friday, 8 A.M.-12:30 P.M.

2839 N. Eastern Avenue
Los Angeles 90032
223-2441

H 13. SITE OF MISSION VIEJA

San Gabriel Mission was founded on September 8, 1771, by Franciscan Padres Jose' Cambon and Francisco Somera. The nearby San Gabriel River subjected the mission to flooding, so it was moved in 1775 to San Gabriel, and the old site became known as "Mission Vieja." A monument in a small public park commemorates the original founding.

More than a century later, in 1914, young Thomas Workman Temple II made a momentus discovery at the same site. Looking for tall wild oats, which he used to snare lizards, the nine year old boy came across an out-cropping of natural gas in a pool on his father's property. The discovery was located on the hillside behind the family home at Temple's Corners, which occupied the original mission site near the banks of the Rio Hondo (formerly called the San Gabriel River). Standard Oil commenced drilling in 1917, and soon the whole Montebello Oil Field was under development.

More than 200 million barrels of oil have been pumped from beneath the Montebello hills, and the output as of 1974 was 1,100 barrels a day. Since 1956, 2.3 billion cubic feet of natural gas have been stored 7,000 feet underground under 21 acres owned by the Southern California Gas Company.

Lincoln Avenue and San Gabriel Boulevard
Montebello 90640

H 14. SOTO-SANCHEZ ADOBE

Rancho La Merced was granted in 1844 to widow Dona Casilda Soto de Lobo, who erected a small adobe house about 1845 with the help of her sons. The 2,363-acre rancho was mortgaged in 1850 to William Workman for $1,225., with an option to purchase for a total sum of $2,225. Workman exercised his option in 1851, and the following year deeded the land to his son-in-law, F. P. F. Temple, and to Juan Matias Sanchez, the latter paying the sum of $1.00. Sanchez was Workman's loyal friend, a trapper who had sold his furs when both were in New Mexico before Workman came to California. When Sanchez came somewhat later, he became Workman's majordomo or overseer. Sanchez lived in the original Soto adobe, and in the mid-1850s he added a new north wing and a fountain in front.

Soto-Sanchez Adobe

When the Temple and Workman Bank was hit by the 1875 financial panic, Workman initially appealed to E. J. Baldwin for assistance. Baldwin insisted that Sanchez mortgage his property as part of the deal in which funds be provided to Workman. When asked to comply, Sanchez reportedly remarked, "No quiero morir de hambre" (I do not wish to die from hunger), but he signed his name to help his friend anyway. Temple and Workman's bank collapsed in 1876, "Lucky" Baldwin foreclosed, and all three lost their fortunes. Sanchez was left with only 200 acres and the old adobe. He died in 1885 and left the property to his widow, and when she died in 1892, Baldwin filed an action and received the adobe and the land from the Sanchez children.

Upon Baldwin's death in 1909 his estate sold the property to a group of men, and when they later divided the land, W. B. Scott chose 45 acres upon which the adobe was located, and in which he and his family took up residence. The building had deteriorated, so a new roof and dormer windows were installed. Eventually the old adobe became a two-story home of mansionlike proportions, with an elaborate garden and full-time caretakers. The ceilings were embellished with paintings and gold-leaf designs.

In 1957 the property was subdivided, but Mrs. Josephine Scott Crocker retained ownership of the adobe and six surrounding lots as an historical landmark, which she restored and later deeded to the City of Montebello in 1971. Architect Eugene E. Hougham was hired to assist the restoration, and furnishings and museum pieces have been contributed by the Montebello Historical Society.

Wednesday, Saturday, Sunday,
    1:00-4:00 P.M.

946-1000 Adobe Avenue
Montebello 90640

H 15. RIO SAN GABRIEL BATTLEFIELD

Near this site on January 8, 1847, American forces commanded by Captain Robert F. Stockton, U.S. Navy, Commander in Chief, and Brigadier General Stephen W. Kearny, U.S. Army, fought Californians commanded by General José María Flores in the Battle of Rio San Gabriel. As the American force of 600 advanced toward Los Angeles, the Californians, several hundred in number, stationed themselves advantageously atop the bluff on the far side of the river. Two cannons were placed opposite to and commanding the ford. Luckily for the sailors, marines, dragoons, and volunteers crossing the quick-sandy river, the Californians' powder was so poor that their artillery fire, which otherwise would have been withering, did not hinder the Americans from fording the river. Instead of a protracted and bloody battle the engagement lasted less than two hours. Only two Americans were killed and eight wounded, and the Californians suffered similar relatively minor losses.

Rio San Gabriel Battlefield

It is most fitting that this battle is commemorated by a small shelter featuring two very old cannons which, though they probably were not used in the battle, once fronted the Los Angeles County Courthouse until it was demolished in 1934, when the cannons were removed to the Armory in Exposition Park. They were brought to the present site in 1941, which was marked with a plaque and dedicated as a state landmark in 1945.

Visitors are often confused by the fact that the monument commemorating the Battle of San Gabriel overlooks the river now called Rio Hondo. During the 1860s and 1880s the flooding San Gabriel periodically left its banks to carve out a new channel, on one occasion destroying much of the Pio Pico mansion near the banks of what became known as the new San Gabriel River, with the rather inappropriate name Rio Hondo ("Deep River") being given to the old San Gabriel river bed.

Washington Boulevard and Bluff Road
Montebello 90640

First Baptist Church of Rivera

H 16. FIRST BAPTIST CHURCH OF RIVERA

The First Baptist Church of Rivera was organized in 1888 with 15 members who met in an old schoolhouse. Friends and neighbors helped to raise funds which eventually totalled $1,119 for the church building, even though many were not members of the congregation. A one-room chapel was erected on the southeast corner of Slauson Avenue and Rosemead Boulevard (Slauson was then called Shuggs Lane and Rosemead known as San Gabriel Boulevard). The building was dedicated in 1889 and a bell hung in the belfry in 1890. At first baptisms were held in the Rio Hondo on the east bank at the Slauson crossing. A baptistry was installed in a new room built on the back of the church in 1904 with donated labor. In 1916 the church building was moved to its present location.

Today the exterior of this simple little wood-framed chapel is little changed from its appearance early in this century. It resembles New England Colonial style, with steep pitched, gabled roof, clapboard siding, narrow, pointed arch windows on side elevations, a small, projected front porch, and a central spire projecting above it on the south facade.

Sunday Services: 8:30 A.M.-10:50 A.M.
  and 6 P.M. (September-May)
  7 P.M. (June-August)

9141 E. Burke Street
Pico-Rivera 90660
698-0095

H 17. VICENTE LUGO ADOBE

This Monterey-style wood and adobe casa occupies a site which was once part of Rancho San Antonio, a 29,413-acre grant originally awarded to Antonio María Lugo in 1810. Don Vicente built this home with its second-story balcony, and about 1850 retired here from the family's townhouse in Los Angeles. Sometimes called the "Beau Brummel of Los Angeles," Vicente Lugo did much to perpetuate his family's reputation for fine hospitality.

Over the years the Lugo family gradually relinquished its once vast land holdings, which were developed by others into the communities of Huntington Park, Vernon, Walnut Park, South Gate, Lynwood, Bell, Cudahy, Bell Gardens, and the City of Commerce. Land which included the Lugo hacienda was sold at a sheriff's auction in 1865 for less than a dollar an acre. Jonathan S. Slauson purchased much of this property in 1883 for $200 an acre, and in 1927 a portion was sold for $7,000 an acre for the Firestone Tire and Rubber Company plant.

Private residence
Not open to the public

6360 E. Gage Avenue (at Garfield Blvd)
Bell Gardens 90201

H 18. GAGE HOME

When Henry T. Gage married one of Lugo daughters, he received this piece of property as a wedding present. Gage was later Republican governor of California from 1899 to 1903. The house was originally built about 1840 and is still occupied as a home.

Private residence not open to the public

7000 E. Gage Avenue
Bell Gardens

H 19. RANCHO LOS AMIGOS (ORIGINALLY COUNTY POOR FARM)

Land was purchased at this site in 1885 and the first building constructed in 1887. In order to provide for infirm indigents of Los Angeles County, the first sixty ambulatory patients were transferred here from the county hospital at the end of 1888. A few years after its founding, the name was changed from the Country Poor Farm to Rancho Los Amigos.

Rancho Los Amigos, c. 1906

The site of the original central administration building with two hospital wings was on 120 acres west of Paramount Boulevard and south of Imperial Highway. More than 400 additional acres were acquired over a period of time until the 1930s. In recent years the facility has sold off much of this land, and now has 200 acres whose assessed valuation as of 1970 is $50 million. After the 1933 earthquake many buildings were condemned; 55 acres were purchased on the north side of Imperial Highway where the new facility has been built.

William Saar, Ombudsman at Rancho Los Amigos Hospital, has an excellent collection of photographs and scrapbooks which graphically depict the growth of this institution.

Visiting hours 10:00 A.M.-8:00 P.M. daily

7601 E. Imperial Highway
Downey 90242
922-7111

H 20. PÍO PICO MANSION

In its heyday Pío Pico's adobe mansion was one of the most pretentious and one of the loveliest country homes of California. Don Pío built the hacienda on the 9,000 acre Paso de Bartola, which he had purchased for $4,600 in 1850 and affectionately named "El Ranchito." In 1883 the rampaging Rio San Gabriel rose above its banks and cut away the soil to the very wall of the mansion, weakening the foundations of the west side until the two end rooms collapsed and the *corredor* roof fell in. At the time he rebuilt the house, Pico found himself temporarily short of funds and had to borrow $62,000. Through fraud and foreclosure on this loan,

Pío Pico Mansion (two views)

secure aid and money in Mexico to fight against the American army, Pico returned to California in 1848 and quickly involved himself in community and business affairs. He served as Los Angeles councilman, founded Picoville, and invested in California's first oil venture.

After Pico's death "El Ranchito" was abandoned and began to deteriorate. In 1907 Harriet Russell Strong, who had once lived in the house herself, worked to save the Pico mansion when the buildings were being demolished for use as a road fill for repaving Whittier Boulevard. With the help of the Governor Pico Museum and Historical Society and the Landmarks Club, the property was purchased and restored, and in 1917 the mansion was given to the State of California. It again deteriorated until 1946, when it was again restored, and the State selected 1870 as the date that should be stressed in interpretation of the mansion's history.

The 13-room hacienda is a "U" shaped structure with the court open to the east between the wings. The adobe walls are between two and three feet thick. A covered porch with stairs to the second floor is on the inside of the "U" and there is a well in the courtyard.

Files at the Pico mansion contain materials on Pío Pico, some of his letters, photographs of Pico and the mansion, and materials on Harriet Strong.

Wednesday-Sunday, 1:00-4:00 P.M.
Admission, adults 50¢, students and
    children 25¢

6003 S. Pioneer Boulevard
Whittier 90606
695-1217

for which Pico had put up all of his property as security, he lost all of his estate. He took the case to court, but the California Supreme Court decided against him in 1892, and within two years Don Pío Pico, the last Mexican governor of California was dead.

A leading political figure in the 1830s and 1840s, Pico participated in several "revolutions" and served as governor in 1845 and 1846, when he moved the capital to Los Angeles and stepped up secularization of mission lands. His term of office was abruptly cut short by the American invasion, and the governor fled to Mexico. Unable to

H 21. GRAVE OF "GREEK GEORGE"

The grave of "Greek George" Caralampo is in Founders Memorial Park in Whittier. He was a camel driver from Asia Minor who came to this country with the second load of camels purchased by Jefferson Davis for the U.S. War Department as an experiment to open a wagon road from Fort Defiance, New Mexico, to Fort Tejon in southern California. Because of the Civil War, the project was abondoned, and in 1876 "Greek George" became a naturalized citizen under the name of George Allen. He built an adobe home on Santa Monica Boulevard.

Founders Memorial Park
Broadway and Citrus Avenue
Whittier 90601

H 22. FRED C. NELLES SCHOOL FOR BOYS

As authorized by the state legislature in 1888, Governor Robert Waterman appointed a board of trustees to establish California's first state correctional institution for boys. Trustee Hervey Lindley of Whittier arranged for a donation of 40 acres along Whittier Boulevard with a bonded option on an adjoining 120 acres at $200 per acre, which the state later purchased. Dr. Walter Lindley became the first superintendent of the Whittier School for Boys, which in 1920 became known as the Fred C. Nelles School for Boys.

Not open to the public

11850 E. Whittier Boulevard
Whittier 90602

H 23. SOUTHERN PACIFIC RAILROAD STATION, WHITTIER

The railroad station in Whittier is one of very few depots built before the turn of the century to survive to the present. It was constructed in 1888 to capitalize on the building and business boom in the new town of Whittier. That community raised $40,000 to help construct a six-mile spur line from the Norwalk area. The building boom came to a halt, but the railroad provided transportation for the burgeoning citrus industry in the 1890s. The depot is a simple wooden structure with ornamentation and is typical of many S.P. stations erected in the late 19th Century. By 1970 the station was no longer

Southern Pacific Railroad Station, Whittier, 1890s.

Southern Pacific Railroad Station, Whittier, today.

needed by the railroad, and it was leased to private interests.

11825 Bailey Street, just off Hadley Street
Whittier

H 24. PARADOX HYBRID WALNUT TREE

Planted in 1907 as part of an agricultural experiment by the University of California, this tree commemorates the fact that the Whittier area was once the largest walnut growing area in the world.

12300 E. Whittier Boulevard
Whittier 90602

H 25. WHITTIER COLLEGE

The 100-acre campus of Whittier College spreads upward over the lower slopes of the Puente Hills at the city's eastern edge, well shaded by trees. Established by Quakers in 1891 as Whittier Academy, it was chartered ten years later as a co-educational, non-sectarian college. The school provides liberal arts and pre-professional curricula for a student body of about 1,400.

The library houses 127,000 volumes, and in addition has the largest collection of Quaker materials west of the Mississippi. There are special collections relating to John Greenleaf Whittier, William Somerset Maugham, the manuscripts of Jessamyn West, and a small Richard Nixon collection.

Open during regular scheduled hours.

13406 E. Philadelphia Avenue
Whittier 90601
693-0771

H 26. BAILEY HOUSE

German immigrant farmer, Jacob Gerkins, built this ranch house about 1868 on 160 acres of land which he claimed under provisions of the Homestead Act. Through purchases and foreclosures in 1880 and 1881, the property came into the possession of John M. Thomas, an Indian farmer who had come to California in 1859 and to Los Angeles in 1868. He raised barley here until 1887, when the Thomas ranch was purchased by the Pickering Land and Water Company, of which Jonathan Bailey was president, and plans to subdivide the area were quickly implemented.

The prospective new community had already been named after New England Quaker poet, John Greenleaf Whittier. Bailey and his wife soon established their home in the old ranch house among the pepper trees, thus becoming Whittier's first citizens. Within a few days Sunday religious services were held on their front porch. The bench on which the worshippers sat is still there. Two weeks later land sales began— $100 to $200 for town lots and $1,000 for 5-acre parcels outside the townsite—and after 2 months the first carload of 15 Quaker settlers arrived from Iowa by train.

For decades the house on the Thomas Ranch property served as a landmark for

Bailey House

travelers. A person making the 2 1/2 hour drive from Los Angeles across the wide plain that is Montebello could look up ahead and see at the base of the Puente Hills near Turnbull Arroyo a patch of green, formed by the pepper trees clumped around the house.

A simple frame structure in a style common to the Midwest, the Bailey House was restored by the Whittier Heritage Association. The house contains furnishings which belonged to the Bailey family and other pioneers of Whittier, as well as photographs and artifacts relating to the town's history.

Wednesdays, 1:00-3:00 P.M.
Admission, adults 50¢, children no charge.

13421 E. Camilla Street
Whittier 90601

H 27. PADDISON HOUSE

Businessman John Paddison, an English emigrant, bought land in the Norwalk area in 1874, and four years later constructed a two-story Victorian home which is still standing. Six acres remain intact with barns

Paddison Home, Norwalk

and out-buildings. The house is being refurbished by a grandson of the original owner and is almost entirely concealed by surrounding trees today.

Private residence
Not open to the public

11951 Imperial Highway
Norwalk 90650

H 28. METROPOLITAN STATE HOSPITAL

Originally named the Norwalk State Hospital, this mental hospital accommodates 400 patients and was self-sustaining when it opened in 1916. Since then the state-owned facility has been considerably enlarged, with 37 wards accommodating approximately 1,300 in-patients.

As an institution for those afflicted with mental illness, alcoholism, and drug addiction, the hospital is open only to visits by friends and relatives of patients.

11400 S. Norwalk Boulevard
Norwalk 90650
863-7011

H 29. GILBERT SPROUL MUSEUM

Gilbert Sproul, founder of Norwalk, built this redwood home for himself and his family in 1870. Many town meetings were held in this house, which was one of the first homes in the Norwalk area. Sproul's granddaughter, Vida Sproul Hunter, donated the home to the City, which moved the building about 100 yards to its present location, where since 1964 it has been open to the public as the Sproul Museum. Inside is the

Sproul House in 1891, now a city museum in Norwalk Park

Hargitt House a few years after construction (c. 1894)

original furniture, much of which dates back to 1870, along with materials relating to the history of Norwalk, such as maps, early school pictures, and other city photographs. In addition there are displays of dolls, guns, and Indian artifacts.

Wednesday-Friday 10:00 A.M.-2:00 P.M.
Weekends 12:00-5:00 P.M.
Admission free

12237 Sproul Street
Norwalk Park 90650
864-9663

Not open at present to the public

12450 Maple Dale Avenue
Norwalk 90650
864-9663

H 31. NEFF HOME

In 1880 Chicago atlas publisher Andrew McNally purchased the 2,378 acre Windemere Ranch in La Mirada, which he planned to sell as 20-acre country estates. Due to tight money problems, the plan was abandoned in 1900, and the remaining 1,500 acres were used to establish the olive and citrus empire of the McNally Olive Company.

A ranch home was constructed for McNally in 1893-94, but his daughter Nannie, and son-in-law, Edwin Neff, were the first occupants. Andrew McNally brought rare plants, trees, and birds here from all over the world. Ed Neff served as secretary and manager of the La Mirada Land Company, and later became president and secretary to the Pasadena Tournament of Roses Association. The Neffs lived in the

H 30. HARGITT HOUSE

D. D. Johnson, organizer of the Norwalk school system, built this beautiful two-story Victorian home in 1891. Following the death in 1975 of Charles Hargitt, Johnson's grandson, who was born and lived his life in the house, the property was donated to the City of Norwalk. The original furnishings have been preserved, and there are plans to open the house as a museum.

Neff Home, Neff Park

McNally Ranch House, La Mirada, c. 1890s.

house until McNally's death in 1904, at which time company accountant, Robert McGill, became manager and moved with his family into the home. Upon McGill's death 40 years later, William Neff, grandson of the original occupants, returned with his family to manage the estate. Sometime later, Neff and his wife, Mina, sold or donated 10 acres around the home to the Southeast Park District for a recreational and cultural center.

La Mirada's oldest home was built as a wood frame structure with some stucco added at a later date. Standing nearby are the George home (the foreman's cottage) and the Neff barn, which housed carriage and stable. Pictures, photographs, and historical materials relating to the Neff home are in the History Room at La Mirada City Hall.

The house is frequently used for group meetings, weddings, and as a craft center.

Neff Park is located in La Mirada between Biola and Valley View Boulevards, just off Stage Road at San Cristobal and San Esteban Streets.

There is no charge for tours of the historical buildings but reservations must be made in advance, either with City Historian Bob Camp at La Mirada City Hall, 137 La Mirada Boulevard, La Mirada 90638 (943-0131), or with the Southeast Recreation and Park District, 12159 East Sproul Street, Norwalk 90650 (864-3794). Neff Park is open at all times.

NOTES

Queen Anne's Cottage, Baldwin estate.

SECTION I

Eastern Los Angeles

1. Mt. Wilson Trail, Richardson House, and Lizzie's Trail Inn, Sierra Madre
   Corner of Mt. Wilson Trail Road and Mira Monte Avenue
2. Los Angeles State and County Arboretum
   301 N. Baldwin Avenue; Arcadia
3. Hugo Reid Adobe
   301 N. Baldwin Avenue; Arcadia
4. The Queen Anne Cottage and Coach Barn
   301 N. Baldwin Avenue; Arcadia
5. Santa Anita Depot
   301 N. Baldwin Avenue; Arcadia
6. Santa Anita Race Track and Arcadia County Park
   285 W. Huntington Drive and 405 S. Santa Anita Avenue
7. Vollmer House
   464 N. Myrtle Avenue; Monrovia
8. Aztec Hotel
   200 Block of Foothill Blvd. (near Magnolia Avenue); Monrovia
9. El Monte Cemetery, Rosemead
   9236 Valley Blvd.; (Mission Rd.)
10. El Monte Historical Museum
    3100 Tyler Avenue
11. William Workman Home, Rancho La Puente
    15415 E. Don Julian Road; City of Industry
12. Workman Cemetery and Temple Mausoleum
    15415 E. Don Julian Road
13. Temple Mansion
    15415 E. Don Julian Road
14. John A. Rowland Home and Lillian Hudson Dibble Museum, Rancho La Puente
    16021 Gale Avenue; City of Industry
15. John Reed Home, Rancho La Puente
    16021 Gale Avenue
16. Two Pylons, Gateway to Adams Tract
    Hollenbeck Avenue near corner of San Bernardino Road; Covina
17. Holy Trinity Episcopal Church
    100 N. 3rd Avenue; Covina
18. Covina Firehouse
    125 E. College Street
19. Walnut Packing House
    Lemon Avenue and Walnut Drive
20. William R. Rowland Ranch House
    Lemon Avenue at Lemon Creek Park; Walnut
21. Phillips Mansion
    2640 W. Pomona Blvd. (near Valley Blvd.); Spadra
22. San Dimas Hotel
    111 N. San Dimas Avenue
23. Mud Springs Monument
    Corner of San Dimas Canyon Road and Palomares Avenue
24. La Verne College
    1950 3rd Street
25. La Casa de Carrion
    919 Puddingstone Drive; La Verne
26. Los Angeles County Fairgrounds
    White Avenue
27. Blessing Land
    458 Kenoak Place; Pomona
28. First Palomares Adobe
    1569 N. Park Avenue; Pomona

29. La Casa Alvarado
    1459 Old Settlers Lane
30. Adobe de Palomares
    491 E. Arrow Highway
31. Palomares Cemetery
    N. San Antonio Avenue and E. Arrow Highway

32. Sumner Hall, First Building of Pomona College
    College Way and Bonita Avenue
33. Denison Library, Scripps College
    Columbia Street and 11th Street
34. Honnold Library, Claremont Colleges
35. Pomona Power Plant
    Mt. Baldy Road, San Antonio Canyon

I 1. MT. WILSON TRAIL, RICHARDSON HOUSE, AND LIZZIE'S TRAIL INN, SIERRA MADRE

This historic trail was constructed in 1864 by "Don Benito" Wilson, with the help of Indian labor. It was first used to bring timber down from the mountains for the family home of John Richardson, which he built the same year. Later, in 1889, students from Harvard University carried all the equipment for the first telescope on Mt. Wilson up this trail. In recent years the trail has been the site of an annual foot race on Memorial Day weekend.

The Richardson House, the oldest in Sierra Madre, has recently been restored and furnished through the efforts of the local historical society.

At the same site, adjacent to the Richardson House, is Lizzie's Trail Inn, which dates from the early 1900s. Located at the base of the trail, this once popular tiny restaurant was abandoned and fell into disrepair for many years. As a Bicentennial project, members of the Sierra Madre Historical Society are restoring it as a small museum.

The Richardson House is open free of charge every Sunday from 1:00-4:00 P.M. The popular 7 1/2 mile Mt. Wilson Trail is open every day except during the summer, when there is extreme hazard from fires. Hikers are urged to respect the rights of residents who live near the base of the trail. Especially beautiful in the spring, the trail demands good physical condition from those who hike it.

Corner of Mt. Wilson Trail Road and Mira Monte Avenue
(near Mountain Trail Avenue)
Sierra Madre 91024

I 2. LOS ANGELES STATE AND COUNTY ARBORETUM

Once the site of a Gabrielino Indian village, the land now occupied by the Arboretum became, in the early 1800s, the center of Rancho Santa Anita, a vast acreage belonging to Mission San Gabriel. In the 1830s and 1840s, Scotch trader Hugo Reid occupied the rancho which was later bought by E. J. "Lucky" Baldwin in 1875.

The Arboretum's rich historical legacy is preserved in the restored Hugo Reid adobe (1839) and "Lucky" Baldwin's ornate Queen Anne Cottage (1881), his Coach Barn (1879), and numerous peafowl, imported in the 1890s, all of which earned for him a reputation for extravagant taste and lavish entertainment.

Most of the Arboretum's 127 acres are devoted to trees, shrubs, vines and groundcovers grown for educational, research, and scientific purposes. The research program includes the propagation, testing and introduction of new plant materials, as well as experimental research into various horticultural and botanical problems such as the relationship of plants and smog, or the eradication of injurious plant diseases and insect pests. The educational program includes field trips, classes and workshops for young people, and formal adult classes in botany, plant taxonomy, practical horticulture, and botanical sketching.

The Arboretum is open free of charge every day except Christmas, from 9:00 A.M. to 5:00 P.M. Tram tours leave every 30-45 minutes on week-days from 12:00 to 3:45 P.M., and on weekends from 10:00 A.M. to 4:00 P.M. Children under 18 must remain with a responsible adult at all times. Dogs and other animals must be left outside.

301 N. Baldwin Avenue
Arcadia 91006
446-8251

I 3. HUGO REID ADOBE

Rancho Santa Anita, a grant of 13,319 acres, was originally part of the San Gabriel Mission lands. Hugo Reid, a Scotsman who immigrated to California, applied for the title in 1839 and received provisional ownership in 1841, later confirmed in 1845.

The three-room adobe house built in 1839 was the "Country seat" of Reid, his Indian wife, Victoria, and the four children of her first marriage. Felipe, the eldest son, seems to have been resident manager, but as the orchards and vineyards developed, the family spent more time here than in their home in San Gabriel. Outside, Indian servants lived in brush shelters called "wickiups." Reid was a rare man for his era in that he was truly interested in the Indians, his wife's people, and in 1852 he published an important account of their history, customs, and beliefs.

Reid sold the ranch in 1847 to his old friend and neighbor, Henry Dalton, for $2,700 (20¢ an acre). Passing through many hands, the Santa Anita Rancho (reduced to 8,000 acres) was purchased by "Lucky" Baldwin in 1875 for $200,000 ($25 an acre).

The three-room adobe, the oldest of the Arboretum's historic buildings, was restored and authentically furnished together with a "ramada," a thatched, open-faced terrace to the west, where Baldwin's frame ell of 1879 once stood.

Hugo Reid's house may be viewed free of charge, any time during the hours the Arboretum is open. Visitors never are permitted inside, but the interior of the small adobe can be seen through the windows. Twice

Hugo Reid Adobe interior

yearly the Arboretum's historical section is opened for special guided tours; check in advance for the dates.

Open daily, 9 A.M.-5 P.M.

301 N. Baldwin Avenue
Arcadia 91006
446-8251

I 4. THE QUEEN ANNE COTTAGE AND COACH BARN

Elias Jackson Baldwin's "Queen Anne Cottage," set beside the spring-filled lake at Rancho Santa Anita, is one of the most picturesque historical landmarks in California. The house's charming name, given to it in later years, comes from a style of architecture popular in the late Victorian era. It is a wood frame house with four gabled roofs, and the bell tower is known as a belvedere. Architect A. A. Bennett spared no expense in the building and construction of the cottage, which he completed in 1881. Bennett is also remembered for designing the State capitol in Sacramento, as well as for being the father of Baldwin's last wife.

Baldwin's principal home was in San Francisco on Nob Hill. The cottage at his Santa Anita ranch was planned solely for the entertainment of guests, and had no cooking facilities. When Baldwin died in 1909, his daughter Anita crated all detachable parts of the house and carefully stored them in the Coach Barn. Over the years the buildings fell into sad disrepair; many people tell of going through the Queen Anne Cottage on horses.

In 1949 restoration of the historical section of what has become the Los Angeles County Arboretum began under the direction of Susanna Bryant Dakin, and since 1954 the completely refurbished cottage has been open to visitors. The formal garden, neglected for years, was beautifully restored by the Pasadena Garden Club.

A walkway leading to the cottage entrance is of marble, as are all the fireplaces inside, including one with a marble hearth. The whole building is surrounded by a very wide porch. Upper portions of most of the windows are pictorially stained and leaded glass. Inside, the delightful music room has a square grand piano, a harp, and other instruments. The study contains a remarkable old desk, and to the rear of this is a bathroom, showing Baldwin's shaving equipment and toilet facilities.

To the rear of the cottage is the Coach Barn, also restored, with much ranch equipment and outside dog kennels. It was built in 1879 before the railroads had come to the San Gabriel Valley, so the original lumber for the building was shipped from northern California and brought to the ranch on wagons from San Pedro Harbor. The barn was one of three buildings which matched the Queen Anne Cottage, but when the ranch fell into disrepair the other two were torn down.

In 1957 and 1958 the State Division of Architecture spent almost a year renovating the Coach Barn. All inside walls of alternating redwood and Port Orford cedar slats, three inches wide, had to be removed and scraped by hand before they could be renailed to new studding. Special fireproofing material was impregnated into the roof rafters. New shingles had to be made especially for the restoration.

In the loft upstairs were the hay storage area and the grain bins. Above the loft is the bell tower room which not only housed the stable boys, but also provides a view of the entire ranch. Downstairs are the stalls for the coach horses with cast-iron hay chutes and bins, fancy brush racks, and dividing grilles. Also on display are Baldwin's coach and runabout buggy, fancy saddles and harnesses, a blacksmith's shop, and an old firefighting wagon.

The Queen Anne Cottage may be viewed free of charge any time during the hours when the Arboretum is open. Visitors ordinarily are not permitted inside, but may view the interior through the windows. A special exception to this rule is made twice annually, when guided tours conduct visitors through the Arboretum's historical section, including the inside of the cottage.

Open daily, 9 A.M.-5 P.M.

301 N. Baldwin Avenue
Arcadia 91006
446-8251

I 5. SANTA ANITA DEPOT

In 1890 the Santa Fe Railroad built this depot on Rancho Santa Anita. E. J. Baldwin had paid $10,000 for the right-of-way to the railroad with the condition that trains would always stop for him upon request, and for the next half century the depot served residents of the area—for many years also as a post office—until it was closed in 1940. With the advent of the Foothill Freeway, members of the community rallied to the defense of the depot and in 1968 had it relocated and restored on the grounds of the Los Angeles State and County Arboretum, there to become part of the already existing complex of historical buildings.

Small stations like this one usually had wooden floors, but Baldwin was always a man to be afraid of fires, as was anyone who had lived in San Francisco during the Gold Rush days. Concrete floors were a new and safer building concept in 1890. The building is unusual, too, in that it has a fireplace in the waiting room; most stations had a large pot belly stove for heat.

The brick and much of the outside framing is original in its Gothic Revival style, while the furnishings are authentic of the turn of the century period. Especially noteworthy in the upstairs living quarters is a "pie safe"—mother could bake several pies at one time and lock them up so the children couldn't get to them; the holes in the sides let the steam out so that the pies could cool.

The Santa Anita Depot may be viewed free of charge any time during the hours the Arboretum is open. Visitors are not permitted inside, but may peer through the windows. A special exception to this rule is made twice annually when guided tours conduct visitors through the Arboretum's historical section, including the inside of the depot.

Open daily, 9 A.M.-5 P.M.

301 N. Baldwin Avenue
Arcadia 91006
446-8251

I 6. SANTA ANITA RACE TRACK AND ARCADIA COUNTY PARK

The original Santa Anita Race track, developed by Elias J. "Lucky" Baldwin, was located on land that is now Arcadia County Park. The grandstand seated several thousand people; beside it was a large paddock, and to the rear were acres of stables that could house as many as 1,200 horses. Twenty thousand spectators attended the opening day in 1907, but after the state legislature in 1909 banned horse racing in California, Santa Anita Park closed its gates forever.

In the early 1930s the state again legalized horse racing. The well intentioned efforts of Anita Baldwin ("Lucky's" daughter) and others to re-establish the sport of Arcadia met with temporary success. Townspeople expressed their approval by a vote of 1,563 to 599 but disclosure of promoter Joe Smoot's financial shenanigans brought the work project to an abrupt halt.

About this time a group of investors which included Hal Roach of Hollywood movie fame, formed the Los Angeles Turf Club. After joining with Dr. Charles H. Strub

Santa Anita Racetrack

of San Francisco, who possessed a racing permit, they selected Arcadia as the site for their new race track, which opened on Christmas Day of 1934.

During World War II, Santa Anita Race Track served as an assembly center for persons of Japanese ancestry who were being "relocated" to concentration camps. By summer of 1942 the government started to evacuate Japanese from the Pacific Coast, and in sixty days the camp was empty. Thereafter, Santa Anita was used as a training center with facilities for approximately 20,000 troops. Near the end of the war, the facility also served as a prisoner of war camp.

As for the original Santa Anita Park race track site abandoned in 1909, it too was used by the military during a world war. Early in 1918, near the end of World War I, E. J. Baldwin's former race track property became Ross Field, or "The Balloon School." Here soldiers were trained to direct artillery fire from observation balloons, and a huge hangar was constructed on the southwest corner of the field.

With the return of peace, Ross Field was neglected and soon became an eyesore in the heart of the city. All attempts to get the land back from the War Department failed until, during the Depression, the Works Progress Administration developed the land into a park and golf course. Constructed almost entirely by hand labor between 1936 and 1938, Arcadia Country Park cost the W. P. A. approximately $625,000.

Santa Anita Race Track
285 West Huntington Drive
Arcadia 91006
447-2171

Arcadia Country Park
405 South Santa Anita Avenue
Arcadia 91006

I 7. VOLLMER HOUSE

Architect Frederick Wallace designed this imposing two-story residence in 1923 for L. B. Vollmer, who was secretary and treasurer of Flower City Ornamental Iron Company of Minnesota, the largest industry of its kind in the country at the time. Upton Sinclair, famous author of *The Jungle* and scores of other novels, who in 1932 was also Democratic candidate for California governor, purchased the house from the original owner in 1942 and resided there for several years.

Private residence
Not open to the public

464 N. Myrtle Avenue
Monrovia 91016

I 8. AZTEC HOTEL

In the early 1920s the citizens of Monrovia, unable to attract outside capital to construct a hotel in their comparatively small town, sought to raise the necessary funds from public subscriptions. An amount of $95,000 was sought, but community enthusiasm was such that a total of $138,900

Aztec Hotel

was pledged. Architect Robert B. Stacy-Judd incorporated elements of Aztec, Toltec, and Mayan architecture, and the hotel was completed in 1926.

Community spirit notwithstanding, the Aztec Hotel was never a financial success. After a new financing plan failed in 1927, the building was sold at an auction to Fidelity Savings and Loan for $50,000. Today various small shops operate their business on the ground level.

200 Block of Foothill Blvd.
(near Magnolia Avenue)
Monrovia 91016

I 9. EL MONTE CEMETERY, ROSEMEAD

This little cemetery, with its scattering of old-fashioned tombstones, is said to be the oldest Protestant burial ground in southern California and possibly the state. Just how many pioneers were buried here after they reached the end of the Santa Fe Trail is unknown. In the days when El Monte was still known as Lexington, many of the headstones were made of wood. Two youths hired to clean up the cemetery decided it would be easier if they burned the weeds and grass off the graves. Many of the wooden headstones burned too, and some were never replaced.

Legend has it that when pioneer families could not afford to bury young children, who succumbed to frequent epidemics, they would slip over the cemetery fence at night and dig small, unmarked graves.

The cemetery's origin dates back to the 1850s, when Henry Dalton, owner of Rancho San Francisquito, stumbled across two unmarked graves on his property. Cactus had been planted around the graves to protect them from coyotes. The graves belonged to families in Lexington, who had traveled to the site to bury their dead because the water table in Lexington was then a scant six feet below the surface. Dalton left the graves and the adjacent land undisturbed as a burial ground for the people of the community.

The cemetery's tombstones and grave markers bear the names of early settlers such as Durfee, Guess, Wiggins, Fawcett, Cleminson, McGirk, and Ellis, all prominent in the history of the El Monte-Rosemead-Temple City area.

Open during daylight hours

9236 Valley Boulevard
(at the corner of Mission Road)
Rosemead 91770

I 10. EL MONTE HISTORICAL MUSEUM

The building which houses El Monte Historical Museum was built by the Works Progress Administration as a library during the Depression. The Library served the community from 1936 until 1967, when it moved into new facilities. The vacant structure was soon occupied by the Historical Society, formerly located at the old high school on Valley Boulevard, its home for the first nine years of its existence.

The museum is divided into three areas. A small archive library contains manuscript letters and diaries of local pioneers, documents, newspapers, books, maps, films, and 2,000 pictures and photographs. Another section displays the interior of a home in the El Monte area circa 1870-1890. A third wing portrays the frontier village of Lexington in the 1850s (the community changed its name to El Monte in 1868), with a general store, barber shop, police department, and school room. There is also a jail in the rear of the building.

Among the various authentic nineteenth century displays are tools, clothing, fabrics, laces, dishes and glassware, furniture, musical instruments, and Indian, Spanish, and Mexican artifacts. In addition there is also a gift shop.

Tuesday-Friday, 10:30 A.M.-4:00 P.M.
Group tours are available by appointment.

3100 Tyler Avenue
El Monte
444-3813

I 11. WILLIAM WORKMAN HOME, RANCHO LA PUENTE

Within a year after their overland immigrant train reached southern California in 1841, the leaders of the Workman-Rowland party were jointly granted 48,470 acres known as Rancho La Puente ("Ranch of the Bridge"). William Workman built the original adobe in 1842 with the help of former mission Indians. The home was said to have been under siege by hostile Indians for three weeks in the early days. A secret tunnel supposedly led toward the present family cemetery and provided access to water unknown to the Indians. Shortly thereafter, a well is said to have been dug in the basement in anticipation of future raids by hostile Indians.

Between 1843 and 1868 the adobe was enlarged into a "U" shaped structure, with two parallel 75-foot wings added southward. An adobe wall which enclosed the south elevation had a massive 50-foot wide wooden gate.

In 1872 an entirely new "H" shaped structure was superimposed over the original adobe. The architect was Ezra F. Kysor, who had previously planned the Pico House Hotel in Los Angeles, St. Vibiana Cathedral and the Mt. Pleasant House. Designed in the style of an English country manor, with steeply gabled roofs and Norman arched windows, the new home was constructed of brick and stone as well as adobe.

Workman, also known as "Don Julian," founded the first banking house in Los Angeles, together with his son-in-law, F. P. F. Temple and I. W. Hellman. In 1876 the bank's failure bankrupted Workman, who shot himself at home in his office. As a result of Workman's death and financial calamities, his half of the once 48,000-acre rancho was reduced to 75 acres. Although the family retained the original homestead, it lost the remaining land through mortgage foreclosures in the 1890s.

In 1919 Walter P. Temple re-acquired the old family homestead, and lived in the Workman home for a few years before building his own residence nearby. During the 1930s the property was used as a boys' military academy. From 1941 until the early 1960s, the surrounding land was used by a convalescent hospital, which carefully preserved the Workman house. About 1962 the City of Industry acquired a portion of this property which included the historic home and family cemetery. Adjacent to the house are a nineteenth century water tower and pump house, both of which are to be restored.

Although not generally open to the public, the Workman home can be visited if one obtains permission from the City of Industry, which owns the property.

15415 E. Don Julian Road
City of Industry 91744

I 12. WORKMAN CEMETERY AND TEMPLE MAUSOLEUM

About 600 feet to the south of the Workman home on what formerly was La Puente Rancho stands the Temple Mausoleum on the grounds of the Workman family cemetery, also known as El Campo Santo and the Little Acre of God Cemetery. Sometime after the Workman family relinquished ownership of the property in the 1890s, it came into the possession of L. F. Lewis. The original family chapel burned down in 1903, and in 1905 Lewis began to tear down the brick walls surrounding the heart-shaped cemetery. Walter P. Temple, Workman's grandson, obtained a court order to stop the destruction, but by this time only the original west wall was left standing.

After he discovered oil in Montebello in 1917, Temple purchased the property surrounding the old family homesite and in 1919 erected a miniature Doric Greek Temple Mausoleum on the site of the original chapel. Within its crypts are buried William Workman, members of his family and their descendants, as well as old family friend Governor Pio Pico and his wife, among others. The Picos were removed from Calvary Cemetery in Los Angeles when it was demolished and redeveloped, and reinterred here in 1921. The site is heavily landscaped with fruit trees, grape arbors, palms, oak, an avenue of arborvitae, and century old rose bushes and other specimens. El Campo Santo, which is believed to be located on the site of a previous Indian burial ground, is the oldest private cemetery in the county.

The cemetery is closed to the public, and the mausoleum is locked to prevent vandalism. Under special circumstances, and by appointment only, it is possible to visit the site. When restoration of the Temple Mansion and Workman House is completed, it is hoped that the entire property, now owned by the City of Industry, may be opened to the public on a regular basis.

15415 E. Don Julian Road
City of Industry 91744

I 13. TEMPLE MANSION

Temple Mansion, also called Temple Hall or Casa Nueva, was built by Walter P. Temple, son of F. P. F. Temple and grandson of William Workman. The house was begun in 1919 and completed in 1923. Its Spanish Colonial Revival architecture was designed by Walker & Eisen of Los Angeles, with a few later modifications by Roy Seldon Price of Beverly Hills.

La Casa Nueva, as Temple named his 16-room home, is significant for its unique and abundant use of custom craftsmanship and decorative art, executed largely by local craftsmen who employed traditional early California construction methods. Two millstones from the nearby nineteenth century Workman mill were incorporated into the architecture. The two-feet thick walls are of hand-made sun-dried adobe bricks. Kiln-fired bricks, also made on the site, are around the window openings, and the roof is tiled. The two-story "U" shaped house has a full basement, and the walls are covered with stucco plaster inside and out.

Special features include carved wooden beams, massive carved double doors at the main entrance, wrought-iron light fixtures, custom crafted decorative tile made by local and Mexican artisans, and one of the earliest self-contained refrigeration systems in the area (the original compressor still exists) for the built-in kitchen cooler. There are many stained-glass and leaded windows, including a master bedroom window depicting the

Workman-Rowland wagon trek to California. In addition there are scenes from the Montebello Oil Fields (Walter Temple discovered oil there in 1914-17) and the family crest. The library features stained-glass windows portraying famous authors, and the music room windows depict similarly famous musicians.

A beehive-shaped smokehouse covered with stucco, reclaimed from the old Temple Block in Los Angeles, built in 1871 by Temple's father, is at the southwest corner of the house and is to be restored.

Except for four wooden stairs on the exterior, added in the late 1930s and 1940s (to be removed), and the roofs over the sundecks, little has been altered since the original construction. The home is surrounded by adobe brick walls, grape arbors and other outstanding landscape features.

The City of Industry owns the Temple Mansion and intends to refurnish it as a museum and cultural facility.

The Temple Mansion ordinarily is not open to the public. For further information, contact the City of Industry, 15651 East Abbey Street, 91744, telephone 333-2211.

15415 East Don Julian Road
City of Industry 91744

I 14. JOHN A. ROWLAND HOME AND LILLIAN HUDSON DIBBLE MUSEUM, RANCHO LA PUENTE

Sixty-one year old John Albert Rowland built this 15-room home in 1855 for his second wife, the 26-year old widow Charlotte Gray, to replace the adobe in which he had lived with his first wife. Rowland was co-leader of the Workman-Rowland party, which arrived from New

Rowland Home, Puente

Mexico in 1841, the first wagon train of immigrants to settle in southern California. A year later Rowland and Workman were jointly granted 48,470-acre Rancho La Puente. Eventually the cities of La Puente, Hacienda Heights, the City of Industry, Rowland Heights, West Covina, Covina to San Bernadino Road, and parts of El Monte, Whittier, and Baldwin Park were carved out of this vast landgrant rancho.

The Rowland family was to a large extent responsible for the two main transcontinental railroads coming through the valley. The Union Pacific passes within a few feet of the original Rowland adobe of 1842, and the Southern Pacific track is a half-mile distant.

Three generations have lived in the Rowland home: John and Charlotte Rowland; Josian and Victoria Rowland Hudson; and William and Lillian Hudson Dibble. Mrs. Dibble had no children of her own, but she maintained a museum for school children in the adjacent round house. She willed the home upon her death to the Hacienda La Puente Unified School District. Several years later La Puente Valley Historical

Society leased the home, renovated it, and opened it for tours to schools and the public.

Though often referred to as an adobe, the two-story home is actually constructed of brick covered with stucco. It has a basement and an attic. The Rowland house was the first brick home in the San Gabriel Valley, and it is one of the oldest fired-brick houses still standing in southern California. The original bricks, made in Los Angeles, have been covered since 1897 with a facade of stucco. Six of the rooms contain original furniture, much of it brought around the Horn from the East, including the bed in which John Rowland was born in Baltimore, Maryland, in 1791. The adobe cookhouse (built of bricks from the 1842 adobe home) has kitchen utensils typical of the adobe period and also utensils dating from the turn of the century. The Dibble Museum has artifacts from the outdoor life of Rancho La Puente, among others.

Access to the Rowland Home and Dibble Museum is through the Hacienda La Puente School District Office parking lot at 15959 Gale Avenue.

Wednesday and first Sunday of each
   month, except holidays, 1:00-4:00 P.M.
Donation 50¢ for adults, 25¢ for children
(Closed August)

16021 Gale Avenue
City of Industry 91744
336-9074

I 15. JOHN REED HOME, RANCHO LA PUENTE

While still in New Mexico, John Reed married Nieves Rowland, whose father led an overland expedition of settlers to southern California in 1841. The Reeds ar-

rived about 1842, and lived in an adobe home on La Puente Rancho until this home was built in 1865. Reed farmed hundreds of acres around his home—wheat, a substantial vineyard, cattle, horses, sheep—until his death in 1874.

When the childless Mrs. Reed died, the home was bought at auction by her nephew, William (Billy) Rowland, who served as sheriff of Los Angeles from 1874-76 and 1880-82. As sheriff, Rowland's most notable achievement was the capture of the bandit Tiburcio Vasquez. After the death of their son in 1902 the Rowlands moved to Los Angeles, but Billy Rowland continued to manage the working ranch.

Sometime later the property was acquired by the Bixby family of Long Beach. The original Reed home was left vacant and the land leased. When Kaiser-Aetna bought the property in 1972, they offered the home to the La Puente Valley Historical Society, who moved it to its present location. One of only three remaining pioneer houses in the area, it is designed in an eclectic style combining elements of Victorian, Gothic, and Greek Revival architecture. Plans for restoring the John Reed Home have not yet been realized.

Not open to the public.

16021 Gale Avenue
City of Industry 91744

I 16. TWO PYLONS, GATEWAY TO ADAMS TRACT

Jack Nelson was a hired hand who worked on the Adams Citrus Ranch around the turn of the century. With little to do during the winter months, he undertook to satisfy his artistic ambition by erecting fancy entrances to the ranch. Nelson carted rocks from the

Pylon Gateway (built c. 1900), Covina

Holy Trinity Episcopal Church

San Gabriel River to construct four pylons, which later served as gateways to the Adams Tract subdivision. Two pylons still remain, located on public land between curb and sidewalk in Covina.

Hollenbeck Avenue near corner of San Bernadino Road
Covina

I 17. HOLY TRINITY EPISCOPAL CHURCH

Holy Trinity Episcopal Church was founded in 1893, and the present edifice was constructed in 1911. The Reverend Alfred Fletcher had visited England, sketching village churches, and these sketches culminated in the plans for the new structure. With stones hauled by wagon from the bed of the San Gabriel River, the contractor (assisted by two stonemasons brought here from Scot-

land) finished the building in a few months. Total cost for the construction, complete with remodeling of Parish Hall, was $13,844. The church is open for Sunday worship and at other times by appointment only.

Sunday Services: 8 A.M. & 10 A.M.

100 N. 3rd Avenue
Covina 91723
967-3939

I 18. COVINA FIREHOUSE

When the Covina Firehouse was constructed in 1911, the town's population was only 1,800. Over the years the building now located behind the city hall, was the scene of many dances and parties for the volunteer firemen and their friends. An adjacent jail, built at the same time as the Firehouse (total cost for both facilities was $6,000), was in use until 1976.

Restoration plans have been made to convert the fire station into a museum for both Firehouse memorabilia and other aspects of Covina's early history, notably the citrus industry.

Covina Firehouse, c. W.W.I

At present the Firehouse has not been restored and is not open to visitors.

125 E. College Street
Covina 91723

I 19. WALNUT PACKING HOUSE

La Puente Valley Walnut Growers Association incorporated in 1912, and the following year completed this packing house, with members pledged to ship nuts harvested from about 2,000 acres through the new association. By 1920 the walnut crop had outgrown the packing facility, which was sold to the Puente Mutual Citrus Association. Thereafter local residents in the town of Walnut used the sizeable building for shipping small crops until 1947, after which time it served as a warehouse. Since 1964 the Walnut Packing House, once the largest of its kind in the world, has stood vacant awaiting almost certain destruction in the indefinite future. This large empty structure is locked and closed to the public.

Not open to the public

Lemon Avenue and Walnut Drive
Walnut 91789

I 20. WILLIAM R. ROWLAND RANCH HOUSE

William R. Rowland built the redwood section of this modest two-room structure of adobe and redwood boards in 1883 as a house for the foreman of his cattle ranch. A rear room was added about 1900. The house is situated in Lemon Creek Park near a small creek whose flow is approximately the same as it was in the 1880s.

Through the efforts of the local women's club, the original structure has been refurnished as it might have been in the 1880s, and the rear addition is furnished as it may have appeared around the turn of the century.

Restoration of the William R. Rowland Ranch House has just been completed, but no specific hours when it will be open to the public have been established. For more specific information, contact the Walnut City Hall, 2055 E. Carrey Road, Walnut 91789, (714) 595-7543.

Tours by request.

Lemon Avenue at Lemon Creek Park
Walnut 91789

I 21. PHILLIPS MANSION

In 1866 Louis Phillips bought Rancho San Jose de Abajo, which was settled by Ricardo Vejar, joint grantee of Rancho San Jose. Phillips erected this stately mansion in 1875 at a cost of $20,000. It was the first brick home in the Pomona Valley area, and was lighted throughout with gas manufactured on the premises.

Phillips encouraged other settlers to move to Spadra. As a crossroads of horse-drawn stage coach and freight lines, his ranch was the village social and trade center. Stage coaches stopped at Rubottom's tavern across the road from his house, and passengers often enjoyed the hospitality of the Phillips family. When the Southern Pacific built its railroad line from Los Angeles, Spadra was the eastern terminus for over a year. The original right of way, which Phillips donated in 1874, still runs across the property. About a half-mile away, on land owned by the Historical Society of Pomona Valley, is the Spadra Cemetery. This site was donated by Phillips, and the first burial was in 1868.

In recent years the industrialist owner of the property announced plans to tear down the mansion and build a factory. The HSPV intervened and in 1966 purchased the home and surrounding grounds.

On the west side of the property is an avocado grove which provides shade for an annual Bar B Q and when restoration is completed it may be used for a public picnic grounds. Future plans also include housing a stage coach, farm wagons, and surreys in the surrounding farm buildings.

Restoration of the Phillips Mansion has not been completed.

Open to the public only by appointment. For further information, contact the Historical Society of Pomona Valley, 1569 North Park Avenue, Pomona 91768 (714) 629-7511.

2640 W. Pomona Blvd. (near Valley Blvd.) Spadra 91768

I 22. SAN DIMAS HOTEL

Throughout the more than 90 years of its existence the 33-room San Dimas Hotel has never had a paying guest. It was constructed beginning in 1885 by the San Jose Land Company in order to lure residents to the company's newly planned community of San Dimas. When it was completed in 1887, the real estate boom of the 1880s was beginning to collapse, and only twelve lots had been sold. The company struck a bargain with a man named Carter, who bought 40 acres of land and agreed to furnish the hotel and operate it for two years, at the end of which time he received it outright. During this period the only persons who stayed in the hotel were Carter and the five land company men who owned it.

Shortly thereafter, Carter sold the hotel for about $25,000 to J. W. Walker, formerly a Kentucky department store owner and a friend of J. W. Robinson. Walker also acquired a 40-acre ranch in the area, and became a pioneer citrus grower in San Dimas, which at one time boasted five packing houses, the largest lemon packing plant in the world, and the world's largest citrus nursery. The first school and first church services were held in the Walker's basement, as were all of the early day club meetings. Since acquiring the hotel in 1889, six generations of the Walker-Carruthers-Brunner family have lived there.

The hotel was originally constructed with lumber floated down the coast from Oregon. Joseph C. Newsom, who with his brother formed one of California's best-known architectural firms in the late 1880s, designed the three-story structure. With its distinctive sunburst decorations, ornamental cupola, balconies, and 140-foot veranda—all painted white with yellow trim—the San Dimas Hotel has been selected by the UC Berkeley School of Architecture to represent the Victorian era in the Oakland museum's permanent exhibit on "The California House." The interior has 30 rooms with 12-

foot ceilings, seven chimneys for 14 fire-places—and only three bathrooms.

Private residence
Not open to the public

111 N. San Dimas Avenue
San Dimas 91773

I 23. MUD SPRINGS MONUMENT

Mud Springs is first mentioned in history as the campsite of Juan Bautista de Anza, who had just blazed a trail across the desert en route from Mexico to establish a presidio at San Francisco. Mountain man Jedidiah Strong Smith, Harrison G. Rogers, and their band of fur trappers later camped here in 1826, having just become the first Americans to reach California overland.

Corner of San Dimas Canyon Drive and
    Palomares Avenue
San Dimas

I 24. LA VERNE COLLEGE

La Verne College was founded in 1891 by the Dunkers and held its first classes in a boom-time hotel. Initially named Lordsburg College, the school was closed for a year or two during its first decade. W. C. Hanawalt, a Philadelphia Dunker who reopened the college in 1903, enabled students to contribute to their own subsistence by raising vegetables and cattle, milking cows, churning butter, and canning food for the winter. Today the college has 1,100 full-time students and several thousand part-time students. It is affiliated with the Church of the Brethren.

The old gymnasium built in 1921 is still in use, although a modern athletic facility has since been constructed. Founders Hall, a three-story tile-roofed concrete structure containing classrooms, and auditorium, and administration offices was completed in 1926.

1950 3rd Street
La Verne 91750
(714)593-3511

I 25. LA CASA DE CARRION

La Casa de Carrion rests in a rural setting which still evokes the aura of its origins. Saturnino Carrion, who built the adobe ranch house, was orphaned at an early age and reared by his aunt, Doña Concepción Lopez de Palomares, and her husband, Ygnacio. The youth received 380 acres of Palomares' vast Rancho San Jose Ariba in 1843, but twenty years passed before Carrion made use of the land. When the drought of the early 1860s hit southern California, Carrion moved his cattle from the area that is now Boyle Heights to the more adequately watered grasslands in the Pomona Valley.

La Casa de Carrion

The "L" shaped shake-roofed Carrion adobe was the first building on Rancho San Jose to be designed by a professional architect, an unknown Italian, and construction began in 1864. Building materials were brought from the pueblo of Los Angeles by ox-drawn carretas. Four years later, Carrion, his wife, Dolores, and their three sons moved into the completed 1 1/2-story home, where five daughters were later born.

Around the turn of the century, Saturnino Carrion stubbornly opposed plans for the creation of Puddingstone Reservoir, which called for inundating a portion of his land. In order to finance his struggle, he was forced to mortgage his land. In the early 1900s the fight was lost, and the remaining family moved to a house in the city of Pomona.

Time passed and the Carrion adobe gradually fell into disrepair. The roof caved in, the weather eroded the adobe walls, vandals carried off the doors and took most of the original hardware.

Since 1941 the Carrion adobe has successively belonged to the Edwin E. Fullers, the Paul E. Taraweeks, and Robert M. Tatsch, all of whom contributed to its restoration. A late vintage addition with modern comforts and amenities has been built on to the original adobe structure and is occupied by the present owner.

An impressive number of documents pertaining to the adobe have been collected, including letters, baptismal certificates, brand registrations, poll tax receipts, papers relating to land sales, and an early survey of Rancho San Jose. Many items relating to the Carrion adobe are on display at the nearby Casa de Palomares, e.g., the oxen yoke used by Saturnino Carrion to haul the original building materials from Los Angeles. Descendants of Saturnino Carrion still live in surrounding townships.

Because La Casa de Carrion is a privately owned home, it is open to the general public only four times a year: New Year's Day, Arbor Day, (March 7th), Admission Day (September 9th), and Columbus Day (October 12th). Access at other times is available by appointment to schools, historical societies and research groups, or "just plain interested individuals." At present there is no entrance fee.

919 Puddingstone Drive
La Verne 91750
(714) 593-5936

I 26. LOS ANGELES COUNTY FAIRGROUNDS

Each year in the 480-acre Los Angeles County Fairgrounds more than a million visitors attend what has long been the largest annual fair in the world. There are fifty-two exhibit buildings with a combined floor space of more than 30 acres. Approximately 45,000 exhibits display such things as plants and flowers, livestock, poultry, machinery, art, household utensils and furnishings, and hand-crafted articles. A half-mile track is the scene of daily horse races, and there are accommodations for 25,000 spectators and pari-mutuel bettors. There is also a sizeable amusement zone, with rides, games, spook houses, etc.

Los Angeles County held its first fair in 1913 at Exposition Park in Los Angeles, and in 1922 the fair was moved to Pomona.

The annual County Fair is held for 17 days beginning in mid-September. Admission is $2.25 for adults and 50¢ for children under 12, and parking costs $1.00. Ad-

County Fairgrounds, Pomona

mission to the horse races is an additional $1, but various other shows, such as the rodeo are free. Costs for the rides and games in the amusement zone vary. (Prices subject to change.)

White Avenue
Pomona 91766
(714) 623-3111

I 27. BLESSING LAND

At this site on March 19, 1837, Padre José María Zalvidea of Mission San Gabriel blessed the land of Ricardo Vejar and Ygnacio Palomares. The two had been jointly granted Rancho San Jose by Governor Alvarado. An old stump of a giant oak tree which stood there holds a marker placed by the Pomona Chapter of the Daughters of the American Revolution. The DAR planted a new tree near the old one after it was cut down.

458 Kenoak Place
Pomona 91750

I 28. FIRST PALOMARES ADOBE

The story of La Casa Primera, the oldest home in the Pomona Valley, goes back to 1837, when Governor Alvarado granted approximately 15,000 acres to Ygnacio Palomares and Ricardo Vejar. Don Ygnacio, who received the upper portion built at least two adobe houses at San Jose Ariba, both of which are extant. The first Palomares adobe, built possibly as early as 1837, is located on Park Avenue near Ganesha Park in Pomona. It consists of five rooms in a row, with a corridor along the front and one side, supported by slender posts of roughly sawed timber. The other larger Palomares home, known as the Palomares Adobe, was completed by Don Ygnacio in 1854 and is located on East Arrow Road.

La Casa Primera is today the property of the Historical Society of Pomona Valley and open to the public on Sunday afternoon from 2:00 to 5:00 P.M. Next door stands the privately owned Casa Alvarado, which Ygnacio Alvarado built around 1840 on land given him by Palomares.

1569 N. Park Avenue
Pomona 91767

I 29. LA CASA ALVARADO

At the invitation of Don Ygnacio Palomares, his intimate friend, Don Ygnacio Alvarado came to Ranch San Jose Ariba and built the adobe which stands today as next-door-neighbor to the Palomares place on Park Avenue in Pomona. It is said that Palomares' invitation was limited but by a single condition—that the new house should contain a chapel. At any rate, the front room of the Alvarado adobe was for almost a half-century used for religious services. During these years, the same room was often gay with dancing in celebration of the fiesta.

When the house was built around 1840, it seems originally to have been "L"-shaped, but the rooms in the rear wing have been destroyed.

Private residence
Not open to the public

1459 Old Settlers Lane
Pomona

Palomares Adobe

I 30. ADOBE DE PALOMARES

During the short-lived prosperity which the gold rush brought to southern California's cattle ranchos, Don Ygnacio Palomares constructed a substantial hacienda on his portion of Rancho San Jose. El Adobe de Palomares, with its 13 rooms, cloth ceiling, and shake roof, was completed in 1854. As a popular regional rendezvous, way station on the San Bernadino stage and 20-mule team freighter route, and resting spot for an occasional band of overland immigrants, the house of Don Ygnacio and his charming wife, Doña Concepción Lopez de Palomares, became known as the "House of Hospitality."

Ygnacio Palomares died in 1864, and in later times the "L"-shaped adobe was used as a tavern. Over the years the once proud structure gradually disintegrated into crumbling ruins until, in 1934, the homesite was acquired by the city of Pomona. With the help of the federal government, numerous civic-minded groups and individuals, and the Historical Society of Pomona Valley, the adobe was restored. Furnishings gathered from throughout southern Califor-

nia include a stove and cooking utensils, tools, branding irons, clothing, furniture, pottery, Indian baskets, an old sewing machine, dolls, a blacksmith's shop, and chest from China. The original landscaping of the spacious courtyard and gardens has been duplicated as nearly as possible. Picnic facilities are available free of charge except in case of excessive use of electricity. The tables will seat about 200. Recreational facilities in the new adjoining Palomares Park are available at all times.

Adobe open Tuesday-Sunday, 2 P.M.-5 P.M.

491 E. Arrow Highway
Pomona 91767
(714) 620-2300

I 31. PALOMARES CEMETERY

Land for this old Spanish cemetery was donated around the middle of the nineteenth century by Ygnacio Palomares, owner of Rancho San Jose Ariba. Four families—Vejar, Carrion, Lopez, and Palomares—each retained a deed to one-fourth of the property. In later years the Archdiocese of Los Angeles acquired part and eventually the whole of the cemetery. Today the Historical

Society of Pomona Valley owns the much vandalized property and eventually hopes to restore the site as an historic monument to the many pioneer settlers of the Pomona Valley who are buried there.

N. San Antonio Avenue and E. Arrow
  Highway
Pomona 91767

I 32. SUMNER HALL, FIRST BUILDING OF POMONA COLLEGE

Pomona College was founded by a group of early settlers in the town of Pomona. Instruction began in September 1888 in a small rented house. Five months later an unfinished hotel (now Sumner Hall) which the Santa Fe Railroad was building, together with considerable land adjacent, was given

Sumner Hall, Pomona College

to the College and the work was transferred there. Although the location was orginally regarded as temporary, Claremont became the permanent home of the College. The name of "Pomona College," however, had

become so definitely fixed to the institution that it was retained.

The first class was graduated in 1894. The first chapter of Phi Beta Kappa in southern California, and the third in the state was established at Pomona in 1914.

Pomona College is the founding member of The Claremont Colleges, a group of six affiliated colleges, of which the other members are Claremont Graduate School, Claremont Men's College, Harvey Mudd College, Pitzer College, and Scripps College. Each institution is autonomous, with its own board of trustees and faculty. The colleges cooperate in their academic programs and in the use of common facilities, including libraries, auditoriums, medical services, counseling center, and business activities.

College Way and Bonita Avenue
Claremont 91711
(714) 626-8511 ext. 2498 (Public Relations)

I 33. DENISON LIBRARY, SCRIPPS COLLEGE

Denison Library on the campus of Scripps College was built in 1930. Architect Gordon Coffman modeled its beautiful design after a Renaissance chapel in Spain of which the donor, Ella Strong Denison, was very fond. It is cruciform shaped with high Gothic arches, featuring stained-glass windows which portray the history of printing, with a figure of Gutenberg in the center. Another set of stained-glass windows represents the symbolism of the alphabet, and the rare book room has windows depicting early printers' colophons. With the addition of the Drake wing in 1969, the library's capacity was doubled so that it now has space for 125,000 volumes.

Library hours vary, and visitors should telephone for specific information.

Columbia Street and 11th Street
Claremont 91711
(714) 626-8511 ext. 3941

I 34. HONNOLD LIBRARY, CLAREMONT COLLEGES

Centrally located Honnold Library is the largest of a number of libraries which together contain almost a million volumes available to students and faculty of the six Claremont Colleges. In addition to its function as the "headquarters" library, the Honnold's special collections emphasize Californiana and Western Americana, American hymnology, the history of aviaition, and authors of American and British literature. Of particular interest to regional history are materials relating to water resources in southern California and the evacuation of the Japanese-Americans from the Pacific Coast during World War II. Other noteworthy holdings are the Henry Raup Wagner cartography collection, the Joaquin Miller manuscript collection, and the Pacific Coast Steamship Companies collection.

Use of library materials is limited to registered students and those who purchase a library card for $15 per semester. Other may use the facilities without charge during the morning before 12:00 noon.

Library hours vary, especially during holidays and vacation periods, but the Honnold is generally opened at 8:00 A.M. Monday through Friday, and at 9:00 A.M. on Saturday.

I 35. POMONA POWER PLANT

California's first hydroelectric installation for long-distance transmission of alternating current at high voltage was built in 1892. The San Antonio Light and Power Company, organized by Dr. Cyrus Grandison Baldwin, president of Pomona College, selected a site below Mt. Baldy on San Antonio Creek. The first high-voltage transformers were built by George Westinghouse and for nine years they provided for transmission of 10,000 volts to the town of Pomona. The site of the original power plant has been designated a state historical landmark and is commemorated with a plaque.

Mt. Baldy Road
San Antonio Canyon
(about a mile below Mt. Baldy Village)

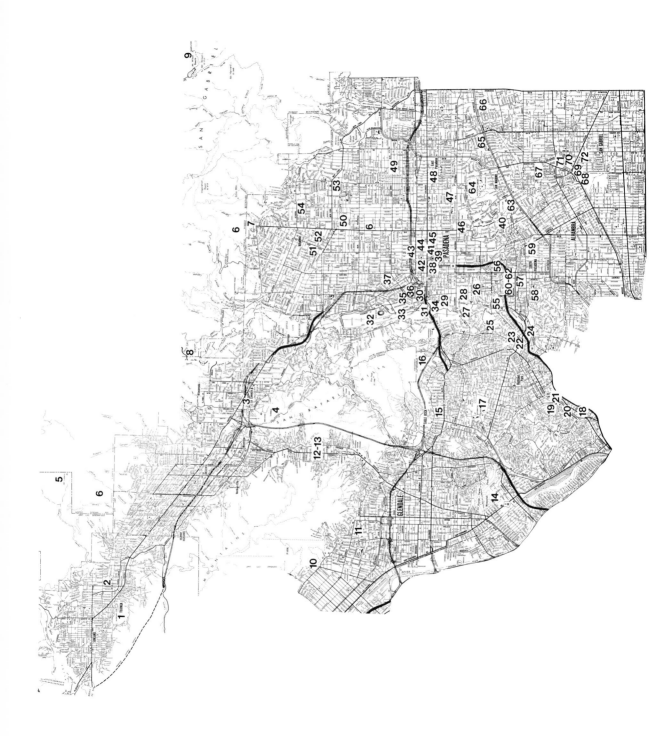

SECTION J

Northeast Area
(Includes Pasadena and San Gabriel)

1. McGroarty Home
   7570 McGroarty Terrace; Tujunga
2. Bolton Hall
   10116 Commerce Avenue; Tujunga
3. Church of the Lighted Window
   1200 Foothill Blvd.; La Canada
4. Descanso Gardens
   1418 Descanso Dr.
   La Canada
5. Mt. Lukens
   North on State Highway 2, 6.7 miles
   from I-210 in La Canada
6. Angeles National Forest
   1015 N. Lake Avenue; Pasadena
7. Echo Mountain
   Hiking trail begins at the end of Lake
   Avenue in Altadena
8. "Old Short Cut"
   North from La Canada on Angeles
   Crest Highway to the Mt. Wilson turn-
   off east to the West Fork Campground
9. Mt. Wilson Observatory
   Mt. Wilson
10. Brand Library and Art Center
    1601 W. Mountain Street; Glendale
11. Casa Adobe de San Rafael
    1330 Dorothy Drive; Glendale
12. Catalina Verdugo Adobe
    2211 Bonita Drive; Glendale
13. Oak of Peace Tree
    2211 Bonita Drive; Glendale
14. Forest Lawn Memorial Park
    1712 S. Glendale Avenue; Glendale
15. Eagle Rock City Hall
    2035 Colorado Blvd.

16. The Eagle Rock
    Freeway 134 and Figueroa Street
17. Occidental College
    1600 Campus Road; Los Angeles
18. The Lummis Home (El Alisal)
    200 E. Avenue 43; Los Angeles
19. Southwest Museum
    234 Museum Drive; Highland Park
20. Casa de Adobe
    4603 N. Figueroa; Highland Park
21. Hiner House
    4757 N. Figueroa Street; Los Angeles
22. San Encino Abbey
    6211 Arroyo Glen; Highland Park
23. Judson Studios
    200 S. Avenue 66; Los Angeles
24. Arroyo Seco Parkway (Pasadena Free-
    way)
    State Highway 11
25. Church of the Angels
    1100 N. Avenue 64; Pasadena
26. The Craven Estate
    430 Madeline Drive; Pasadena
27. Irwin House
    240 N. Grand Avenue; Pasadena
28. Clapp House
    549 La Loma Road; Pasadena
29. The Wrigley Estate
    391 S. Orange Grove Blvd.; Pasadena
30. Norton Simon Museum of Art
    411 W. Colorado Avenue; Pasadena
31. Colorado Street Bridge
    Over the Arroyo Seco into Pasadena
    from the west.

32. The Rose Bowl
Arroyo Seco Park; Pasadena
33. Sheep Corral Springs, Pasadena
Brookside Park, south of the Rose Bowl
& north of Ventura Freeway
34. La Casita del Arroyo
177 S. Arroyo Blvd.; Pasadena
35. The Gamble House
4 Westmoreland Place; Pasadena
36. The Fenyes Estate (Pasadena Historical
Museum)
470 Walnut Street (corner of N. Orange
Grove Blvd.)
37. Townsend House
931 N. Orange Grove Avenue; Pasadena
38. Hotel Green
50 E. Green Street; Pasadena
39. The Moreton Bay Fig Tree, Pasadena
S. Marengo Avenue, north of Cordova
Street
40. Huntington Hotel
1401 S. Oak Knoll Avenue; Pasadena
41. Pasadena Civic Auditorium
300 E. Green Street; Pasadena
42. Pasadena City Hall
100 N. Garfield Avenue; Pasadena
43. Pasadena Library
285 E. Walnut Street; Pasadena
44. The Grace Nicholson Building
46 N. Los Robles Avenue; Pasadena
45. The Pasadena Playhouse
39 S. El Molino Avenue; Pasadena
46. Polytechnic School
1030 E. California Blvd.; Pasadena
47. California Institute of Technology
1201 E. California Street; Pasadena
48. Octagon House
85 S. Allen Avenue; Pasadena
49. The "Hermitage"
2121 Monte Vista Street; Pasadena
50. Dane House
1460 N. Michigan Avenue; Pasadena

51. Christmas Tree Lane
Santa Rosa Avenue from Woodbury
Road north to Foothill Blvd.; Altadena
52. Woodbury House
2606 Madison Street; Altadena
53. Fair Oaks Home
2072 Oakwood Street; Altadena
54. Zane Grey Home
396 E. Mariposa Street; Pasadena
55. Garfias Adobe Site
424-430 Arroyo Drive
South Pasadena
56. Oaklawn Bridge and Waiting Station;
South Pasadena
Between Fair Oaks Avenue and Oaklawn Avenue along Santa Fe Railroad
tracks
57. Meridian Iron Works
913 Meridian Avenue; South Pasadena
58. Wynyate
851 Lyndon Street; South Pasadena
59. Miltimore House
1301 Chelten Way; South Pasadena
60. Garfield House
1001 Buena Vista Street; South Pasadena
61. Howard Longley Residence
1005 Buena Vista Street; South Pasadena
62. Adobe Flores
1804 Foothill Street; South Pasadena
63. El Molino Viejo
1120 Old Mill Road; San Marino
64. Huntington Library, Art Gallery, and
Botanical Gardens
1151 Oxford Road; San Marino
65. Michael White Adobe
2701 Huntington Drive; San Marino
66. L. J. Rose Home
7020 La Presa Drive; San Gabriel
67. Church of Our Savior
535 W. Roses Road; San Gabriel
68. Ortega-Vigare Adobe
616 S. Ramona Street; San Gabriel

69. San Gabriel Civic Auditorium
    320 Mission Drive; San Gabriel
70. San Gabriel Mission
    537 W. Mission Drive; San Gabriel
71. Lopez de Lowther Adobe
    330 N. Santa Anita Street; San Gabriel
72. Rancho Las Tunas Adobe
    315 Orange Street; San Gabriel

Pasadena looking toward Mt. Lowe, 1900.

J 1. McGROARTY HOME

The McGroarty home was constructed in 1923 as the residence of John Steven McGroarty and his wife. McGroarty (1862-1944), a prominent figure in southern California history, was a journalist for over 40 years for the Los Angeles *Times;* the author of eleven books and seven plays, his Mission Play ran for many years at the San Gabriel Mission Playhouse. He also served as a representative in Congress. In 1933 the California legislature named him the poet laureate of the state.

In 1953 the Los Angeles Department of Recreation and Parks purchased the McGroarty home and about twelve acres of land for $30,000; since then the home has been used as a cultural art center. The McGroarty library contains an extensive collection of McGroarty materials including photographs, correspondence, and scrapbooks. Public transportation to 1/2 mile of location.

Monday-Friday, 9:30 A.M.-5:00 P.M.
Monday-Thursday, 6:30 P.M.-9:30 P.M.

7570 McGroarty Terrace
Tujunga 91042
352-5285

J 2. BOLTON HALL, TUJUNGA

Bolton Hall, a beautiful old stone building, was constructed in 1913 as a meeting place for the Little Lands Colony, the first residents of the Tujunga area. George Harris designed the building for Marshall V. Hartranft, and the colonists built the building with stones gathered from the site and from the Tujunga Wash.

Bolton Hall has served a variety of purposes. From 1913-1922 it was a community center; from 1922-27 the American Legion used it as a meeting hall; and from 1927-57 it was the city hall for the City of Tujunga, continuing as a municipal building after Los Angeles annexed Tujunga in 1932. With the completion of a new municipal building in 1957, Bolton Hall was abandoned. Efforts are now under way by the Little Landers Historical Society to restore the building as an historical museum. Public transportation to three blocks of location.

Not open to the public

10116 Commerce Avenue
Tujunga 91042
no phone

J 3. CHURCH OF THE LIGHTED WINDOW

The Church of the Lighted Window in La Canada receives its name from the Tiffany window in its sanctuary which has been lighted at night since April 9, 1925, when it was installed as a memorial to Jacob and Ammoretta Lanterman. The Lantermans provided the land on which the original church was built in 1898. The sanctuary dates from 1924, and a recent rebuilding took place in 1974.

The church long served La Canada residents as a Congregational church, becoming part of United Church of Christ in 1961. It has many stained glass and chipped glass windows and a hand-carved altar. Church records include pictorial history books dating from 1897 to the present, as well as minutes of church groups, information about La Canada history, and manuscripts. Public transportation available to location, which is also easily reached by automobile from I-210 or State 134.

Monday-Friday, 10 A.M.-4:00 P.M.
Church services 10:00 A.M. Sundays

1200 Foothill Blvd.
La Canada 91011
790-1185

J 4. DESCANSO GARDENS

The aura of Spanish rancho days blends with modern horticultural beauty on this 120-acre site maintained by the County arboretum. Descanso, which in Spanish means "tranquility; rest from labor," was part of the Rancho San Rafael granted in 1784 to José María Verdugo by Pedro Vages. On the death of Verdugo, the northern half of the grant passed into the hands of his daughter Catalina, who named it Rancho La Canada. Much of it was covered by a stand of California live oak, hundreds of years old, and many of them still grow in Descanso.

In 1937 the property was purchased by Los Angeles newspaper publisher Manchester Boddy, who built a 22-room home overlooking the gardens, and planted thousands of contemporary plants— camelias, roses, chrysanthemums, rhododendrons—which blend well with the original flora, such as poppy and yucca. The County acquired the property in 1953 and maintained and expanded Boddy's plantings. Today tour guides conduct visitors through the gardens, but a solitary stroll through the quiet oak groves gives one a better sense of history.

Open 9 A.M.-5 P.M. daily.
Tours on the half-hour,

Friday-Saturday, 1 to 4 P.M.,
Sunday, 11 to 4.
Admission free.

1418 Descanso Drive (south of Foothill Blvd.)
La Canada
790-5571

J 5. MT. LUKENS

At elevation 5,074 feet, Mt. Lukens is the highest point in the City of Los Angeles—the lowest being sea level. Mt. Lukens is named for Theodore P. Lukens, an early conservationist. The mountain was earlier known as Sister Elsie Peak, in honor of a nun who operated an Indian orphanage in the La Crescenta-La Canada area.

To reach a good point from which Mt. Lukens may be climbed, drive north on State Highway 2, 6.7 miles from I-210 in La Canada. Hike the fire road, keeping left at .5 and 1.5 mile junctions, to the ridge road at 3 miles. Then turn right, and 2 miles to the summit and a commanding view of the Los Angeles basin.

J 6. ANGELES NATIONAL FOREST

The Angeles National Forest dates back to December 20, 1892, when President Benjamin Harrison set the area aside as the San Gabriel Timberland Reserve. On March 2, 1907, the title was changed to the San Gabriel National Forest. Until 1925, when it became known as the Angeles National Forest, the area also included the San Bernadino Mountains. The San Gabriel Mountains, which are included in the Angeles National Forest, provides valuable watershed protection for Los Angeles County. The highest peak in the range, Mt. San Antonio ("Old Baldy"), is 10,064 feet in elevation.

Today the Angeles National Forest encompasses 691,000 acres—1/4 of Los Angeles County. The U.S. Forest Service administers the forest in five districts. State Highway 2, the Angeles Crest Highway, was constructed from 1929-56; it connects La Canada with Wrightwood. The forest provides extensive picnic and camping facilities at dozens of campsites, several skiing locations and nature trails. Developed campsites are easily reached by automobile.

Fees at improved campgrounds $1-$3 per day, 14 day limitation.

Angeles National Forest Headquarters
1015 N. Lake Avenue
Pasadena 91104
557-0050 (National Forest Service)

J 7. ECHO MOUNTAIN

For more than four decades beginning in the 1890s, one of southern California's favorite excursions was a ride up the Mt. Lowe Railway, which carried passengers to the top of Echo Mountain, site of two hotels, a zoo, a post office, and what was once the world's largest telescope. The railway was constructed for Professor Thaddeus Sobieski Constantine Lowe; it was more than 3,000 feet long, with an average grade of sixty per cent. Under the direction of chief engineer David Joseph MacPherson, timbers and materials were dragged up the mountainside with long manila ropes by a mule team stationed at the summit.

When Professor Lowe's "Railway to the

Incline to Mt. Lowe-Echo Mountain, turn of the century

Echo Mountain trail today

Clouds" opened on July 4, 1893, the crowd sang "Nearer My God to Thee" as the first white chariot of passengers rumbled up the incline. The railway carried 60,000 passengers the first year. Echo Mountain housed the three-story Chalet Hotel, built in 1893, and the Echo Mountain House, considered one of the finest resort hotels in the world when it opened in 1894.

From atop the mountain a giant 3 million candle-power searchlight probed the sky, visible at night up to 150 miles out to sea. Lowe purchased it from an exhibit at the 1893 Chicago World's Fair.

Two fires led to the destruction of this delightful tourist attraction, and it closed down in 1938. Ties, rails, and the gears that hoisted the cars up the incline are still visible to hikers. The remaining foundations indicate the massive size of this unique "City on the Mount."

One of the finest hiking trails in southern California begins at the end of Lake Avenue in Altadena. Maps can be obtained from the Altadena Chamber of Commerce, 2526 El Molino Avenue, 794-3988. Allow 1 1/2 hours for the climb. Use of the trails is free, and picnicking and camping are permitted. Hiking after dark is not advisable, and no open fires are allowed.

J 8. "OLD SHORT CUT"

California's first ranger station (and possibly the first in the U.S.) was built on the west fork of the San Gabriel River in 1900 by Louis Newcomb and Philip Begue, early forest service men. The cabin took its name from the Short Cut Canyon Trail as the structure was one of the main stopping points on this trail. At a cost of about $70 the cabin was constructed of alder logs and incense cedar. It was in continual use as a ranger station headquarters until the 1950s. Since then it has been used only for storage.

The future of this historic ranger station is threatened by the ravages of time, termites, and dry rot, but there are hopes of preserving the cabin and even reopening it as a museum.

To get to "Old Short Cut" drive north from La Canada on Angeles Crest Highway to the Mt. Wilson turn-off, where the Red Box Ranger station is located. Look for the sign which says "Red Box-Rincon Truck Road." Drive east six miles along this dirt road to the West Fork Campground, where the cabin is marked with a plaque.

J 9. MT. WILSON OBSERVATORY

Mt. Wilson was considered for many years as a choice location for an observatory. In 1889 Harvard University astronomers packed a 13-inch telescope to the summit and operated it from Signal Point for over 40 years. The Mt. Wilson Observatory itself dates back to 1903 and the work of astronomer George Ellery Hale of the Yerkes Observatory. The Mt. Wilson Observatory began operation of a 60-inch telescope in 1909 and the 100-inch Hooker telescope (second largest in the world) in 1917, as well as other telescopes. The lights of the growing metropolitan area below dictated that the location of a 200 inch telescope be somewhere other than Mt. Wilson; the Palomar

Mt. Wilson Observatory

Observatory near San Diego was chosen for it. The Carnegie Institution of Washington D.C., and the California Institute of Technology operate the Mt. Wilson telescopes. For many years visitors to Mt. Wilson's Skyline Park could visit the observatory, but as of January 1, 1976, the park was closed and the access road to the observatory closed to the public.

J 10. BRAND LIBRARY AND ART CENTER

Located in Brand Park, high in the Glendale foothills overlooking the San Fernando Valley, the Library and Art Center is housed in a multi-story mansion built in 1904, to which a large gallery and music complex was added later. The original mansion was built by Leslie C. Brand, who called it "El Miradero," meaning high place overlooking a wide view. The design was suggested by the East Indian Pavilion, which attracted Brand when he visited the Columbian World Exposition in Chicago in 1893. The architecture is essentially Saracenic—the crenellated arches, bulbous domes, and minars combine characteristics of the Spanish, Moorish and Indian styles. In contrast to the uncluttered elegance of the cool white exterior, the interior followed the Victorian decor. In addition to bedrooms, there was a parlor, drawing room, dining room, solarium, and music salon cum library. Many fine woods were used, and the windows contain Tiffany leaded glass. The wall coverings were silk damask and oriental carpets covered the floors.

Brand died in the house in 1925. He bequeathed "El Miradero" to the City of Glendale although Mrs. Brand retained rights of residence. The will provided that the property should be used exclusively for a public park and public library. Mrs. Brand died in 1945, and by 1956 the mansion had been converted into Brand Library. Ten years later the city council authorized construction of additional rooms for art exhibitions, lectures, concerts, and art and craft studios. The new facilities were dedicated in 1969.

The library collection includes works on history, theory, criticism and techniques, specialized encyclopedias, dictionaries, indexes and other guides to art and music literature, a total of more than 23,000 volumes. A collection of print reproductions is available to provide study aids as well as for home decoration.

Entrance to all library service is through the original front doors of the Brand residence. Use of materials is limited to persons of high school age or older; younger children must be accompanied by an adult.

From the Golden State Freeway, exit at Western Avenue and drive northwest to Mountain Street. From the Ventura Freeway, exit at San Fernando Road, go northwest to Grandview, and north to Mountain.

Library hours are 12:00-6:00 P.M. Wednesday, Friday, and Saturday; 12:00 to 9:00 P.M. Tuesday and Thursday. Closed Sunday and Monday. Groups desiring docent tours may call the assistant librarian to arrange suitable dates.

1601 West Mountain Street
Glendale 91201
956-2051

J 11. CASA ADOBE DE SAN RAFAEL

Casa Adobe de San Rafael has been owned by the City of Glendale since 1930. Originally built about 1870 as a home for Tomás A. Sanchez, the house and surrounding property were sold, re-sold, and divided many times until purchased by the California Medicinal Wine Company in 1930. Under orders from the company, workers started to cut down the towering eucalyptus trees preparatory to demolishing the house. The neighbors were horrified, and succeeded in getting the contractor to stop for a day to see if something might be done to save the historic site. The City of Glendale arranged to buy the property, and within several years the house was restored.

Casa Adobe de San Rafael is presently furnished with many nineteenth century antiques which were donated for this purpose. The eucalyptus trees still growing on the property have grown from seeds planted by Phineas Banning.

There is no charge for entering this old adobe, but it is open only by group request.

1330 Dorothy Drive
Glendale

J 12. CATALINA VERDUGO ADOBE

Catalina Verdugo was the daughter of José María Verdugo, soldier in the mission guard at San Gabriel, who received in 1784, Ranch San Rafael, one of the first private land grants in California. When Don José died in 1831, his vast holdings were bequeathed to his son Júlio and his daughter Catalina. Thirty years later the brother and sister divided the land equally between them, Júlio taking the southern portion and Catalina the northern half.

For the most part Doña Catalina's half was rugged and mountainous country, cut up into many many canyons, with small streams, willows, sycamores, and majestic

Verdugo Adobe, Rancho San Rafael

live oaks. But the beauty of these living landscapes was not for the eyes of Catalina Verdugo, for she had become blind when still a young girl. She had never married, and now she was growing very old, without even a house of her own. After years of moving about the rancho living with one and then another of her brother's thirteen sons, at last it was arranged with nephew Teodoro, when he had married, that he should build an adobe on her land and that he and his family and Doña Catalina should live together.

Constructed by 1875, this adobe house is the last one built by the Verdugos and is the only one remaining of the several adobes they erected on the rancho.

Private residence
Not open to the public

2211 Bonita Drive
Glendale 91208

J 13. OAK OF PEACE TREE

On the grounds of the Catalina Verdugo Adobe in Glendale stands an old oak tree once thought to have been the spot of the signing of the treaty in which California forces under General Andrés Pico surrendered to Lieutenant-Colonel John C. Frémont. Although Cahuenga Pass has long since been established as the place where the American conquest was formalized, an emissary from Frémont did meet with Pico at this tree to advise him to capitulate with Frémont rather than Stockton in order to secure more generous terms of surrender.

Private residence
Not open to the public

2211 Bonita Drive
Glendale 91208

J 14. FOREST LAWN MEMORIAL PARK

Forest Lawn Memorial Park is much more than just another cemetery. Founded by Hubert Eaton in 1917, it has become the most celebrated, controversial, and financially lucrative institution of its kind in the world. There are several churches and museums as well as notable works of art; branches of Forest Lawn have also been established in Hollywood, Covina, and Cypress.

The Forest Lawn Museum contains works of art and sculpture, including the largest collection of original bronze statuary in America, rare jewels, ancient coins, art objects, and documents. Each of the three churches houses an historical room with letters, mementos, and memorabilia. Statuary and mosaics are placed throughout the Park, and in the mausoleums and churches are stained glass windows.

The Hall of the Crucifixion-Resurrection was built to show Jan Styka's "The Crucifixion," the world's largest religious painting. Dramatic presentations of this work and

Entrance to Forest Lawn, 1940s.

its companion painting, "The Resurrection," are shown daily every half hour, from 11:00 A.M. to 5:00 P.M.

The Last Supper Window, a stained-glass re-creation of Leonardo da Vinci's masterpiece, is presented in Memorial Terrace of the Great Mausoleum on the half hour, daily from 10:00 A.M. to 4:00 P.M.

Daily, 10 A.M.-5 P.M.

1712 S. Glendale Avenue
Glendale
254-3131

J 15. EAGLE ROCK CITY HALL

In 1922, 11 years after Eagle Rock incorporated as a city, a city hall was built to house local government. For one year the three-level Mediterranean-style structure housed the city's government, water and fire departments, and police officer. When Los Angeles annexed Eagle Rock in 1923, the building became the first of many city halls which the city of Los Angeles acquired by annexation in the decade.

During World War II, the edifice was used by the federal ration board. The fire department occupied part of it until 1959, and it also served for years as headquarters for the local YMCA.

In 1968 in response to a resolution of the Eagle Rock Valley Historical Society, the Los Angeles City Council approved expenditures to remodel the city hall into a community building. In 1971, the structure was re-opened to the public as a museum for the Eagle Rock Historical Society, a meeting room, and an art gallery. The building also contains a councilmanic field office. The museum displays silver loving cups won in the Tournament of Roses and paintings, pamphlets, maps, and historical miscellany.

Museum open Friday 2:00 to 4:30 P.M. Admission is free.

2035 Colorado Boulevard
Los Angeles 90041
255-8780

J 16. THE EAGLE ROCK

This massive sandstone rock, 150 feet high, has been a center of interest since the days of the Indians. It was noted by Spanish explorers, and prominent in the days of the ranchos. Its distinguishing feature is the figure of an eagle in flight, a natural formation. Threatened over the years by vandalism

The Eagle Rock, 1890.

and erosion from curiosity-seekers as well as natural causes, it has stubbornly resisted the vicissitudes of twentieth-century progress. According to Carl S. Dentzel, director of the Southwest Museum, "the Eagle Rock is the most distinctive natural landmark in the City of Los Angeles."

The Eagle Rock is on the northern terminus of Figueroa Street, at the northeastern border line of Los Angeles separating it from Pasadena. It is on private property belonging to James Real, and can best be viewed if one travels east on Freeway 134 between Glendale and Pasadena.

J 17. OCCIDENTAL COLLEGE

Occidental College, a four-year institution of higher education in the liberal arts and sciences, was founded in 1887 by a group of Presbyterian ministers and laymen, but since 1910 has been completely independent in governance. The first baccalaureate degree was conferred in 1893, and graduate instruction leading to the Master of Arts degree was instituted in 1922.

The original site, at the time of founding in 1887, was in Boyle Heights. Occidental moved to the present Eagle Rock campus in 1914 from Highland Park where the college had been located since 1898.

Architect Myron Hunt designed the Eagle Rock campus, including Johnson, Fowler, and Swan Halls, which still form the nucleus for the college. Hunt's landscaping included tiny eucalyptus seedlings which have grown to match the expanded campus of 31 buildings and 1,750 students. Hunt also designed the Clapp Library (1924), the first dormitory, Orr Hall (1925), and Thorne Hall auditorium (1938).

The Mary Norton Clapp Library has 290,000 catalogued volumes. Noteworthy

Occidental College

among special collections are: Robinson Jeffers; E. T. Guymon, Jr., Collection of Detective and Mystery Fiction; Earle V. Weller Collection of Romantic Literature; Elmer Belt Collection of Upton Sinclair; imprints of the Ward Ritchie Press; the F. Ray Risdon Lincoln Collection; the John K. Northrop-Richard W. Millar Aviation Collection; the Robert Glass Cleland Collection on Latin America; a collection of William Jennings Bryan's papers; the Max Hayward Collection of Californiana; the Edwin W. Pauley-Charles B. Voorhis Collection of Western Americana; the John Lloyd-Butler Collection of Railroadiana; the William B. Pettus Collection of Chinese paintings; and the M. N. Beigelman Collection of Fine Books.

Occidental College is not far from three freeways, the Pasadena, the Ventura, and the Glendale. From the Pasadena Freeway take the Avenue 52 exit, left on Figueroa to Avenue 50 and north to college. From the Glendale Freeway take the Verdugo Road exit to Eagle Rock Boulevard and east on Westdale. From the Ventura Freeway exit on Colorado Boulevard or Harvey Drive to Colorado; go south on Eagle Rock Boule-

vard and east on Westdale. RTD buses service Eagle Rock Boulevard. The campus is open throughout the year and buildings are open during class hours. Call the library for its special schedule.

Library: 259-2649

1600 Campus Road
Los Angeles 90041
259-2974

J 18. THE LUMMIS HOME (EL ALISAL)

El Alisal (Spanish for "The Sycamores") is a large two-story stone house, occupying a 2 1/2-acre site on the west bank of the Arroyo Seco, which Charles F. Lummis built for himself between 1897 and 1910. Waterworn granite rocks from the arroyo, handhewn timbers, and used log telephone poles went into construction of this 13-room "castle," which Lummis intended to "last for a thousand years." El Alisal was never completed, nor did Lummis intend it to be, for

The Lummis Home (El Alisal)

he regarded it as a kind of gymnasium which he required to counterbalance his extensive mental pursuits.

When "Don Carlos" Lummis died in 1928, El Alisal reverted to the Southwest Museum, together with his archaeological collections and library. The State acquired the property in 1941, but not until 1965 was El Alisal opened to the public. It is also the home of the Historical Society of Southern California.

Sunday-Friday, 1:00-4:00 P.M.
(Closed Saturday)

200 E. Avenue 43
Los Angeles 90031
222-0546

Southwest Museum, exterior

Southwest Museum, interior

J 19. SOUTHWEST MUSEUM

The Southwest Museum was the brainchild of Charles Fletcher Lummis, author, editor, crusader for Indian rights, preserver of missions, defender of Spanish conquest and colonization, outdoorsman, and *afficianado* of America's Southwest. In 1903 Lummis founded the Southwest Society, forerunner of the Southwest Museum, as a branch of the Archaeological Institute of America, and in four years secured 260 members, four times as many as those in the parent organization. The Southwest Museum was incorporated in 1907, and its first collections were displayed in two rooms in the old Los Angeles Chamber of Commerce Building.

When Lummis proposed that the Museum should have a home of its own, Henry W. O'Melveny raised $22,000 for the purchase of 17 acres where the museum now stands, and himself gave an additional $7,000. Mrs. Carrie M. Jones bequeathed $50,000 for the

first building, and the cornerstone was laid in 1913. The imposing fortress-like structure, with its 125-foot high Caracol tower named for Lummis, was completed in 1914 at a cost of about $80,000. The museum opened that year with Dr. Hector Alliot as curator, but its equipment of exhibit cases was not complete until 1923, when Dr. Norman Bridge contributed $17,882 for this purpose.

Realizing that the hilltop site, while beautiful, was rather inaccessible, Dr. Bridge and Mr. J. S. Torrance contributed $50,000 between them for the construction of a 260 foot tunnel to be driven horizontally into the rocky hill at street level and connected with a 108 foot vertical shaft equipped with an elevator for conveying passengers to the museum. This service began in 1920. A series of dioramas, or miniature groups, illustrating American Indian life, may be seen in the tunnel.

In 1940-41 a wing was built by Colonel John Hudson Poole and John Hudson Poole, Jr., to house the Caroline Boeing Poole Collection of American Indian Basketry. This collection, numbering 2,446 specimens, contains baskets from most of the tribes west of the Mississippi and is one of the finest of its kind.

Also on the museum's upper floor are an auditorium, the Lummis Hall of Prehistory, the Plains Hall, and the research library. The lower floor contains the Hall of California Indians, the Hinchman Hall of Southwestern Ethnology, a lobby, offices, and a Special Exhibits Hall.

The museum library, housed in the spacious Torrance Tower, represents the lifetime accumulations of Dr. Joseph A. Munk (Arizoniana), Judge Grant Jackson (Californiana), George Wharton James (Western Americana), Mrs. Eva S. Fenyes (Californiana), and the Hector Alliot Memorial Library of Archaeology, maintained by the Ruskin Art Club. In addition there are numerous valuable manuscript collections, such as the Frederick W. Hodge and Frank H. Cushing papers. Rich in works on the American Indians, as well as on the history of California and the Southwest, the library now contains more than 100,000 items which are available to students and research workers.

The museum is open without charge every
   day from 1:00 to 4:45 P.M., except
   Mondays, New Year's, Fourth of July,

Thanksgiving, Christmas, the last two weeks in August and the first two weeks in September. The library is closed Sundays and Mondays, and otherwise open during the same hours as the museum. Guides and lecturers are available by appointment to schools and other groups.

234 Museum Drive
Highland Park 90042
221-2163

J 20. CASA DE ADOBE

Casa de Adobe had its inception in 1914 when an Hispanic Society of California was conceived by Henry W. O'Melveny, Mrs. Randolph Huntington Miner, John G. Mott, and Hector Alliot. The Casa was painstakingly designed in the authentic style of early California, and its construction completed within a few years, but the dislocation of World War I postponed efforts to furnish the building until 1925. According to Dr. Hector Alliot, at that time director of the Southwest Museum, Casa de Adobe was intended to represent "the home of a young Californian of good family, of some means,

Casa de Adobe

who had just been married and was establishing a home of his own." With more than two dozen rooms organized around a large patio, with fountain and gardens, proportions of the "casa" may strike some visitors as more nearly resembling a Franciscan mission than a home for newly-weds, but the overall flavor of this impressive edifice is unmistakably authentic.

Each room is furnished as it might have been in the first half of the nineteenth century. Among the many *cuartos* (rooms) are a *sala* (parlor), *comedor* (dining room), *cocina* (kitchen), dispensa (pantry), *horno* (bake-oven room), *sala de música* (music room), *portal* (porch), *zaguán* (entry), *baño* (bath), *cuarto del capellan* (chaplain's quarters), *capilla* (chapel), and an *entrada del corral* (entrance to corral). Two bedrooms contain furnishings used by the Sepúlveda and Pico families.

In the mission museum room are displays of religious articles, tools, and methods of production, as well as the Caballeria collection of 34 old paintings, most of which once hung in missions. A smaller rancho muséo room contains branding irons, lariats, household utensils, playing cards, clothing, swords, and firearms.

Historical and patriotic organizations are invited to meet at the Casa by appointment. Casa de Adobe is located at the foot of the hill occupied by the Southwest Museum, with which it has always been intimately associated.

The Casa is open to the public free of
    charge on Wednesdays, Saturdays, and
    Sundays from 2:00 to 5:00 P.M.
Southwest Museum now manages tours by
    appointment.

4603 N. Figueroa
Highland Park 90042
221-2163

J 21. HINER HOUSE

This distinctive stone house with steeply-pitched shingle roof was the home of Dr. Edwin M. Hiner, conductor of the "Los Angeles Band" during the 1930s and an instructor of band music at UCLA. The ten-room house was built for Dr. Hiner in 1922 by Carl Boller, who specialized in theatrical architecture. Stone from the San Gabriel River bed was transported at $5 per wagon load; twenty loads or more were required. Its sturdy construction has withstood earthquakes with no damage.

Many great musicians have been entertained here, including John Philips Sousa, who came for dinner during two different visits to the Pacific Coast with his United States Naval Band. Dr. Hiner had his music studio in the smaller stone house, known as the "Sousa Nook," just south of the larger home residence, where he gave lessons to both professional musicians and students. Dr. Hiner's step-son has for many years occupied the home.

Private residence
Not open to the public

4757 N. Figueroa Street
Los Angeles 90042

J 22. SAN ENCINO ABBEY

Clyde Brown began to build San Encino Abbey in 1915 to surround himself with an atmosphere of medievalism in which to live and work. The construction incorporated rocks and bits of masonry from old castles, monastaries, and European ruins. Brown's love of the Middle ages is reflected in his original name for the house, "Oldestone Abbey." California's mission era is represented by a round stained-glass window at the front of the Abbey depicting an Indian and a padre pulling a handpress. Brown brought an old handpress to the Abbey, where he produced a limited number of books. Much of his finest work was done for Occidental College, for which he was the printer.

Private residence.
Visitors not welcome at present.

6211 Arroyo Glen
Highland Park 90042

sumably some of the Arroyo craftsmen. After a fire partially destroyed the structure in 1910, it was rebuilt.

Near York Boulevard between Pasadena
   Freeway and Figueroa Street.
Entrance Hall and gallery open 9 A.M. to
   4 P.M. daily. Tours Thursdays by appointment at a nominal charge.

200 S. Avenue 66
Los Angeles 90042
255-0131

J 23. JUDSON STUDIOS

Renowned for its stained glass and mosaic craftsmanship, Judson Studios has been in the hands of a single family since 1897. Judson Studios has designed stained glass windows for churches throughout the world, including that of the Air Force Academy. The present owner, Walter Judson, is the grandson of the founder, Walter H. Judson, who received apprentice training in Canada. From modest beginnings in Mott Alley near the Los Angeles Plaza, Judson Studios became the largest on the west coast.

The studios moved to the present location in 1920, when the USC School of Fine Arts vacated the site. (William Lees Judson, father of the studios' founder, had headed the USC art school since 1900.) The area along the Arroyo Seco was southern California's first art center, noted not only for stained glass and mosaics, but also for distinctive architecture and for its colony of writers, painters, printers and binders.

The original cement slab, stone, wood frame, and shingle building now occupied by Judson Studios was designed by architects Train and Williams about 1900, with details by William Lees Judson, students, and pre-

J 24. ARROYO SECO PARKWAY (PASADENA FREEWAY)

After a quarter century of planning and four years of construction, the Arroyo Seco Parkway was dedicated on December 30, 1940, by Governor Culbert L. Olson and Mayor Andrew O. Porter of South Pasadena. This "Highway of Tomorrow" was the first and still vital link in California's State Freeway System. Built as a Public Works Administration project for the State Highway Commission, it was financed with federal, state, and local funds. At the same time the PWA also constructed the flood control channel in the Arroyo Seco (the "dry" arroyo sometimes got quite wet) at a cost of about $7 million. Together with approximately $5 million for the Parkway, the total expenditure was around $12 million.

Under the direction of District Engineer S. V. Cortelyou and State Highway Engineer C. H. Purcell, two separate highways were built, separated at first only by a raised curb. Three lanes in each direction, each 11 or 12 feet wide, were constructed alternately of asphalt concrete and Portland cement so as to provide color differentiation between the four lanes nearest the center. Eighteen

Arroyo Seco Parkway in 1942

bridges are spaced along a total length of 8.2 miles.

No trucks are allowed on what is now known as the Pasadena Freeway, State Highway 11. It remains much as was originally planned, with preservation of the natural sycamores wherever possible. Over the years emergency parking and telephones have been added. The entrance and exit ramps and the curving 45 mph speed limit stretch north of Avenue 64 are reminders of the freeway's pioneer origins.

J 25. CHURCH OF THE ANGELS

The Church of the Angels was built by Mrs. Alexander Campbell-Johnston in memory of her husband as a place of worship for the people of the village of Garvanza. The cornerstone was laid Easter eve, 1889, and the church was consecrated on September 29 (St. Michael and All Angels Day) of the same year. For many years called the Mission Church of the Angels, it became a parish of the Episcopal diocese of Los Angeles in 1928.

Designed by English architect Arthur Edmond Street, the church was patterned after Holmbury St. Mary's Church, near Dorking, Surrey, England, although it is not an exact copy. Another English architect, Ernest A. Coxhead, who was then living in Los Angeles, adapted the church for the topography and site. The church is set in a garden of three acres—part of the enormous Spanish land grant Rancho San Rafael, a portion of which was owned by the Campbell-Johnston family.

The structure is faced with sandstone hauled from quarries in the San Fernando Valley. The San Rafael ranch, of which Garvanza was a part, supplied the red stone which was incorporated into the structure. The interior walls of red pressed brick and the redwood ceiling have mellowed through the years to give a soft warmth of feeling. The magnificent memorial window, which depicts the discovery of Jesus' open tomb on Easter morning, was designed and executed in London and is considered one of the finest examples of stained glass in America.

Wood from two olive trees said to have been over 100 years old, from the grounds of Mission San Gabriel, was used in the veneer of the altar and chancel furniture. The lectern, carved in the form of St. Michael the Archangel, was designed by English sculptor W. R. Ingram and executed in a carving school in Belgium. The body is made from one solid piece of Bog oak believed to have been over four centuries old. The carved pulpit of English oak with white Portland stone base was erected at the church's 40th anniversary.

Sunday Services: 8, 10, & 11 A.M.
Saturday and Tuesday Services, 11 A.M.
May be viewed by appointment.

1100 N. Avenue 64
Pasadena 91103
255-3878

J 26. THE CRAVEN ESTATE

This spacious three-story French chateau-style house was built on a large estate during the late twenties at a cost of $1,250,000 as the home of Mr. and Mrs. John S. Craven. The architect was Lewis P. Hobart, of San Francisco; the builder, P. J. Walker & Company; the interior decorator, Raymond Gould of Los Angeles.

Through much of its history, the Craven Estate has been associated with the Pasadena Chapter of the American National Red Cross. Both Mr. and Mrs. Craven were strong supporters of this organization, and it is therefore quite appropriate that the estate has become the permanent home of the Pasadena Red Cross Chapter, which is helping to preserve it as a cultural landmark.

Monday-Friday 8:30 A.M.-5:00 P.M.

430 Madeline Drive
Pasadena 91105
799-0841

J 27. IRWIN HOUSE

A small cottage built for Katherine Duncan in 1901 was expanded into a larger house for Theodore M. Irwin in 1906 by the firm of Greene and Greene. The house has a distinctive oriental quality, and is designed around a small interior patio.

Private residence
Not open to the public

240 N. Grand Avenue
Pasadena 91103

J 28. CLAPP HOUSE

Erected by W. T. Clapp in 1874 at the southwest corner of California and Orange in Pasadena, this house was one of the first (7th) homes built on land subdivided by the San Gabriel Orange Grove Association. Clapp was a Congregational minister, and in this residence the decision was made to establish the Pasadena Congregational Church. Pasadena's first school was located in the parlor of this house in 1874. In later years the building was moved to its present location.

The oldest frame building in the city, the Clapp house is the only remaining example of a home built in the earliest days of Pasadena. There are two stories, with a simple gable end facing the street and a one-story porch across the front. The rear porches have been enclosed, but the house is otherwise unaltered on the exterior.

From 1874 to the present there have been only three owners of this house.

Private residence
Not open to the public

549 La Loma Road
Pasadena 91105

J 29. THE WRIGLEY ESTATE

Built by George W. Stimson and designed by his architect son, G. Lawrence Stimson, the imposing edifice known as the Wrigley House was eight years in the planning and construction. By the time of its completion in 1914, the house proved too large for Mr. and Mrs. Stimson, who had occupied a portion of the building during the construction, and it was purchased by Mr. and Mrs. William Wrigley, Jr., of the famous chewing

Wrigley Estate

gum family. The Wrigleys occupied the mansion from 1914 until 1958, and in 1959 the Wrigley heirs donated the estate to the City of Pasadena as the permanent headquarters of the Tournament of Roses Association. This impressive structure exemplifies the type of elegant home of South Orange Grove Boulevard that in former years gave Pasadena a reputation as one of the finest, wealthiest and most exclusive residential communities in the nation.

The Wrigley Estate, also called the Tournament House, is open to the public each Wednesday from 2:00 to 4:00 P.M. Groups of thirty persons or more may make special arrangements by contacting the Tournament of Roses office. The grounds are always open.

391 S. Orange Grove Blvd.
Pasadena 91105
449-4100

J 30. NORTON SIMON MUSEUM OF ART

As one of the earliest of the splendid homesites along Pasadena's Orange Grove Avenue for which the city became justly famous, the Ezra Carr estate was particularly noted for its lovely landscaping. Planted with shrubs and trees from all over the world, it became known as Carmelita Gardens. Today the site is occupied by an $8.5 million structure dedicated in 1969 as the Pasadena Art Museum. Subsequently the Norton Simon Foundation absorbed the museum in 1974 and renamed it the Norton Simon Museum of Art, which houses world-renowned paintings, tapestries, and other art objects from the famous Simon Collection.

Thursday-Sunday, 12:00 noon-6:00 P.M.
Admission: adults $1.50; children over 12, 50¢; under 12 free.

411 West Colorado Avenue
Pasadena 91101
449-6840

J 31. COLORADO STREET BRIDGE

High atop a majestic series of arches, the Colorado Street Bridge curves over the Arroyo Seco into Pasadena from the west. It was not built on a curve for purely aesthetic reasons; at this point no suitable bedrock

Colorado Street Bridge

footing was available upon which to erect a straight bridge. Merecereau Bridge and Construction Company built the bridge in 1913 for the City of Pasadena and County of Los Angeles at a cost of about $240,000.

So many people leaped off the structure to their death far below that in the 1920s it became known as "Suicide Bridge." The City of Pasadena stretched high fencing topped with barbed wire along both sides of the bridge in 1937, ending the suicides, but the gruesome appellation still persists.

The Rose Bowl

J 32. THE ROSE BOWL

The "grandaddy" of all bowl games, the annual Rose Bowl New Year's Day football contest began in 1902 when Michigan defeated Stanford by a score of 49-0. The game was discontinued until the first day of 1916, when Washington State defeated Brown University 14-0, and the contest has been renewed annually ever since, except during World War II when the game was played at Durham, North Carolina. Until 1922 the contest was known as the "East-West" game and played at Tournament Park on the campus of the California Institute of Technology.

The present Rose Bowl—built in 1922—was used for a regular season game between USC and California prior to the first Rose Bowl game in the stadium on New Year's Day, 1923. It was originally horseshoe shaped and seated 57,000 persons. The south end was enclosed in time for the 1929 game and enlarged to seat 76,000 spectators. Subsequently enlarged in 1932, 1938, 1949, and 1971, it now accommodates 104,699, although a record crowd of 106,689 managed to squeeze into its 77 rows of seats for the 1973 renewal of the contest.

Twenty-eight miles of lumber are said to have been used to provide seats for the Rose Bowl. The fence surrounding the stadium is one mile in circumference, and over 3,000 rose bushes of some 100 varieties are planted between the fence and the bowl.

The Rose Bowl has many "firsts" to its record. On January 1, 1927, radio stations across the nation were linked together for the first coast-to-coast broadcast. The first west-to-east color telecasts on a nationwide hook-up were the Rose Parade and Rose Bowl game on New Year's Day 1954.

The Bowl was constructed, paid for, and then donated to the City by the Tournament of Roses Association, which also sponsors the famous floral parade staged annually in Pasadena every New Year's Day since 1890.

Arroyo Seco Park
Pasadena

J 33. SHEEP CORRAL SPRINGS, PASADENA

First use by Mission San Gabriel shepherds who grazed and watered their sheep in the vicinity, these springs became part of Pasadena's early water supply and still contribute to that city's water system. A pumping plant was later erected on the site, which is at the foot of the north slope of Reservoir Hill in Brookside Park, Pasadena.

The easiest access to the park, which is south of the Rose Bowl and north of the Ventura Freeway, is via Arroyo Boulevard. Brookside Park is always open, and there is no charge for use of the facilities.

J 34. LA CASITA DELL ARROYO

Situated on the upper rim of the Arroyo Seco, La Casita del Arroyo is a symbol of Pasadena's resourceful community efforts to cope with the economic problems of the Great Depression. Recognizing the need to help the unemployed, the Pasadena Garden Club in 1932 raised over $1,100 toward construction costs, and federal funds were provided through the Works Progress Administration. Prominent community women on the Pasadena Block Aid Committee determined those who were in the greatest need of employment.

Local architect Myron Hunt volunteered his services for the building's design. Construction utilized readily available materials such as sand and boulders from the Arroyo, fallen trees from further up the canyon, and the abandoned bicycle track left from the 1932 Olympic Games.

The building cost Pasadena nothing, and rental fees have helped defray maintenance costs.

La Casita, which includes kitchen facilities, is regularly used by a number of organizations for meetings and has recently been redecorated. Call the Pasadena City Hall Cultural Heritage Commission for rental information.

177 S. Arroyo Blvd.
Pasadena 91105
Pasadena City Hall: 557-4206 or 557-4000

J 35. THE GAMBLE HOUSE

The Gamble House was built for Mr. and Mrs. David R. Gamble (of Procter & Gamble) in 1908—an outstanding example of the design and workmanship of the famous architectural firm of Charles and Henry Greene. It is the best preserved example of the "California Bungalow" and is one of the finest examples of the American Craftsman Movement. Its style evolved from the architects' deep study and love of wood, an appreciation for the integrity of Japanese architecture, a respect for the Swiss, a love of nature and natural materials, and a desire to relate to social and regional characteristics. Greene and Greene went beyond the design of structure, and included landscape, interior design, and such diverse specialties as the design of rugs, furniture, stained glass, light fixtures, finish hardware, and picture frames. The front door contains laminated pieces of Tiffany stained glass in the design of the characteristic gnarled California oak tree.

The basic structural material is Oregon pine, with lesser amounts of redwood and oak; and the exterior is sheathed with hand-split shakes. Characteristic elements are hand-shaped heavy beams supporting broad overhanging eaves, projecting rafters, open sleeping porches, and shingle-clad exterior stained to soft greens to blend with the landscape. The interior wood—teak, mahogany, maple, Port Orford cedar—was hand polished to a glasslike finish, with rounded corners. Wooden pegs were used frequently to join wood together, and the same treatment was used in furniture.

The Gamble House

In 1966 the Gamble family presented the deed of the Gamble House to the City of Pasadena in a joint agreement with the University of Southern California, who operate and administer its programs through the USC School of Architecture and Fine Arts.

The Gamble House is situated 1/2 mile north of Colorado Boulevard (Interstate Highway 134, Route 66) parallel to Orange Grove Boulevard between Arroyo Terrace and Rosemont. Westmoreland Place, a private street, is entered through driveways intersecting the 300 block of North Orange Grove Boulevard.

Conducted tours are given on Tuesdays and Thursdays, from 10:00 A.M. to 3:00 P.M., and on the first Sunday of the month, from 12:00 noon to 3:00 P.M. The entrance fee is $2 for adults; children under 12, and members of the military are admitted free of charge. Individual groups may make arrangements for a visit with a month's advance notice.

4 Westmoreland Place
Pasadena 91103
793-3334 or 681-6427

J 36. THE FENYES ESTATE (PASADENA HISTORICAL MUSEUM)

Surrounded by four acres of beautiful gardens and landscaped with many rare trees, formal terraces, a wandering stream, and several pools, the Fenyes Estate has long been a familiar Pasadena landmark and has been the location for a number of motion pictures. Noted architect Robert Farquhar designed the home for Dr. Asalbert Fenyes and Mrs. Eva Scott Fenyes, and it was completed in 1905.

In 1947 Mrs. Fenyes' granddaughter and her husband, the Honorable Y. A. Paloheimo, established here the headquarters of the Finnish Consulate. Because of frequent large social gatherings at which the Paloheimos were hosts, the estate was popularly known as "The Finnish Embassy." Here, in 1953, Consul Paloheimo founded the "Finlandia Foundation."

The residence (including turn-of-the- century and antique furnishings, paintings, tapestries, and objects of art which have been preserved for four generations) was donated in 1970 as a home for the Pasadena Historical Society by Mrs. Thomas E. Curtin (daughter of Mrs. Fenyes) and Consul and Mrs. Paloheimo. As the Pasadena Historical Museum, the main floor of the Fenyes Estate has been maintained in its original condi-

Pasadena Historical Museum (Fenyes Estate)

tion. The downstairs basement has been converted into a display of Pasadena history, with memorabilia, painting, photos, artifacts, and a reference library containing books, manuscripts, letters, and documents open to researchers.

On the outside grounds are a unique Finnish folk art exhibit and authentic "Sauna House," a furnished model of a sixteenth century Finnish farm house.

Tuesday and Thursday, last Sunday of the
    month, 1:00-4:00 P.M.
Donation $1.00

470 Walnut Street
(corner of N. Orange Grove Blvd)
Pasadena 91103
577-1660

J 37. TOWNSEND HOUSE

When erected by David Townsend about 1879, this two-story frame residence was one of the six most pretentious homes in Pasadena. The Townsend home was one of the earliest to be constructed in the Lake Vineyard tract, the first subdivision added to the original Pasadena settlement. Today it survives as the city's third oldest frame structure and its third oldest home. Typical of the dwellings of farm families who developed the horticultural community, it has a one-story kitchen area, two corbeled chimneys (originally there were three), a bay window, and two porches. The bay window and porches have been enclosed and a veranda added, and a sun room has been built over the front porch and windows cut into the east gable.

Private residence
Not open to the public

931 N. Orange Grove Avenue
Pasadena 91104

J 38. HOTEL GREEN

Pasadena's first fine hotel was built through the efforts of two men, promoter E. C. Webster, who began its construction, and Colonel G. G. Green, whose sizeable personal fortune enabled him to complete the building after Webster became insolvent. Colonel Green had come to southern California in 1888 from New Jersey and purchased a 10-acre homesite in Altadena, where enthusiasm for his new surroundings prompted him to name his newly-born daughter and his private railroad car "Altadena."

The Webster, later known as Hotel Green, officially opened on January 1, 1890, under Webster's management, and it immediately received the enthusiastic patronage of fashionable high society. The visit of President and Mrs. Benjamin Harrison in 1891 was a memorable event in which both Pasadena and the Hotel Green took much pride.

In 1893-94 Colonel Green doubled the size of his hotel, but the growing flood of guests soon necessitated further additions. With the construction in 1897-99 of a 110-room

Hotel Green, c. 1910

"annex," connected to the original building by a three-arch bridge extending from the second floor and spanning Raymond Avenue, the Hotel Green boasted a total of 360 rooms. More than 1,000 guests were invited in January 1899 to inspect the completed annex. Ironically, Colonel Green, whose fortune was made in patent medicine was confined to bed with a severe case of influenza.

Architecturally, the eclectic Hotel Green drew from Moorish and Roman styles; a half-dozen flagged-topped domed turrets in combination with various rectangular and circular-shaped roofing topped the multi-storied complex.

In 1890 it was estimated that guests of the Hotel Green spent about $150,000 in Pasadena during the winter months, a sizeable economic boost to a community of less than 10,000. By the 1920s, however, the Green had lost much of its former luster. The original structure on the east side of Raymond Avenue was demolished in 1924, except for a small one-story portion of the building at the corner of Green Street, and the south portion of the annex became the "Castle Green" apartments under separate management. The famous bridge was torn down in 1928. After a long series of ownership changes, the hotel was condemned as unsafe by the City Board of Directors and closed in December 1964. Subsequently renovated, it now serves as a retirement community for senior citizens.

50 E. Green Street
Pasadena 91105

J 39. THE MORETON BAY FIG TREE, PASADENA

Towering above the Conference Center on property now owned by the City of Pasadena, this Moreton Bay Fig was planted about 1880 by Thomas Early in the garden of his home. Mr. Early was mayor of Pasadena from 1907 to 1914, and during his term he entertained President William Howard Taft in his home.

When the Conference Center was constructed several years ago, the city of Pasadena insured this majestic botanical monument for $15,000. The Moreton Bay Fig (Ficus macrophylla) was imported from New South Wales, Australia, and other giants of its kind may be seen in the Plaza in downtown Los Angeles.

S. Marengo Avenue, north of Cordova Street
Pasadena

J 40. HUNTINGTON HOTEL

General Marshall C. Wentworth in 1907 started construction on the "hotel of his dreams," so that every room in the all reinforced concrete structure would receive direct sunlight sometime during the day—a startling innovation in a hotel building at that time. It opened as The Wentworth—and closed after one disasterous season, aggravated by heavy and "unusual" winter rains. In 1913-14 it attracted the attention of Henry E. Huntington, railroad tycoon and art collector, who reopened it as the Huntington Hotel, January 8, 1914.

Originally the present patio was a drive-in entrance with the driveway coming through the present Mirror Room. Huntington moved the "motor" entrance to its present location and also added the 5th and 6th floors.

Management was in the hands of D. M. Linnard, who ultimately gained ownership of the Huntington to be succeeded by his son-in-law, Stephen W. Royce, until the hotel's acquisition by the Sheraton Hotel

Huntington Hotel

Corporation in 1954. In 1974 Sheraton sold the hotel to Keikyu U.S.A., Inc., and retained Sheraton management on a long-term contract.

Still considered one of the loveliest hotels in southern California, the Huntington is surrounded with beautifully maintained gardens, shrubs, and handsome old trees, intertwined with numerous pathways. The crystal chandeliers in the Viennese Room were fashioned in the same ateliers that created the chandeliers for the palaces of Ludwig the "Mad King of Bavaria."

1401 S. Oak Knoll Avenue
Pasadena 91109
792-0266

J 41. PASADENA CIVIC AUDITORIUM

Pasadena's Civic Auditorium, the third and final building included in the original Civic Center design, was dedicated in 1932. Italian Renaissance style was followed by the architects Edwin Bergstrom, Cyril Bennett, and Fitch H. Haskell. William C. Crowell was the contractor.

For more than 40 years this Pasadena cultural center staged events ranging from grand opera to ballet, from light opera to musical comedy. Seminars, travelogues, and conventions are also very popular. There was a complete halt in activity at the Auditorium during construction of the Pasadena Center facilities in 1973. The Auditorium is now part of the convention center.

Charges for admission depend upon the event.

300 E. Green Street
Pasadena 91101
577-4343

J 42. PASADENA CITY HALL

The Pasadena City Hall was designed by San Francisco architects John Bakewell and Arthur Brown who worked within the original Civic Center design conceived by Bennet, Parsons, and Frost of Chicago. The second building to be completed within the Civic Center group, it opened in 1927. Architect Bakewell described the design as a modern interpretation of the sixteenth century Italian Renaissance style of Andrea

Pasadena City Hall, c. 1930.

Palladio, who himself had studied and admired the Roman architect Vitruvius. Interestingly enough, respected architectural historians have described the City Hall's style as "Spanish Neo-Baroque."

Monday-Friday, 8:00 A.M.-5:00 P.M.
The beautiful courtyard is open at all
    times.

100 N. Garfield Avenue
Pasadena 91101
577-4000

J 43. PASADENA LIBRARY

Following national competition for civic center design, the City of Pasadena in 1923 accepted the plans of Bennet, Parsons, and Frost of Chicago for a library, city hall, and civic auditorium. The Main Library, designed by Pasadena architect Myron Hunt, with W. C. Crowell as builder, was opened to the public in 1927, the first structure in the civic center group to be completed. The library houses more than 600,000 volumes and an estimated 151,000 documents. The California Room houses an excellent state and local history collection. In front of the Mediterranean style edifice is a courtyard with a fountain adapted from Mirador de Daraza at the Alhambra.

Monday-Thursday, 9:00 A.M.-9:00 P.M.
Friday-Saturday, 9:00 A.M.-6:00 P.M.
Sunday, 1-5 P.M.

285 E. Walnut Street
Pasadena 91101
577-4066

J 44. THE GRACE NICHOLSON BUILDING

This authentic example of traditional North Chinese courtyard architecture was conceived in 1924 by Miss Grace Nicholson in order to house and display valuable art objects she had imported from the Far East. The papers, notes, and pictures of interior and exterior details she had studied for fifteen years were used by architects Mayberry, Marston, and Van Pelt in the design of the building. All the roof tiles, finials, and stone carvings were brought from China, as were Chinese craftsmen to lay the tiles, and gardeners to plan the patio garden.

Miss Nicholson conveyed the building to the City of Pasadena in 1943, with the Pasadena Art Institute to be the lessee, and with Miss Nicholson retaining the use of her apartment in the northwest portion of the second floor. The Pasadena Art Museum remained here until 1969, when it moved into its new building. Since then, the Pacificulture Foundation has leased the Grace Nicholson Building and presents continuing exhibitions of the art and cultures of the Far East and Pacific Area.

Wednesday-Sunday, 12:00-5:00 P.M.
Donations of $1.00-$2.00 welcomed

46 N. Los Robles Avenue
Pasadena 91101
449-2742

J 45. THE PASADENA PLAYHOUSE

The Pasadena Playhouse is the oldest theatrical producing organization in western America. It dates back to 1916, when Gilmore Brown and his Savoy Stock Company moved into the "Old Savoy" on North Fair Oaks Avenue, replacing burlesque with

Pasadena Playhouse

the plays of Shakespeare, Ibsen, Barrie, and Shaw. The Community Playhouse Association, later called the Pasadena Playhouse Association, was incorporated in 1918. When the Old Savoy was condemned by the Fire Department, the Community Players raised funds in a door-to-door campaign for purchase of land and the building of a new home.

In 1925 the new Playhouse opened to the public. The building's multilevel Spanish Colonial architecture, constructed around a rough-flagged courtyard was designed by Elmer Gray.

In 1928, with the world premiere of Eugene O'Neill's "Lazarus Laughed" gaining for it a position of prominence in theatrical circles, the Playhouse Association opened its School of Theatre Arts, and the first class was graduated in 1930. Because of its policy of presenting both premieres of the work of leading dramatists as well as plays by obscure writers, the Playhouse became an active force in stimulating local drama. In 1937 the California State Legislature designated it the "State Theatre of California."

The Playhouse stood vacant from 1970 until it was acquired by the City of Pasadena in 1975. The City is now engaged in a program of major restoration.

The facility is presently closed for major renovation. Upon its reopening, charges will be made for admission to dramatic productions.

39 S. El Molino Avenue
Pasadena 91106
577-4343

J 46. POLYTECHNIC SCHOOL

With its patios, open-air corridors, lavish use of windows, and H-shaped single story design, Polytechnic Elementary School was a precursor of California school architecture by almost half a century. In an effort to find appropriate housing for the projects and programs of John Dewey's teaching theories, Pasadena architects Myron Hunt and Elmer Gray broke away from the usual depressing box-like buildings several stories high, characteristic of elementary and secondary school architecture until then. Plans were drawn up in August 1907, and the building was occupied in the middle of October.

Within this well lit and spacious environment, pupils can supplement their academic training with workshops in pottery, woodworking, leather, and metalwork. In the event of an emergency all classrooms can be cleared in a few seconds.

Polytechnic School occupies a 2 1/2-acre site originally part of an orange grove. Many trees were necessarily removed during construction; during much of the school's history, the others not only adorned the campus, but also—because of the abundance and quality of the fruit—supplied an unexpected source of income to a non-profit educational institution. The redwood-clad structure is the oldest school building in continuous use in Pasadena.

Monday-Friday, 8:00 A.M.-4:30 P.M.

1030 E. California Blvd.
Pasadena 91106
792-2147

J 47. CALIFORNIA INSTITUTE OF TECHNOLOGY

The California Institute of Technology began in 1891 as a small vocational school, founded by Amos G. Throop, one time mayor of Pasadena. In 1910 it was moved to the present campus and its name changed from Throop Polytechnic Institute to Throop College of Technology. At that time it was the only institution west of the Mississippi exclusively devoted to the training of engineers. Under the presidency of Dr. Robert A. Millikan, from 1920 to 1945, the school attracted nationally known scientists and educators, secured financial assistance for prominent philanthropic individuals and foundations, and in later years assumed its present name. Today Cal-Tech's annual operating budget is in excess of $30 million.

Renowned as one of the world's foremost scientific and engineering schools, Cal-Tech has had 14 Nobel laureates among its faculty and 13,000 alumni. Albert Einstein worked there for a time after fleeing Germany in the 1930s. Dr. Lee DuBridge, former president of the school, was scientific advisor to the Nixon administration. Jet Propulsion Laboratories (JPL), which Cal-Tech operates for NASA, sent the Ranger and Surveyor rockets to the moon. The Bicentennial landing on Mars of the Viking Project was also controlled from JPL as was part of the Apollo Project, which led to a manned landing in 1969. In conjunction with Hale Observatories, Cal-Tech operates the Mt. Wilson and Mt. Palomar observatories and the solar observatory at Big Bear.

The school's 1,500 students are evenly divided between graduates and undergraduates. Women have been admitted as graduate students since 1953, and the undergraduate program has been co-educational since 1970, with women now comprising more than 10 per cent of all students.

In recent years the original 32 acre campus has expanded northward, and there are now 90 acres with 64 buildings. Although Throop Hall, built in 1910, was so badly damaged in the 1971 earthquake that it had to be removed, several of the older facilities still remain. The two buildings comprising the Gates and Crellin Laboratory of Chemistry were erected, respectively, in 1917 and 1927. The Norman Bridge Laboratory of Physics was constructed in 1922, the Mediterranean-style Debney Hall of the Humanities in 1928, and the Athenaeum Building housing the Faculty Club in 1930.

Open during scheduled school hours

1201 E. California Street
Pasadena 91106
795-6811

J 48. OCTAGON HOUSE

In the chilly northern climate of his native state of Maine, Gilbert Longfellow had long dreamed of living in an octagon-shaped house—to receive maximum sunlight. He came to Pasadena around 1880, purchased a 15-acre homesite, and fulfilled his dreams by constructing the unique Octagon House.

85 S. Allen Avenue
Pasadena 91106

J 49. THE "HERMITAGE"

Built for James Craig in 1869—five years before the founding of Pasadena—the "Hermitage" is the oldest adobe residence in the area. It is partially constructed of thick adobe walls, has five fireplaces, and is surrounded by a lovely garden.

Private residence
Not open to the public

2121 Monte Vista Street
Pasadena 91107

Christmas Tree Lane, Altadena

J 50. DANE HOUSE

Presently occupied by the fifth generation of the family who built it in 1885, the Dane house was originally a ranch house surrounded by 160 acres of fruit and livestock in territory then outside the Pasadena city limits. The land was annexed by the city in 1909 and subdivided in 1912. The two-story New England type home, with simple straight walls and trim, hip roof, and cupola, has had no alterations other than plumbing and electricity. A garage was attached prior to 1923.

Private residence
Not open to the public

1460 N. Michigan Avenue
Pasadena 91104

J 51. CHRISTMAS TREE LANE

That portion of Santa Rosa Avenue known as Christmas Tree Lane was originally laid out as the driveway to the home of John Woodbury. Fred Woodbury, John's

brother, had his ranch foreman, Tom Hoag, plant the two-foot seedlings along the roadside. John Woodbury was so impressed with the East Indian cedars which he had admired on his trips to Asia that he had some seeds sent to him. The seedlings were grown for two years under glass before being planted in their present location. The first Deodar Cedar trees in the United States, they are now thirty years beyond their life expectancy.

The stately Deodars were lighted for the first time in 1920 by Fred C. Nash, founder of the Christmas Tree Lane Association. Beautiful enough at any time of the year, the trees take on their greatest splendor during the third week of December, when over 10,000 lights are turned on to welcome in the Christmas season. The lane has been dark only twice since 1920, once during World War II, and again in 1973 during the energy crisis. Every year the Christmas Tree Lane Association holds an opening ceremony when the switch is turned on to "Light the Lane."

The Deodar trees are more than 90 years old, over 80 feet tall, and measure 60 feet around. Ninety percent of these trees are the original Deodars planted in 1882. New trees grown from seeds gathered from the cones are presently being grown by the Christmas Tree Lane Association. Last year was the first time in seven years that the trees had coned.

This celebrated double row of cedars stretches for more than a mile along Santa Rosa Avenue, from Woodbury Road north to Foothill Boulevard. Buses run along Woodbury Road from Pasadena.

J 52. WOODBURY HOUSE

During the 1880s the Woodbury brothers, Frederick and John, purchased seven large tracts from the Arroyo Seco to Lake Avenue, and began to develop what was the largest subdivision of its time. Among those who built homes on this property, which included all of present day northwest Altadena, were Colonel G. G. Green, owner of the Hotel Green, and Andrew J. McNally, of the famous map company.

Captain Frederick Woodbury's redwood frame home was begun in 1880 and completed in 1885 with labor supplied by hired hands. Hampton Story purchased the house in 1892 and added a 1,200 square foot music room with redwood beams. The Goddard family owned the house for three decades, beginning in 1922, during which time it was used variously as a residence, a tea house, sheriff station and Sunday school. Most of the five acres surrounding this, the oldest existing residence in Altadena, were subdivided in the 1950s.

Private residence
Not open to the public

2606 Madison Street
Altadena 91001

J 53. FAIR OAKS HOME

This old ranch house was built in 1862 for the widow of General Albert Johnston, who was in charge of western Confederate forces and killed at the battle of Shiloh. When Judge Benjamin S. Eaton purchased the Fair Oaks Ranch in 1865, he moved the house from its original site on Roosevelt Avenue above Washington Boulevard. Eaton planted more than 30,000 grape vines on the previously unproductive ranch, and irrigated

Woodbury House

Fair Oaks Home

the land by diverting water from the canyon that bears his name.

The original entrance to the home is now at the side of the house at the bay window. The Fair Oaks Home is between Allen Avenue and Pepper Drive one block south of New York Drive.

Private residence
Not open to the public

2072 Oakwood Street
Altadena 91001

J 54. ZANE GREY HOME

This Spanish style residence was built originally for Arthur H. Woodward, president of International Register Company in Chicago. His wife, Edith Norton Woodward, had nearly perished in a fire in a Chicago theater, so when the family moved to California their two-story home was constructed of concrete reinforced with steel to make it as fireproof as possible. The Woodwards lived on the site from 1906 until 1918, when it was purchased by Zane Grey, his

Zane Grey Home

wife Lina, and their three children. The Greys added a third level, which became his writing studio, for he was then America's most prominent writer of "Western" novels and short stories. In 1928 a 2-story east wing, with specially milled huge wooden beams was added to the main house.

Although Zane Grey had a summer home in Avalon on Catalina Island and a hunting lodge on the Tonto Rim in Arizona, this was his home and writing studio. Grey died in 1939, his wife in 1957; son Romer Grey continued the family corporation here until the property was sold in 1970.

The original 5-acre site is now 1 1/4 acres, presently owned by the family of Charles and Rosejane Rudicel. The Rudicels have collected Zane Grey's early writings, photos, and magazines which serialized his stories in the early twenties. These and other artifacts are on display in the east wing.

The Zane Grey home is a block south of Altadena Drive halfway between Lake Avenue and Allen Avenue north of the Foothill Freeway.

Private residence
Open by appointment only

396 E. Mariposa Street
Altadena 91001
797-1450

J 55. GARFIAS ADOBE SITE

No structure remains, but visitors may drink in the "aura" of one of Los Angeles County's better-known sites, that of the Manuel Garfias Adobe. Built at considerable expense in 1853 on the east bank of the Arroyo Seco, this elaborate adobe served as headquarters for Rancho San Pasqual until it was sold and subdivided. The adobe ruins

Ruins of Garfias Adobe, 1880s.

Oaklawn Bridge and Waiting Station

were removed in the 1880s when the property was divided into town lots. In the 1930s the site was converted into the studio and gardens of Charles Gibbs Adams, a landscape architect. His influence is still visible, as is Garfias Springs, which run, appropriately, in the spring of the year. Across the street is a monument erected in 1953 to mark the location of "cathedral oak," which local legend maintains was utilized by Portolá and Father Crespi for an Easter service.

424-430 Arroyo Drive
South Pasadena

J 56. OAKLAWN BRIDGE AND WAITING STATION

One of the first concrete reinforced structures in the area, Oaklawn Bridge was designed by architects Greene and Greene and built by contractor Carl Leonardt in 1906. Details of the bridge are the work of Italian Michael de Palo. With a total length of 240 feet, it was originally planned with five spans, the highest point 27 feet from the rails below to the crown of the arch. An additional pillar was added to the center

span making a total of six arches, although architects Greene and Greene felt this addition was unnecessary. The original pylon lighting fixtures have been removed from the bridge.

The purpose of the bridge was to provide easy access for Oaklawn residents to the Pacific Electric Line along Fair Oaks Avenue, which ran between Los Angeles and Pasadena. The tiled-roof, cobblestone Waiting Station at the east end of the bridge was designed in the Greene brothers Craftsman style. Cost for the bridge alone is estimated at $20,000.

This picturesque historic site is located in South Pasadena between Fair Oaks Avenue and Oaklawn Avenue spanning the Santa Fe Railroad tracks.

J 57. MERIDIAN IRON WORKS

A popular subject for artists, the Meridian Iron Works was originally built around 1890 as a grocery store with hotel living quarters above. It was located in the center of South Pasadena's early business district, and there is still an old watering trough across the street. Next door was the Santa Fe Railroad

Meridian Iron Works

Wynyate

station (now demolished), which may explain why small models of the box-shaped redwood frame Meridian Iron Works have been made for miniature railway buffs. On the walls and ceiling are the original tongue and groove paneling. Newspaper lining dated 1896 was discovered behind wallpaper in the northeast room.

Not open weekends

913 Meridian Avenue
South Pasadena 91030

J 58. WYNYATE

Wynyate, which in Welsh means "vineyard," was built for Donald M. Graham, the first mayor of South Pasadena, and his wife, author Margaret Collier Graham. Architect W. R. Norton designed the Victorian style redwood home, which served as a center of cultural activities in the area over many years. A crest with the date, 1887, is under the eaves on the east side. Shingles of fish scale design completely cover the 2nd and 3rd floors.

Few changes have been made in the house, except for the removal of the porte-cochere and a change in the exterior color of the window frames. Wynyate occupies a beautiful site overlooking South Pasadena; a lemon eucalyptus tree planted by John Muir, stone pine, live oaks, and toyon cover the slopes. One of the first pretentious homes in South Pasadena, Wynyate is one of the few remaining structurss which are almost as old as the City itself.

Located south of Monterey Road near the intersection of Meridian, the house is not near public transportation.

Private residence
Not open to the public

851 Lyndon Street
South Pasadena 91030

J 59. MILTIMORE HOUSE

With the flagrant destruction of the Dodge House in Los Angeles in 1970, the Miltimore House is now the most significant surviving example of architect Irving Gill's

Miltimore House

Garfield House

work in this area. Constructed for Mrs. Paul Miltimore in 1911, the center of this simple two-story wood frame and stucco residence is cubic in form, with wings at the northeast and northwest of one story which gives the plan a T shape. The flat roof, recessed openings for windows and doors, and sheer, plain walls painted off-white all add to the cubic theme. Gill extended the house into the garden by using trellises extending from projections on two sides of the house supported by columns.

Private residence
Not open to the public

1301 Chelten Way
South Pasadena 91030

J 60. GARFIELD HOUSE

Lucretia M. Garfield, widow of President James A. Garfield, lived in this house, built for her by Greene and Greene, from 1904 until 1918. This architecturally outstanding example of the Greene brothers' Craftsman or California bungalow style reveals a dis-

tinct oriental influence. It has two stories, with a cedar shingle siding and roof, and the foundation and chimneys are of stone and brick. A sun porch in the rear has been enclosed, where it is remembered that Mrs. Garfield enjoyed relaxing on the porch swing.

Private residence
Not open to the public

1001 Buena Vista Street
South Pasadena 91030

J 61. HOWARD LONGLEY RESIDENCE

As the earliest surviving work by Greene and Greene in California, the Howard Longley residence, built in 1897, reflects the architects' Eastern seaboard style, while the Garfield house next door is designed in their later California Craftsman style. Pioneer Craftsmen Henry and Charles Greene were almost exact contemporaries of Frank Lloyd Wright. Architectural historians rank them among the half-dozen "most distinguished architects to immigrate to California in two

Howard Longley Residence

Adobe Flores before restoration

centuries." They, along with Willis Polk, Bernard Maybeck, Ernest A. Coxhead, and Irving Gill, arrived between 1886 and 1893.

The slightly curved roof line of the Longley House, with finials at the edges and butterfly crackets on the down spouts, reflects an oriental theme which the Greenes were to develop more fully in the Gamble House. In 1910, the Greene brothers remodeled the two-story wood frame home for Mr. and Mrs. Frank G. Bolt, and the original stained-shingle siding is now painted off-white.

Private residence
Not open to the public

1005 Buena Vista Street
South Pasadena 91030

J 62. ADOBE FLORES

La Casa de José Pérez, "Adobe Flores" as it is called today, is one of the most beautifully restored buildings from the Mexican era in California which is still a private residence. The west ell of the building is the older portion, built by Don José Pérez sometime before his death in 1840, while the other

Adobe Flores today

wing was added a little later. By default the land reverted to public domain and was taken up by Manuel Garfías, who later served as an officer on the staff of General José María Flores whose Mexican forces opposed the American army under John C. Frémont. The ranch building served as temporary headquarters for the Mexican army, and was the site of a meeting of General Flores, Andrés Pico, Garfías, and José Antonio Carrillo, to draw up their terms of surrender, which were later signed at Cahuenga on January 13, 1847. The Adobe

Flores has subsequently been used as a residence, a golf house, real estate office, and again as a residence.

Private residence
Not open to the public

1804 Foothill Street
South Pasadena 91030

J 63. EL MOLINO VIEJO

Situated on a hillside about two miles northwest of Mission San Gabriel, El Molino Viejo (Old Mill) was constructed about 1816 by neophyte Indians under the supervision of Padre José María Zalvidéa. The 5 foot thick lower walls of the water powered grist mill are composed of oven-baked brick and volcanic tuff; walls of the upper level are adobe. Rafters, ceilings and beams are made of local pine and sycamore. Mortar made from lime deriving from burnt seashells covers the exterior surface, and the roof is tiled. Buttresses supporting two corners supplied strength to counteract vibration of the grinding machinery. A third was added later.

After a new mill adjacent to the mission began operating in 1823, the original less-efficient mill was relegated to an auxiliary role and became known as "El Molino Viejo." Used occasionally for fiestas, it also ground grain for the pueblo of Los Angeles.

Following secularization, the mission lands surrounding the Old Mill were sold by Governor Pío Pico to William Workman and Hugo Reid. Confusion attendant upon the adjudication of Mexican land grant titles enabled James S. Waite, editor of Los Angeles' first English language newspaper, the *Star,* to settle upon 160 acres, including El Molino Viejo, in 1850.

El Molino Viejo

For $500, Waite sold the mill in 1859 to Dr. Thomas White, prominent Los Angeles physician. In 1860, for one dollar and "his natural love and affection," Dr. White deeded the property to his daughter, Fannie Kewen. Fannie and her husband, Confederate sympathizer and later state Assemblyman Colonel E. J. C. Kewen, converted the old adobe structure into a pleasant residence with garden, vineyard, and orchard, extending to 500 acres.

Colonel Kewen's last years were marred by debt and he died in 1879 shortly before financier J. E. Hollenbeck foreclosed upon his home and sold it to retired building contractor Edward L. Mayberry. In 1903 the property came under control of Henry E. Huntington. When the hotel bearing his name opened in 1914, the Old Mill served as a clubhouse for the hotel golf course. When the golf course was later subdivided, ownership of El Molino passed in 1927 to Mrs. James Brehm, widow of Henry Huntington's only son, Howard, who decided to rescue the ancient adobe from disrepair, convert it into a residence, and preserve it as an "authentic legacy of California's past."

To perform the renovation, the Brehm's hired Frederick H. Ruppel, a contractor who had restored San Juan Capistrano mission.

Whenever possible, Ruppel used construction methods and materials contemporary with the mission period.

Upon their deaths in 1962, the Brehms bequeathed the mill to the City of San Marino, which in 1965 invited the California Historical Society to establish its southern California headquarters there. The Society's office and reference library on the west side of the building is in a room adjoining the original cistern, or water tank, and was formed in part from another cistern. The present entrance room served as El Molino's grinding room. The upper room, originally the granary, is used by the Society for changing exhibitions depicting aspects of California history. Tours may be arranged by appointment.

Tuesday-Sunday, 1:00-4:00 P.M.
Closed Mondays and holidays
Admission free

1120 Old Mill Road
San Marino 91108
449-5450

J 64. HUNTINGTON LIBRARY, ART GALLERY, AND BOTANICAL GARDENS

Art museum, botanical wonderland, historical research paradise, the magnificent estate known as the Huntington Library attracts more than a half-million visitors each year. Henry Edwards Huntington began serious collecting of books and paintings around 1910, about the time he relinquished control of the Pacific Electric interurban railway system to the Southern Pacific, and shortly before he married Arabella Yarrington Huntington, widow of Henry's uncle, Collis P. Huntington. With his own im-

Huntington Library in the 1940s.

mense fortune, augmented by that of his wife, Huntington was able to acquire works of art and even whole libraries at a time when many valuable collections came to the market. Arabella is credited with having stimulated Henry's interest in painting several years before their marriage in 1913, but it appears to have been his decision to specialize in English painting before the Georgian era. Sir Thomas Gainsborough's "The Blue Boy" and Sir Thomas Lawrence's "Pinkie" are probably his most famous acquisitions, along with a vellum copy of the Gutenberg Bible, which he purchased in 1911 for the then unheard of price of $50,000. The library building in which these priceless works are displayed was designed in 1919 by Myron Hunt and constructed in 1920.

Development of the botanical gardens dates from 1904, when Huntington hired William Hertrich, a 26-year old landscape gardener, as superintendent of his ranch. At the time, the approximately 600-acre property was a working ranch, about three times the size of the present grounds. Gathering plants from all over the globe, Hertrich supervised the development and maintenance of the splendid Huntington gardens until he retired in 1949, serving thereafter in an advisory capacity until his death in 1966 at the age of 88. Among the botanical marvels which Hertrich engineered are the Shakespeare garden, the Japanese tea garden, sprawling lawns, stately live oaks, and vast areas devoted exclusively to individually labeled roses, palms, and cacti.

Henry Huntington died in 1927 and the Library opened to the public the following year. According to the trust indenture of 1919, the Library received an endowment of $10.5 million, which by 1978 had grown to $27 million (providing 75% of operating income; the rest comes from donations from friends of the Huntington). Since 1928 the number of books and manuscripts have grown almost three-fold. Modest acquisitions have been made in paintings, but relatively few compared to the original Huntington collection. Superlative holdings in English literature make the Library a haven for distinguished scholars, and the collection of Californiana is second only to the Bancroft Library on the Pacific Coast.

The research library is open only to qualified scholars admitted by special permission.

The art gallery, grounds, and botanical gardens are open free of charge from 1:00-4:30 P.M. daily except Monday and during October.
Gardens open Sundays, 10:30 A.M.
Sunday reservations required.

1151 Oxford Road
San Marino 91108
792-6141

J 65. MICHAEL WHITE ADOBE

The Michael White, or Blanco Adobe, was built by an English seaman, Michael White, whose name was translated into Spanish as

Michael White adobe, 1947.

"Miguel Blanco" after he arrived in California in 1829. He received a parcel of land from Governor Pío Pico north of Mission San Gabriel, which he called Rancho San Ysidro. It was here in 1845 that he built his adobe house, which was surrounded by his vineyard and orchard. Eventually he sold the property to L. H. Titus, and still later it was acquired by James Foord.

At one time a two-story frame wing was added on to the original adobe, and as late as the 1930s the structure was surrounded by an orange grove. The frame wing has long since been torn down, and today the old adobe stands in the middle of the campus of San Marino High School. Because the Blanco Adobe cannot be seen from the street, it is little known to the public.

The San Marino Historical Society is developing plans to make the adobe accessible to the public. It is presently still being used by the school district, and tours may be arranged through the school or the Society.

2701 Huntington Drive
San Marino 91108
School district number: 289-3691
Society: 284-2130

J 66. L. J. ROSE HOME

Leonard J. Rose came west from Iowa in 1858, and in 1862 he built this home near the headquarters of his famous 1,300 acre Sunnyslope Ranch. The modified Victorian ranch house was located below La Presa (The Dam). Sunnyslope was a show-place of vast orchards, vineyards, fine wines and brandy, and champion trotting horses. The town of Rosemead is located on former Sunnyslope Ranch lands and bears the name of its founder.

The house has been moved a block, but it is well maintained. The original homesite is now occupied by Clairborne School at 8400 Huntington Drive.

Private residence
Not open to the public

7020 La Presa Drive
San Gabriel 91775

J 67. CHURCH OF OUR SAVIOR

Possibly the oldest Protestant church in the San Gabriel Valley, the Church of Our Savior was founded in 1867. The simple Gothic wing of the present church edifice was constructed in 1871 using bricks from B. D. Wilson's nearby ranch and dedicated in 1872. Funds were provided by Mrs. Amos Vinton, a Rhode Island philanthropist. Since then the church has been enlarged considerably, but the original building remains unchanged. Distinguishing highlights are the church's stained-glass windows depicting historical subjects, great nave, and park-like setting. The adjacent cemetery, also laid out in 1871, was the first Protestant cemetery in the area.

Daily 9:00 A.M.-5:00 P.M.
Sunday services: September-May, 7:30, 9:00 and 11:00 A.M.
June-August, 8 and 10 A.M.

535 W. Roses Road
San Gabriel 91775
282-5147

J 68. ORTEGA-VIGARE ADOBE

One of the oldest adobes in the county, this house was started by Don Juan Vigare, possibly as early as 1795. Originally built in the shape of an "L" it is now only half its former size. The remaining living quarters are spacious, and the ceiling is unusually high. The ancient beams have been covered by a modern roof above and a flat ceiling below. The old lean-to adobe *cocina* (kitchen) which used to extend at the rear has fallen, and the former *corredor* has become a "front porch."

In 1859 the adobe became the property of Don Jean Vigare, and in the early 1860s, as San Gabriel's first bakery, it was separated from the mission's lime orchard by a high cactus wall. Dona Luz Vigare, a great granddaughter of Juan Vigare, a soldier of the mission guard, lived there until the 1930s. Today the adobe is in a good state of preservation and is owned by the Blessed Hope Church of San Gabriel, which until recently used the building for religious services.

Not open to the public at present

616 S. Ramona Street
San Gabriel 91776

J 69. SAN GABRIEL CIVIC AUDITORIUM

Originally called the Mission Playhouse, this city-owned auditorium was designed especially for John Steven McGroarty's Mission Play. Prior to completion of the present auditorium in 1927, McGroarty's play was staged in the old Mission Playhouse, located nearby in what is now Plaza Park. With its colorful pageantry and a cast of over a hundred, the play was long a favorite attraction for tourists in southern California.

Between 1912 and 1932 it was performed more than 3,000 times before an audience of over 2.5 million, establishing a world record for consecutive seasonal performances not broken until the 1950s and 1960s by Lerner and Loewe's "My Fair Lady" in London, England.

Architect Arthur Benton patterned the facade of the new playhouse after Mission San Antonio de Padua in Monterey County, with a curvalinear gable and flanking belfries. Two workers were killed in the construction, one of whom still lies entombed within his concrete grave in the wall of this building. Inside the auditorium are wall hangings presented by King Alfonso of Spain which depict heraldic shields of the major provinces in Spain. In the adjoining courtyard are replicas of the 21 Franciscan missions in California.

Monday-Friday, 2:00-5:00 P.M. plus
  scheduled events

320 Mission Drive
San Gabriel 91766
284-3277

J 70. SAN GABRIEL MISSION

The fourth of the 21 Franciscan missions in California, San Gabriel was founded on September 8, 1771. Within five years, floods forced the mission to move from nearby what is today the Rio Hondo (Deep River) four miles north to its present site. San Gabriel grew to become the "Queen of the missions," one of the most prosperous in California. It once controlled a million and a half acres, extending from the mountains to the sea. Between 1806 and 1830 San Gabriel's neophyte population averaged 1,700 and 40,000 cattle roamed its widespread ranges. With the coming of secularization in 1833, the mission deteriorated, and in 1846 most of its lands were given by the Mexican government to Hugo Reid and William Workman. This transaction was rescinded within two months, and division of the lands among many owners followed. In 1874 the U.S. government granted a patent to the present 13-acre mission property to the Catholic Diocese of Los Angeles. Since 1908 the pastorate has been administered by the Claretian Fathers, who restored the church, built the parochial school, and converted the monastery into a museum.

San Gabriel, Mission, 1924.

The massively buttressed mission church was constructed by Indian labor about 1791 to 1805, using stone, mortar, and brick. Beneath the altar of the sanctuary lie the remains of eight padres who served the mission. Outside in the cemetery, the bones of approximately 5,000 neophytes are buried together in a common grave.

In an often photographed belfry at the end of the church building hang five bells in arches of graduated size. Two of the bells were cast in 1795, two in 1828, and the largest in 1830.

The museum in the former priest quarters contains vestments, tools, some mission records, and Indian artifacts. Especially noteworthy are the stations of the cross painted by an unknown neophyte Indian who was at the San Fernando mission.

Daily, 9:30 A.M.-4:00 P.M.
Admission 50¢

537 W. Mission Drive
San Gabriel 91776
282-5191

J 71. LOPEZ DE LOWTHER ADOBE

On the grounds of Mission San Gabriel is an adobe home, thought to have been built around 1806, which was originally one of the buildings of the west wall of the mission. Don Juan López and his descendants occupied the house from 1849 until 1964. In the 1920s it was redecorated by María López de Lowther. The adobe houses family memorabilia and a doll collection.

Sundays 1:00-4:00 P.M. or by appointment

330 N. Santa Anita Street
San Gabriel 91776

J 72. RANCHO LAS TUNAS ADOBE

Rancho Las Tunas Adobe is the oldest continuously occupied home in southern California. The handsome residence is said to have been built several years before the San Gabriel mission church was erected. The adobe originally consisted of three rooms, a dining and storage room, a granary, and a room for the padres who supervised the Indians constructing the mission. An adobe addition was made to the original long rectangular structure shortly before the American conquest, so that the home now has fifteen rooms shaped somewhat like a "T," with *corredores* outlining the new wing and the exposed ends of the old front.

Judge Volney E. Howard bought the adobe in 1852 from a Mr. Hildreth. There is evidence that Hugo Reid once owned the property, which was known as Rancho Las Tunas, and Henry Dalton appears also to have been an owner previous to hildreth. It was probably in Judge Howard's time that the new wing and shingle roof were added. The brea covering of the *corredores* was retained until much later.

For much of the nineteenth century, the little rancho was surrounded by a hedge of cactus or *tuna* such as the friars planted to protect their groves and orchards. In 1880 this hedge was about 50 feet thick.

When a room in the older portion was renovated in 1927, a floor of 6-inch pine, laid forty years earlier, was taken up. Beneath that, a floor of 8-inch redwood was found and removed, and beneath that lay irregular planks of native live oak, almost completely disintegrated. At other times about the house and grounds, old Dutch coins, small cast-iron cannon balls, and bronze grape shot have been unearthed.

Private residence
Not open to the public

315 Orange Street
San Gabriel 91776

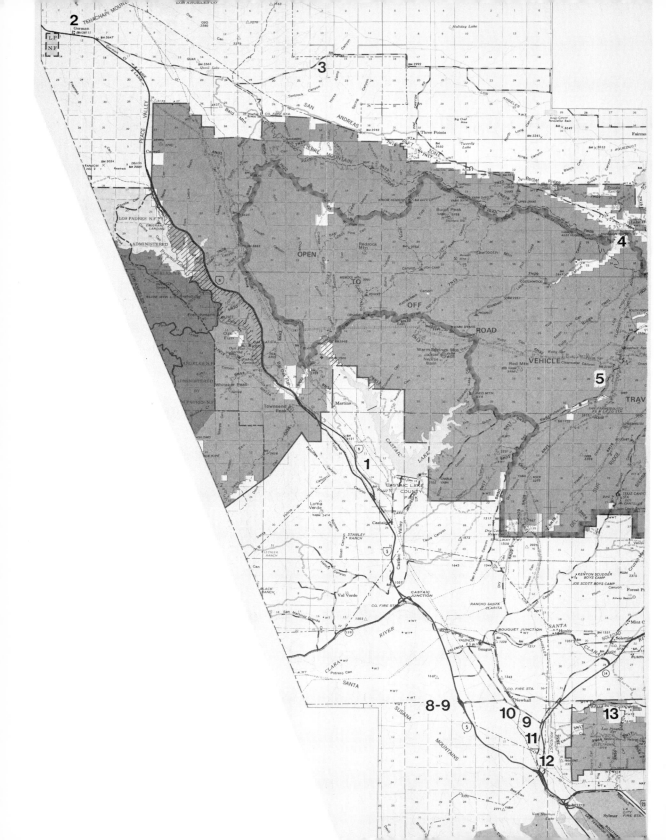

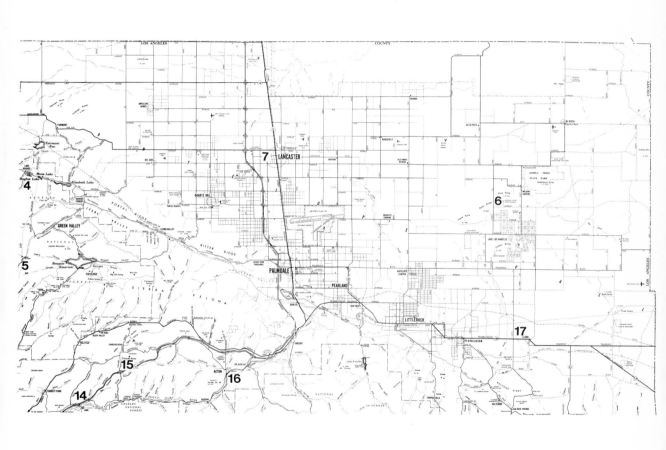

Grape Vine loops, early in the century.

SECTION K

Northern Los Angeles County (Canyon and Desert)

1. Old Ridge Route
   North of Interstate 5 in Castaic
2. Gorman
   Interstate 5 to Gorman exit
3. La Casa del Rancho La Liebre
   Interstate 5, southeast of Gorman, then
   10 miles east
4. La Casa de Miguel Ortiz
   Elizabeth Lake Road
5. St. Francis Dam Disaster Site
   From Interstate 5, take Valencia turn-off, go north on the San Francisquito
   Canyon Road
6. Antelope Valley Indian Museum
   Wilson Route at Piute Butte;
   near 770th St. & Ave. M East-22 mi. E.
   of Lancaster or Palmdale
7. Western Hotel
   557 W. Lancaster Blvd.
8. Mentryville
   Pico Canyon Road, near Newhall
9. Pico No. 4 and the Pioneer Oil Refinery
   Pico Canyon near Newhall

10. William S. Hart County Park
    24151 Newhall Avenue
11. Lyons Station Stagecoach Stop
    San Fernando Road, south of Newhall
12. Beale's Cut
    East of Highway 14, 1 mile north of
    Interstate 5
13. Placerita Canyon State Park
    19152 W. Placerita Canyon Road
14. Lang
    Soledad Canyon Road, 10 miles east of
    Saugus
15. Vasquez Rocks County Park
    San Andreas Fault north of Antelope
    Freeway
16. Acton
    Cory Avenue off Crown Valley Road in
    Acton
17. Ruins of Llano Utopian Community
    Highway 138, west of the Llano post office

K 1. OLD RIDGE ROUTE

The modern highway known as the Ridge Route, crossing the Tehachapi Mountains north of Newhall, has seen several earlier incarnations. The first was constructed in 1914 along the crest of the mountain ridges from Newhall on to Bakersfield. On its completion the route was hailed as a force for promoting the unity of the state, as at the time several efforts had been made to separate California into two states. But the original Ridge Route was a winding road 48 miles in length, with so many curves that a driver in effect traveled over 100 complete circles.

Ridge Route, c. 1920.

With increased traffic, the route was relocated in 1933 to become Highway 99, again remodeled in the 1940s, and then again in 1966-67. The successive improvements reduced mileage distance, eliminated curves, and brought the road up to interstate highway standards. The old Ridge Route had been deserted almost overnight when Highway 99 was created. However, portions of the original route can still be traveled. Drivers go north on Interstate 5 to Castaic, turn right on Elizabeth Lake Road, proceed one mile, and turn left. Ruins of old resorts and gas stations can be seen.

K 2. GORMAN

Gorman, a rest stop on the Ridge Route, was homesteaded in 1864 by Henry Gorman, who had served in the U.S. Army at Fort Tejon. For many years Gorman served as a relay station for stagecoaches; it successfully continued its existence into the automobile era. Today the small community offers such roadside services as gas stations, restaurants, a motel, and a post office. The area is noted for its springtime display of wildflowers. Automobile transportation recommended to location, north on Interstate 5 to Gorman exit.

K 3. LA CASA DEL RANCHO LA LIEBRE

Rancho La Liebre was part of a large area of land in northwest Los Angeles and southern Kern counties acquired in the 1850s by General Edward F. Beale. Beale built an adobe ranchhouse in Canon de las Osas to serve as headquarters. Forty years later the property, including both Rancho La Liebre and Fort Tejon, was purchased by a Los Angeles-based syndicate (the *Times* publisher was a partner), the Tejon Ranch Company, which still exists.

From Interstate 5, southeast of Gorman, drive east ten miles along the San Andreas rift zone. La Casa is a half mile south of this point.

Privately owned
Not open to the public

K 4. LA CASA DE MIGUEL ORTIZ

Miguel Ortiz was a muleteer employed by General Edward F. Beale, commandant at Fort Tejon in the 1850s. Beale gave some land to Ortiz in the Elizabeth Lake area, and Ortiz constructed a one-story adobe home there. The stage road connecting Saugus to Fort Tejon ran past the Ortiz adobe. During the 1870s outlaw Tiburcio Vasquez frequented the area. The adobe still may be seen on Elizabeth Lake Road. Automobile transportation recommended.

K 5. ST. FRANCIS DAM DISASTER SITE

The Owens Valley aqueduct water project, begun by William Mulholland in 1905, was expanded by further construction in the 1920s. The 185-foot high St. Francis dam was built in 1926 to store water. On March 12, 1928, at the end of its first winter season, the dam collapsed. Cascading waters destroyed hundreds of homes and killed nearly 500 persons, with bodies and debris swept down the San Francisquito Canyon. The dam was not rebuilt, but a pile of rubble still marks the site.

From Interstate 5, take the Valencia turn-off, drive north on the San Francisquito Canyon Road. After passing County Detention Camp Number 17 and before reaching Powerhouse Station 2, the rubble may be seen west of the road.

Antelope Valley Indian Museum

K 6. ANTELOPE VALLEY INDIAN MUSEUM

Located at Piute Butte, this novel museum is built into the native rocks and is devoted to the cultures of the early and later Indians of the area. Other cultures such as those of the Southwest, Plains, and Latin America, are found in various rooms with a natural passageway running between them. This is a non-profit private museum. A separate building houses the Antelope Valley Archeological Association.

Closed during summer
$1 adults; 50¢ children

Wilson Route, Box 167
Lancaster 93534
Near 170th Street and Avenue M East
(Approximately 22 miles east of Palmdale or Lancaster.)

K 7. WESTERN HOTEL

This hotel was constructed in 1874 by the Gilroy family. George T. Webber purchased the hotel in 1902 and named it Western

Hotel. During the construction of the Owens Valley-Los Angeles Aqueduct between 1907-1913 the hotel was used by the city's construction crews. The hotel served as an important center of commercial and social activity in Lancaster. It is currently under restoration.

557 W. Lancaster Blvd.
Lancaster 93534

K 8. MENTRYVILLE

Mentryville was a settlement serving the first commercially successful oil development in the area in the 1880s. It was built by Alex Mentry, pioneer oil man, who died in 1900. Three old buildings, a schoolhouse (c. 1885), a house (c. 1889) and a barn, have been renovated by a team composed of the Newhall Women's Club and the Santa Clarita Valley Historical Society, who hope to eventually open them to the public at regular hours. Mentryville was dedicated as a State Historical Monument on October 8, 1977.

From Interstate 5, drive west on Pico Canyon Road into the Santa Susana Moun-

Mentryville, looking away from Newhall, after construction of house which stands today.

tains. After three miles a locked gate is encountered, but the buildings are easily seen from this point.

Tours arranged by correspondence with
Mrs. Carol Lagassee
27201 W. Pico Canyon Road
Newhall 91321

Pico Canyon Road, near Newhall

K 9. PICO NO. 4 AND THE PIONEER OIL REFINERY

The discovery of oil in Pico Canyon in 1876 marked the beginning of the petroleum industry in California. The possibility of a major oil discovery in the area dated to 1854 when oil seepage was used for lighting purposes by local residents. Well No. CSO-4, as Pico No. 4 was officially known, was the first commercially successful oil well in California. Its production was modest by modern standards, as its initial flow was 30 barrels a day, later increased to 150 barrels when the well was deepened from 300 to 600 feet. The well site consists of 850 acres and

Mentryville, Pico Canyon, facing Newhall, before construction of Pico Cottages

includes buildings dating back to the well's first operations.

The success of Pico No. 4 resulted in the construction of California's first commerical oil refinery in 1876. It was operated by the Star Oil Company, a predecessor of the Standard Oil Company of California. The refinery was restored in 1930 and is open to the public. Automobile transportation is recommended.

Pico No. 4; in Pico Canyon west of
Newhall, beyond Interstate 5
Not open to the public
Refinery: east of Newhall, near San
Fernando Road and Pine Street, west on
Pine Street to location.
Admission free, open during daylight hours

K 10. WILLIAM S. HART COUNTY PARK

William S. Hart, famed star of the silent films, bought the Horseshoe Ranch in Newhall in the early 1920s as a retirement residence. Occupying over 250 acres, the ranch includes a ranch house built in 1910, Hart's residence built in 1925-28 and named La Loma de Los Vientos (the Hill of the Winds) by Hart, and stables. Hart died in 1946, and in his will he deeded the ranch to "be maintained by Los Angeles County . . . exclusively as a public park and pleasure grounds—for the amusement, recreation, and pleasure of its inhabitants—that a charge or fee never be made to the public for admission."

Visitors to the park will find 110 acres preserved as a wilderness area. Buffalo can be seen, presented to the park in 1962 by Walt Disney. The original ranch house, used by Hart as a movie set, has collections of saddles, lariats, spurs, and bridles. Hart's residence contains numerous works of art by

such foremost western artists as Charles M. Russell and Frederic Remington. The park offers picnic facilities, a barnyard zoo, and hiking and nature trails. Best reached by automobile, with parking available at the lower level.

No fees
10:00-7:30 seven days a week
Home tours Tuesday-Sunday,
10:00 A.M.-5:00 P.M., every 15 minutes

24151 Newhall Avenue
Newhall 91321
(805) 259-0855

K 11. LYONS STATION STAGECOACH STOP

Lyons Station, named for Sanford and Cyrus Lyons, was a stopping place for early California stage lines in the 1850s and 1860s. Facilities included a post office, telegraph office, tavern, and stagecoach supplies. Long since superseded by railway connections and a succession of evermore modern highways, the site is now marked by its pioneer cemetery, the Eternal Valley Memorial Park. Automobile transportation recommended.

San Fernando Road, south of Newhall

K 12. BEALE'S CUT

This historic site still exists over 100 years after it was first constructed. Movement over San Fernando Pass, which was named Frémont Pass after John C. Frémont's forces crossed over it during the Mexican-American War, was extremely difficult ow-

Beale's Cut

ing to the steepness of the terrain. In 1859 General Edward F. Beale, in charge of Fort Tejon, had his men cut fifty feet from the summit of the pass. The result was a remarkable steep-sided passageway that in the twentieth century became a favorite spot for western film-makers. Tom Mix even jumped his horse across the cut. Beale's Cut made passage much easier for vehicles to make the crossing, and it continued in use until superseded by more modern roads. The cut is located about 1/4 mile east and north of a parking area on the east side of Highway 14, 1 mile north of the junction with Interstate 5. Automobile transportation recommended to parking area, with a 1/4 mile hike to location.

K 13. PLACERITA CANYON STATE PARK

Seven years before gold was discovered at Sutter's Mill in northern California, southern California experienced a gold rush of its own. Three herdsmen discovered gold in Placerita Canyon in March 1842. One of the herdsmen, Francisco López, in pulling up some wild onions, discovered particles of gold clinging to the roots. By May over 100 prospectors were searching for gold in the canyon. Although some gold was found, the amount just was not worth the effort involved, and California's major find had to wait another half-dozen years in another area.

After statehood Placerita Canyon became public domain, but by 1900 it had been successfully homesteaded by Frank Walker. The Walker family owned the canyon for over 50 years, during which time the area proved attractive to local moviemakers. In 1949 the Walker family sold the first of three parcels to the State of California to create Placerita Canyon Park, the other two parcels being acquired by the state ten years later.

Today the Los Angeles County Parks and Recreation Department operates Placerita Canyon Park for the State of California. A nature center built in 1971 has proved a major attraction, as have the nature trails and the very oak under which Francisco López is said to have dreamed of finding gold before pulling up his wild onions. Recommended transportation by automobile to location.

No fees
Park open seven days a week, dawn to dusk. Nature Center open daily until 5 P.M.

19152 W. Placerita Canyon Road
Newhall 91321
(805) 259-7721

K 14. LANG

On September 5, 1876, an event of major historic importance occurred at this spot in Soledad Canyon. The Southern Pacific Railroad completed its connection between Los Angeles and San Francisco. Leland Stanford, Charles Crocker, and other Southern Pacific officials and dignitaries were present to witness the driving of a gold "last spike." With the completion of this link in the Southern Pacific network, Los Angeles ended its period of isolation and began its climb towards major metropolitan status.

The golden spike in the holdings of the California Historical Society in San Francisco was returned to Lang for display at a ceremony commemorating the centennial in 1976. Also participating were members of

Lang Station in 1936.

the Chinese historical society, for the labor of four to five thousand Chinese workers made the railroad possible.

The Lang station was dismantled in the late 1960s, in spite of efforts to preserve it, but visitors may view three monuments and the rails, and experience the stiff winds blowing through the pass. Automobile transportation recommended to site.

Soledad Canyon Road, 10 miles east of Saugus.

K 15. VASQUEZ ROCKS COUNTY PARK

The Vasquez Rocks are Los Angeles County's most dramatic segment of the famous San Andreas Fault, which extends through California and caused the San Francisco earthquake in 1906. These unusual geologic formations are said to have been a magnet for early Indian tribes. They are also reputed to have been the hide-out of the notorious bandit Tiburcio Vasquez in the early 1870s.

A popular recreation area, Vasquez Rocks was assumed by the County Parks Department in 1969. The Antelope Valley Freeway (Route 14) runs through the park, but most of it lies to the north.

It is open to the public from 7:30 A.M. to one half hour before dark daily.

K 16. ACTON

Located on the northern side of the San Gabriel Mountains, in the foothills above the Antelope Valley, Acton traces its history back to the 1870s. Between 1873-1876 Acton served as a railroad camp while the Southern Pacific constructed its line connecting Saugus to Mojave. The small community was also the base for a local gold mining boom that stretched from the 1880s to the 1940s. Automobile transportation is recommended to the location, north on Highway

14 to Acton exit. Numerous mines can still be found in the Acton area.

The Soledad-Acton school district is one of the oldest in the county. Formed in the 1860s, it included all of the county north of San Fernando. The first adobe schoolhouse was built in 1869. The present brick structure was constructed in 1890 at Cory Avenue off Crown Valley Road in Acton and has been dedicated a point of historic interest.

K 17. RUINS OF LLANO UTOPIAN COMMUNITY

The socialist movement in Los Angeles was strong in the first decade of the twentieth century, particularly after the 1907-08 depression. Socialist Job Harriman narrowly lost the mayoralty campaign of 1911. He participated in the defense of the McNamara brothers, who were convicted of bombing the *Times*. In 1914 Harriman and other socialists, most of them from the area,

Ruins of Llano

founded a utopian community in the Antelope Valley north of the Angeles National Forest. For a time the colony thrived, but inadequate water reserves drove it out of the state in 1918. Ruins of the Llano hotel may be seen on Highway 138, west of the Llano post office.

APPENDIX

Suggested Readings

For further reading: *A Dozen Books about Historical Times and Places in Los Angeles*

Reyner Banham, *Los Angeles, The Architecture of Four Ecologies* (1971; paper).

Lynn Bowman, *Los Angeles: Epic of a City* (1974).

John and LaRee Caughey, *Los Angeles, Biography of a City* (1976; paper).

Robert M. Fogelson, *The Fragmented Metropolis* (1967).

David Gebhard and Robert Winter, *A Guide to Architecture in Los Angeles and Southern California* (1977; paper).

Richard Lillard, *Eden in Jeopardy* (1966).

Carey McWilliams, *Southern California, an Island on the Land* (1946; paper ed. 1973).

Remi Nadeau, *Los Angeles from Mission to Modern City* (1960).

Harris Newmark, *Sixty Years in Southern California* (1916; 4th Ed. 1970).

Leonard Pitt, *The Decline of the Californios* (1966; paper).

Jack Smith, *The Big Orange* (1976).

John D. Weaver, *L.A.: El Pueblo Grande* (1973).

PHOTO ACKNOWLEDGMENTS

Photographs printed in the Guide were donated by the sources listed below. Those photos appearing with a site description are numbered according to the site (e.g., A-10); others are listed by page number.

Altadena Historical Society: J-7 (lower), J-51, J-52, J-53, J-54

A.M.A.I. (Avalon): F-23, F-25 (2), F-26

Angeles Abbey: E-38

Arcade Building Management: A-48

Automobile Club of Southern California: end maps

California Historical Society: pp. 8, 18, 20, 27, 28, 29 (center left), 34, 172; F-21, J-62 (top), J-63

California State University, Dominguez Hills, Archives: pp. 29 (center, rt), 38 (rt), 110; F-1, G-2 (lower), J-64

Chatsworth Historical Society: B-16

Camp, Bob (La Mirada Historical Com.): p. 25; H-31

Covina Valley Historical Society: E-16, E-18

Dunbar Museum: E-28

El Pueblo State Historic Park: map-48; pp. 14, 15, 36 (rt), 50; AA-1 (2), AA-2, AA-3 (2), AA-4 (2), AA-5, AA-6, AA-8 (2), AA-10, AA-12, AA-13, A-1, A-3

Gamble House (Marvin Rand, photographer): J-35

Garfield Building Management (Jordan Grinker): A-44

Golden State Mutual Life: E-2 (2)

Gordon, Dudley: J-18

Grenier, Judson: p. 44; A-6, C-6 (2), C-8, C-9, C-13, D-4 (2), D-5, G-2 (upper), G-13 (2), G-14, H-2, H-5, H-8, H-9, H-15, H-20 (2), H-23 (lower), J-14, J-19 (2)

Harrington, Marie: B-4, B-5, K-6, K-14

Huntington-Sheraton Hotel: J-40

Leonis Adobe: B-17

Lomita Railroad Museum: F-8

Los Angeles, City Department of Recreation and Parks: F-14, F-15 (2)

Los Angeles, City Department of Transportation: p. 45

Los Angeles, County Department of Military and Veterans Affairs: E-13

Los Angeles, County Museum of Natural History: pp. 2, 3, 4 (2), 9, 11, 16, 17, 21, 22, 23, 24, 28 (3), 29 (upper left and lower), 31, 36 (upper left), 38 (left), 39 (2), 40, 94, 264, 305; A-5, A-50, B-2, B-6, B-25, C-16, C-18, D-11, D-32, E-5, E-16, E-20, G-5, I-3, J-16, J-38

Los Angeles Police Academy: A-10

Los Angeles Port Authority: pp. 41 (2), 43, 192; G-6, G-15

Los Encinos State Historic Park: B-22

McPherson, Rolf: p. 63; A-18

McPolin, Father Pat: G-1

Manhattan Beach Historical Society: p. 29 (upper rt); F-2, F-3

Mentry, La Verne: K-8 (2)

Matthews, Miriam: A-53, E-23 (photo by Harry Adams), E-26, E-29 (photo by Harry Adams)

Norwalk Historical Heritage Committee: H-27, H-29, H-30

Occidental College: J-17

Pasadena, City of: J-45

Pasadena Historical Society: J-36

Paramount Studios: D-16

Rancho Los Amigos Hospital: H-19

Santa Fe Railroad Co.: F-4

Security Pacific National Bank: pp. 13, 36 (lower), 125, 147, 240; AA-10, A-23, A-42, A-49, A-58, A-59, A-62, A-65, B-1, B-26, C-7, C-10, C-12, C-19, C-20, D-1, D-2, D-10, D-19, D-22, D-26, D-29, D-37, D-38, E-8, E-15 (2), E-21, E-24, F-12, F-24, G-4, G-7, G-12, G-13, I-6, I-14, I-26, I-30, I-32, J-7 (top), J-9, J-12, J-20, J-31, J-42, J-69, K-1, K-12, K-17

Sitton, Thomas (Los Angeles County Museum): A-24, A-27, A-29, A-32, A-33, A-34, A-37, E-6, E-7, E-10, E-12, E-14, F-20, G-10, G-16, G-17, G-21, G-22, G-24 (2), H-14, H-16, H-23 (top, originally from Whittier Daily *News*), H-26, I-8, I-17, I-25

South Pasadena Cultural Heritage Commission: J-24, J-55, J-56, J-57, J-58, J-59, J-60, J-61, J-62

Torrance Historical Society: F-5, F-7

Tournament of Roses Association: J-29, J-32

Twenty-eighth Street YMCA: E-27

St. Vincent de Paul Church: E-9 (2)

Sears-Roebuck Corporation: p. 218

Southern California Quarterly: map-p. x

INDEX TO SITES

This index is a guide to locations. It is not a compendium of the names, dates or events which are contained in the historical section or in the site entries. Purpose of the Index is to facilitate use of the guidebook and to enhance understanding of historical places in Los Angeles county. The numbers refer to the pages in the book in which the principal entry occurs. Information in parentheses indicate whether the entry is illustrated and if additional references to the item appear in the book.